Project Risk Quantification

Project Risk Quantification

A Practitioner's Guide to Realistic Cost and Schedule Risk Management

by John K. Hollmann

Probabilistic Publishing

Associate Editor: Nancy Winchester
Cover Illustration: Haesel Charlesworth Holbrook

Initial printing: June, 2016

Probabilistic Publishing   www.decisions-books.com
                                          e-mail: dave@decisions-books.com
Florida:
5715 NW 67th Ct
Gainesville, FL 32653

Texas:
1702 Hodge Lake Ln
Sugar Land, TX 77478
281-277-4006

Written, designed, and printed in the United States of America.

Library of Congress Control Number: 2016943376

ISBN: 1-941075-02-9   Kindle version: 1-941075-06-1
ISBN 13: 978-1-941075-02-9   Kindle version: 978-1-941075-06-7

To my wife Cindy with whom risk and reward are everyday realities.

Reviews

"Working at a private equity firm that invests in mining projects, Mr. Hollmann's *Project Risk Quantification* text is a must read and will be my go-to-guide for many years to come. Private equity investment is all about identifying risks and how to capture these risks quantitatively. John's book takes a smart two-part approach that lends itself perfectly to understand and implement risk quantification at any stage in the project life cycle. It is clearly and concisely written and fills a gap that currently exists in the field of risk management." –Edward van Doorn, Project Controls Manager, Resource Capital Funds.

"John Hollmann's *Project Risk Quantification* text makes an important contribution to the practice of project appraisals and to project risk management. Realistic quantitative methods–*absolutely*–are needed for calculations and meaningful communication. I found special interest in the parametric cost estimation details and the novel discussion of and methods for projects tipping into chaos." –John Schuyler, Principal Consultant and Instructor, Decision Precision and PetroSkills; author of *Risk and Decision Analysis in Projects*.

"For those in the trenches of project cost engineering in general, and risk analysis in particular, it is difficult to find practices that are practical and reliable; i.e., that will work on every project. John Hollmann's book not only lays out an integrated set of methods in detail, but documents their basis in empirical reality. The stories are interesting too. For credibility, organizations need strong risk quantification competency in-house and this book provides a great guide for building that competency –Prashant Srivastava, Manager, Cost Engineering Systems, Enbridge Pipelines, Inc."

"John Hollmann is well known for his necessarily blunt honesty about project performance and risk, and as a result he is a rare and valued resource to clients and colleagues alike. He tells it as it is, and offers advice in a pragmatic fashion, often accompanied by vigorous debate. Characteristically, this book does the same, imparting decades of hands-on capex risk management and quantification experience in a readily-accessible, engaging, and conversational tone. It provides a practical guide to projects as dynamic systems, and risks that impact both project decision-making and performance. Run, do not walk, to your nearest bookseller." –Alexia Nalewaik, Vice President of Major Projects and Program Management, WT Partnership.

"John's book demonstrates to users how realistic estimates and forecasts can be created using historical data and proven techniques. A thought provoking guide that delivers a practical starter tool for those who are new to risk quantification and provides experienced parametric estimators with a laser sight for large and small projects." –Laurie Bowman, Principal, Synchrony.

"Currently, no book in the marketplace addresses the question of integrated project risk analysis and quantification in a realistic way. As Mr. Hollmann makes clear, the prevalent methods fail to predict the cost and schedule overruns that frequent process and other industry projects. His book finally addresses the age-old challenge of how to realistically forecast cost and schedule accuracy while also keeping it practical. The book is comprehensive and addresses all the issues in detail along with interesting examples and anecdotes. Everyone will enjoy reading and using this book!" –Kul B. Uppal, Consultant, AACE Technical Director, and former Estimating/Risk lead at oil & gas majors.

"At a time when capital-intensive industries are very prudent with their investments and tempted to demand certainty from project teams, this book comes in handy to equip risk professionals and management with the framework and toolset required to understand, quantify and communicate project risks. Whether you are risk pro or a senior manager, set aside your pre-conceived notions about what makes capital projects successful; follow John as he debunks industry beliefs about capital projects risks and guides you through tried-and-tested methods you can apply to quantify them. Once your organization produces reliable base estimates, the next challenge is to understand, quantify and communicate the uncertainties inherent to capital projects. Whether you are a risk practitioner or a senior manager, John's approach will help you frame the challenge based on years of research and experience, and offer an extensive toolset that can be readily applied by professionals." –Julien Saillard, Team Lead-External Benchmarking, Royal Dutch Shell

"Nobody knows for sure what will happen tomorrow, but it is critical that we make the best predictions possible for the cost and schedule of our projects and programs. John Hollmann's book on *Project Risk Quantification* provides owner cost engineers and decision-makers with tools and methods that are practical and, as the book demonstrates, realistic in order to improve our return on capital. It offers the first truly integrated approach to project risk quantification over the project life cycle that I have seen. It will be my guide for training." –Andres Pereira, Cost Engineer, Strategic Asset Management, Ecopetrol

"This is a great guidebook and reference on risk quantification for cost and schedule professionals in the process industries but also for those in infrastructure and elsewhere. It is a particularly great resource for owner companies for investment decision making, including national-owned companies. It contains a wealth of practical experience including useful examples. I recommend that everyone in the capital project business get a copy of this book" –Johnson Awoyomi, General Manager Cost Engineering, Nigerian National Petroleum Corp.

"John Hollmann's new book on risk quantification is an engrossing and thought provoking read for anyone dealing with capital investment in the process industries. He starts by providing a very good summation of the common errors and misconceptions that are prevalent in dealing with uncertainty and risk. In this, his use of real life examples adds relevance to the text. He then goes on to propose practical methodologies to account for uncertainty and risk that draw on his many years of experience in the field. His emphasis on the need to seek practical solutions that can be proven to work is refreshing." –Gordon Lawrence, EMEA Manager, Capital Project Consulting Practice, Asset Performance Networks LLC.

"John Hollmann's work has opened up a world of empirical knowledge and a type of common sense that have had a profound impact in my career. This book gives everyone access to a breadth of knowledge and practical advice regarding risk analysis in capital projects which cannot be found in existing literature. I am confident that other professionals will find this book to be an invaluable tool for dealing with all the challenges risk analysis poses for capital projects and portfolios." –Claudia Villegas Timm, Lead Portfolio Management Improvements, Wind Power Projects, Vattenfall.

"This book is a must read for any owner, contractor or business person who needs to understand risk quantification and accuracy of estimates and schedules on capital projects and programs and how to avoid the pitfalls. John Hollmann demystifies risk analysis, challenging common industry practices and pointing the way forward with methods that provide greater confidence and credibility for informed judgement and decision-making on capital investments. It is a straight talking guide backed up by a lifetime of industry experience, anecdotes, research and recommended practices." –Les McMullan, Global Director, Project Controls, EPC Firm

"John Hollmann shares his vast expertise while giving you practical, functional tools and a pragmatic guide to implement risk quantification methods at your own organization. I can confirm that the integrated, empirically-based methods that John shares are simply the fastest, least cost and, most importantly, the most accurate available. If you are frustrated with your organization's inability to accurately quantify risk and tired of unexpected cost overruns and schedule slips, this book is your answer!" –Matthew Schoenhardt, Principal at MS Consulting.

Preface and Acknowledgments

My first thanks must go to my mentor in cost estimating, Mr. Bruce Elliott of Conquest Consulting Group. Bruce taught me the basics of estimating and, as my supervisor, carved out a sandbox of budget and time for me to develop and apply creative approaches on a wide array of projects at Kodak in its heyday.

My thanks also go to Mr. Edward Merrow, owner of Independent Project Analysis, Inc. (IPA) and my analyst colleagues there. For seven years, IPA offered a different sort of sandbox: a database of thousands of actual projects, their practices, and their outcomes. One cannot fully understand risk quantification as covered in this text without first understanding their foundational research on cost and schedule growth.

Further thanks go to AACE International, which provided a sandbox to publish, present, and test ideas against those of my peers. The practices in this text are largely aligned with AACE International Recommended Practices; an under-appreciated industry resource of practical, consensus-based how-to guidelines.

Special thanks to my publisher/editor Dave Charlesworth for his encouragement and efforts as well as fellow author Patrick Leach for allowing me to borrow some of his excellent work on decision making. As a companion text focused on decision making, I recommend Patrick Leach's *Why Can't You Just Giv°e Me the Number?*

Finally, thanks to Haesel Charlesworth for the excellent cover art, and to Dr. Douglas Gransberg and Mr. Tony Jervis for reviewing the draft manuscript. Thank you Dr. Nancy Winchester for your diligent final document edits.

–John K. Hollmann, June, 2016

Publisher's Note

When John contacted us to explore publishing his manuscript, we were immediately interested. I have some experience in the area of cost and schedule risk, including co-authoring a paper with my former colleague Jack Bess (Chevron), which we presented at a DAAG conference. I also facilitated Jack's workshops on several occasions.

I also had extensively and carefully studied Rand's work (which was led by Ed Merrow) on project performance in the mid 1980's while working as a Research Supervisor at the Savannah River Lab (now SRNL). The DOE-funded Rand reports are timeless and are still on my bookshelf. John draws heavily on this work and his experience working at IPA. I was able later to meet and talk with Ed at one of the Chevron CPDEP Forum sessions a few years ago and express my appreciation of his work.

To be honest, I wish I had been able to read John's book thirty years ago! The concepts that he lays out so clearly in this book are things I had to learn the hard way, by trial and error. *Every* engineer involved in any kind of manufacturing, process, and/or project work needs to read this book, which goes far beyond risk quantification. This book will help you improve the way you approach, implement, fund, and manage projects. It can also serve as a primer to help project engineers understand how projects are developed, planned, and implmented and the myriad of ways that projects can go wrong.

We would like to hear your comments relative to this book, especially successful examples of applying the concepts; please e-mail dave@decisions-books.com. We sincerely wish you success in your future projects.

And, we repeat John's appreciation to Haesel Charlesworth Holbrook for the cover illustration and to Nancy Winchester for her astute comments and corrections.

–Dave Charlesworth, June, 2016 Probabilistic Publishing

Contents

"...suddenly a White Rabbit with pink eyes ran close by her. There was nothing so very remarkable in that; nor did Alice think it so very much out of the way to hear the Rabbit say to itself "Oh dear! Oh dear! I shall be too late!" (when she thought it over afterwards it occurred to her that she ought to have wondered at this, but at the time it all seemed quite natural); but, when the Rabbit actually took a watch out of its waistcoat-pocket, and looked at it, and then hurried on, Alice started to her feet, for it flashed across her mind that she had never before seen a rabbit with either a waistcoat-pocket, or a watch to take out of it, and burning with curiosity, she ran across the field after it, and was just in time to see it pop down a large rabbit-hole under the hedge. In another moment down went Alice after it, never once considering how in the world she was to get out again."

– Lewis Carroll from "Alice's Adventures in Wonderland"

1

Introduction: Why Risks are Poorly Quantified

Project risk analysis and quantification can seem to be an "Alice in Wonderland" world where nothing is reliable: a world where strange things happen and cost and schedule outcomes seem impossible to predict (although many people tell you they can do so). In the project world, significant cost and schedule overruns are the norm. Blowouts are common and rarely predicted, despite applying seemingly sophisticated risk analysis methods.

For example, a 2014 Ernst & Young (E&Y) study of 205 major (greater than US$1B) oil and gas industry projects found that the estimated cost at completion was on average forecast to be 59%

above the initial estimate.[1] And this is before the final cost came in! E&Y later reported that the average overrun of initial estimates for mining and metals was 62%.[2] These are just recent examples of what 50 years of similar research has found.

So, why do our project cost and schedule risk quantification outcomes miss the mark so often?

As an introduction, I will list ten reasons why risk quantification fails that I have discovered in my twenty-plus years of studying and working on major process industry projects (as an estimator/cost engineer/controls engineer, then as an analyst at a capital project benchmarking firm, and finally as a consultant for major owner companies). But first, an anecdote...

> After conducting a major project cost and schedule risk analysis and presenting my findings of significant cost uncertainty to a business unit vice president (the project sponsor), he asked how the worst case could be so bad when, "Industry standards call for a much tighter percentage cost range."
>
> The answer was one that I knew he would not want to hear: "First, there is no industry standard range; your company's standards have no basis in reality. Second, your company's project system is frankly not capable of managing such a complex project effectively even if the scope had been well defined."

This exchange highlights the fact that risk quantification failures largely result from poor internal capital and project management practices and our failure to recognize our weaknesses or to take ownership of them if recognized. The problem is typically not about poor base estimates or schedules and usually is not even about risk events in and of themselves. Taken together, the project strategy, processes, practices, organization, and stakeholder interaction are a system. If this *system* is immature, weak, or broken, that is the risk that matters most!

Furthermore, project systems function within changing external political and economic systems, which are moving targets. When a risk event happens (a change is made or the market shifts), a weak project system and/or one misaligned with the external system will respond ineffectually and the project will overrun. In

1   "Spotlight on Oil and Gas Megaprojects," ey.com/oilandgas/capitalprojects, 2014.

2   "Opportunities to Enhance Capital Productivity; Mining and Metals Megaprojects," ey.com/miningmetals, 2015.

the worst cases, it will overrun chaotically and will blowout. In the end, the risks that matter most, the *systemic* risks, are usually not in the risk or issue registers. In short, what is not identified (and they can be) cannot be quantified.

Most systemic risks belong to senior business managers because they control the internal "system," i.e., strategy, processes, people, and money. These managers also most often interact with external partners (e.g., ventures) and politicians, i.e., key stakeholders. If a project process or system is bypassed or short circuited, it is usually the senior manager's decision to do so. Hence, identifying systemic risks means questioning and rating what senior business managers and project managers do and how they think (bias). This is an almost impossible expectation for a lowly project or cost engineer, risk analyst, or even consultants (who want to keep their job or get called back for another assignment).

In the end, this situation has resulted in process industry owner companies applying seemingly sophisticated technical analysis and quantification methods and tools that neither address the risks that matter nor predict the outcomes that actually occur. The risk quantification methods in prevalent use are at best generating numbers that business managers want to hear, and those numbers have little or no basis in reality. Risk quantification (our profession) will always be suspect so long as we chase methods, wondrous as they seem, *without evidence that they work.* In this "Alice in Wonderland" world, we are sometimes like rabbits with a methodological watch leading managers down a rabbit hole.

This book is about facing reality and considering what *works* and *what does not work* (how to avoid the rabbit hole). Only then can capital and project outcomes be improved.

So here are my top ten reasons that risks are so poorly quantified. If you recognize one or more of these rabbit holes in your workplace, this book will help you avoid going where they lead and help you find a way out.

Top Ten #1: I want it fast and cheap!

The pressures to complete a project as early as possible and to keep costs low are immense. Everyone feels it. At the board level, reputations are at stake to close a deal. Vice Presidents (VPs) may be accountable for promises based on budget numbers whose origin they can no longer recall. The VPs are often competing for scarce capital with other VPs. The VPs in turn influence their managers to view their role as being hard-nosed cost cutters. At the team level, the pressure can be about survival.

As the mining CAPEX "super-cycle" was ending in 2012, I recall an owner project manager whispering before a risk analysis that, "If this project does not fly, everyone in this workshop will be out of a job, including our contractor." That is pressure. For large projects, all of this results in a prevailing bias towards aggressive cost and schedule targets and increases risks that nobody is willing to recognize or talk about openly, let alone analyze.

Top Ten #2: If you miss the milestone or overrun more than 10%, your career is over!

Pity the project manager (PM) who has had the "fat" cut from his or her budget and schedule and who then must deliver the project on target or earn the dreaded "*does not meet expectations*" rating (from which few careers recover). There is only one rational but perverse response from a PM, estimator, and/or planner, and that is to add extra time and money ("fat") in greater doses than even the business suspects. The practice is more pernicious than simply adding fat (often subconsciously); the practice destroys capital discipline by turning the system into a game with unrealistic budgets and plans that nobody buys into and analyses nobody believes in, increasing the chance of a serious blowout.

Top Ten #3: I never had an overrun greater than 10% (oh *that* project; it was an exception)!

I have met scores if not hundreds of PMs and I have yet to meet one who told me, "On average my projects overrun by more than 10%." This is contradictory to the reality that most large industry projects overrun by more than 10%. So, why is there such a disconnect between PM memories and industry experience? Is the PM world so Darwinian that all PMs who overrun are fired and therefore the survivors are speaking the truth? Or, is it just selective memory or optimism bias?

In any case, most companies have a decided lack of project history to realistically judge the risk; everything is based on opinion that usually differs markedly from reality. The culture is to look ahead with hope and never look back.

Top Ten #4: If you were a better estimator, the range would be +/-10% (and even tighter for schedule).

Many managers believe that estimators and planners can influence the uncertainty range (best and worst cases) by doing "better" estimates or schedules. In reality, other than some nominal uncertainty resulting from the estimating/scheduling work processes, the estimator/planner has little to no influence on or control of the range. If management does not like the range, the *manager* must change the project. This is because uncertainty results from risks that are what they are for a given system and project scope and the estimator/planner can do little about them.

However, there is one caveat. If a company's culture is punitive (Top Ten #2), the estimators/planners can indeed influence the range: they can just hide fat in the body of the estimate or activities to obtain a narrow range that is more likely to be within the artificial range that management dictates. Punitive cultures are expensive!

Top Ten #5: The more rigorous the model, the better the analysis will be!

Many practitioners become enamored with methodological elegance, complexity, and/or arcane statistics. Some become experts in it, anchored to complex software tools with endlessly evolving and expanding features. Consultants, intentionally or not, benefit from methods that are difficult to comprehend and/or perform.

However, in my experience, if the team is getting involved in debates about "correlation coefficients" or "merge bias," they are likely missing the fact that risk elephants (e.g., systemic risks) are roaming the room undetected or ignored. A focus on statistical minutiae also replaces caring about empirical reality (Top Ten #3). To use the old idiom, many are not seeing the forest for the trees.

Top Ten #6: Let the contractors do it; they are the experts!

Contractors are very good at what they do, which is to execute engineering, procurement, and construction (EPC). To the contractor's bottom line, risk is cost they will incur that the owner won't cover. An estimating manager at a major EPC contractor once admitted to me that, "We don't have any idea how much our historical projects overran the owner's budget. It's not in our database. All we know is how far our income came in the black or the red…" (the "red" being the amount of any cost increase that they did not recover from the owner).

For EPCs, claims recovery is in effect a profit center. A project that is a disaster for an owner can be a gold mine for the contractor. For example, I once reviewed a megaproject disaster in progress that was blowing out by several billion dollars. A few weeks later I read the EPC's quarterly stock analyst conference call minutes in which the EPC's unit VP bragged to the analysts about how their backlog

increased. The increase was the exact amount of the disaster overrun I had just reviewed.

The lesson is that EPC contractors simply do not have the
empirical knowledge or incentive to perform valid cost and schedule risk quantification for owners. It's not an ethical issue, it is just
their point of view. *Risk quantification is an owner responsibility*
and must therefore be a core competency for the owner.

Top Ten #7: It's Lump Sum. Therefore, this is all the contractor's risk

Lump sum contracts are a favorite of banks and National Oil
Companies (NOCs) for the perceived reduction of uncertainty they
provide. However, a saying I share: *"There is no such thing as fixed
cost."* Lump Sum only transfers a nominal portion of the risk to the
contractors.

For example, a published study that I led once showed that
the cost penalty for deficient owner project control practices was the
same for lump sum and reimbursable projects.[3] Both approaches
overran the base cost estimates by the same amount, with the only
difference being that the lump sum projects locked in or "bought"
about 10% of risk cost in their bid, leaving no opportunity for the
owner to underrun that portion. For the statistically minded reader,
that means the distribution of outcomes of lump sum project costs
have a truncated tail on the low end, but the long tail on the high
side remains.

Top Ten #8: Escalation is Inflation (just ask Finance)

From 2004 to 2008, the costs of commodity materials and EPC
services increased dramatically in the process industries. Commodity demand from China resulted in a glut of capital investment.
However, the supply chain of goods and services to projects is slow
in meeting demand spikes, so suppliers were able to increase their
prices in line with supply and demand. Plus, the suppliers had their
own risks. Therefore, everyone paid higher prices.

However, many owner Finance departments continued to in-
sist that project teams fund *escalation* using their internal *inflation*
guidelines even though inflation was minimal. Even the construction or plant cost indices from the magazines failed to track price
increases because they reflected cost inputs (for example, wages)
and did not escalate prices for services. Project cost escalation is

---

3   Hollmann, John, "Best Owner Practices for Project Control," AACE
Transactions, 2002.

not monetary inflation (although it includes it); escalation varies by the product or service in question and by the applicable supply and demand conditions. To make matters worse, very few companies estimate escalation risk probabilistically despite the fact that it represents the most uncertain cost for some projects.

Top Ten #9: The Standards say so. What more is there to talk about?

There are no industry standard cost accuracy ranges. That statement surprises many people. AACE quotes a wide "range of ranges" in their Estimate and Schedule Classification series of Recommended Practices (RPs). AACE further tell us that range can only be determined through risk analysis because every project's risks are different. Unfortunately, most companies have created their own internal "standard" ranges that often refer to non-existent AACE recommendations. Fixed range criteria create a pressure to conform by estimators – and conform they do (Top Ten #4). Once a company sets pre-determined ranges as policy, meaningful discussion about risk quantification ends and becomes largely irrelevant to decision making.

Top Ten #10: You talkin' to me?

A senior business manager once told me after a risk analysis that, "If I wanted advice on how to manage my business, I'd hire McKinsey." That probably wasn't a bad idea long term, but it was not very helpful to his project-funding situation at that moment. As we will discuss later, the greatest risks on projects generally do not belong to the project manager or team: they belong to the business.

Some typical systemic risks include:

♦ Immature capital project processes,
♦ Indecisiveness,
♦ Poor communication,
♦ Weak skills, and
♦ Resource shortages.

In a weak system, otherwise nominal risk events in the presence of complexity can compound into disasters.

So when I tell project management that the worst case for their complex project is a potential 50% or 70% or more overrun, they are often at a loss for words. They have never heard of a worst case of more than, say, +30% for CAPEX. Furthermore, when told the only way to significantly reduce the worst case is for the *business to strengthen their system* (or do a different project), their response is sometimes like the lead-in quote. System strengthening requires organizational change and industry experience with organizational change projects, which are among the most difficult and least successful types of projects to undertake, and they take years, not weeks or months. Meanwhile, the Board of Directors meeting to review the manager's project proposal is next week (if I had a Top Ten #11, it would be about performing analysis too late to matter). There is no better time to strengthen your system than now. If the CAPEX budget is slow, this could be an even better time.

In summary, at any one company, you might find several of these situations in operation; in some cases, all ten of them. Suffice it to say the objective, reliable, and empirically valid risk quantification is nearly impossible to do at one of these companies. The rest of the book addresses ways to remove these roadblocks to successful risk quantification.

"Janus am I; oldest of potentates! Forward I look and backward and below. I count – as god of avenues and gates. The years that through my portals come and go... My frosts congeal the rivers in their flow, My fires light up the hearths and hearts of men."
– Henry Wadsworth Longfellow from "The Poet's Calendar"

2
Risk – God of the Gate; Creator and Destroyer of Value

Among the ancient Roman gods and myths, Janus is the god of beginnings and endings and thereby of doors and gates. The Janus gate of Rome was opened for the legions to march forth in times of war, and closed after the legions returned and peace prevailed.

Projects also have *gates* – that is the name given to the milestones when investment decisions are made to commit and send forth resources to execute all or some portion of a capital project. Janus has two faces – one looks into the future and one into the past; every decision must consider both. Janus not only looks across time, but also sees both the fire of hope, opportunity, and added value in the future and the frost of failure and lost value in the past. Hot optimism alone might consign one to disappointment or disaster, while cold pessimism might lead to indecision and entropy. When deciding to go forth at the gate, one hopes for the wisdom of Janus to see and consider all: past and future to balance risk and value, hope and fear, optimism and pessimism. Unfortunately, our vision is clouded.

What we see is uncertainty of the future and imperfect understanding of the past. Good decisions and good beginnings depend on the understanding of risk, informed by the past. And, to the extent that decisions are based on numbers, risk quantification is vital.

In project systems, we usually apply risk quantification at project decision points or gates. The purpose is to identify sources and causes of risk and quantify their resultant uncertainty in potential outcomes. Uncertainty is a characteristic of every element of the as-yet unrealized project, be it scope, resources, cost and/or time. A subsequent purpose of risk quantification is to fund specific allowances or budget allocations for risk in cost and time based on the general risk quantifications and the decision maker's risk attitude and risk tolerance.

Cost and schedule risk quantification, done appropriately, is what makes or breaks most owner project decisions. Over the last 30 years, I have supported, prepared, or reviewed hundreds of project cost estimates. I have found that *base estimates*, i.e., the estimate before making allowance for risk, are reasonable representations of the known project scope (albeit with biases). The quality of base estimates varies of course, but base estimate quality risk is miniscule compared to the uncertainty resulting from other risks. Unfortunately, what passes for risk quantification in most project systems today is actually estimate quality quantification, e.g., how well quantities were measured from the drawings or models, is pricing based on vendor quotations, and so on.

It is similar for schedules. Project schedule risk quantification assumes that the project scope will not change, performance will go as planned, and no risk events will occur. These are, of course, unrealistic assumptions for a major project. Because most estimates and schedules are done in similar ways, at most companies the risk analysis outcomes always look the same regardless of project differences (e.g., contingency of 10% for cost). Therefore, their risk analysis and quantification add no value to project decision-making.

In fact, fifty years of research tells us that the greatest risk is the project scope:

♦ What is (or will be) the project scope?
♦ How well is the scope defined?

Other key risks are project complexity and the status of team development. The more complex the scope and execution strategy, the more important the strength and resilience of the team becomes.

In the end, a project depends on human behavior that can be very unpredictable as well as biased, particularly when faced with confounding circumstances, changes, and risk events. The human nature of risk manifestation is that most project failures are characterized by an overrun of labor hours for management, engineering, and construction. *Systemic risks* include how mature and biased a project system is, how well that system defines and manages the scope, and the degree of team development. And, as described in the Introduction, in most cases, systemic risks are neither identified nor quantified.

Poor risk quantification provides no differentiation of project options at early decision gates (all get more or less the same contingency percentage regardless of risk) and no basis on which to kill overly risky projects at the final decision gate. The net effect is project overruns, late first production, and poor return on capital investment.

Who Should Read This Book?

First, this book is focused on the process industries: oil and gas, petrochemicals, chemicals, mining, metals, power, pipeline, utilities, pharmaceuticals, and to some extent manufacturing and assembly. These are characterized by being process equipment or machinery centric rather than structure centric (i.e., no architects) although there is plenty of civil, structural, and infrastructure work involved in process projects. It is also focused on owner companies (the investment decision makers); however, the methods in the second half of the book apply to contractors as well. In addition, Chapter 15 provides insight into risk quantification for non-process industry projects and for contractors.

The book addresses three audiences. The first audience is investment and bidding decision makers including the C-level officers, VPs, and senior business managers. This also includes the project's financiers. They must understand the concepts of capital project cost and schedule risk and its quantification and how these relate to basic investment and bid decision making, i.e., is the risk information good enough to support the decision at hand, and if so, how should it be applied? The book's focus is on managers in growing companies without cadres of decision and risk analysis specialists; these companies usually have a hunger to improve. In the smallest companies, the managers may be doing the analyses themselves (the methods here are within your reach). Managers in major companies will find new ideas here for consideration, although they will likely face the difficult challenge of changing legacy approaches.

The second audience is program directors, project managers, and project engineers who must understand the needs of senior management while also understanding their own needs for tactical level decision making and project control. In addition, they need to understand the basics of performing risk analysis and quantification that they are ultimately responsible for, even if they are not actually performing it themselves. In a small company, these people may have a direct hand in the investment decision.

Finally, the book is for team members participating in or performing risk analysis and/or risk quantification. The later chapters delve into the methods and modeling specifics; however, the book as a whole is not specifically for technical experts. It is about practical analysis that is within the grasp of an experienced project engineer or cost and schedule practitioner with training and a modest budget for software or consulting. Overemphasis on statistical minutiae and overly complex (but poorly fitting) models has been detrimental to effective day-to-day risk quantification for projects in growing companies.

This book is also intended to fill a gap in the literature between general project or risk management texts that touch lightly on risk quantification, texts on decision analysis that look at all inputs to investment decisions (not just capital cost and schedule), and texts for technical experts ("quants") or consultants that dive deep into statistics and modeling for all sorts of applications. It is focused on aligning:

- The business manager who is framing the project and who, working with decision analysis experts, will help decide on the investment,
- The project manager, who will execute the project, and
- The team members who analyze and communicate cost and schedule risk for management's consideration.

Some might ask why the book skips revenue, OPEX and operability, interest rates and other NPV or IRR calculation inputs. The reason is that CAPEX *risk* (as opposed to the amount financed or borrowed, which certainly get a lot of attention) gets less respect than deserved; CAPEX is deserving of a book on its own. CAPEX is of immediate concern. If it blows out or if the production starts late (with no counter balancing revenue), the results can be devastating for the owner. You get one chance with CAPEX; there is no 20-year life to optimize it like revenue, operability, or OPEX.

Another unique aspect of the book is that all of its recommended methods have been shown by empirical research (by Rand Corporation, Construction Industry Institute, IPA Inc., and others) to be reasonably reliable. Most treatments on risk analysis do not address whether a method actually works or not; therefore, practices have entered the risk management literature and practice without the slightest evidence of their efficacy. There is also an unfortunate tendency to become enamored by the elegance or complexity of a model rather than ask if the method is practical day-to-day.

If you are already doing risk quantification, ask yourself two questions about the methods your company is now using:

♦ Are they *empirically valid*, i.e., demonstrated to work compared to actual outcomes?

♦ Are they *practical* for available in-house resources to apply on every project regardless of size, type, phase, or quality of definition and planning?

If you answered "no" or "I am not sure" to one or both questions, please read this book! However, be forewarned that the methods described in the book are not commonly used.[1] If you propose these methods for your company, be prepared to answer questions along the lines of, "Why not use the method our competitor uses?" The first answer is, "Because these methods actually work and they're practical," but also be assured that the methods in this book are aligned with the Recommend Practices (RPs) of AACE International, the premier association for Cost Engineering (RPs are practices for which there is a general consensus as to their reliability). In addition, the book shares examples from owner and EPC companies that are using these methods successfully. I will also describe how research has shown that the most common model-based quantification method in use (i.e., line-item ranging) has been a disaster for industry.

As a final note, given the theme of quantifying the future while paying homage to the past, the book includes some history. I hope you share some of my amazement at how little of what we do is truly new. For example, the topics in this book were hot buttons in the

---

1   There is one exception to this statement. IPA, Inc. has run its empirically-based parametric contingency analysis model (CAM) on many thousands of projects for scores of companies since 1987. However, their analysis is run as a 'benchmark' that companies rightly do not apply verbatim. Unfortunately, most companies have not internalized the IPA quantification approach and too often do not heed the benchmark lessons.

1830s when canal and railroad projects were overrunning significantly and giving birth to civil engineering as a formal profession. In fact, it is arguable that cost and schedule risk quantification has not improved since the advent of the steam engine. Maybe we can change that!

What is Risk?

Risk is uncertainty. AACE defines risk as *"an uncertain event or condition that could affect a project objective or business goal."* It includes both threats and opportunities. It's something that acts on your project, or a condition that interacts with what you are doing, in all cases adding uncertainty to outcomes. Per AACE, the goal of risk management then is to *"increase the probability that a planned asset, project, or portfolio achieves its objectives."* Just about everything on a project other than what has been completed and spent is subject to uncertainty, particularly the behavior of the people and organizations involved. Projects take place in physical, social, economic, political, and other milieu whose state and behavior are also uncertain. Quantifying all that uncertainty is intimidating, and frankly impossible in a reductionist way. Uncertainty is well, uncertain. As a first rule, we must remain humble about our ability to identify risks and forecast their outcome. We are not Janus, but identify risks and quantify them we must.

A premise of this book is that everything that is uncertain can be identified and quantified (albeit not always very well). Whether we do or do not address a risk depends on whether the risk *matters*. What matters is what history tells us has mattered and what our current analysis shows is reasonably likely to apply to our project situation, i.e., the two faces of Janus. At quantification, there are no "unknown unknowns (U-U)." While U-U phraseology is philosophically interesting, its usage usually precedes the user disavowing responsibility for poor outcomes. Owning all risks does not mean you should fire a manager for being over budget, but it does mean we should expect our worst cases to be something resembling the worst.

The U-U idiom has the distinction of winning a "Foot in Mouth Award" from the Plain English Campaign for comments that run counter to ensuring "information is delivered in a clear manner." US Secretary of Defense Donald Rumsfeld used this winning statement in 2003: "As we know, there are known knowns; there are things we know we know. We also know there are known unknowns; that is to say we know there are some things we do not know. But there are also unknown unknowns — the ones we don't know we don't know."[2] What this phraseology conveniently leaves out is *what we do not like or want to know* (i.e., unknown-knowns). Projects never fail for something that could not have been anticipated to some degree: weak systems, poor competencies, political flip-flops, regulatory indecision, storms, strikes, accidents, incompetency, and even "black swans." They have all happened before and will happen again. In risk quantification there are just varying degrees of uncertainty as to potential occurrence and impact. We need to own it all. There are no unknown-unknowns, only what we decide does not matter.

I must also point out an issue with "issues." In some risk management practices, a risk that occurred or is certain to occur (e.g., "the team is inexperienced") is labeled an "issue" rather than a "risk." Risk analysts then move it to an issue log for some poor manager to deal with. However, at the decision gate, most of these issues remain unresolved, and, no longer being on the list of risks, do not get quantified. Philosophically, they become unknown-knowns or inconvenient truths that nobody wants to deal with or even talk about. From experience, we do know that if the "team is inexperienced" and a disruptive risk event occurs, the impact of the risk event will be amplified significantly. The interaction of issues and risk event response is often what matters in risk quantification. In other words, issues tend to result in ineffective risk response, and in the worst case, chaos. In sum, all sources of uncertainty that matter must be quantified, known/unknown, risk/issue or whatever; don't let philosophical or managerial labels get in the way.

That is not to say that risk categories do not matter. This book categorizes risks in a way that ties to the method best suited for quantifying them. At the highest level, the categories are simply *systemic* and *project-specific* risks (and with respect to cost, *escalation* and *exchange*):

♦ *Systemic* risks, as the word implies, are artifacts of system attributes (the internal project system, its maturity, company culture, complexity, bias and so on), and the project's interaction with external systems (regional culture, political, and regulatory systems). Some have called these *background* or *strategic* risks. Others call them issues. Research has shown that systemic risks are the greatest source of uncertainty on projects.

---

2   Plain English Campaign (http://www.plainenglish.co.uk/)

♦ *Project specific* risks are the conditions and events specific to our project scope and strategy (strikes, weather, soil conditions, and so on). Some have called these *event* or *tactical* risks. Systemic and project-specific risks are often not independent in occurrence or impact, e.g., a weak team may result in a strike, or amplify the impact of a risk event due to inappropriate response.

Other types of risk for cost are *escalation* and *exchange*. These are somewhat related risks that stem from general economic and monetary conditions external to the company and project. Their quantification requires input from economists via integrated price index (escalation) and currency exchange forecasts (exchange). Escalation and systemic risks or issues such as skilled labor shortages are also related. In sum, while these categories help us align risks with ways to quantify them, you must try to avoid allowing methodology to get in the way of holistic understanding.

What Is Risk Quantification? (It is More Than Contingency)

While writing this book, a fellow consultant asked, "Why not title the book "Contingency;" after all, that is what everyone in the CAPEX picture gets excited about." I must admit the thought crossed my mind as well. When a young professional asks me what they should write a paper on, I always say, "Put *contingency* in the title and you are sure to fill the room and get a good debate going."

The problem is that contingency is not risk. It is not uncertainty. It is in fact a *number* – a control budget account to be funded, not unlike concrete and steel. But unlike concrete and steel (which everyone understands: what it is, how it is measured, how its cost is estimated, and so on), contingency is often seen as a game, a guess, or worse: a given or token pittance.

To project teams, contingency is defined as an amount of money or time in the budget and schedule to cover uncertainties (i.e., risks) that statistically speaking *we expect to be incurred* just as we expect to spend for concrete and steel. However, to business management, contingency is often seen as an amount of money that will be returned to them if the project team does its job right, that is, *they do not expect it to be incurred*. This misunderstanding is one of the top reasons why risk quantification (and project control in general) fails.

In any case, contingency is the "tail of the risk dog." We need to look at what matters, and that is understanding and identifying risk first, quantifying it second, then funding the risk third (e.g., contingency). That is the approach of this book.

Risk quantification is a *probabilistic estimate of risk impact*, optimally with the estimation of cost and schedule impact being integrated. It combines cost estimating with planning and scheduling in probabilistic modeling approaches. Furthermore, quantifying systemic risk requires behavioral understanding (e.g., biases), economics insight, and good communication skills. Finally, the methods must be informed by the past, i.e., historical analysis and metrics. This combination of skills and knowledge is hard to find in most workplaces. Unfortunately, people with only some of these skills and knowledge do the majority of project risk quantification and there is a dearth of project risk history to work with. Lacking in-house competencies, consultants are often depended upon. Given in-house weaknesses and/or the variability of consulting services, this often results in lost credibility of risk quantification, its methods, and practitioners. One must at least have practical, robust methods to deal with less than ideal practitioner competency.

Procedurally speaking, risk quantification is also a step in the Risk Management (RM) process within capital project management. Many are familiar with one or more of the industry RM processes and models (e.g., PMI PMBoK®,[3] AACE TCM®,[4] ISO 31000®[5]). Without getting into detail, these all include the steps of *risk planning, assessment, treatment,* and *control* (the AACE names) that are done throughout the project life cycle. You are always managing risk, implicitly or explicitly. These processes all include quantitative risk analysis (QRA) or risk quantification in the risk assessment box. However, quantification is sometimes an orphan because it is only performed occasionally at decision gates while ongoing *qualitative* assessment gets most of the attention (the green-yellow-red scoring matrix approach most are familiar with). AACE has the only RM process that highlights the sporadic, decision-centric, post risk treatment nature of risk quantification; their approach is the technical basis of this book.

---

3   Guide to the Project Management Body of Knowledge (PMBoK), Project Management Institute.

4   Total Cost Management Framework (TCM), AACE International.

5   Risk Management – Principles and Guidelines (ISO 31000), International Organization for Standardization.

Done well, risk quantification also involves some contingency planning; i.e., not contingency estimating, but pre-planning risk responses (or range of responses) to risk conditions or events if they were to occur. This requires that the risk quantification method quantify cost and schedule risk in an integrated way by explicitly addressing trading cost for schedule.

For example, assume the business owner's cost/schedule objective is *schedule driven* (i.e., willing to trade cost for schedule, which is quite common given the importance of an early revenue stream) and there is a risk of the construction site being flooded. Not considering the owner's cost/schedule objective, the construction manager (CM) may say the schedule slip will be two months on the unspoken assumption that the goal is minimizing extra direct costs (the unstated risk response is just stand-down and let the flooded site dry out). However, if the CM was told that the completion date cannot slip, he may reply, "Well, for $2 or $3 million there are some things we could do to get the place back in full swing in a week or so." If the owner is unclear about their objective, then who knows what they will ask the CM to do when the risk actually occurs (it will be a surprise). If the objectives are unclear, one must include both long delay *and* high direct cost impact in the range of possible impacts. In short, risk quantification is not just numerical analysis – it forces contingency planning.

Why Focus on Risk Quantification?

As stated earlier, risk is God of the Gate. We need to know the chance of success of the capital investment or bid proposal. Our company's profitability depends on it (the typical metric being return on capital or return on equity). If there are options, we need to understand the difference between alternative risk profiles because by the time of the decision gate, viable alternatives tend to have similar mean valuations (EMV, IRR, NPV, ROCE[6]). If all alternatives being considered are judged identically at, for example, +30%/–10% on cost or +6/–2 weeks on schedule because these are the company norms or because of the repetitive outcome of our methods, then there is no way to objectively make good *risk-aware* decisions.

When risk quantification is empirically valid, it is not uncommon that the worst case in one or more option's risk profiles will

---

6   These acronyms stand for Expected Monetary Value, Internal Rate of Return, Net Present Value, and Return on Capital Employed, respectively.

be seen to significantly hurt the business's profitability. Obviously, we need to expose this. For megaprojects, the worst case value may drive the business to bankruptcy.

I recall one project by a mid-size firm with weak capabilities. The company decided to build the world's largest process unit of its kind while also employing new technology in a downstream process unit. The final cost came in double the budget, reducing the company's credit rating to junk. It took ten years to restore their rating to investment grade. The risks of scale-up and new technology combined with a weak project system and other systemic risks were eminently knowable, but the company's biased risk quantification ignored these risks and the lessons that history tells us about them (the unknown-knowns or inconvenient truths).

As an example of how far off industry's prevailing risk quantification is from reality, I did a study in 2012 of the available empirical research on estimate accuracy in the process industries ("Reality"), and I compared that to my knowledge of the accuracy forecasts that are presented to management for their consideration at the time of project authorization ("As Estimated").[7] Here was the result: the high end of cost overrun reality is about two to three times that which our risk quantification is forecasting (see Figure 2.1).

Another reason to focus on risk quantification is that, if done well, it serves a unique quality assurance or governance function at the gate. The methods recommended here explicitly rate the project system and how well it was applied (among other risk driving practices), so project teams that cut corners in discipline, definition, team building, and so on will be penalized with much greater uncertainty in outcomes and much higher contingency (or at least worst cases and reserves). After a few projects get killed or sent back for further scope definition, everyone gets the message to strengthen their process and be more disciplined in its application.

I know of one owner company that was so successful in creating effective processes and instilling discipline that its risk quantifications (using the methods in this book) rarely showed much uncertainty; i.e., the final costs were both competitive and within the proverbial +10/–10% range. When this is achieved, someone will inevitably ask, "Why are we wasting our time and money on this risk analysis?" The answer is that effective risk quantification is in part what assures these good outcomes.

---

7   Hollmann, John, "Estimate Accuracy: Dealing with Reality," *Cost Engineering Journal*, AACE International, Nov/Dec 2012.

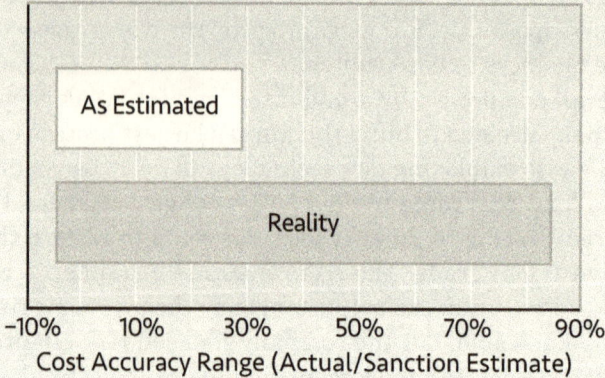

Figure 2.1: Cost Accuracy Ranges: As-Estimated versus Reality

Myths, Misdemeanors, and Felonies

A warning at the start: if you are prejudiced against Monte Carlo Simulation (MCS), or enamored with Critical Path Method (CPM) risk quantification methods, the recommendations of this book are going to challenge your thinking. Similarly, if you believe that overruns result mostly from endemic systematic lying or misrepresentation and/or corruption, the book will ask you to think again.

First, some are of the opinion that MCS is an inherently "bad" method for risk quantification. This book will explain why some of what you read or heard about MCS is wrong. I note this up front because MCS is one of only two probabilistic methods in the "practical" toolbox. You simply cannot do cost and schedule risk quantification without MCS (in combination with the other practical, empirically-based method of parametric modeling). However, it is true that MCS applied to an inappropriate underlying model and/ or not using proper MCS protocol results in bogus and sometimes dangerous outputs.

Without getting into details here, MCS is an algorithm that starts with a deterministic model (a spreadsheet that comes to a bottom line or a schedule with a completion date) and through repeated sampling from possible inputs to the model generates a probabilistic outcome. For risk analysis, MCS obviously requires an underlying model that has risk among its inputs (i.e., the causes or drivers of risk). As obvious as that statement may seem, the most prevalent methods in industry use do not have risk drivers as inputs. These methods are *line-item ranging* for cost and *activity ranging* for schedule. Furthermore, when applying MCS, many users skip the essential protocol to define how model variables are correlated (e.g., are risk events A and B related?). Combine these gross violations of first principles and the result is bad outcomes and the myth that MCS is at fault. Some also argue that MCS cannot model the way projects behave or at least replicate the outcomes; this book will show that this is also not true.

Second, in the misdemeanor category (because it's a good news/ bad news situation), is the application of resource-loaded CPM schedule-based models in cost and schedule risk analysis.

First the good news: research shows that resource loaded CPM modeling is an effective approach to developing a robust, risk tolerant base project execution plan. By using it in risk analysis to debug and stress test a project plan, you improve both the integrity of the plan and schedule and how it deals with uncertainty (for example, test if there is an alternate logic that will result in better performance with relatively less uncertainty). However, in quantifying cost and schedule uncertainty in an absolute sense (coming up with the right budget numbers or worst case value), the CPM approach can be an impractical rabbit hole, especially for cost.

CPM model weaknesses start when a significant risk event occurs. The actual risk response of the team will often be to change the schedule logic. However, CPM risk analysis, as practically applied (i.e., without probabilistic branching in the model) does not do this; it just stretches the duration like an accordion.

Second, it is not practical to deal with cost/schedule trading with CPM models. In reality, when a risk event occurs, projects may do everything in their power to either not incur a delay (trying to save money), or recover from it (see changed logic for risk response). In other words, the impact to schedule activities is often insignificant because we make it so. However, the direct cost of mitigation or recovery is often huge, including the knock-on impact (secondary risk) of lost discipline and control given that change is disruptive, particularly when the system is weak (in the worst case, a project spends money to recover schedule and fails – both cost and time blowout).

Next, most CPM-based analyses do not address systemic risks objectively if at all (although there are ways to do it; see Appendix A).

Finally, the method requires a high quality resource-loaded CPM schedule that research shows we usually do not have, or the project is in an early phase and the schedule is just a bar chart or only a completion date.

In short, the CPM-based method is sub-optimal for quantifying cost risk, limited in applicability by phase, and generally not practical day-to-day. That is not to say a highly experienced consultant cannot address these weaknesses, but this book is predicated on not requiring a highly experienced consultant on every project. The rabbit hole is that the method is enticing to analysts and convincing to management given the elegance of the model and math and the availability of software. That said, you should always strive to develop a quality, resource-loaded CPM schedule and use it in risk analysis to improve the plan. For those who use CPM-based risk quantification, Appendix A provides details on how to make sure its outcomes are as realistic as possible in consideration of systemic risks.

Finally, in the felony category is lying and/or corruption. Perhaps the best known and most cited researcher of project cost overruns is Dr. Bent Flyvbjerg. His work has focused on large public infrastructure projects. His Oxford University website profile says, "…his ideas on optimism bias (the tendency to take an overly positive view of planned actions), and strategic misrepresentation (deliberately misstating the likely outcomes of actions) have been incorporated into project evaluation techniques around the world."[8] Of optimism bias, there is no question that it is a fact of project life. Of the need for empirically valid methods and the long established practice of estimate validation, again, these are fundamental requirements of effective risk quantification. (Dr. Flyvbjerg calls his approach to validation the "outside view" or "reference class forecasting.")[9] However, when strategic misrepresentation (lying) becomes your operative presumption, then you give into the dark side of Janus's vision. The misrepresentation view presumes there is little hope of improving practices or outcomes in the future; there is only repeating of past failures (the reference class) that tends to become viewed as fate.

Also, weak processes and practices allow lying's cousin, corruption, to flourish. The 2014 Corruption Perceptions Index (CPI) by Transparency International rates countries on a scale of 0 (highly corrupt) to 100 (very clean). For example, the CPI rating for Brazil

---

8   http://foresightpress.net/member/bent-flyvbjerg/.

9   Flyvbjerg, Bent, "Curbing Optimism Bias and Strategic Misrepresentation in Planning: Reference Class Forecasting in Practice." European Planning Studies, January 2008.

was 43.[10] At the time of this book's writing, the outfall of an alleged corruption scandal involving Petrobras, some of its major contractors, and others, rocked Brazil's economy.

We are unlikely to ever forecast when corruption's leakage bursts into a deluge, but clearly this was not a system unknown-unknown.

The Organization of This Book

In the "Who Should Read This Book" section, three audiences were identified: senior management, project management, and risk quantification practitioners. To address these various audiences, the book has two parts:

♦ Part 1 introduces basic concepts of capital project systems, scope development, and investment decision making as well as the risk analysis and quantification needed to support them. This is the business case for and context of risk quantification; i.e., when, where, how, and why it is applied. Part 1 is intended for senior management as well as the general audience, keeping the details of risk quantification methods to a minimum. It offers anecdotes and examples to highlight and help explain the concepts.

♦ Part 2 is for the project manager, teams, and risk quantification professionals. It covers the details of practical risk quantification methods and models while also explaining why they are needed; i.e., how do they support the senior business manager's decision needs and the project manager's control needs. This part is a technical reference book.

Because the terminology used in the risk analysis world is often not well understood, the book includes a glossary and sidebars to define important terms as they come up. Finally, the book includes an index for handy reference. This chapter has provided a summary of risk quantification, its importance, and potential pitfalls in its application and hence serves as a foundation for the rest of the book.

---

10 Transparency International (http://www.transparency.org/cpi2014).

Questions

1) What is risk in respect to project objectives?

2) What message is the Janus meme attempting to convey?

3) Why is good risk quantification important to investment decision making and what has empirical research shown to be true of the risk quantification in typical industry cost estimates?

4) What should a company expect from risk quantification methods that "work"?

5) What are the drawbacks of the known/unknown logical construct?

6) List and describe the main risk types in respect to alignment with risk quantification methods?

7) Describe the risk type some call "Issues" and why care is needed in applying this categorization?

8) Define what is meant by "Contingency" and its relation to "Risk Quantification" in general?

9) What is "Contingency Planning" and how does that relate to Cost/Schedule Trading ?

10) Why has Monte Carlo Simulation (MCS) been perceived by some as unreliable? When is it a reliable practice?

11) What are the good and the not-so-good points about using Critical Path Models (CPM) as the basis of risk quantification?

12) What is meant by the term "Strategic Misrepresentation" and what would it mean if this was the operative mode of behavior of a project system or point-of-view of the risk quantifier?

"No work process or business system creates advantage, only the disciplined execution of the process creates advantage."
– Edward Merrow from Industrial Megaprojects[1]

"...the race is not to the swift, nor the battle to the strong... but time and chance happeneth to them all."
– Ecclesiastes 9:11

3
Phase Gate Capital Project Systems

Coming out of World War II, the oil and chemical industries were on a roll. New developments in polymers and petrochemicals rolled out of R&D departments. Demand for quality fuels soared as the number of automobiles increased. The 1950s saw growing prosperity and capital spending but also intensifying competition. Manufacturing processes for materials such as polymers and metals were maturing and lower margins on these commodities led to a drive to scale up plant capacities. Other companies pursued higher margin specialty products using new technology from R&D.

However, the cost of scale-up and the cost of new technology projects often overran their budgets badly. On the other hand, the maturity of business organizations was increasing. Projects transitioned from being heroic endeavors during the war to more systematized business processes. Businesses worked to bring order to the

---

1   Merrow, Edward, *Industrial Megaprojects; Concepts, Strategies and Practices for Success*, John Wiley & Sons (2011).

jumble of capital investment ideas coming through their door for decisions. And high on business's list of capital management goals was increasing the accuracy of cost estimates.

It was in this environment in the chemical engineering arena that the newly formed American Association of Cost Engineers (now AACE International) published its first proposed standard in 1958, creating four types of capital cost estimates.[2] The types were designed to support business's capital management needs for logical, phased project scope definition and incremental investment decision making, with the intent to improve accuracy. The estimate types with their respective scope definition deliverables at that time are summarized in Table 3.1.

Estimate Type	Key Scope Definition Deliverable and Status
Order of Magnitude	Type, quantity, and quality of product
Preliminary	Preliminary flow charts and plot plans
Definitive	Final flow charts and plot plans
Detailed	Detailed engineering completed

Table 3.1: AACE Estimate Type Standard (1958)

Phasing of project scope and estimate development was not new in 1958,[3] but from that point on it was codified, at least in the AACE world (oil, chemicals, petrochemicals, materials, and utilities). There is little need to debate the need for project scope development *phasing*; it has always been accepted wisdom that businesses and investors need to have confidence in *what their capital is buying and how much it will cost.* It is also common sense that if the scope of what you are buying is not well defined, you cannot have much confidence in cost estimates.

Given that risk management's goal for capital investments is to increase the probability that a project achieves its objectives, *scope development and estimate phasing is perhaps the first standardized project risk management practice.* And it remains the most fundamentally important one to this day. The details have of course evolved since 1958 as will be described in this chapter, but the fundamentals remain the same.

---

2   Derived from Gorey, J., "A Proposal by the Estimating Methods Committee-Estimate Types," AACE Bulletin, Vol 1, No 1, 1958.

3   Nichols, W. T., Capital Cost Estimating, Industrial and Engineering Chemistry Division of American Chemical Society, 1951, 43 (10).

What management really wants from phasing are *reliable* accuracy ranges in cost estimates. Accuracy range is perhaps the most fundamental risk quantification metric; if nothing else, it is easy to understand the math. Accuracy is usually expressed as the percentage that the actual cost or duration outcome will vary from the estimate. For example, +100%/–50% accuracy means that the final actual cost of a project estimated at $100 will range from $200 (+100%) to $50 (–50%). So, given management's need, the AACE technical committee documented typical accuracy ranges one might expect for estimates at the various phases in 1958. To get a feeling for history, the original ranges were as shown in Table 3.2.

Estimate Type	Accuracy (% that actual will vary from estimate)
Order of Magnitude	+100%/–50%
Preliminary	+/–40%
Definitive	+/–10%
Detailed	+/–5%

Table 3.2: AACE Estimate Type Accuracy Range Expectations (1958)

Quoted ranges such as these have been both a blessing and a curse for risk quantification ever since. They have been a blessing for conceptually communicating the *relative* improvement of accuracy that results from developing better scope definition before approving full project funding. They have been a curse because management has often interpreted these ranges *as standards in an absolute sense*, i.e., they assume that the ranges apply or should apply to every project estimate. This is a false and dangerous assumption because the level of scope definition is only one uncertainty among many and it often is not the greatest risk. Pre-determined ranges do *not* apply to any given estimate. In fact, research shows that the high ranges in the table above are on average too low by a factor of two to three times (2X to 3X) for large industry projects. That is why realistic risk quantification is required; *there are no standard ranges* (as AACE clearly states in the current version of the above table in their RP18R-97).

Just as there have always been scope development *phases*, there have been incremental *decisions* to approve spending and obtain resources as needed for R&D, preliminary design, and eventually, full funding for the process plant engineering, procurement, fabrication, construction, and startup. Managerial and engineering economics practice was well evolved in the 1950s and the capital investment profitability estimation was a key focus of AACE at its founding. What has evolved since then is increasing systemization of scope development phases and their intermediate, incremental *gates* (decision points) as formalized management processes. In this chapter I will describe the typical features of these evolved *phase gate capital project systems* and the role of risk quantification in these systems, keeping in mind that phase gating is about risk management.

Systems

Throughout this book, the word *system* appears, particularly with respect to capital project management systems and *systemic risk*. My years of benchmarking, research, and consulting experience have taught me the value of viewing capital and project management as *systems* – something with parts that interact to form an integrated functioning whole. It seems natural in the project world where one deals constantly with work breakdown, process flow diagrams, and organization charts. In addition, there are external economic and social systems in which businesses operate and capital project systems interact.

I am not alone in seeing things from a systems point of view. For example, one author said over 40 years ago that "Cost Engineering must be viewed as an integral part of systems engineering."[4] Also, the AACE's Total Cost Management (TCM) Framework text, which is the foundation of all its technical products, also takes a systems point of view (i.e., TCM is an annotated process map).

It also does not take much experience for one to see that project systems are also dynamic; the system elements and interactions change over time. An active area of risk quantification research involves systems dynamics (SD), which studies how complex systems behave over time. SD modeling has found many uses, particularly in regards to system technical risks. For project management, it has also evolved fascinating models using feedback loops (e.g., rework). Work by Cooper and many others since the 1970s have demonstrated SD application on projects, particularly in claims analysis.[5] Unfortunately, SD models and tools are not practical for cost and schedule

---

4   Uriegas, Carlos T., "Towards a Scientific Approach to Cost Estimating", AACE Transactions, AACE International, Morgantown, WV, 1971.

5   Cooper, Kenneth G., "Naval Ship Production: A Claim Settled and a Framework Built", Interfaces, Informs, Catonsville, MD, December, 1980.

risk at this time because of the complexity of and skills required for building unique SD models for each project.

While this book does not include SD modeling, it does cover methods that borrow the system concept of risk *interaction*, including the behavior and biases of people in these interactions. What research shows us is that risk conditions and events can amplify and compound, resulting in non-linear impacts (i.e., impact is disproportional to the sum of each risk, otherwise known as chaos and blowouts). But before we get into systemic risks and their impacts, let's look at today's prevailing capital project systems and how they came to be.

Project Management and Systems Evolution in the Process Industries

We have all come to know the profession of Project Management since it blossomed along with the use of the PERT (Program Evaluation and Review Technique) and CPM (Critical Path Method) methods of scheduling in the 1960s. It is hard to imagine that when AACE was founded there were few professional schedulers and that becoming a project manager (PM) was seen as an extension of one's engineering or construction career. PMs had no association of their own and scheduling was often just another task for the project or construction engineers.[6] As process and project complexity grew and computers became more practical, capital management became more systematized, and roles such as scheduling more specialized.

This systemization is highlighted in a classic 1965 text that I still use today (and encourage others to read) entitled *Control and Management of Capital Projects* by John Hackney, an AACE founder.[7] Not only does he describe project management, organization, and control, but Mr. Hackney was a strong proponent of the "Janus" view. In terms of Risk Quantification, his book was ground breaking in that it not only recognized the phased approach in capital management, but it provided the first practical empirically-based model for quantifying project cost risk. Though largely forgotten today, I believe the "Hackney Model," which in our terminology is

---

6   Traub, A., et. al., "Can the Application of the Critical Path Method Assist Cost Control," Report of the AACE Cost Control Committee, May 1963.

7   Hackney, John A., *Control and Management of Capital Projects*, Wiley (1965). The 2nd edition (1991) is available from AACE International (from www.aacei.org).

a parametric, systemic risk model, is superior to many of the risk quantification methods in common use today (this method will be covered in more detail in Part 2).

By the 1970s, mainframe computer applications for project estimating and scheduling were common, but the systems seemed to be burying themselves under their own weight. By 1976, Mr. Hackney and his Mobil Oil colleague James Bent had this to say, "Many contractors have invested heavily in the development of PERT and CPM techniques and control systems. In spite of this investment, and resulting sophisticated systems with their associated heavy running costs, owners continue to experience poor execution of the planning and scheduling function. We believe this is due in part to the increasing size and complexity of projects mentioned above, but principally to the reduced quality of scheduling personnel, failure to appreciate owners' real objectives, and lack of *system integration*."[8]

By 1979, project system failures continued to occur, leading Hackney to add, "The final indictment of present cost control methods is the repeated incidence of project overruns of hundreds of millions, and even billions of dollars without adequate warning. These unanticipated overruns have often exceeded 50%, and in some cases have been more than 100% of initial estimates... What cannot be excused is the fact that so many of these overruns have come as shocking surprises to management, well after the occurrence of events that made them inevitable."[9]

Given these perceptions at the time of increasing complexity and failures, the US Department of Energy, working with 34 major oil and chemical companies, hired the Rand Corporation to perform a study to seek "...a better understanding of the reasons for inaccurate estimates of capital costs."[10] The study acknowledges Mr. Hackney for helping to inspire it. Fittingly, the study starts with a summary of an industry consensus project phase gate scope development and decision process or system (although it did not use the words phase gate). Scoping activities and estimate deliverables in each phase of this system were succinctly described. It notes that "These estimates shape allocation decisions..." and, "Each estimate derives from its own knowledge base."

---

8   Bent, J. and J. Hackney, "Owner Approach to Planning and Scheduling" 1976 AACE Transactions. Emphasis added by the author.

9   Hackney, John, "Key Cost Control for Capital Projects," 1979 AACE Transactions.

10   Merrow, E., et. al., *Understanding Cost Growth and Performance Shortfalls in Pioneer Process Plants*, R-2569-DOE Rand Corporation, 1981.

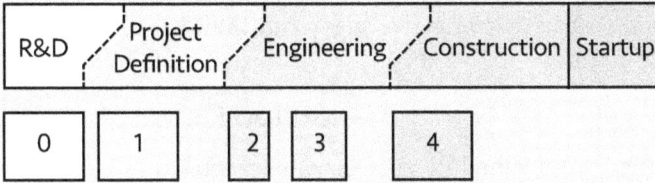

Figure 3.1: The Original Project Phase-Gate Process (Rand, 1981)

This study will be further described in Part 2; however, in terms of cost growth risk quantification, its major contribution was to add statistical horsepower to the Hackney Model concept (Rand covered 44 projects from 34 companies) and link it more tightly to the well-defined, industry consensus phase gate process shown in Figure 3.1. From the moment of its publication, there was no excuse for any process industry company for failing to use its findings and basic methodology. There is still no better empirically supported risk quantification model available in the public domain. Also, refined versions of its phase gate process have become ubiquitous in the process industries since the 1990s. Virtually every major company and contractor has incorporated a version of this model in its own capital project management system (if your company does not have one, it is time to catch up).

Dissemination of phase-gating was facilitated when Edward Merrow, the lead researcher of the Rand study, founded the benchmarking firm Independent Project Analysis, Inc. (IPA) in 1987. He acquired the Rand database and, building on the original studies, began conducting independent risk analyses of industry projects. IPA and its clients continued to evolve the phase gate process definition, calling it Front-End Loading, or "FEL." That FEL concept is similar to the old bidding term that describes the practice of disproportionately "loading" indirect and other cost into the unit price of work items to be completed early in construction to increase income cash flow. In scope definition terms, "loading" refers to doing as much scope definition as practical before or in front of project full-funding authorization. In FEL there is a "best practical" definition beyond which research shows there is little further reduction in cost and schedule risk.

Given the success of the FEL concept and the fact that most companies now have a FEL-like process in place, you would assume that these companies also use it as part of risk quantification. This would be incorrect. The typical company with a FEL-like process does not use formal parametric risk analysis, they do not consider systemic risk in any effective way, and their methods are not empirically sound.

Scope Definition and FEL

If cost and schedule risk are a concern (and if you are reading this book, they are), it is necessary for capital managers, risk analysts, and all other project professionals to understand the FEL phase gate model concept and its foundations. There is no better reference than IPA. I recommend reference to their training Institute (http://www.ipainstitute.com) and their other research sources for in-depth understanding (e.g., Paul Barshop's *Capital Projects*[11]). However, to provide some basic background, Figure 3.2 outlines the five basic phases, their intermediate decision gates, and a final closeout gate (note that for projects applying new technology, R&D may be done before and during FEL 1).

The following outlines the phases and gates above. The names such as "Assess" vary in practice, but the ones shown are common and will be used in this book (see Glossary for acronyms). After this discussion, I will describe the associated industry standard "Estimate Classes" that align with the gates and what they mean with respect to risk quantification.

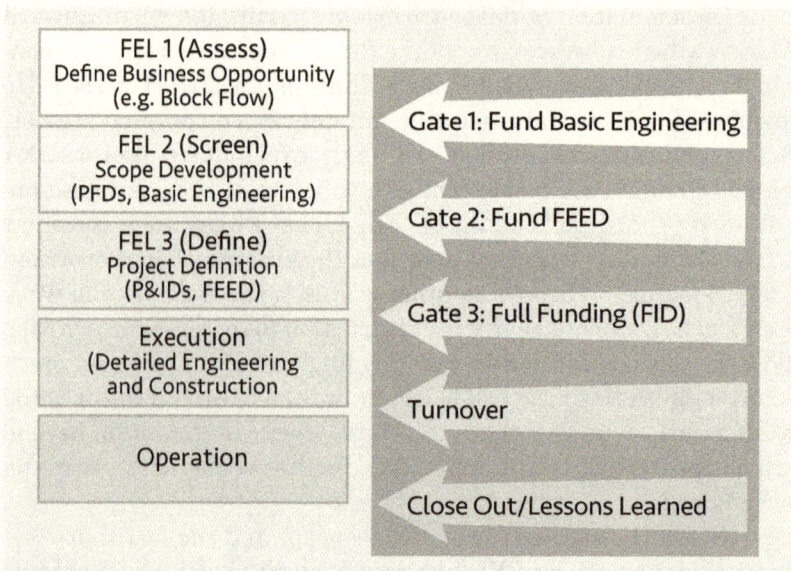

FEL 1 (Assess)
Define Business Opportunity
(e.g. Block Flow)

FEL 2 (Screen)
Scope Development
(PFDs, Basic Engineering)

FEL 3 (Define)
Project Definition
(P&IDs, FEED)

Execution
(Detailed Engineering
and Construction

Operation

Gate 1: Fund Basic Engineering

Gate 2: Fund FEED

Gate 3: Full Funding (FID)

Turnover

Close Out/Lessons Learned

Figure 3.2: Typical Front-End Loading Phases and Decision Gates

---

11 Barshop, Paul, *Capital Projects*, John Wiley & Sons, 2016.

FEL 1 (Assess)

In this phase, the business unit works to frame and define the business opportunity (other names are scoping, screening, appraisal, conceptualization). Alternatives to address business needs are outlined; these may include capital projects, operational changes, or other solutions. Project scope information may be limited to the type, quantity, and quality of product, and deliverables include block flow diagrams and general site locations. Costs incurred during this phase are relatively minor and are typically expensed. At the decision gate, several viable alternatives may be slated for further scope development with a business case documented for them.

It is important that risk quantification is good enough to screen out alternatives that have the worst risk profiles while flagging those with high potential value that can be capitalized on. Resultant cost estimates provide information for long term capital budgets and to support funding for the next phase. Common unresolved risks at this gate include ongoing R&D and incomplete results from pilot tests and a myopic view as to shaping (not considering all the aspects of the business case). High risk often offers high reward, so this phase should try to apply the Janus view to avoid killing potential game changers because of an overly pessimistic view.

FEL 2 (Select)

In this phase a technical team is assigned to flesh out the scope of the alternatives that passed the first gate. Enough scope definition is required to narrow the alternatives in broad outline to one and to obtain sufficient confidence that the business case is in fact solid for that selected alternative. Selection implies a commitment bias, even if not a financial one, so doing this phase well is of utmost importance. The next stage may consume 5 to 10% of the project's total capital cost, so the FEL 2 decision is never trivial.

This also means that risk quantification should be good enough to assure that the selected option has a viable risk profile, particularly in the worst case scenario. Key defining scope deliverables to obtain confidence include completed process flow diagrams (PFDs), preliminary plot plans, and preliminary specification of the most critical pieces of equipment. Developing this scope is often called "Basic Engineering" (in mining, it is "Pre-Feasibility"). Value improving practices are applied as applicable. Resultant cost estimates provide information to update capital budgets and to support funding for the next phase (which may include procurement of very long lead items).

Projects that require early commitments and agreements to go forward to FEL 3 (such as joint ventures) are often fully funded at this gate (e.g., upstream oil, transport/transmission carriers) and therefore the shaping or framing of the business case must be solid in all dimensions, including R&D and pilot tests. Common unresolved risks at this gate are residual uncertainties in the technology and/ or the business case.

FEL 3 (Define)

In this phase, the scope of the selected alternative is defined to the extent that a reliable basis of execution cost and schedule control is established. The business should have full confidence in the quality of this decision basis including, as with FEL 2, that risk quantification assures the project has a viable risk profile, particularly in the worst case.

Key defining scope deliverables include completed piping and instrumentation diagrams (P&IDs), final plot plans, and specification of all major equipment. Developing this scope is often called "Front End Engineering and Design" or FEED (in mining, it is called "Feasibility"). Resultant cost estimates and schedule are based on a defined execution plan and provide the owner with a complete basis for cost and schedule control, and support full funding for the project. A common unresolved risk at this gate is that P&IDs including HAZOPs (Hazard and Operability Studies) and execution and control basis planning are not quite complete.

Execution

In this phase, detailed engineering, procurement, fabrication, construction, and pre-commissioning work through mechanical completion are done in accordance with the plans established in FEL 3. There are milestones during this phase where critical risks and assumptions tend to be resolved or defined. For example, after tendering and issuance of the major procurements and contracts, there may be an intermediate gate to assure that FEL 3 planning assumptions are still valid and to re-baseline the execution plan and control basis to align with contractor inputs as needed. Also, after fabrication and construction are underway, assumptions about site conditions, labor availability, and productivity become known facts to address.

Startup and commissioning planning, which was preliminary in nature in FEL 3, will take place in earnest well before the planned mechanical completion date. This phase concludes with turnover of the functional asset to the business owner. After turnover, feedstocks are introduced with the intent of producing saleable product. The capital cost is booked after startup and asset depreciation begins.

A common unresolved risk at turnover is that functionality or operability is well short of expectations, particularly when new technology or scale-up is involved. It is not uncommon for the project to be booked to the asset ledger with long term debugging being carried on by operations for some time.

Operation

In this phase, the plant is operational; however, the operator must often work to bring the asset up to full operating capacity at the required product specification. In many cases production capacity and/or quality fall short. This may necessitate starting FEL 1 on debottlenecking or modification options to resolve the shortcomings, sometimes during the first maintenance shutdown (turn-around).

Historically speaking, the final cost of these follow-up projects are rarely added to the cost of the original project. As bad as project cost overruns and schedule slip look in the historical record, they are often understated because they do not include all of the work, time, and money spent to achieve the full original objectives.

For example, in one case a major manufacturing plant for a new product simply failed to operate. So, at the point in time where costs were about to go over by more than 10%, the project was declared "complete" and a major new modification project began to make it operational. In two other cases, the most important piece of equipment failed at startup and had to be replaced in its entirety; again, the replacements were declared new projects.

Close Out/Lessons Learned

Most project systems have a final review gate that is conducted a year or so after the turnover of the asset to operations. This review considers lessons learned and studies the asset's initial operability. In terms of risk quantification, at this point final historical risk information is captured for use in improving future analysis methods.

System and Process Maturity and Quality

While FEL-like processes are now widely used, they are typically immature in development, and/or they are not applied in a disciplined way. To repeat this chapter's lead-in quotation, *"No work process or business system creates advantage, only the disciplined execution of the process creates advantage."* A common system weakness is lack of disciplined and/or integrated sub-processes to support the overall phase gate process. The success of the decision gates hinges on the phase yielding high quality deliverables upon which management can base their decisions, including risk analyses and quantification deliverables. However, many companies have weak functional level processes.

For example, the FEL process requires a "Class 3" estimate to support the FEL 3/Define decision gate. However, the company may not have a well-defined process for producing a Class 3 estimate (as we will discuss later, AACE "Class" says nothing about the estimate process or quality). It is common for owners to accept contractor deliverables (e.g., a FEED estimate or CPM schedule) more or less "as-is" based on an assumption that being prepared by a large contractor, the estimate must be good quality. This is not a safe assumption. I bring the maturity and quality issue up because these are systemic risks that must be assessed and considered in risk quantification; it is not enough to simply have a phase gate process and list of deliverables.

System maturity and deliverable quality can be objectively measured. An example process maturity model is the Cost Engineering Maturity Model (CEMM) developed by Lance Stephenson based on the AACE Total Cost Management (TCM) process framework.[12] The CEMM provides "an objective assessment that identifies any deficiencies and gaps of an organization's process and enterprise capabilities and outlines where necessary improvements are required for future success." It includes a score card with quantitative measures for every aspect of the process and organizational capabilities. Figure 3.3 shows an example of a process maturity rating at the highest level, where level one is "just getting started" and four is "best in class."

There are also companies who will benchmark a company's project system maturity, competencies, and so on. I do this at a functional level. Similarly, you can perform independent review of the quality of deliverables (particularly cost estimates and risk analyses in our case). The goal is to improve the quality of the process, deliverables, and performance discipline. With quality defined as conformance to requirements, the road to quality starts with

---

12 Stephenson, Lance, "Cost Engineering Maturity Model (CEMM)" Cost
    Engineering Journal, Oct 2011. AACE International.

Total Cost Management (TCM) Maturity Assessment

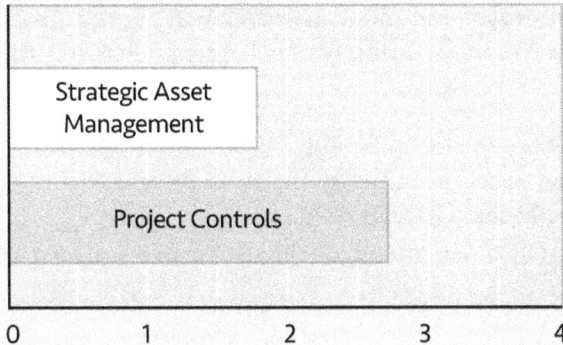

Figure 3.3: Example Process Maturity Model
(permission granted by Lance Stephenson)

establishing requirements that address the company needs and the project needs that tie back to company strategy. Then you simply assure that the deliverables meet these requirements.

If there are no company or project-specific requirements, you can fall back on seeing if the work aligns with industry practices (e.g., AACE Recommended Practices). However, if a company does not have its own well defined requirements for estimating, risk analysis, and so on, I have found that regardless of how pretty the deliverables look, the outcome will likely be disappointing. Making things up as one goes along is not a reliable approach. In Part 2, ways to measure these systemic risks and apply them in risk quantification will be described in more detail.

Scope Definition Metrics

As previously stated, the FEL phase gate process guides the incremental development of project scope definition, and scope definition is characterized by the status of defining deliverables (e.g., P&IDs, estimates, schedules, risk analyses). Each phase has a defined set of required deliverables, including expected content and quality. In a disciplined phase gate process, the gate keeper will first assure that the deliverables meet the stated requirements so as to not waste decision maker time due to inadequate or low quality information (garbage-in).

As with the process maturity example, most project systems use a type of scorecard to assess and quantitatively rate the status of the defining deliverables. Over fifty years of industry empirical research shows that quantitative ratings of scope development are strongly correlated with cost growth and schedule slip. Again, this is why project systems and scope development are at the front of the book. There are three rating systems in common use by the industry, including the following:

- ◆ IPA Front-End Loading Index (FEL Index),
- ◆ Construction Industry Institute Project Definition Rating Index (CII PDRI®), and
- ◆ AACE International Estimate Classifications (Classes).

Each of these rating systems is discussed below.

IPA FEL Index

IPA's FEL Index was the first widely used scope definition measure that is accompanied with a formally defined process. The FEL Index has been central to IPA's benchmarking approach since the company's founding in 1987. As discussed, its roots in capital projects were the work of Hackney and Rand. However, the IPA rating, while widely published in summary form, is proprietary to IPA and IPA's clients.

In summary, the rating has a scale from 1 to 3, which aligns with the FEL phases. An index rating of 3 is "best practical" at FEL 3/Define (note that better definition than best practical is not correlated with markedly improved outcomes). FEL is what I call a "threshold index;" i.e., if you have not achieved the desired state for all key deliverables, you do not get the score. For example, it does no good to have a detailed estimate and schedule based on incomplete P&IDs. If the P&IDs have not been reviewed and signed off by operations then, *no signature – no FEL 3 rating.*" This is important because projects that rate their own status are too apt to give themselves credit for incomplete work (e.g., "we think this will be done before the gate review meeting so we will give it a 3"). Many teams call the P&IDs and infrastructure definition "complete" when they are far from being so, particularly for OSBL (outside battery limit) systems where late definition causes major late changes.

CII PDRI:

With the success of the FEL Index, there was demand from general industry for a non-proprietary rating scheme and corresponding research. In 1997, the Construction Industry Institute (CII) sponsored a team of owners and contractors that published the first Project Definition Rating Index (PDRI) for process plants

A. MANUFACTURING OBJECTIVES CRITERIA	G. PROCESS/MECHANICAL (CON'T)
A1. Reliability Philosophy A2. Maintenance Philosophy A3. Operating Philosophy	G10. Line List G11. Tie-In List G12. Piping Specialty Items List G13. Instrument Index
B. BUSINESS OBJECTIVES	**H. EQUIPMENT SCOPE**
B1. Products B2. Market Strategy B3. Project Strategy B4. Affordability/Feasibility B5. Capacities B6. Future Expansion Considerations B7. Expected Project Life Cycle B8. Social Issues	H1. Equipment Status H2. Equipment Location Drawings H3. Equipment Utility Requirements
	I. CIVIL, STRUCTURAL, AND ARCHITECTUAL
	I1. Civil/Structural Requirements I2. Architectural Requirements
C. BASIC DATA R&D	**J. INFRASTRUCTURE**
C1. Technology C2. Processes	J1. Water Treatment Requirements J2. Loading/Unload./Storage Facilities Requirements J3. Transportation Requirements
D. PROJECT SCOPE	**K. ELECTRICAL AND INSTRUMENTATION**
D1. Project Objectives Statement D2. Project Design Criteria D3. Site Characteristics Available vs. Required D4. Dismantling and Demolition Requirements D5. Lead/Discipline Scope of Work D6. Project Schedule	K1. Control Philosophy K2. Logic Diagrams K3. Electrical Area Classifications K4. Substation Requirements Power Sources Identified K5. Electric Single Line Diagrams K6. Instrument & Electrical Specifications
E. VALUE ENGINEERING	**L. PROCUREMENT STRATEGY**
E1. Process Simplification E2. Design & Material Alts Considered/Rejected E3. Design for Constructability Analysis	L1. Identify Long Lead/Critical Equipment & Materials L2. Procurement Procedures and Plans L3. Procurement Responsibility Matrix
F. SITE INFORMATION	**M. DELIVERABLES**
F1. Site Location F2. Surveys & Soil Tests F3. Environmental Assessment F4. Permit Requirements F5. Utility Sources with Supply Conditions F6. Fire Protection & Safety Considerations	M1. CADD/Model Requirements M2. Deliverables Defined M3. Distribution Matrix
	N. PROJECT CONTROL
	N1. Project Control Requirements N2. Project Accounting Requirements N3. Risk Analysis
G. PROCESS/MECHANICAL	**P. PROJECT EXECUTION PLAN**
G1. Process Flow Sheets G2. Heat & Material Balances G3. Piping and Instrumentation Diagrams (P&ID's) G4. Process Safety Management (PSM) G5. Utility Flow Diagrams G6. Specifications G7. Piping System Requirements G8. Plot Plan G9. Mechanical Equipment List	P1. Owner Approval Requirements P2. Engineering/Construction Plan & Approach P3. Shut Down/Turn-Around Requirements P4. Pre-Commissioning. Turnover Sequence Requirements P5. Startup Requirements P6. Training Requirements

Table 3.3: PDRI – Industrial "Elements" (2008)

(now in its third edition).[13] They have since developed PDRIs for building and infrastructure project types.

Many of the CII participants were by then knowledgeable of IPA's FEL, and CII was advised by Mr. Hackney, so it is no surprise that the rating schemes have similar characteristics. The CII PDRI rates 70 "elements" (i.e., deliverables) as shown in Table 3.3.

Each deliverable is given a rating from 1 to 5 by the team, with 1 being "complete definition" and 5 being "incomplete or poor definition" (0 is "not applicable"). Criteria are provided for what these ratings mean for each element. Each element is weighted and a normalized overall score is calculated that may range from 0 to 1000 with 1000 being the least defined. I call this a "continuous index" as opposed to the FEL threshold approach. For example, you can get a target PDRI rating score (for example, 300) without completing all key deliverables. From a definitional quality and risk standpoint, incomplete P&IDs are not much better than having no P&IDs, so be careful to assure that if PDRI is used, threshold criteria are also implemented.

AACE Estimate Class

As with CII, the cost estimating community also desired a non-proprietary scope definition rating scheme that also met estimating needs. The estimate is a key deliverable because most investment stage-gate decisions hinge on cost. The estimate is also the final manifestation of scope definition – the estimate takes of all the other deliverables and translates their technical and programmatic information into monetary terms (if one assures the estimate, one is assuring all definition).

In 1997, the AACE Cost Estimating Committee published Recommended Practice 18R-97 for process plants. At its heart, it includes a table of the key deliverables used to prepare an estimate and the rating of each deliverable's expected development status at each of five estimate classes (Class 5 to 1 with 5 being least defined). Table 3.4 from 18R-97 is shown (with permission).[14] Note that:

- ♦ "S" is Started,
- ♦ "NR" is Not Required, and
- ♦ "C" is Complete.

---

13 Construction Industry Institute, *Project Definition Rating Index (PDRI)– Industrial Projects*, 3rd edition (2008).

14 AACE International, *Cost Estimate Classification System – As Applied in Engineering, Procurement and Construction for the Process Industries*, Recommended Practice RP18R-97, refer to latest revision.

CLASSIFICATION	CLASS 5	CLASS 4	CLASS 3	CLASS 2	CLASS 1
GENERAL PROJECT DATA:					
Project Scope Description	Preliminary	Preliminary	Defined	Defined	Defined
Plant Production/Facility Capacity	Preliminary	Preliminary	Defined	Defined	Defined
Plant Location	Preliminary	Preliminary	Defined	Defined	Defined
Soils & Hydrology	Not Required	Preliminary	Defined	Defined	Defined
Integrated Project Plan	Not Required	Preliminary	Defined	Defined	Defined
Project Master Schedule	Not Required	Preliminary	Defined	Defined	Defined
Escalation Strategy	Not Required	Preliminary	Defined	Defined	Defined
Work Breakdown Structure	Not Required	Preliminary	Defined	Defined	Defined
Project Code of Accounts	Not Required	Preliminary	Defined	Defined	Defined
Contracting Strategy	Not Required	Preliminary	Defined	Defined	Defined
ENGINEERING DELIVERABLES:					
Block Flow Diagrams	S/P	P/C	C	C	C
Plot Plans	NR	S/P	C	C	C
Process Flow Diagrams (PFDs)	NR	P	C	C	C
Utility Flow Diagrams (UFDs)	NR	S/P	C	C	C
Piping & Instrument Diagrams (P&IDs)	NR	S/P	C	C	C
Energy and Material Balances	NR	S/P	C	C	C
Process Equipment List	NR	S/P	C	C	C
Utility Equipment List	NR	S/P	C	C	C
Electrical One-Line Drawings	NR	S	P/C	C	C
Specifications & Datasheets	NR	S	C	C	C
General Equipment Arrangement Drawings	NR	S	C	C	C
Spare Parts Listings	NR	NR	P	P	C
Mechanical Discipline Drawings	NR	NR	S/P	P/C	C
Electrical Discipline Drawings	NR	NR	S/P	P/C	C
Instrumentation/Control System Discipline Drawings	NR	NR	S/P	P/C	C
Civil/Structural/Site Discipline Drawings	NR	NR	S/P	P/C	C

Table 3.4: AACE 18R-97 Estimate Input Checklist and Maturity Matrix
(Revised March 1, 2016)

The RP expands on this rating somewhat for the key deliverables (e.g., the P&IDs are to be "issued for design" at Class 3); however, it does not offer a detailed deliverable specification. For example, one would expect that a "defined" P&ID has undergone a hazard and operability (HAZOP) review, but this is not stated.

AACE has since developed Class tables for building, mining, and other project types. AACE has also developed a parallel Schedule Classification RP. As with CII, many of the AACE committee members were knowledgeable of FEL, so the rating schemes align closely:

♦ Class 5 is FEL 1/Assess,

♦ Class 4 is FEL 2/Select, and

♦ Class 3 is FEL 3/Define.

Correlating Class to PDRI is more problematic given PDRI's continuous and non-linear nature. Conversions of these ratings are discussed further in Chapter 13.

Both FEL and Class are "threshold" approaches; e.g., there is no Class "3.1." A project's definition should not be called Class 3 or FEL 3 until all deliverables meet the threshold. If it has not reached the goal, call the estimate "Class 3 with exceptions" to make sure management is aware that there are gaps and residual risk. As mentioned with the FEL Index, teams typically over-rate their scope development ("class creep"). Teams are often so proud of completing their P&IDs that they call them Class 2, having previously overrated their incomplete P&IDs as Class 3. As a general rule, if your team tells you that their FEED estimate is Class 2, it is not.

Scope Definition: Driver of Cost Growth and Schedule Slip

As stated in Chapter 2, over fifty years of industry research tells us that the greatest cost and schedule risk is not fully knowing what the scope is at project authorization. We have described the tools for scope definition, but what is their empirical reason for being?

In each rating system, from Hackney, Rand, IPA, to CII, there have been empirical studies demonstrating the correlation between the level of scope definition and other systemic risks and cost growth and schedule slip. The correlation is so powerful and well proven that *it makes no sense doing risk quantification without starting from that point*. This part of the Chapter is in effect the business case for deciding to evaluate your systemic project risks using para-

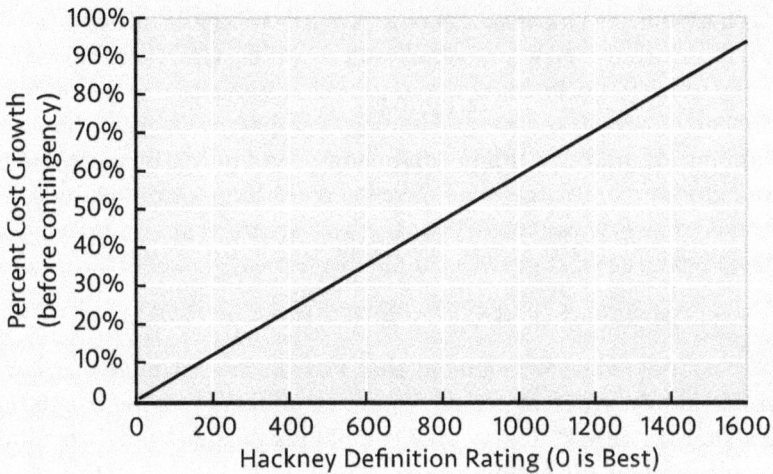

Figure 3.4: Hackney Study: Percentage Cost Growth from Base Estimate (1965)

metric methods. The highlights of each of the key research studies are described below. Part 2 of the book will cover the methods that have evolved from these studies in more detail and how to put them into practice.

Hackney - Cost (1965; updated 1991)

John Hackney examined cost growth data from a group of 30 projects from his personal records.[15] He measured cost growth as a percentage from the *base* or bare estimate without contingency after normalizing for escalation (growth from the base estimate is the estimator's viewpoint). His definition rating scheme was based on his own experience and judgment (i.e., his weightings were not statistically tested). His index includes 117 elements in 29 groups in the following six broad categories (there are notable similarities to the CII table that he advised on later):

♦ General process basis,
♦ Process design,
♦ Site information,
♦ Engineering design,
♦ Detailed design, and
♦ Field Progress.

---

15 Hackney, John A., *Control and Management of Capital Projects*, Wiley (1965). The 2nd edition (1991) is available from AACE International (www.aacei.org).

The sheer number of items in his rating system, as with CII, is both a strength and a weakness. It serves as a great checklist of definitional attributes that a risk analyst should consider. However, having so many items tends to dilute the impact of any one item. For example, Hackney under-rated new technology's impact relative to the later Rand study findings. Figure 3.4 shows his finding for percentage cost growth versus the level of scope definition, with 0 being fully defined in every way (100-200 is the best practical at authorization). As you can see, cost growth can be dramatic.

Rand – Cost and Execution Schedule (1981 and 1986)

As described previously, Rand examined cost growth data provided by a group of major US process industry companies to the US DOE in 1981.[16] Thirty four companies participated, providing usable data on 106 estimates for 40 plants. The cost growth data is relative to the total estimate *including* contingency (the executive viewpoint) after normalization for escalation, capacity or product changes, regulatory changes, and unforeseeable risk events. It looked at only risk factors *"internal to the nature of the project"* (i.e., what this book refers to as systemic risks). The statistically significant cost growth drivers ($R^2 = 0.83$) were:

- The level of scope definition (0 to 8, with 8 as worst; 3 is best practical),
- Interaction of scope definition with process development (i.e., is R&D underway or scale-up from small pilot),
- Percent of capital cost in technology unproven in commercial use,
- Impurities in process flow,
- Process complexity, and
- Estimate inclusiveness.

Figure 3.5 shows the study's findings of percentage cost growth versus the level of scope definition. The upper line is for processes for which R&D is underway or that were scaled up from a small pilot. For this chart, the other risk drivers were set at typical values. Note that Rand included contingency (because it is difficult to find estimate breakouts years after the fact), unlike Hackney, who looked at

---

16 Merrow, E. W. et al., *Understanding Cost Growth and Performance Shortfalls in Pioneer Process Plants*, Publication R-2569-DOE, Rand, (1981).

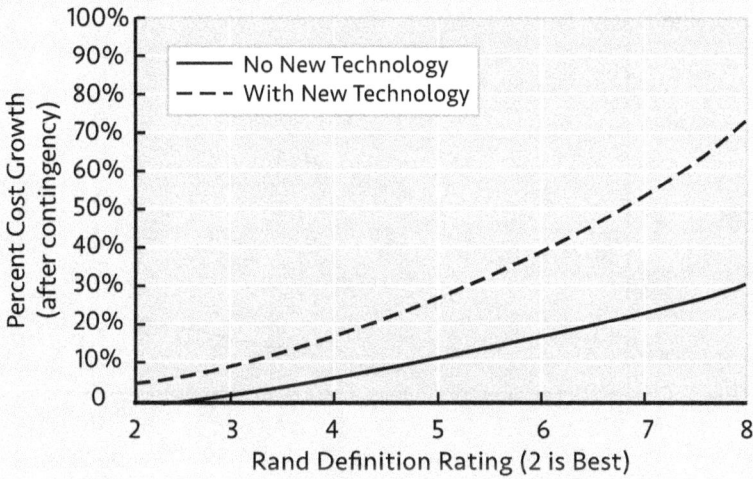

Figure 3.5: Rand Study: Percentage Cost Growth from Total Estimate (1981)

growth from the base estimate. From my benchmarking experience, is reasonable to assume that most estimates included from 5 to 20% contingency; therefore, to convert the findings to growth from the base estimate (the estimator's viewpoint), adding 5% to the level 2 definition and scaling up to 20% for level 8 is suggested.

Later, using the same database as for cost growth, Rand examined construction schedule slip. Fewer drivers were significantly correlated with schedule duration than for cost growth and the model fit was not as good. This is probably because of the paramount importance of the first production milestone. Trading of cost for schedule is common, i.e., schedule achievement can be bought, so the connection of risk drivers to schedule is masked. The statistically significant construction schedule slip drivers ($R^2 = 0.65$) were:

♦ The level of scope definition (0 to 8, with 8 as worst; 3 is best practical),

♦ The interaction of technology and the percent overlap of engineering & construction schedule, and

♦ Process includes solid or semi-solid feedstocks (ore, tars, powders, and so on).

Figure 3.6 shows the study's finding of percentage construction schedule slip versus the level of scope definition. The upper line is for plants whose process technology is exploratory or predevelopment or R&D is underway at sanction (with an assumed 50% overlap of

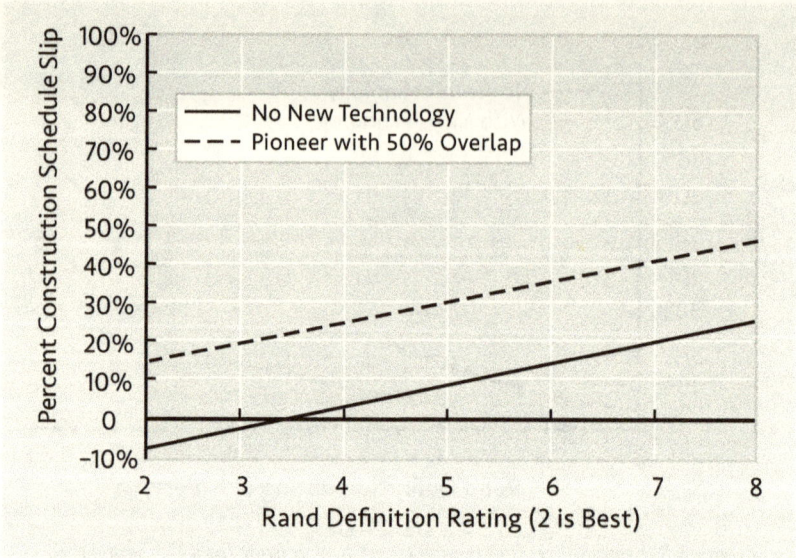

Figure 3.6: Rand Study: Percentage Construction Schedule Slip (1986)

engineering and construction activities). The relationship shown is reasonably applicable to the entire execution phase duration. Also, the study looked at slip in absolute months of large projects, but it found the months and percentage slip measures were 88% correlated; based on that the months were converted here to percentages.[17] To put the percentages in perspective, if the execution schedule was 30 months, the expected slip would be three months at the Rand midpoint rating of 5. A question you may want to ask about your own major project schedule risk analyses is, *"How many of your schedule risk analyses show three months slip as typical?"*

CII – Cost and Schedule (1995)

CII did an empirical validation of its original Industrial PDRI in 1995. They examined the cost growth from the authorization estimate, including contingency. The range of PDRI ratings in the sample of 23 estimates only went up to about 500 out of 1000 (i.e., it did not cover AACE Class 5). The study did not show a mean trend line; however, using its data the mean trend is shown in Figure 3.7 ($R^2 = 0.33$). The estimates included contingency, so adding 10% to the values in the chart would be a reasonable approximation of cost growth from the base estimate (the estimator's viewpoint).[18]

---

17 Myers, C. W. et al., *Understanding Process Plant Schedule Slippage and Startup Costs*, Publication R-3215-PSSP/RC, Rand (1986).

18 Gibson, G. and P. Dumont, *Project Definition Rating Index (PDRI) for*

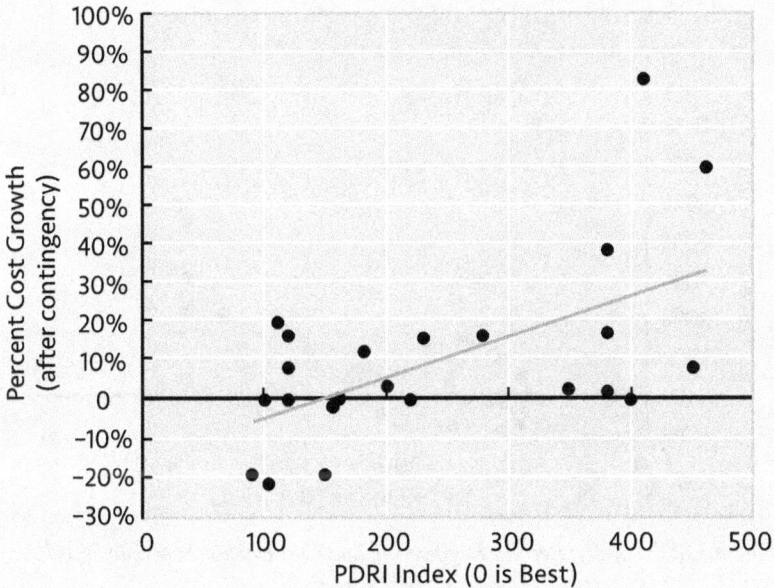

Figure 3.7: CII Study: Percent Cost Growth from Authorization Estimate (1995)

The CII team also examined the execution phase (engineering & construction) schedule slip. Again, the study did not include a mean trend line; however, using its data the mean trend is shown in Figure 3.8 ($R^2 = 0.53$). In this case we find a 10% schedule slip at the best practical definition rating. CII researchers went on in later years to improve upon this data analysis.[19] However, the original findings suffice to demonstrate the importance of scope definition to both cost and schedule duration.

These findings about scope definition are presented to drive home three points:

♦ These studies are all in general agreement; this is not a fluke,

♦ They are timeless; research finds the same outcomes today, and

♦ For the typical company, the impacts are very damaging to capital performance and can be catastrophic in the worst case. As was shown in the accuracy Figure in

Industrial Projects, Construction Industry Institute, 1995.

19 Trost, S., et.al., "Predicting Accuracy of Early Cost Estimates Using Factor Analysis and Multivariate Regression," Journal of Construction Engineering and Management, ASCE, March/April 2003.

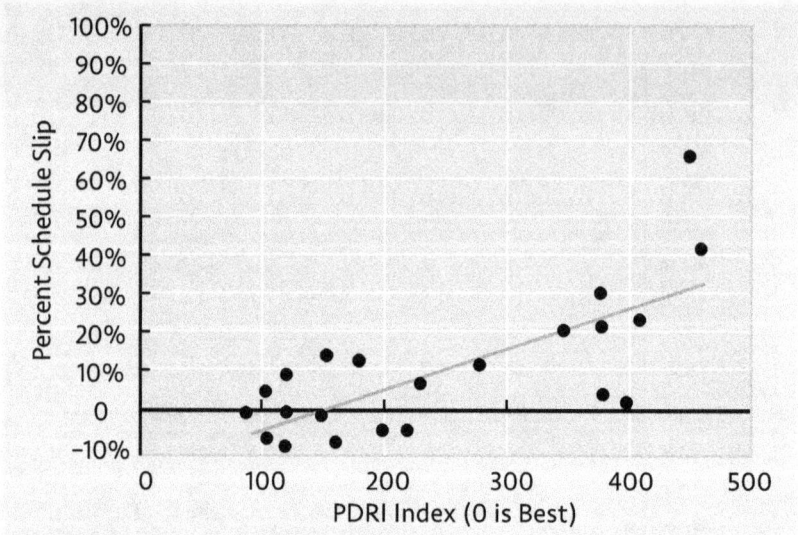

Figure 3.8: CII Study: Percent Engineering and Construction Schedule Slip (1995)

Chapter 2 (Figure 2.1), prevailing risk quantification methods are not predicting these outcomes.

Of course, these charts should not be used directly in risk quantification. There is more to risk than just scope definition. Each project is different and ongoing research has elaborated on other key systemic risks, including:

♦ Process and project complexity,
♦ Team development, and
♦ Project control practices.

In addition, weak systems can compound the impact of risk events, which requires a holistic treatment of all risk types. Finally, as was noted, the findings of these studies excluded escalation impact, and, in the Rand case, excluded significant risk event impacts! Part 2 will describe a full quantification approach.

In summary, the take-away message of this chapter is that the maturity and capability of the project system and discipline in its application are extremely important in risk quantification and ultimate project outcomes. This is not to diminish other systemic risks (e.g., technology, complexity), but it starts with the project system. The next chapter elaborates on not only the absolute cost and schedule impacts covered here, but also the uncertainty or range of those impacts (accuracy).

Questions

1) What was the driving purpose behind formalized phase gate project systems?

2) Describe an advantage and disadvantage of published accuracy range expectations by phase.

3) What is a system and how might capital and project management be viewed as one?

4) For process industry projects, briefly outline the historical chain of development of phase gate systems and the modeling of what is called Systemic risk by AACE.

5) Name the five typical phases and gates of FEL-like project scope development processes and describe a key defining design deliverable for each of the three pre-sanction phases for process industry projects.

6) What is the purpose of measuring system maturity and how might that relate to risk analysis?

7) Name at least three scope definition metric systems, identify if the metric is threshold/stepped or continuous in nature, and describe a caution with continuous measures.

8) The chapter summarizes a number of empirical research studies showing the relationship of objective scope definition measures and cost growth and schedule slip. Name two general learnings that one should take away from these (not specific numbers).

1835..."*When we reflect on the ruinous projects in which a confiding community have embarked their fortunes – the estimates which have encouraged, and the disappointments which have resulted from them – we must rather regret then deny the justice of their incredulity.*"
– Charles Ellet, Jr. in "The Cost of Railroads," Documents of the New York Assembly, 1835.

1840..."*It would appear the engineers have improved a little, and instead of blunders of 180 percent, they have reduced them to something under 100%, in the latter cases, which we must own looks like doing better – like having gained something from their experience. If they go on progressing thus, it is possible in another half century engineers' estimates will come to something near the mark.*"
– Editor from *Engineers and their Estimates*, Journal of the Franklin Institute, January 1840.

1981..."*The unreliability and uncertainty surrounding the accuracy...vastly exceeded any normal range of expected uncertainty associated with capital cost projections. These estimates...proved so highly unreliable and uncertain as to have effectively distorted, or at best confounded, efficient capital planning.*"
– Rand Study on *Understanding Cost Growth*, 1981 (ibid).

4

Accuracy: Confidence and Credibility

As we can see above, cost estimating, as measured by accuracy, is perhaps unique as an area of engineering skills and knowledge that has not improved much since the advent of the steam engine. Well, maybe some – the accuracy reported in the 1840 article about English railroads represents a 50 percent chance of overrunning the estimate by 130% or more and ten percent chance of overrunning

Accuracy and Accuracy Ranges

Accuracy is industry's shorthand for expressing the uncertainty of estimates. Accuracy is defined by AACE as: "An expression of an estimate's predicted closeness to final actual costs or time. Typically expressed as high/low percentages by which actual results will be over and under the estimate along with the confidence interval these percentages represent."[1]

Simplicity in the math makes *accuracy range* a good communication tool. In the example, the accuracy range of the $100M case is (140/100)–1 or +40% on the high side and (85/100)–1 or –15% on the low side. This results in a –15/+40% accuracy range.

To complete an accuracy statement, two qualifiers must be defined:

♦ The first qualifier is "what reference point is the low/high range relative to?" Sometimes it is the base, point or bare estimate without contingency (e.g., Hackney's estimator view); other times it is the total estimate including contingency (e.g., Rand and CII executive view).

♦ The other qualifier is "what confidence does the range represent?"

AACE recommends reporting an 80% confidence interval (see the definition given for Confidence).

---

[1] AACE International, *Cost Engineering Terminology*, Recommended Practice 10S-90.

by 410% or more. But with respect to confidence and credibility, the term "incredulity" would still seem to apply. In Chapter 3, the average impact of systemic risks in terms of project cost growth and schedule slip were described. However, when it comes to credibility of the quantification, we also need to understand the uncertainty or *range* of those potential impacts, i.e., their *accuracy*.

To provide an example of the importance of accuracy to investment decisions and credibility, consider two capital investment alternatives:

♦ Option A has a base estimate of $100M, while
♦ Option B's is $105M.

Without considering accuracy, Option A's $100M looks best. However, if an empirically-valid risk quantification method was used and Option A's high range was $150M, while Option B's was only $120M, the decision might change to Option B because it avoids the potential negative consequences of $150M on economics and reputation.

Now suppose the analyst uses a risk quantification method or a rule-of-thumb yielding a more or less "standard" high range of

Confidence Levels and Confidence Intervals

Confidence has a meaning in probability and statistics that the book will use. When we speak of *"p90 value,"* that means that value has a 90% probability or "confidence level" of being underrun (the high end of accuracy ranges). Correspondingly, *"p10"* would have a 10% chance of being underrun (the low end). If you say the +/- range has an 80% *confidence interval*, p80 defines the width of the range: 90% - 10% = 80% confidence interval.[1]

Why do we use 80% and not 100% for the range confidence interval? Because actual cost overrun distributions are usually highly skewed - a long tail of all too common disasters. The high end tail becomes flat (asymptotic) above *p*90 such that small increments in *p* value (e.g., *p*95 value versus *p*90 value) result in very large and unreliable increases in costs or schedule impact. If you see an analysis of a large project that has a *p*100 value that looks economical, then you should probably doubt the reliability of the analysis.

Note that some may report range in terms of +/- standard deviations (SD). For example, the actual accuracy of industry funding estimates at one SD is about +/- 20% (based on my benchmarking experience). For normally distributed data, one SD includes about 68% of outcomes and two SDs includes 95%. However, SD does *not* communicate the true range for unsymmetrical skewed distributions such as for cost growth. It is better to use confidence levels and intervals.

------

[1] AACE RP18R-97.

about +25%. Then, Option A's worst case of $125M ($100M x 1.25) looks even better compared to Option B's $138M ($105 x 1.25)! Two years later, the actual cost comes in at $140M – a surprise that should not have been.

Accuracy Range: Expectation versus Reality

As quoted in the chapter epigraph, the Rand study found that the actual range *"vastly exceeded any normal range of expected uncertainty."* So what is the expected range? A representative answer is found in the 1958 AACE Estimate Type standard presented in Chapter 2: +/–10% for a "definitive" estimate. These general expectations have not changed in 60 years. What these ranges really represent is an ideal case or a target that assumes mature systems, quality planning, good management with competent teams, no pronounced estimating bias, no new technology, typical complexity, nominal design changes, and no significant risk events. Projects where all or even most of these attributes are true are extremely rare. It's like living in Lake Wobegon where "all the children are above average" (to quote Garrison Keillor) or, using the Janus meme, management's expectation is the optimistic face looking forward.

This rosy expectation reflects one of the following two schools of thought (usually unspoken assumptions) as to the responsibility of the estimator for quantifying risk:

◆ Estimators are only responsible for quantifying the uncertainty in the given facts, or

◆ Estimators are responsible for quantifying all risk.

This is a very old confusion. Consider the following dialogue in an Engineering News article in 1904. A certain Mr. Whinery discussed "...the prevalent distrust of engineering estimates." Whinery believed the cause of the distrust was that the engineer was only responsible for some of the risks, while the business owner expected the estimates to address all the risks. The editor of a competing journal quickly countered that the engineer should be responsible for all the risks (the point of view of this book).[1] Whinery identified the top 10 risks and his view of partial responsibility as follows (and here we stand today):

Engineers' (or Estimators') Responsibility?

1. Quantity and character of the work
2. Physical conditions
3. Method of execution
4. Unit costs
5. General expense

Business's Responsibility?

6. Market fluctuations
7. Ability and skill of execution
8. Integrity and honesty in execution
9. Fortuitous incidents
10. Plan and scope of work changes

Figure 4.1 illustrates the ideal expectation of business management for accuracy wherein the ranges at each phase have short tails on the high end and the *p*50 stays the same for each estimate from gate to gate.

The reality, however, is illustrated in Figure 4.2, which compares the AACE 1958 "expected" ranges to the Rand 1981 study "actual" ranges converted to an actual/estimate format (the AACE data was modified to line up with the Rand estimate class designations). The high and low accuracy bounds are shown for each source

---

1   "Engineers' Estimates of Cost," Engineering News, Aug 11, 1904, and a response editorial, Engineering and Mining Journal, Sept 22, 1904.

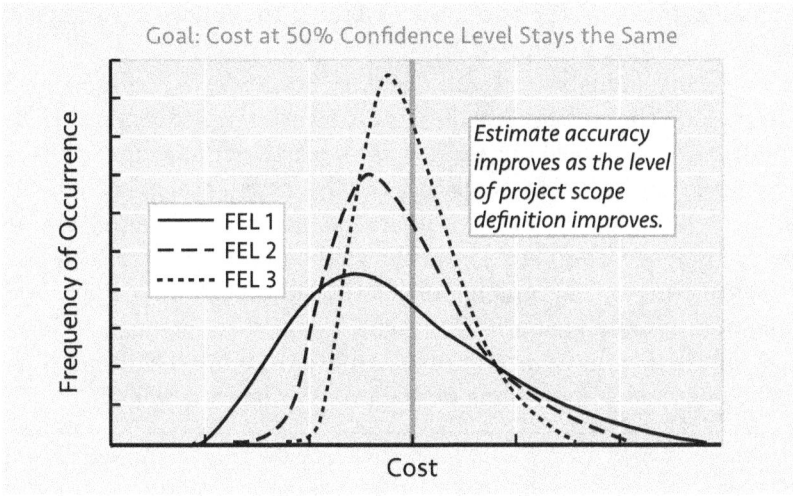

Figure 4.1: Industry Expectation for Accuracy Evolution in a Phase Gate System

(actual/estimate –1 in percentages). The 1958 AACE standard did not qualify what the range represents in terms confidence interval; however, the Rand curves represent an 80% interval. (Note that these are the statistics from the Rand data, not regression model results.)

Both ranges illustrate the concept that accuracy improves as the scope definition gets better (moving from left to right). But what is glaringly obvious is an industry underestimation bias. The majority of the Rand study project actual costs never underran the estimated cost, and the overruns were about *three times* (3X) *the expected high range.* As will be discussed later, the 3X bias factor will show up in other empirical studies as well, and not just for pioneer plants, but any large reasonably complex project. This is

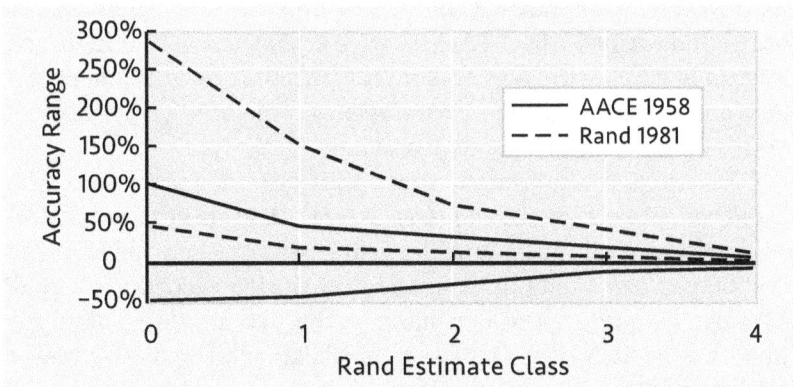

Figure 4.2: Industry Expectation for Accuracy Evolution in a Phase Gate System

a manifestation of the two faces of Janus: the failures of the past versus hopes for the future.

To the industry's credit, the AACE standards have evolved since 1958. The current AACE RP 18R-97 attempts to communicate there are *no* standard ranges because uncertainty has many causes besides scope definition. It also defines the confidence interval (80%) and reference point (total estimate including contingency set at p50 confidence level). Table 4.1 shows the new concept, which is a range-of-ranges. There is no longer the suggestion that there is a single standard distribution for each Class of estimate (e.g., a Class 5 estimate may have a range as narrow as –20 to +30% or as wide as –50 to +100%, depending on the project's specific risks).

| | EXPECTED ACCURACY RANGE OF RANGES | |
| | (around the estimate total, including contingency) | |
ESTIMATE CLASS	Low (*p*10)	High (*p*90)
Class 5	–20% to –50%	+30% to +100%
Class 4	–15% to –30%	+20% to +50%
Class 3	–10% to –20%	+10% to +30%
Class 2	–5% to –15%	+5% to +20%
Class 1	–3% to –10%	+3% to +15%

Table 4.1: Accuracy Range-of-Ranges, AACE Recommended Practice 18R-97

This is clearly an improvement in terms of avoiding the presumption that risk is somehow predetermined. However, even the RP's widest ranges are still too narrow and the high range too low compared to actual outcomes. For example, Figure 4.3 overlays the RP18R-97 range-of-ranges (shaded bands) with the accuracy findings of a 2014 study of Canadian hydropower project estimates (boxes and dashed lines).[2] Again, we see that the actual high end overrun is 2 to 3X the AACE "expected" accuracy bound; there is a huge underestimation bias of contingency evident in *every* empirical study of large project that I have found.

Figure 4.4 summarizes the actual accuracy situation. Predicted cost growth, and to a lesser extent schedule slip, are underestimated at each phase, but particularly so at early phases. The final actual cost tends to be outside the stated accuracy range of our early estimates, and is usually at the *p*70 or *p*80 point of our funding estimate range. Our risk quantification estimates represent

---

2   Hollmann, J. et. al., "Variability in Accuracy Ranges: A Case Study In the Canadian Hydropower Industry," AACE International Transactions: 2014.

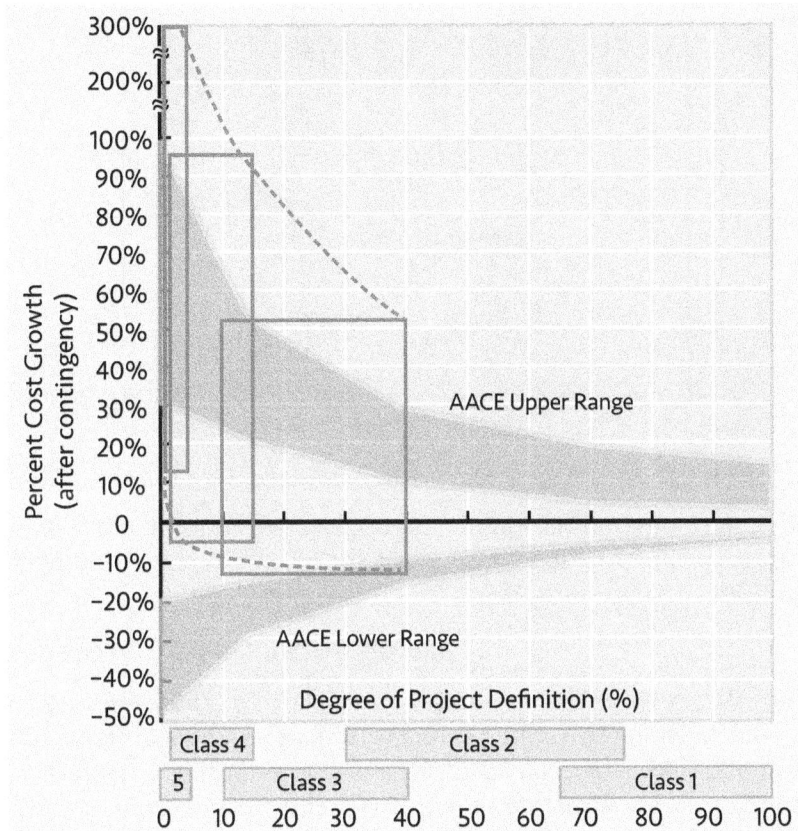

Figure 4.3: AACE Range-of-Ranges (18R-97) vs. Hydropower Project Study (2014)

Whinery's partial engineer's view (some of the risk); the actuals represent the business's view (all the risk). This disconnect in expectations is a prescription for lost confidence and credibility. And thanks to *unknown-unknown* rationalization, we all have convenient cover for 180 years of failing to address the *unknown-knowns*, our inconvenient truths.

Non-Process Industries

Most of the *controlled* research on accuracy has been on the process industries. However, many of the published studies on accuracy have been on public infrastructure projects. Most of those studies are *uncontrolled* for known risk drivers (such as the level of scope definition at sanction), so their conclusions as to the cause of overruns and slip are suppositional. Chapter 15 takes an in-depth comparative look at some accuracy studies for various industries

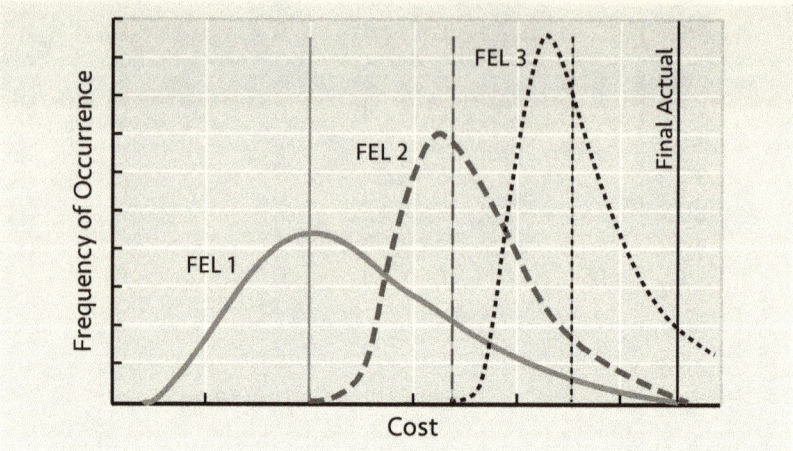

Figure 4.4: Industry Experience – Understatement at Each Estimate Phase

and concludes that the findings of the process industry research can be reasonably applied across most construction-related industry projects.

Large versus Small Projects

The prior charts are for large projects, i.e., those whose size would individually have a meaningful impact on a company's overall capital performance, but not "mega" such that a single project has the potential to devastate a company's profitability and/or valuation. There is less empirical research of small project estimate accuracy because these projects are individually less of a threat to overall profitability and shareholder's perceptions.

However, we know that the realities of small and large projects differ; small projects are biased to overestimating and underruns. As stated by one researcher, "When a project team sets a soft [cost] target, about half of the unneeded funds are usually spent...about 70% of small projects underrun."[3] This research also indicated that in small project systems, overruns tend to be punished. To avoid punishment (in less disciplined cultures), teams avoid overruns by including "fat" (above-the-line contingency, often called allowances) in the base estimate because high visibility contingency is often poorly received by management for any project size. This can bias a company's perception of risk and partly explain their misguided expectations.

---

3   Kulkarni, Phyllis, "Stop Punishing the Overruns," InSites, IPA, Inc., Sept 7, 2011.

Figure 4.5 shows a typical distribution of actual/estimate values observed by the author for a small project portfolio. Often, no projects overrun by more than 10% (finance usually allows a 10% overrun before raising alarms). In this "cresting wave" pattern, many projects spend all their funds, while some return all or some of the excess. The long tail on the low side is a good thing because it means that unused funds were returned rather than wasted, i.e., good post-sanction control discipline. If your primary goal is to keep the plant running and running safely, using this over-estimate and underrun practice on capitalized maintenance work makes some sense. Perversely, a bad sign for these systems is too good of an accuracy outcome (i.e., a tight distribution around 1.0). This is usually achieved by over-funding projects by about 20% and then wasting any excess on "urban renewal" tasks and/or doing work on other projects that would otherwise have overrun (cost shifting). Everyone comes out on budget!

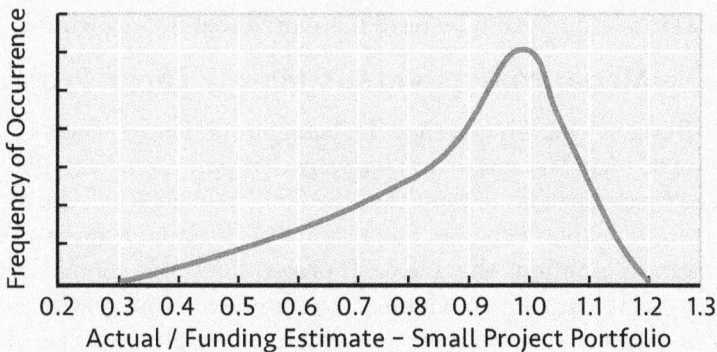

Figure 4.5: Typical Accuracy for a Small Project Portfolio

The small versus large project overrun dichotomy can induce a kind of corporate schizophrenia. Many owner companies have major project organizations that are separate from small or plant-based organizations. A newly formed major project group will often inherit the small project system cultural trait of expecting underruns or always being on budget. Small project managers may not appreciate that FEED contractors for major projects prepare base estimates with little or no fat. The game on large projects is "get 'er funded" as opposed to "get 'er done" on small projects. Project or business managers conditioned to under runs can lead to disasters when they bring that mind set to large projects, or a small company takes on a rare, "once-in-a-blue-moon" megaproject.

Looking at an entire company's portfolio of projects of all sizes, the combined distribution of the number of under-running small projects and over-running large projects can look serenely *normal* (as in normally distributed). The "all size" accuracy distribution of major companies has a p10/p90 range of about +/–20% around the funding estimates. The company probably doesn't realize that this reflects the overlap of separate populations. Overruns are primarily a large project phenomenon, but because large projects dominate company capital budgets and overall return on capital, they are what matters most.

As a last note on the "cresting wave," this underrun behavior is not limited to small project systems. It can occur where OPEX (e.g., feedstocks) is low, funds are available, and pressure is off the economics (for example, some Middle Eastern national oil companies). Unlike small projects where "over-fund-and-under-run" (or spend) has some rationale, it makes no sense for large ones because of the potential for waste and/or corruption, not to speak of the locked up capital funds that could be used more productively elsewhere.

Megaprojects versus Merely Large Projects

Research has shown that the behavior of megaprojects is in a class of its own. Merrow, in his *Industrial Megaprojects* text, defined megaprojects as those larger than US$1 billion in 2003 dollars, which is about $2 billion in 2016. For risk quantification, a more useful measure to highlight these special projects involves *complexity*, of which size is a significant element. In complexity theory, size is *one* way to measure *complication* (an element of complexity). Size being a key element of complexity, there *is a threshold size above which the project becomes complex* – no more questions need be asked. A $2 billion threshold is appropriate, and if you consider what some call the super-mega projects (greater than $10B), then complexity is a given.

That being said, size is not the whole story of complexity. For example, a $500 million integrated chemical plant with many continuously linked process units and new infrastructure, multiple licensors, multiple EPC contractors, and multiple venture partners can be relatively more complex than a merely large project over $2B (for example, a straightforward LNG plant with multiple trains, single EPC contractor, no venture partners, etc.).

Complexity and mega scale exact an extra cost penalty for poor practices. For example, there is an increasing penalty for poor scope

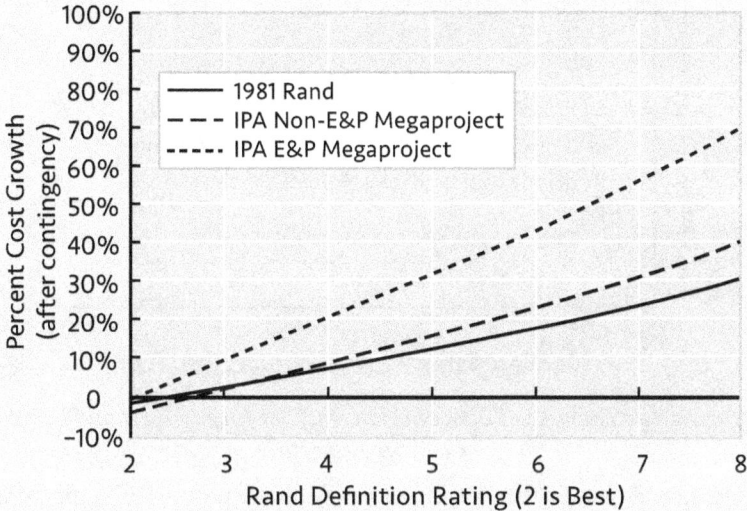

Figure 4.6: IPA and Rand: Megaproject Cost Growth from Authorization Estimate (2012)
(note: IPA's qualitative rankings were converted to Rand ratings per IPA "Best" = Rand "2" and "Screening" = Rand "8")

definition. Figure 4.6 compares 2012 IPA findings about megaproject cost growth (including in exploration and production) with the 1981 Rand chart of general industry projects. The Figure shows the significant cost penalty for poor megaproject scope definition.[4] Note that schedule outcomes do not necessarily follow this pattern because companies will often trade cost for schedule.

However, the worse cost uncertainty of megaprojects (and complex projects in general) is not just a matter of having somewhat more cost growth (a longer tail) than merely large projects. Complex project accuracy outcomes often reflect a unique *mode of failure* – the accuracy distribution becomes *bimodal*.

Complexity and the Disorder Dichotomy

Mega and complex project cost growth is either similar to that of merely large projects or it is in a class of its own – classic blowouts. Most blowouts are characterized by a doubling or tripling of direct and indirect labor hours for engineering, construction, and sometimes fabrication (particularly if fabrication is on site). If labor-related costs are half of total costs for a labor intensive process plant

---

4   Merrow, E, "Oil and Gas Industry Megaprojects: Our Recent Track Record," Oil and Gas Facilities, April 2012.

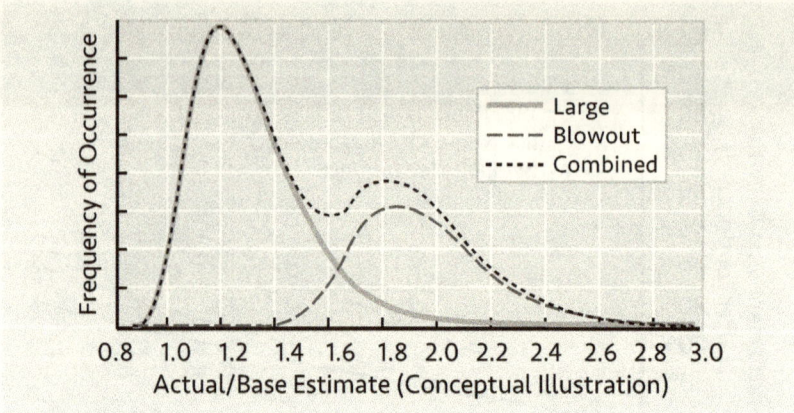

*Figure 4.7: Example of Bimodal Outcomes for Megaproject and Large
Complex Projects*

project, a blowout with double or triple labor hours will experience
a 50% to 100% overall cost overrun.

The blowout failure mode occurs when project management
and labor behavior transitions or *tips* from an orderly state where
traditional project control is effective, to a disorderly or chaotic
state where traditional control fails and intervention is required to
restore order. The *tipping point* most often occurs when complexity
combined with systemic weakness (business indecisiveness, poor
team development, and poorly defined scope) is confronted with
high stress (aggressive requirements, multiple risk events, adverse
markets). The transition from order to disorder gradually ramps up
to the point of collapse; i.e., the approach of disorder is usually first
evident as multiple engineering and procurement delays that start
to accumulate. When construction is about 30% to 50% complete,
this trend changes into an unambiguous blowout.

As previously noted, an attribute of complexity and a trigger of
blowouts is the severity of requirements, i.e., high stress put on the
project by businesses or other demands. In particular, IPA research
has shown that the stress of aggressive schedule requirements is
apt to push a megaproject over the tipping point. In his *Megaproject*
book, Merrow calls this business-driven stress a "pathology" that
he captured in the phrase "speed kills." The methods in this book
expose the pathology.

Figure 4.7 illustrates the tipping point dichotomy. The accuracy
distribution of large projects in an orderly state is on the left (solid
line) versus the distribution of large projects that have crossed the
tipping point into a disorderly state with a 50% or higher cost overrun

Substandard Resources?

Most project professionals have read stories of or have been involved in disputes between owners and contractors. However, it is rare for them to surface in the industry press. An example is a law suit made by Exxon Mobil Corp against Australian contractor WorleyParsons over the "Arkutun-Dagi" project, which was reportedly one of the largest offshore oil drilling platforms in the world. Per the Wall Street Journal (WSJ) in March 2015:

"Exxon claims the Australian contractor made so many mistakes designing the platform that the work took 2.7 million man-hours more than originally estimated and delayed the project by a year, according to a lawsuit in the Supreme Court of New York."

The article continues with, "... WorleyParsons denies this, saying Exxon's complaint 'is replete with unfounded, spurious allegations.' The contractor says it didn't commit to a fixed deadline or price, and that Exxon 'decided to retain the risks of cost overruns and delays rather than pay' WorleyParsons to bear them."

The article further says, "After promising to use its 'A' team and all necessary resources when pursuing the project, WorleyParsons staffed the project with its 'C' team and used substandard resources Exxon alleges. WorleyParsons denies this, saying the project took longer largely because Exxon increased the scope of work required."[1]

Shortly after the WSJ article, the dispute was reported as settled. The Business Spectator reported that, "WorleyParson said the settlement of the dispute, over the Sakhalin-1 Arkutun-Dagi project's offshore platform, has normalised the business relationship between all parties. The full settlement totals $US78m and includes cash payments of $US55m."[2]

---

1   Gilbert, Daniel, "Exxon Suit Highlights Energy Cost Fears", Wall Street Journal, March 8, 2015.

2   Neems, Mitchell, "WorleyParsons, Exxon settle dispute", Business Spectator, May 21, 2015.

on the right (a classic blowout; dashed line). Put all of these projects into one database and the dichotomy may appear as a two-humped camel, which is a bimodal distribution (dotted line).

Of course, in reality the dichotomy is not that clear-cut – as noted in one study major cost overruns can have many causes and not all major cost overruns reflect chaos.[5] Also, depending upon the labor content of the project, a doubling of labor may not have as

---

5   Ogilvie, Alexander, "A Tale of Two Tails; Chaos in Estimating Predictability," AACE International Transactions, AACE International, Morgantown, WV, 2016.

(Substandard Resources, Continued)

This illustrates the concept of risk allocation and how risk impacts differ between owner and contractor. Exxon reported a 2.7 million hour overrun and one year delay which likely resulted in hundreds of millions of dollars in additional capital cost and interest, not to speak of lost revenue. The contractor's reported impact was $US78 million.

♦ "Substandard resources" and "mistakes" were mentioned as factors in the law suit. What types of risks are these and, considering the project size as well, how might an owner company quantify the cost and schedule impact of these types of risk?

♦ If you are a contractor working in a capex market experiencing skilled labor shortages, how might you quantify labor shortage and design error risks in a reimbursable bid such as this one? In a lump sum bid?

notable an impact on total cost. However, for large projects with a major labor component, this bimodal outcome is somewhat predictable in risk quantification using an objective metric that combines measures of complexity risk (including stressors), systemic risk, project-specific risks, and escalation (external market stress). As that measure nears the tipping point, the probability that the project will cross into disorderly behavior increases. This concept is applied in the models in Part 2 (Chapter 14).

While this book is not about risk management and mitigation per se, the potential for devastating blowouts calls for risk management to have a two-level objective:

1. First, Thou Shalt not Blowout! Monitor for early disorder warnings (as covered in this book's quantitative approach) and apply a crisis intervention and containment approach; traditional control will not restore order.

2. Once safely within an orderly state, apply traditional control and risk management.

Lump sum contracts offer minimal protection for owners in these cases. First, the owner is often the root cause of blowouts: weak owner systems, owner changes, and/or indecisiveness. As losses become too much for contractors to bear, claims and disputes result (valid or otherwise) – and they will be costly. In some cases, the owner may change contractors and end up paying for most of the losses. While liquidated damages and other treatments can help, an owner can *never* fully recover the lost revenue if the project completion is late.

Programs and Portfolios

Another feature of megaprojects is that they are usually not a single project. They are almost always made up of several large sub-projects such as Inside Battery Limit (ISBL) process areas, Outside Battery Limit (OSBL) utilities, and offsite infrastructure, with each element having its own project manager, reporting to an overall project director or equivalent. The sub-projects that make up a megaproject are usually executed more or less in parallel, hence the overall duration of a megaproject is usually not much longer than the duration of the largest sub-project (project execution duration tends to max out at five years or so). The sub-projects may also be sponsored by multiple business units (e.g., refining, transport, and petrochemicals) and in some cases venture partners. Megaprojects therefore share similarities with programs.

A *program* is a set of projects that are administratively grouped together to address an overarching business strategy. They may all be included in a single high-level master schedule. Above that is an even broader category called *portfolios*. A portfolio is a group of projects and programs tied together by an overarching organizational goal. The phrase "capital portfolio" is often used in respect to the capital budget and budgeting process; this is a form of portfolio management. The demarcation between projects, megaprojects, programs, and portfolios is not always clear. The main issue in their naming and also in their risk quantification application is, *"How interdependent are the parts?"*

The elements of a project Work Breakdown Structure (WBS) are of course integral to the project's Critical Path Method (CPM) network logic and all the work is usually under one project manager (PM). In terms of risk quantification, the project gets its own funding and a PM will usually own the contingency. Megaprojects and programs are usually made up of fairly interdependent projects, captured in a master schedule, but often tied together firmly only by some key milestones and shared resources. They usually have multiple PMs under a director. Each sub-project may be funded separately by an overarching program business entity, often incorporated in its own right (e.g., a limited liability company or similar), keeping an eye on the total. For risk quantification, this means the decision makers are going to want to see outcomes by project and for the program as a whole.

In terms of risk quantification, the main issue in how to analyze a program is *dependency*. A program will have an overarching strategy, and to varying extents common organizations, shared resources, practices, and so on. External commercial, market, regulatory, and other environmental influences will be common to all the projects to some extent as well. In short, the projects are not independent. If a risk affects one, it will likely affect the others. As complexity deals with the interaction of parts in a system, programs are complex to the degree its projects are interdependent. And, like complex mega-projects, their cost overrun and schedule slip behavior tends to be bimodal. If the company's system (e.g., FEL, competencies) is weak, and one project starts to blow out, other parts will be stressed and may suffer as well. Risks can cross-infect and compound.

This book addresses ways to analyze and quantify risks at a program level. In summary, this involves assessing the sub-projects at one level, and then assessing common and integrative risks at the program level, viewing them through a complexity lens. Cost and schedule contingency and other risk funding can be quantified at each level.

The Cost of Time and Money (Escalation, Exchange, Interest)

All of the empirical research studies referenced so far have excluded *escalation*, i.e., the historical cost growth data was normalized to remove escalation impacts. This was done under the assumption that teams can neither control nor predict external economic risks, and also because escalation impact (i.e., pricing levels) is relatively easy to identify after the fact and to hedge before the project begins.

However, escalation is a major risk and, depending on market volatility over the duration of the project, it can be the dominant capital cost risk if it is not mitigated. A particular example was the 2003-2014 commodities "super-cycle," during which prices of many materials and services escalated quickly.

The same is true for currency exchange rates, which can also be volatile and expensive if you must pay for goods and services with currencies other than the one with which it is funded.

Finally, interest rates may change over time and, depending on how the project is financed, can also add risk. In each case, these risks tend to be compounding factors that add a further penalty price to the impact of other cost risks. For example, the cost impact of a risk event in the later years of a project will incur greater escalation than earlier risks, and the cost of a completion delay will include

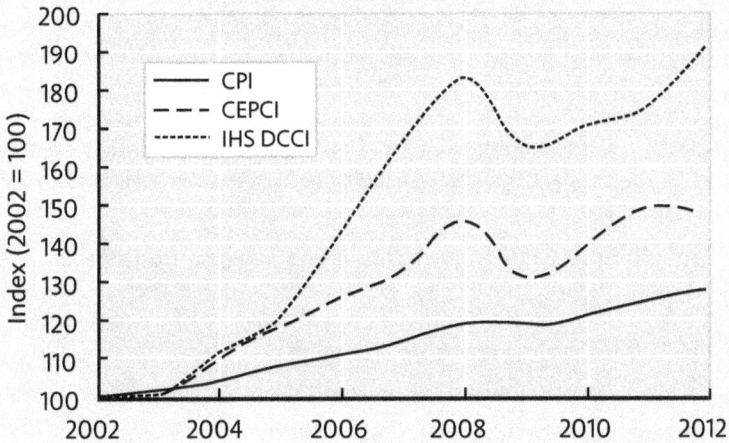

Figure 4.8: Inflation versus Contractor Cost Escalation/Owner Cost Escalation

additional escalation if prices go up rapidly in the later years. Also, escalation and other risks seem to go hand-in-hand – when CAPEX markets are hot, there will be both elevated escalation and increased labor shortages and low productivity (more stress).

All of this seems rather obvious and quantifying these risks would seem fairly straightforward mechanically speaking (forgetting for the moment the difficulty of economic prognostication). However, like systemic risks, the industry has tended to misunderstand and underestimate escalation, and rarely treats it as a risk (i.e., they use deterministic estimates). There are two areas of misunderstanding:

♦ Confusing escalation with inflation (as was highlighted in the Introduction Top-10 list), and

♦ Confusing contractor's internal cost escalation (e.g., wages) with how they price their services (e.g., bid unit prices), which is the cost to the owner.

As an example of what how this confusion can lead to very poor estimates and accuracy, Figure 4.8 compares three alternate price-level measurements for the period from 2000 to 2012, which included the commodity super-cycle and the global 2009 recession. These indices include:

♦ US Consumer Price Index (CPI): this is an inflation measure used by many companies in their capital evaluations. Given that almost none of the items in the

Who Says You Can't Underrun?

It is not often that one hears about massive large project cost underruns. A famous example was construction of the Empire State Building in New York City. Constructed from 1929 to 1931 at the start of the Great Depression, it was completed in just 15 months from first steel placement – 3 months faster than planned! The construction cost, excluding land, was estimated at about $43 million. Its final construction cost was only about $25 million.[1]

While the project benefited from the use of innovative construction techniques, the cost underrun was primarily due to market driven de-escalation. It is instructive to compare the project's cost underrun of about –40% to the reduction of US price and economic indices from 1929 to 1931:[2]

♦ Consumer Price Index (CPI): about –10%

♦ Producer Price Index (PPI): about –20%

♦ Industrial Production: about –35%

♦ Steel Scrap Price: about –40%

♦ Dow Jones Industrials: about –45%

However, upon completion, the building had trouble attracting tenants. It was called by some the "Empty State Building." Because of low revenue, the investment was not profitable until 1950.

A lesson learned from this case is that care must be taken in selecting price indices for risk quantification purposes (e.g., Steel versus PPI in example). Also, for services that are bid (such as construction), it is indices of demand that rule in volatile times (Industrial Production in example), not input cost indices such as the PPI. Finally, when capital spending in the market drops due to market collapses, it is likely that revenue will too.

---

1   Bob Moore Construction, "Empire State Building," (www.generalcontractor.com).

2   Yardeni, E., "US Economic History: Great Depression", Yardeni Research, Inc., February 19, 2014.

CPI basket are items that go into a capital project, this is a particularly poor choice (Ref: US Bureau of Labor Statistics – USBLS).

♦ Chemical Engineering Plant Cost Index (CEPCI): this uses USBLS input cost data for items that go into a chemical plant project, but it reflects cost to a contractor (e.g., wages), not the price an owner must pay for services (e.g., bid price).[6]

♦ IHS Downstream Capital Costs Index (DCCI): this is

---

6   See www.chemengonline.com/pci-home.

based on the actual sell price that IHS owner clients actually experienced for downstream process plant projects. For owners in this industry, *this is escalation.*[7]

As can be seen, the contractor costs (CEPCI) increased at a rate about twice (2X) that of inflation (CPI), and owner cost (DCCI) increased about four times (4X) inflation and 2X contractor costs. This is because the CEPCI included more commodity items such as steel and pipe that increased significantly in price during the super-cycle, and DCCI included the bid price for fabrications and labor services, which also increased significantly due to shortages of skilled labor and the ability of contractors to raise their mark-ups (and cover their own increased risks). Obviously, accuracy of escalation estimating depends not only on economic prognostication (forecasting market turns such as in 2004 and 2009), but on using the appropriate measure of prices.

Opportunity as Threat

Upon reviewing an early outline of this book, a fellow consultant suggested I focus more on "opportunity" – the positive side of uncertainty. It was a good suggestion; however, from an empirical point of view, my take on the topic is not what he may have expected.

Recall that "risk" is anything that adds uncertainty to the outcome whether it is positive (an opportunity) or negative (a threat). From a quantification viewpoint, the methods are agnostic – the models work the same with positive impacts as negative (which is why my original outline did not emphasis the topic). However, from a management viewpoint, opportunities should be directed to a value improvement program to be sure to capitalize on them (e.g., reduce costs and/or duration) rather than letting them lie dormant in risk management registers. However, there is one quantification issue that analysts must be aware of and that is that opportunities often come with a high price. There is an accuracy aspect to consider as well.

To explain, consider a project where the team has identified a cost reduction opportunity that they have sent to a value improvement workshop to analyze (this concept applies to schedule reduction and revenue enhancement opportunities as well). Let us say the workshop identifies that this change will reduce the base estimate by some amount as indicated in the "Cut Base" arrows of the Figure 4.9.

---

7 See www.ihs.com/Info/cera/ihsindexes/index.html.

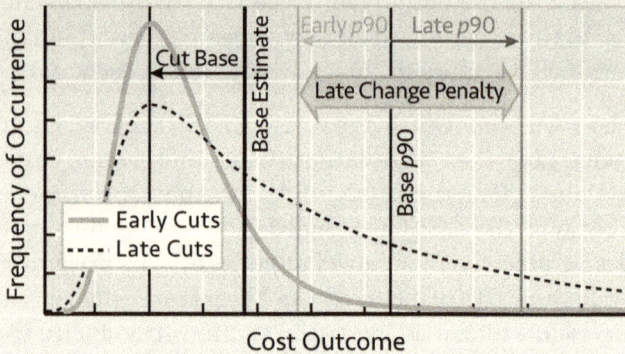

Figure 4.9: Opportunities and the Uncertainty Penalty

Most teams and estimators look at such cuts as a number, i.e., the most likely outcome, and that reduced number is often an enticing prospect. But before you decide to make the change, risk quantification analysis needs to be brought in to the workshop. The risk quantifier will focus on the uncertainty or accuracy, and *not just the number*. Here is where opportunities can become a threat, depending on what phase the project is in.

If the project is in pre-sanction (prior to commitment of significant resources), opportunities often add unalloyed improved value because they decrease cost without increasing uncertainty. Because we have not finalized the scope yet, we can make the change and optimize the plan around it. However, if the project is post-sanction (in execution), the story is entirely different. In that case, *every* scope change is a potential threat to project discipline, particularly if the system is weak or fragile. Late changes almost always increase uncertainty (worse accuracy) and add stress. A decrease in base cost that comes at the price of significantly increased risk is not value improvement.

Figure 4.9 illustrates this with three overlain distributions. The base case cost "base estimate" and "base $p90$" are labeled lines. The early cut distribution is the bold line, and the late cut distribution is the dotted line. The arrows show the movement of the mode value resulting from a cost cut and the movements of the $p90$ values. For the early pre-sanction cut both the mode and the $p90$ are reduced – a good value! However, for the late post-sanction cut (late change), the mode is reduced by the size of the cut but the $p90$ value increases as the accuracy worsens (distribution widens or becomes more uncertain). The difference between the early and late cut $p90$s is the late change penalty. As a rule-of-thumb, I advise my clients that for every dollar they save in a late cost cutting exercise, they will need to add a dollar to the contingency and two dollars to the worst case.

This situation reflects the hard fact that late change in an otherwise orderly project system is highly disruptive. The penalty usually shows up as a reduction in productivity and delays. For a mega or large complex project, late cost reduction exercises not only weaken and disrupt the system, but add stress by adding more aggressive requirements. This alone can push a project past the tipping point. I will generally not accept consulting assignments to facilitate late cost reduction or "value" exercises because there is too much pressure to cut – *regardless of the risk.*

In summary, opportunities should be capitalized on early (before completion of the Define phase) by an organization using value management (i.e., value improving practices or VIPs such as constructability, value engineering, and so on, which are the topics of other books). However, early or late, the risks of changes must be quantified with a cold, unbiased, empirically-informed eye on the likelihood of deterioration of control and performance, which for late changes is almost inevitable.

Dealing with Reality

Again, the reason for showing all these empirical studies is to emphasize that you cannot be complacent about the uncertainty of cost estimates or schedules, even when prepared in most mature project systems and by the most experienced estimators and planners. For large projects, the expected accuracy ranges are too tight, and are biased too low. For small projects, the bias is too high. For mega and large complex projects, the risk of blowouts gets added. In addition, long time horizons open the door to greater escalation, exchange, political, and financial risks (which are often misinterpreted).

The good news is that we know these things. They are quantifiable with reasonable confidence. This situation is not about "unknown-unknowns," but *unknown-knowns* (inconvenient truths in Rumsfeldian parlance) – we know the risks and we know how to assess and quantify them – but too often industry simply chooses not to. In Part 2 of the book we will show how to put all this research to work.

As a final note, for those doing risk quantification for a living, this disconnect has created a conundrum. Do you give the customer what is empirically valid, or what they expect and want? Or is it best to not even ask the question (keep it an unknown-known)? Excluding the agnostics as to risk quantification methods, you face two potential types of customers:

- ♦ Realistic managers who have lost confidence in risk quantification (often blaming Monte Carlo or economic "voodoo"), so they rely more on their judgment or rules-of-thumb. These customers will not call.

- ♦ Optimistic managers (or those who really want their project approved) who find comfort in analyses that align with their unrealistic expectations. They have no problem with sophisticated analyses, realistic or not. These are the customers who call. However, if you complete empirically-valid risk quantification and the numbers do not meet their optimistic expectations, it may well be the last call.

This chapter's title is about credibility and confidence. In my view, one has no choice but to try to re-align industry expectations and then deliver empirically valid results. Anything but the full Janus view is deception.

Questions

1) When expressing the –/+ (low/high) percentages of "Accuracy Range" of a cost or duration estimate, what two additional pieces of information are needed as well to understand what it means?

2) Statistically speaking, what are the two types of "Confidence" and what do they represent?

3) The assumption of the estimator often differs from the expectation of business owners as to what project risks the Estimator is responsible for quantifying. Describe the assumptions and expectations.

4) AACE International provides Recommended Practices for classification of estimates aligned with industry phase-gate processes and it includes indicative estimate accuracy range information. What is special about the accuracy information in respect to management accuracy expectations?

5) Describe the typical difference of cost over/underrun distribu-

tions for large projects managed by a project organization and small projects managed by a plant organization. Why is there a difference?

6) What distinguishes a *megaproject* from other large projects?

7) How does the distribution of cost overrun of complex projects (including megaprojects) often differ from that of low complexity projects?

8) Define what a *program* is and risk considerations it might add for quantification.

9) Describe two common areas of confusion as to the definition and nature of *escalation* that can detract from reliable quantification.

10) In terms or risk, describe how the nature of *opportunities* varies depending on when in the phase-gate process the opportunity presents itself.

"Chaos of Thought and Passion, all confus'd; Still by himself, abus'd or disabus'd;... Go, teach Eternal Wisdom how to rule; Then drop into thyself, and be a fool!"
– Alexander Pope from "An Essay on Man"

"Why, sometimes I've believed as many as six impossible things before breakfast."
– Lewis Carroll from "Alice's Adventures in Wonderland"

5
Investment Decision Making at the Gate

To this point I have described the reality of project cost and schedule risk in the process industries, and industry's inadequate and too often disastrous efforts to quantify that risk reality. This chapter changes the subject to the *use of risk quantification*. Project cost and schedule risk quantification is done primarily to support strategic capital investment or bidding decision making by businesses as well as tactical decision making by project teams. Therefore, we need basic understanding of the decision making process, and the role of CAPEX in that process, so that risk quantification meets decision making needs.

In a capital project system, the major decisions are made at defined scope development milestones commonly referred to as decision gates as illustrated in Figure 3.2 of Chapter 3. The industry body of knowledge concerning decision making, decision theory, and decision analysis is extensive and cannot be covered well in a single chapter. I particularly recommend the book *Why Can't You Just Give Me the Number?* by Patrick Leach; some of the material in the chapter is derived from Leach's text.[1] However, this chapter will address the following:

♦ Typical investment decision making and analysis processes and methods,

♦ Where and how project cost and schedule risk quantification information is used in decision making at the gate, and

♦ Insights as to decision maker risk attitudes and biases to help ensure the risk quantification story is communicated.

As an experienced owner company cost estimator moving into the world of benchmarking analysis, I gained more insight into what happens in the executive board room. I was somewhat shocked to learn that the elaborate project risk analyses I had been involved in as part of project teams in the past were often not being used in the investment decision-making process (at least not in the sophisticated way I had imagined). Now, a bit more seasoned, I am often asked by project teams to help facilitate cost and schedule risk quantification exercises, usually a few weeks before the gate review meeting. When I ask the project risk lead how the decision makers will use the resulting risk information, their answer is usually, "*I am not sure.*" Do the decision makers use sensitivity analysis? Probabilistic NPV? Arm wrestling? Decision makers and the analysts that support their NPV analyses are often reluctant to open their commercially sensitive doors to project cost and schedule analysts. In any case, general ignorance of the company's business decision-making process and methods is the prevailing point of view at the project level.

On the other hand, behind the board room doors, I have found that senior managers and their NPV analysts often do not know enough about project cost and schedule risk quantification to know what to ask for from the team or how that information might help with NPV evaluation. I recall supporting a 2-hour presentation on a new project cost and schedule risk analysis method being inaugurated by a risk management department. At the close, the capital

---

1   Leach, Patrick, *Why Can't You Just Give Me the Number?* Probabilistic Publishing (2006). (Note that a second edition of Patrick Leach's book was published in 2014.)

projects division manager, in whose department risk management resided, took me aside in the hallway and said, "John, I have no idea what was just said in there. *P*50, ranges, Monte Carlo and so on – it looks impressive, but what am I supposed to do with that?" Being a bit embarrassed, he had asked no questions in the room, but had me come into his office privately after the meeting so I could walk him through it. I started by saying, "First, tell me how your organization analyzes investment decision options, then I will tell you how what you just heard from the project team can be applied." That is the approach used in this chapter.

Decision Making and Decision Analysis

AACE's capital asset management process, the *TCM Framework*, has a chapter on "Investment Decision Making" (in fact, decision making is the centroid of the field of cost engineering covered by TCM, but that is another story). That chapter outlines an integrated process that starts with establishing decision policy, applying systematic Decision Analysis, and using quantitative, probabilistic modeling to give decision makers objective decision support information. Decision Analysis as outlined in the TCM Framework includes:

1. **Structuring** – identify and layout (i.e., frame or shape) the problem or opportunity,

2. **Evaluation** – analyze the alternatives identified in structuring,

3. **Agreement** – develop formal agreement on the selected alternative, develop the implementation plan, obtain decision maker approval, and

4. **Implementation** – implement the selected alternative.

Decision Analysis is consistent with the capital project systems discussed in Chapter 3 and illustrated in Figure 3.2. In the project system, the FEL 1/Assess phase is focused on business opportunity shaping and FEL 2/Select on agreeing on a single capital solution alternative. FEL 3/Define ends with agreement on and approval of the final investment decision (FID) and its implementation. The concern of cost and schedule Risk Quantification is primarily on the *Evaluation* step and providing information to facilitate agreement and implementation. Because the FEL 2/Select gate agrees on a single alternative, this is perhaps the most important gate for risk quantification in terms of value; however, the FEL 3 gate is the last chance to assure that it is the right decision.

Evaluation from a quantitative point of view includes heuristics and algorithms that focus on a key measure of investment profitability that is defined in the company's decision policy. The evaluation question is, *"What are the economics?"* The methods usually apply time-honored "engineering economics" approaches that evaluate technical and economic factors considering the time value of money and estimated cash flows over time. The most common profitability measures of interest in Evaluation include:

♦ Net Present Value (NPV): the net value of a cash stream for an alternative that has been discounted to the present at a given interest rate (usually representing the cost of capital or a minimum acceptable rate of return, sometimes known as the "threshold" or "hurdle" rate).

♦ Internal Rate of Return (IRR): The interest rate that makes the NPV of all cash flows for an alternative equal to zero. This calculated rate should exceed the company's "hurdle" rate. It does not indicate the benefit in absolute terms.

This book assumes that most business people and engineers understand basic engineering economics (time value of money and present value calculations). The profitability measure for the entire company is usually some version of return on capital, equity, or assets (ROCE, ROE, RONA). The presumption in decision making is that the better each project's return is, the better the company's metric will be; both look at return on capital investments.

There are two ways these measures are used in decision making:

♦ To decide between alternatives, select the alternative with the highest NPV or IRR.

♦ To make a go/no go decision on a single option, it will be "go" economically if the NPV is greater than zero (or if the IRR is greater than the hurdle rate).

The NPV calculation involves multiple cash flow streams. The one that often gets the earliest attention is the one that is the project's reason for being – the revenue stream. That stream starts with the first sale of product from the operating asset. NPV and IRR and hence the investment decision are usually highly sensitive to changes in inputs that affect revenue (e.g. production rate, sale price, and start date of revenue). Everyone understands the importance of sales price. As to production rate, if the plant does not produce the design capacity, the business case is likely hurt; therefore, operability related technical issues are a major (but often underappreciated) risk.

However, in this book, our concern with revenue is *timing*, which equates to project schedule. Schedule slip not only results in greater CAPEX (including escalation risk), but greater financing costs, lost initial revenue, and greater discounting of the later revenue stream. That said, it is fortuitous that the systemic risks that drive capital cost and schedule risk are also key drivers of operability. If we reduce the uncertainty of one risk, we tend to reduce the uncertainty of them all.

The NPV primary cash outflow streams are capital and operating expenditures (CAPEX and OPEX) and financing costs. The focus of this book is on CAPEX – the amount that gets booked into the asset register when the asset is mechanically complete and depreciated in the income statement after turnover of the asset to operations. OPEX (including general and administrative costs) are expensed costs of operating and maintaining the asset after turnover. Financing costs are primarily interest charges on borrowings to cover the CAPEX investment (or equivalent costs if internally funded).

CAPEX is of crucial immediate concern. It is the earliest cash outflow and it is not mitigated much by discounting. Finance or borrowing costs and rate risks are substantial; however, our main interest in them is schedule risk because if repayment of debt is delayed, or if further borrowing is required, interest charges accumulate. In short, finance needs to understand the schedule risk. Not to diminish the importance of these NPV variables, but you have many years to optimize production, sales, and/or operating efficiency for revenue and OPEX. CAPEX and depreciation are locked-in up front. Also, commodities producers are "price takers" and seem to find ways to defend their operating margins over time as needed. If the IRR is marginal, one can be assured the CAPEX and first production date uncertainty will become of paramount interest to decision makers, the investors, and others (e.g., banks) providing the funds. Nobody wants to take a write-down for an uneconomic asset.

The attention that CAPEX gets depends in part on the type of capital investment. *Strategic* capital is for projects that take a company in a new market direction or will increase production. As there is new income to the company, there is a strong emphasis on

revenue uncertainty. *Sustaining* capital (and capitalized maintenance) is focused on maintaining production, e.g., opening a new
section of a mine as an old one is worked out. Both strategic and
sustaining capital projects are evaluated using NPV or IRR. However, because sustaining capital maintains the prevailing production
and revenue stream, its economics tend to focus more on minimizing
CAPEX and financing costs. Investments made for policy, safety,
regulatory, reputational, or other non-economic reasons are generally not as focused on NPV or IRR because there is no revenue cash
stream (other benefits must be considered). However, like sustaining
capital, non-economic projects tend to focus on minimizing CAPEX
to obtain the desired benefit.

In boom times, strategic and large projects will make up the
lion's share of capital budget (the Pareto principle of 80/20 is common for the proportion of the budget for large/small). In booms,
the focus is often on chasing revenue with fast schedules. In busts,
strategic projects are deferred and sustaining capital becomes very
important. The focus then shifts to capital cost discipline as cost
cutting becomes the rule. The pressures to speed up the revenue
stream and/or cut CAPEX will be discussed later.

Decision Models and Applied Risk Quantification

Many (if not most) companies explicitly address uncertainty
in their Decision Analysis evaluations of NPV. The following are
three common methods used in the evaluation of process industry
projects (see Leach's "Number" text for more complete coverage of
these methods, which I have summarized below):

♦ Sensitivity Analysis and Tornado Diagrams
♦ Decision Trees
♦ Monte Carlo Simulation (MCS)

Sensitivity Analysis and Tornado Diagrams

The goal of sensitivity analysis is to determine which decision
model input (e.g., CAPEX) has the greatest effect on the output
(e.g., NPV). This evaluation is usually plotted on a tornado diagram.
Figure 5.1 shows a typical example.

A tornado chart used in sensitivity analysis requires three
values for every continuously uncertain input of interest: low (usually $p10$), most likely, and high (usually $p90$). For discrete uncertain
inputs, two values are required (e.g., NPV for yes/no or with/without).

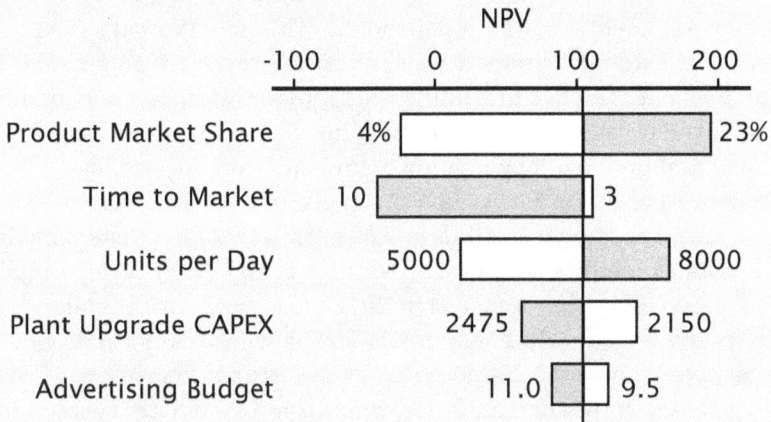

Figure 5.1: Example Tornado Chart Evaluating NPV
(Leach, with permission)

In a first pass, you first set all the inputs to their most likely value and calculate the NPV or other metric of interest. This forms the center line of the tornado diagram. You then set one parameter to its low value, keeping all others at their most likely, and recalculate the NPV. You repeat the calculation with that input parameter set to its high value, and the two outcomes are become the low/high arms on the tornado diagram for that parameter (discrete risks will have only one arm to left or right). This is repeated for each input.

In the example, the most likely NPV is $110M, and the product market share can be seen to be the greatest uncertainty and driver of value. CAPEX, which in the high case reduces the NPV to a still positive $60M, is only fourth on the list. It is not unusual to find revenue drivers at the top and CAPEX well down the list in sensitivity analyses tornado diagrams. It is also not unusual to find that the high/low values reflect subjective opinion, or in the case of CAPEX, predetermined ranges based on company policy or standards (e.g., +20% worst case for FEL 3 estimates). Readers of this book should have seen enough so far to be asking themselves, *"What if the CAPEX high case was really three times (3X) that shown in the Figure?"* The answer is that, assuming a linear relationship with NPV, the resulting NPV would be negative and CAPEX would rank nearer to the top of the list. This is not an extreme example – recall from Chapter 4 that research has shown that actual capital cost growth averages about two to three times (3X) of most company expectations. To paraphrase Rodney Dangerfield, "CAPEX risk gets no respect" in economics.

A shortcoming to be aware of for tornado diagrams is that they treat each input as independent. This is not a safe assumption. For example, product price and EPC costs are correlated in volatile times. A case in point is the "super-cycle" when commodity prices and revenue increased rapidly due to increasing demand from China and limited global supply. Commodity producers chased revenue by racing to get new capacity in place to catch the price wave. However, they forgot to allow for the parallel CAPEX cost trend. In the end, chasing revenue resulted in virtually every large mining company CEO being replaced in 2012 after metal prices collapsed, projects were cancelled, and write-downs were taken. Companies rediscovered cost discipline. What is unfortunate is that we know from research that commodity revenue and CAPEX are correlated; this outcome was predictable.

So, what do we need to provide to management's NPV analysts if simple tornado diagrams are the company's decision evaluation method? In that case, our *risk quantification must provide the low, most likely, and high case values for CAPEX cost and schedule.* The low and high numbers are not usually set to the absolute best and worst case (the true worst possible case is almost always an unqualified disaster), but, as discussed in Chapter 4, we use reasonable bounds such as a 10 and 90 percent chance of underrun ($p10/p90$ range).

If the project risk analyst is producing cost and schedule distributions using Monte Carlo simulation, the full distribution they are generating is not likely to be used by management's NPV analysts. Decision makers should understand that by using a 3-point estimate, they are losing risk information. For example, the arithmetic mean of a high side skewed triangular distribution will be greater than the mean of a PERT (Program Evaluation and Review Technique) distribution with the same 3-point values.

For some companies, the decision evaluation concludes with tornado diagrams. In a go/no go decision, if none of the arms of the bars reach into negative NPV territory, the project is good to go. The tornado diagram also shows how the most likely NPVs vary for alternate cases, and visually shows how sensitive that value is to the most uncertain inputs, but judging the relative risk/value is still left somewhat to the eye of the beholder. A more probabilistic approach will help clarify the situation as one departs from the most likely value.

Decision Trees

The next step up in sensitivity analysis in terms of useful information is to assess the 3-point values in a decision tree model, albeit without decisions incorporated (i.e., with chance nodes, but no intermediate decision nodes). A decision tree structures the evaluation so every possible combination of low/most likely/high for every important input parameter is calculated. It is fairly simple to do – it just requires a lot of calculation. Adding probabilities to the each branch allows a single risk-weighted "Expected Value" (EV or expected NPV) to be calculated.

Figure 5.2 from Leach shows a decision tree for the three most influential input parameters in the prior example. The only new information you need to input are the probabilities for each of the 3-point values. In the example, as suggested by Leach, the 30/40/30 probabilities are rule-of-thumb values that reasonably replicate the mean and variance of a full distribution. The example tree has 27 branches or possible combinations (i.e., 3x3x3). Once plotted, the first step is to calculate the NPV of each branch going from left to right; the probabilities are ignored. The second step is to calculate the risk-weighted EV by calculating 27 values from right to left, this time weighting each calculation by the probability for each input, then summing the 27 weighted values. The EV (about $32M in this case) is useful information if somebody just wants a *number*; however, it does not provide any information about the *confidence*.

To address confidence, plot the non-weighted 27 NPVs from the left-to-right calculation as a cumulative probability distribution. For example, in Figure 5.3, the probability of the NPV being less than or equal to –300 is 1/27 (0.037). The probability of it being less than or equal to –190 is 2/27 (0.074), and so on. We now see that there is a 37% chance of losing money but a 10% chance of making $200M or more.

So, what do we need to provide to management's NPV analysts if a risk-weighted decision tree is used as the company's decision evaluation method? *Risk quantification must provide the low / most likely / high case values (e.g., for CAPEX) and a probability for each.* As mentioned, the rule-of-thumb probability of 30/40/30 is generally adequate for the L/ML/H was expressed as a *p*10/*p*50/*p*90 of a continuous distribution.

The decision tree literally gives us confidence. However, the decision tree still suffers from some shortcomings. Visually, the probability curve is choppy and, for better or worse, this tends to

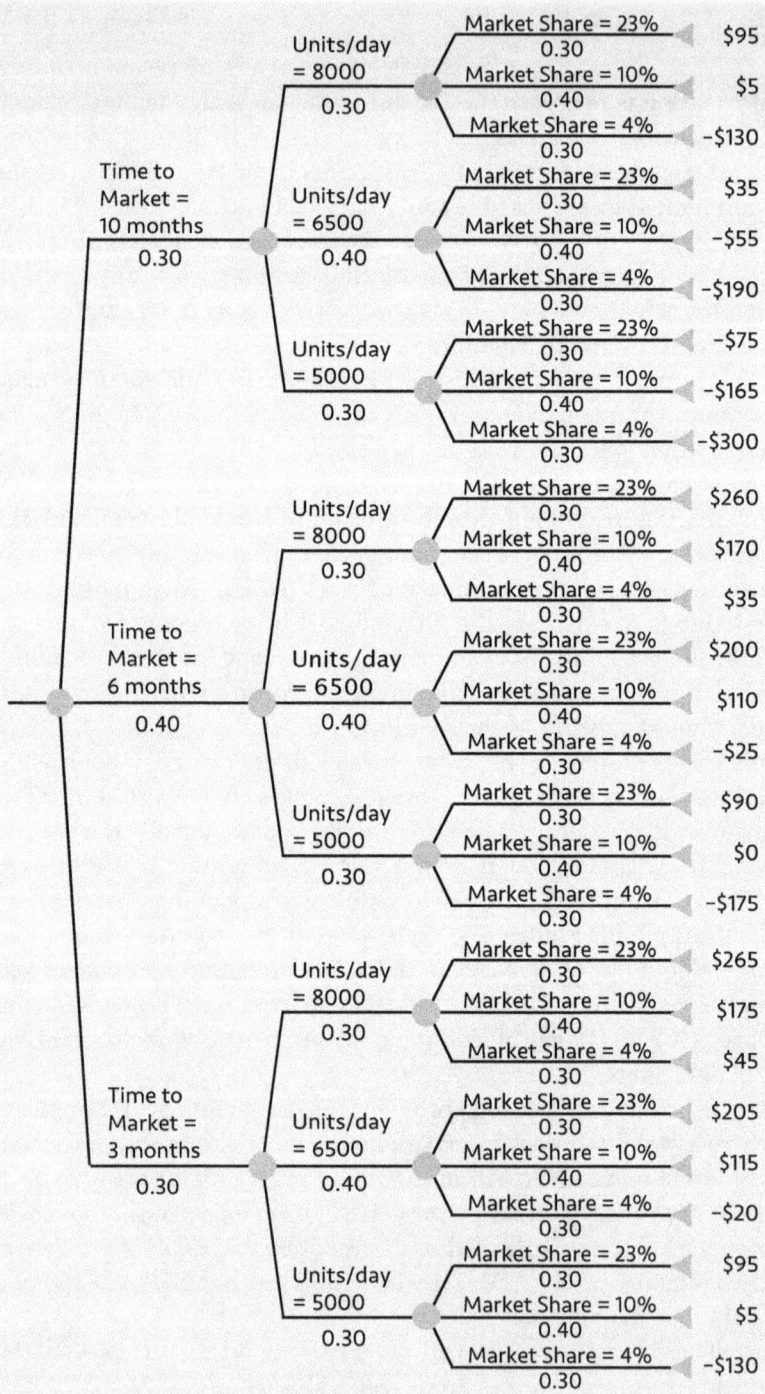

Figure 5.2: Example Decision Tree Evaluating NPV
(Leach, with permission)

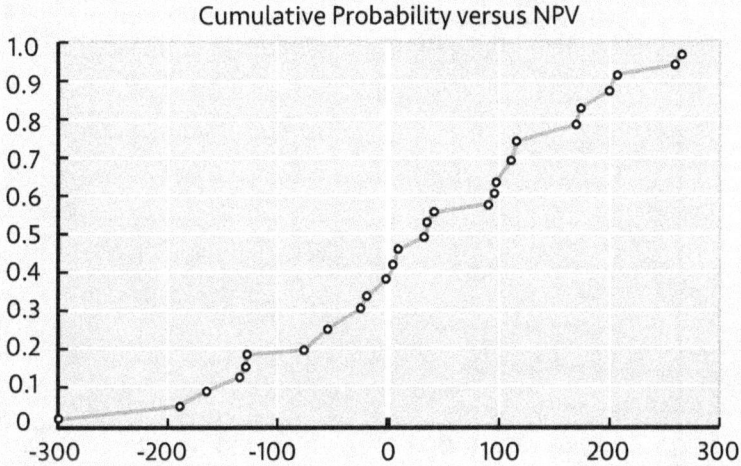

Figure 5.3: Example Cumulative Probability for the NPV Decision Tree
(Leach, with permission)

detract from the message by implying a noisy method. If the tree includes only one or two dominant input parameters, the choppiness can become so pronounced that the chart has big step changes that may lead to incorrect conclusions. It also becomes cumbersome to use if more parameters are added (e.g., adding CAPEX to the example takes the number of branches to 81). Next, the probability weightings assume a typical Pert-like distribution, which may not be true for every input. Finally, it still ignores the dependency issue – for example, revenue and CAPEX may be highly correlated. These issues can be addressed by applying Monte Carlo Simulation to the NPV model.

Monte Carlo Simulation (MCS)

Since the introduction of practical PC-based MCS add-ons for spreadsheets in the 1980s, MCS use has become common both in project cost and schedule risk analysis and in decision analysis. In a do-it-yourself mode, the method starts with creating an NPV model in a spreadsheet. The user then replaces the fixed values of the uncertain variables (e.g., CAPEX) with a distribution of possible inputs that the MCS add-on allows a user to select. If no better information is available, common distributions used are Triangle and Pert because the user can easily define these with 3-point values. The MCS algorithm is then initiated. The MCS algorithm calculates the spreadsheet thousands of times, each time sampling from the

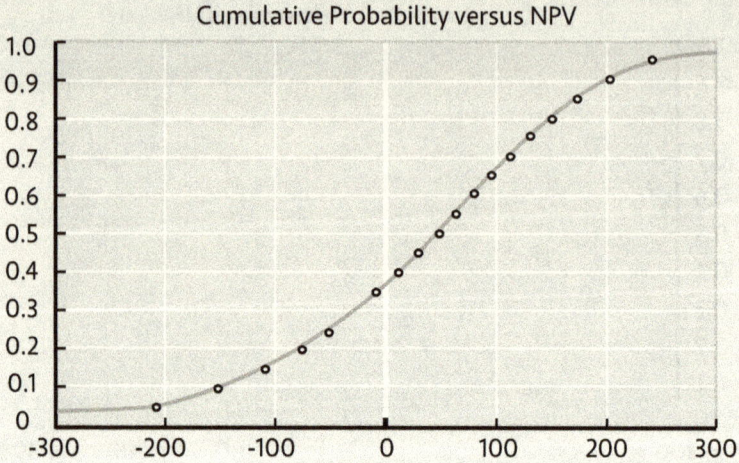

Figure 5.4: Example Cumulative Probability for the NPV model using MCS
(Leach, with permission)

input distributions and recording the answer, in this case the NPV. It remembers and can plot the distribution of all these thousands of outcomes. Figure 5.4 provides an example probability curve from an MCS run. Compare that to the choppy decision tree plot shown in Figure 5.3.

Where MCS really shines is that it allows one to define relationships between the uncertain input distributions. Indeed, one must define these relationships for an MCS model to be valid. This is done by entering correlation coefficients for related inputs (we will get into the details of how to do this in Part 2). Some common correlations are that high commodity sale price tends to drive higher CAPEX costs, and project schedule delay drives escalation and financing costs. Another MCS advantage is that you can enter more realistic input distributions if something better than 3-point estimates are available. These will include true worst cases. In our case, the NPV model input distributions for CAPEX and first production date (start of revenue) will be the output distributions from our MCS evaluation of cost and schedule risks.

So, what do we need to provide to management's NPV analysts if MCS-based NPV models are used as the company's decision evaluation method (unfortunately, not as common as it should be)? *Risk quantification must provide the distribution of possible values for each input (e.g., CAPEX), as well as information about correlations.*

Care must be taken to follow defined protocol in entering and reporting model structure, input distributions, and correlations to avoid misuse of the tool. MCS's poor reputation is in part due to shoddy and/or biased application.

The Story

It must be noted that none of the models above are true risk analysis models per se. As presented here, all the decision maker sees from their models are possible outcomes with no information as to *why* the outcomes are what they are! The diagrams are mute. Therefore, you must tell the capital project *risk story* to the management team, i.e., what risks do the low/high CAPEX and early/late completion date represent?

You cannot assume that the business NPV analysts will know the typical cost and schedule stories. They are often experts in business (marketing), finance, operations, or other areas and not engineering and construction. For example, if the high CAPEX case reflects the contracting department's opinion that the construction market will be hot with high labor cost and escalation, the NPV analyst must be told this so that they can make sure that revenue, OPEX and financing reflect the same "hot" market assumptions. If MCS is used by the NPV analysts, they can define these dependencies explicitly. Similarly, if the decision is between two alternatives, you must assure that both business decision and project teams use common input assumptions where applicable.

For alternatives, Figure 5.5 from Leach below shows how the decision makers may view the alternate risk profiles. In the Figure example, strategy "C" has a higher *p*50 NPV than strategy "B" ($150M vs. $100M) and offers potentially greater value on the high end; however, it also has a higher chance of losing money (20% vs. 0%). This is great information for a decision maker. If they are risk averse (seek to avoid risk), they might avoid strategy C. If they are risk takers, strategy C may be just what they want. However, if you are not using *realistic* risk quantification (e.g., one is using subjective or one-size-fits-all +/− ranges), then it is a "garbage in, garbage out" situation.

A concluding take-away from this section is that what matters to good decision making is not the most likely value (as in the example above, these values often tend to be close), but the best and worst case values. If your analysis does not result in low and high values in a realistic ballpark and you do not credibly communicate

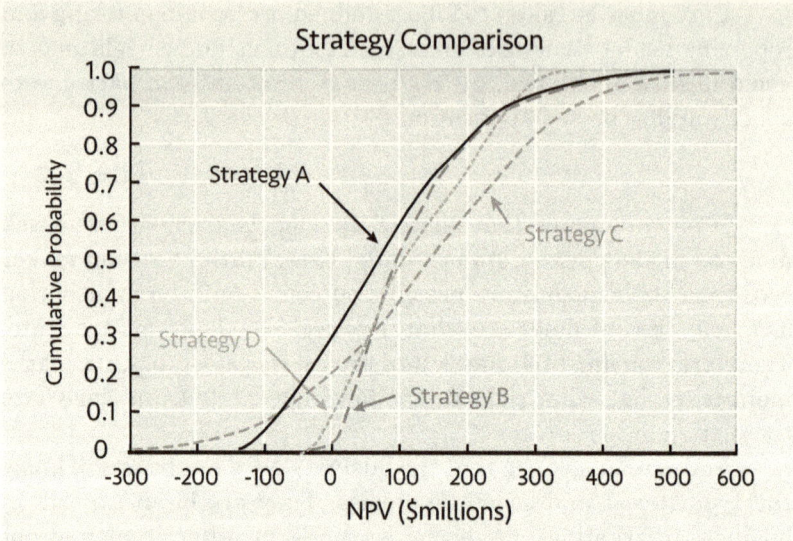

Figure 5.5: Example Comparison of Alternative NPVs
(Leach, with permission)

the story behind those values, then risk quantification will be largely irrelevant to these decisions.

Gate Keepers, Stakeholders, and Behaviors

In a decision making process, the roles and responsibilities for those involved in evaluating the decision at the gate should be well defined. Often a "gate keeper" is assigned. This person understands the project process and is responsible for assuring that procedures and protocol are followed, as well as facilitating group efforts to keep things in balance. The roster of decision makers (e.g., a decision board or panel) will be decided on for each project, program, or portfolio, depending on the decision's strategic importance, ownership of the asset, equity participation, sustainability issues, and so on. In any case, the input from the stakeholders to the asset and the project decision is obtained.

Each party has their own interests and expertise with respect to the decision at hand. The business sponsor should understand the market opportunity (and if a portfolio, the overall balance with other businesses) and external environment. Operations has interest in the design, functionality, and OPEX. Finance is often focused on cash-flows, cost of capital and funding mechanisms. Engineering and construction should understand the technology, design, and CAPEX. And, if applicable, a project management office (PMO) lead will understand the project execution, and along with the engineering head, its capital cost and schedule risk. Of course, the Project Director is invited to present the case for the project along with the business sponsor.

If a mature and disciplined capital project system is in place (e.g., a FEL-like process), you can reasonably assume that all parties *conceptually* understand the relative importance of project definition to capital cost and schedule uncertainty. It is why the company has phases and gates in the first place. However, as covered in Chapters 3 and 4, it is not safe to assume that all parties understand the *reality* of CAPEX cost and schedule uncertainty in absolute terms. In fact, as seen in the tornado chart diagram example, it may be unusual for CAPEX risk to appear in the list of priority NPV issues because empirically valid risk quantification is unusual. For example, when researching this book I came across a reference that showed an oil refinery NPV analysis in which the CAPEX was treated as a constant (after all, the project team had a lump sum quote – see the Introduction's mistake #7)!

Getting general management to appreciate the empirical reality of cost and schedule accuracy is a challenge. However, the more painful message to get across is that much of the uncertainty is driven by *systemic* risks that, to one extent or another, the people in the boardroom own. Clarity of objectives, system maturity, team and competency issues, resource shortages, decision making, bias... the list goes on. If management does not take ownership of these risk drivers, then they are less likely to accept the accuracy message. This is a classic Catch-22 (and a reason for this book).

The only management participating in the decision that most project risk analysts interact with may be the Project Director and the PMO and Engineering department heads or similar. Therefore it is essential that these people understand and communicate the real CAPEX risk story to other senior managers. In any case, we need to understand the biases of the parties involved to the decision so that we can craft a story to communicate up the chain.

Risk Attitude

For individuals, *risk attitude* defines how to approach trade-offs between threats and opportunities. It is a mind set that drives decision making behavior. For an organization, the corporate risk attitude may be expressed as a stated *risk policy*. In any case, an organization will have a mind set, recorded or not.

For example, most company cultures are punitive with respect to project cost and schedule risk. If a project manager overruns or is

Carajás: A Roller Coaster Strategy (Building in the Dips)

"It seemed to be a recipe for disaster: A state-owned company in a financially squeezed, developing nation embarks on a huge iron-ore export project when demand for metals is tumbling worldwide. 'So what are we doing entering an industry that is in decadence?' asked Eliezer Batista, president of Brazil's Companhia Vale do Rio Doce (CVRD), adding cheerfully, 'That is some question when you're spending $4 billion... The project's cost – partly financed by borrowing abroad – came in under budget,' Mr. Batista said."[1]

The above 1985 article is about CVRD's (now Vale) Carajás iron ore development program in Brazil. The project defied a risk that has led to overruns on countless others – political risks. As the article states, "In an economy dominated by such giant state enterprises ... CVRD has somehow managed to shield itself from the usual political interference. We've had a combination of luck and recognition by the Government of the company's special role,' Mr. Batista said."

What is more unusual is that 30 years later Vale seems to be repeating history at Carajás with its S11D expansion project. A 2015 article said, "Vale told investors it expects the S11D expansion in the Brazilian Amazon to be completed by the end of next year and that it has trimmed the project's budget by as much as $2.6 billion to around $14.5 billion....Vale said it was able to reduce cash costs to just $12.70 per tonne (it's in the high teens at Rio Tinto and BHP) and that S11D could push costs below $10 a tonne, thanks largely to the weak real."[2]

Vale's investments reflect a high stakes strategy (in 1985 and 2015) of adding high grade, low cost production to raise market share and squeeze out rivals. Also, by building when mining markets have collapsed, construction costs tend to be better (competitive bidding and labor priced in reals). However, Vale has also reported about negative $2 billion free-cash flow in 2015 and its stock price had declined by over 90%.

- Considering the process industry's cost growth history, what project cost risks, including the worst case, did Vale likely face in its capital investment decisions?
- What influence might Vale's negative free-cash flow situation have on the S11D project's schedule strategy and risk?
- What future market situation is Vale likely predicting that would make this capex strategy attractive?

---

1   Riding, Alan, "Mining for Profits in the Jungles of Brazil," New York Times, May 19, 1985.

2   Els, Frik, "Vale says S11D to push costs down to $10 a tonne," Mining.com, Nov. 6, 2015

late, it will be detrimental to their reputation, if not their career. Individual behavior therefore tends to reflect a risk averse attitude.

However, if you look at the company mission statement, you will find statements such as, *"We take calculated investment risks to maximize shareholder value."* This would seem to be a risk tolerant approach.

A classic case of risk attitude and behavior disconnect is the "death march" project where risk-seeking decision makers approve a risky project (that they may not see as risky) after cutting the budget submitted by the risk averse project manager and handing it back to the project manager with the direction to "deliver or else." This project's legion is doomed from the first marching step out of the Janus gate.

Some companies express their risk attitude by establishing a standard confidence level for the amount of funds it authorizes for a project once it has been decided upon. For example, they may state that, *"We fund capital projects at the p70 level of our risk quantification."* Theoretically, the $p50$ or mean reflects a risk neutral attitude while a $p70$ or $p80$ level would reflect a risk averse one. However, what the research in Chapter 4 tells us is that the $p80$ of our analysis is the $p50$ of reality! The corollary is that the $p80$ of reality would kill most projects. In other words, companies that fund at $p70$ or $p80$ know that the token −10/+20% or whatever "standard" range they apply in sensitivity is not real and they are "closet risk neutrals."

As a particular case in point, my experience is that $p80$ funding has become a de facto standard in the mining industry for this reason. If a company does fund projects at a $p50$ or mean level, it may mean that:

♦ They have their act together,
♦ Their analyses are shaky but they are risk seeking,
♦ They have a large portfolio to adjust to cover some overruns; and/or,
♦ The risk averse teams are savvy and pad the base estimates.

Policy be what it may, we need to communicate risks to individuals. The following list categorizes risk attitudes or expectations you can expect to find (based partly on Ingram's approach).[2]

---

2   Ingram, D. and M.Thompson "What's Your Risk Attitude? (And How Does It Affect Your Company?)," Harvard Business Review, June 11, 2012.

♦ **Pragmatists**: projects are uncertain and unpredictable (risk tolerant; cynic),

♦ **Conservators**: projects are perilous and high risk (risk averse; pessimist),

♦ **Maximizers**: projects are low-risk; exceptions will average out (risk seeking; optimist), and

♦ **Managers**: projects are risky, but we can manage the risk (risk intolerant; didactic).

To change behavior, we need to change or at least influence risk attitude for the case at hand. Risk attitudes can change, but that will only happen after many surprises hammer the message home that there is a fundamental disconnect between what our analyses are predicting will happen and what management is expecting.

The "Surprise Table" (Table 5.1) shows how managers of various mindsets might react to the risk messages presented to them. As risk analysts, we need to be prepared to address their reactions or, if we are managers receiving the message, understand our own reactions. Note that the premise of this book is that our risk quantification will be realistic (consistent with historical experience). Therefore we may present any of the four cases depending on the project's real risks and can explain clearly why it is so. This assumes there is no bias in our risk analyses and quantification.

		COMMUNICATED ACCURACY SITUATION			
		UNCER-TAIN (WIDE)	SKEW RIGHT (OVERRUN)	SKEW LEFT (UNDER-RUN)	MODERATE (AVERAGE)
BUSINESS OR PERSONAL EXPECTATIONS	PRAGMATIST	No surprise	What did you miss?		
	CONSERVATOR	What did you miss?	No surprise	Are you kidding?	Did you really do an analysis?
	MAXIMIZER		Are you kidding?	No surprise	
	MANAGER	Thanks, but we will ensure it won't happen			No surprise

Table 5.1: "Surprises" – Where Risk Messages Meet Risk Attitudes

The following describes the reactions to each of the four reported accuracy situations:

♦ **Uncertain**: There is no strong pattern to the project risk situation; things may turn one way or the other. Often, the system is somewhat immature and undisciplined but has pockets of excellence. The Pragmatist's view is confirmed. Surprised Managers will be defensive while Conservators and Maximizers will suspect bias or lack of rigor in the analysis.

♦ **Skew Right** (Overrun): There is a combination of risk events and system weakness that present significant threats (common with megaprojects). The Conservator's view is confirmed. Surprised Managers will be defensive while Pragmatists and Maximizers will suspect bias in the analysis.

♦ **Skew Left** (Underrun): This is typical of smaller projects with overestimation and loose control, or there may be opportunities in the scope. The Maximizer's view is confirmed. Surprised Managers will be defensive while Pragmatists and Conservators will suspect bias in the analysis.

♦ **Moderate**: The moderate risk situation happens to look very much like industry average expectations. The Manager's view is confirmed; things are in control while all others will suspect bias or lack of rigor in the analysis.

Which of these attitudes is most common in industry? I have no data, but experience suggests that most executives are either Maximizers (i.e., optimists who hope and believe they'll get lucky – the bright side of Janus) or Managers (i.e., optimists not about luck but in their own power to control – they think they *are* Janus).

Pessimists (the dark side of Janus) do not last long at the C-level because they are paid to grow the company and that cannot be done without taking risks (although with the increasing use of earnings to buy back shares, one wonders). However, most project managers and those under them tend to be risk averse. They have no golden parachute and they want to survive to manage or work on the next project. Perhaps the hardest to deal with are Pragmatists who cynically play or game the uncertain situation to their advantage (see "Strategic Misrepresentation," which is discussed later in this chapter).

Behavioral Science and Bias

Most companies strive to improve the governance and objectivity of their decision making by using standard project processes, decision analysis, decision policy, quantitative analysis methods, and so on. However, the reality is that people using their judgment make decisions. There are branches of science (behavioral science or behavioral economics) that use empirical data to study how people and organizations behave and interact when deciding. This book will not review the science, but risk analysts and their clients need to understand "where the decision makers are coming from" and behavioral science offers some clues to that, particularly with respect to people's cognitive biases. Here are a few of those biases that are particularly prevalent in the capital project world:

BIAS	DESCRIPTION
Ascription of Causality	Ascribe causation although evidence only suggests correlation
Anchoring	Unduly influenced by initial information; shapes our view of later information
Attribution Asymmetry	Attribute success to our abilities; attribute failures to bad luck
Confirmation Bias	Gather facts that support certain conclusions; disregard other facts
Escalating Commitment	Increase support of a decision over time (over-value sunk costs)
Group Think	Peer pressure to conform to the opinions held by the group
Illusion of Control	Underestimate future uncertainty because we believe we have control
Inertia	Keep thought patterns that we have used in the past despite new circumstances
Optimism Bias	See things in an unjustifiably positive light (or planning fallacy)
Premature Termination	Accept the first alternative that looks like it might work
Recency	Place more attention on more recent information
Repetition Bias	Believe what we are told most often and by the most different sources
Selective Perception	Screen-out information that we do not think is important

Table 5.2: Biases in the Capital Project World

Typically, more than one bias will be at work in project decision making. Table 5.3 provides some common ways (and my names for them) that biases manifest themselves in risk quantification and how you might deal with them in communicating with decision makers.

THE "MAGIC 10s" (OPTIMISM, REPETITION, ILLUSION OF CONTROL, INERTIA)	
Evidence	"If you did your job, we would have +10/–10% range; you get 10% contingency."
Reality	Industry range at authorization is about +20/–20% at 1 std deviation (68% confidence).
Result	The illusion is pernicious! Add a punitive culture and result is "fat" estimates.
Response	Use empirically valid methods and collect your own history to prove it.
"MAGIC TRIANGLES" – COUSIN OF THE MAGIC 10s (SEE ABOVE)	
Evidence	Three-point estimates are always multiples of –1/+2; i.e., –10/+20, –15/+30, –50/+100.
Reality	Actual accuracy has a lognormal distribution with a high end of 2X to 3X those above.
Result	Constant surprises when overruns occur.
Response	Use empirically valid methods and collect your own history to prove it.
THE "NUMBER" (ANCHORING)	
Evidence	The first estimate number published takes on a life of its own.
Reality	The first number to go into the capital budget is always too low! Often it is only a fraction of reality.
Result	Pressure to cut to force the cost into the number box; overruns; death march projects.
Response	Reconciliation of current to past estimates; the only way to cut cost is to change scope.
"SCOPE CREEP"– COUSIN OF THE "NUMBER"	
Evidence	Scope keeps getting added, but the capital budget stays the same.
Reality	Early estimates will miss necessary scope; count on it.
Result	See the "Number."
Response	Reconciliation of current to past scope.
"WELCOME TO WOBEGON" (OPTIMISM, ATTRIBUTION ASYMMETRY, SELECTIVE PERCEPTION, ILLUSION OF CONTROL)	
Evidence	No systemic risks (issues) appear in the risk register (see, hear and speak no evil).
Reality	Immature and/or undisciplined systems, weak teams, and so on are common.
Result	Constant overruns; everything is ascribed to "unknown-unknowns."
Response	Use empirically validated methods that objectively rate systemic risks.
"PET PROJECTS" (OPTIMISM BIAS, SELECTIVE PERCEPTION, ESCALATING COMMITMENT)	
Evidence	Irrational business defense of a project or option (also see, hear and speak no evil).
Reality	Everyone but the champion sees that it is a "dead parrot" (Monty Python).
Result	Uneconomic decisions followed by overruns; plant may not even go into operation.
Response	See all of above; Just try to stay objective and document everything.

Table 5.3: Biases and How to Address Them

A common theme in most of the situations above is *optimism bias* and the single most effective response is to use and continue to validate (using historical data from a robust system) empirically valid risk quantification methods.

Strategic Misrepresentation

Optimism bias is the more or less subconscious attitude of senior decision makers that can be mitigated by best practices. However, there is a pernicious form of optimism bias called "Strategic Misrepresentation," or, as one researcher puts it, "lying."[3]

This is the realm of Pragmatists who cynically play the uncertain situation to their advantage. Dr. Flyvbjerg has suggested that this is the predominant mode of operation for publicly funded projects. In that realm, the politicians and promoters are the ultimate pragmatists. Their behavior is to overstate revenues and understate CAPEX, OPEX and finance costs to get the project approved.

Unlike optimism bias, this presumes the sponsor is largely aware of the reality. They are not surprised by the actual overrun, but if you actually predict it, they will try to hide the message (if not the messenger). Once approved, escalating commitment bias takes over (i.e., over-valuing sunk cost) because nobody wants to cancel a project once reality starts showing its costly face. A classic quote confirming that strategic misrepresentation is real comes from Mr. Willie Brown, former mayor of San Francisco, who wrote in 2013...*"In the world of civic projects, the first budget is really just a down payment. If people knew the real cost from the start, nothing would ever be approved."*[4]

Dr. Flyvbjerg's prescription is to take the decision analysis evaluation out of the hands of the promoters by (or at least govern it by) applying an outside view to the revenue forecasts and cost estimates – a view that assumes the past will repeat. However, as stated in Chapter 1, when Strategic Misrepresentation or lying becomes your operative presumption, then you are giving in to the dark side of Janus's vision. The liar view presumes there is little hope of improving practices or outcomes in the future. That is not a viable solution in a competitive environment. While the outside view is important, that view must be focused on not only gate decisions, but on long-term process improvement.

---

3   Flyvbjerg, B., "Underestimating Costs in Public Works Projects," Journal of the American Planning Association, Vol. 68, No. 3, Summer 2002.

4   Willie Brown, quoted in the San Francisco Chronicle, July 27, 2013.

Nobody Wins

The following utility project, which made its way into case law books and the news, is an example of how both owners and contractors lose when a project has cost overruns and late completion and technical problems.

The project was the 440-mw Red Hills Lignite Power Plant in Mississippi owned by Choctaw Generation Limited Partnership (CGLP) and built by its EPC contractor, Bechtel Power Corporation. The capital cost estimate was about $500 million in 1999 ($1.1m per mw). The contract was reported as "...fixed-price, date certain, turnkey EPC contract, which is guaranteed by Bechtel, and contains liquidated damages for up to 30% to cover delayed startup and performance."[1]

One source summarized the risk impact situation as follows: "The project was completed almost 16 months late, resulting in claims between the parties exceeding $500 million to address responsibility for the delays. The case featured claims by Bechtel for labor force majeure and owner interference with the execution of the work, as well as some complicated technical issues associated with the Alstom-furnished boilers and lignite and limestone handling systems."[2] Completion was delayed from late 2000 into 2002.

The magnitude of the potential losses (claims about equal to the original project estimate) put all parties under pressure. The contractor went so far as to make force majeure claims "for certain costs and schedule delays due to alleged labor shortages."[3] If successful, such a claim would essentially equate escalation with a force majeure risk event. In any event, CGLP was able to draw liquidated damages against Bechtel's surety.

On the owner side, there were obligations with the coal supplier on one end and the power buyer (TVA) on the other. Revenue losses added financial pressure. In 2001, Moody's and Standard & Poor lowered the credit rating on CGLP debt securities and ten years later the owner was in default: "CGLP defaulted at the end of 2012 after underperforming for an extended period because of a turbine design flaw and a series of equipment failures. The project did not achieve its contracted heat rate, and extended outages hurt revenues."[4]

♦ What risks did Bechtel assume with a turnkey approach with liquidated damages including performance guarantees?

♦ What assumptions do you think Bechtel's upper management made about their ability to use change orders and claims against the owners to offset project implementation risk?

♦ What risks did the CGLP assume with this approach?

---

1   Moody's Investor Service, Global Credit Research, February 9, 1999.

2   http://www.cp-strategies.com/Indestries_PowerGeneration.html.

3   Standard & Poor's, Feb. 1, 2001.

4   Moody's Investor Service, Global Credit Research, May 30, 2001.

A culture of Strategic Misrepresentation (and/or its cousin, corruption) is a very difficult environment for the estimating and risk professional to work in. If you produce empirically valid results, they will not be well received (to say the least). The resulting projects often become "death marches" for those on the team. On the other hand, these projects are often highly visible and monumental. Many see them as feathers in one's cap after the immediate pain of failure passes and is forgotten.

In any case, having made the investment decision, good or bad, there will be a project to execute. This takes us to the next contextual topic, which is risk quantification's role in the realm of Project Control and its special needs.

Questions

1) Describe the steps of Decision Analysis and how they align with typical phase-gate system gate decisions.

2) What are two common engineering economic metrics studied during the decision analysis Evaluation step? Briefly describe them in words including the main inputs.

3) The book focuses on CAPEX and its timing. In terms of NPV evaluation, why is CAPEX an important concern and what in terms of NPV evaluation is the importance of the project completion date?

4) In terms of NPV evaluation, what is the major difference between Strategic and Sustaining capital investments?

5) In a typical process industry project NPV Sensitivity Analysis, how would CAPEX range relative to Revenue? Also, what effect would the outcomes of prevailing industry risk quantification methods (as reflected in studies in Chapter 4) have on this ranking?

6) If a risk-weighted decision tree, with NPV as the key measure, is used as the company's decision evaluation method, what CAPEX information do we need to provide for the NPV evaluation? Also, if Monte-Carlo Simulation (MCS) is applied to the decision tree, what CAPEX information is then needed?

7) Describe the typical Risk Attitudes of a project manager and team relative to that of the business or corporation. What risk quantification behavior might a difference in their risk attitudes induce in a project team?

8) Describe what effect "anchoring" bias in business managers might have on project risk quantification in a phase-gate system.

9) What does the "Magic 10s" behavior mean and what management biases might this behavior reflect?

6

Budgeting for Risk

This chapter continues exploring risk quantification's context by looking at its role in the project after a decision has been made. If the decision was made at the FEL 1/Assess or 2/Select gates as discussed in Chapter 5, the next phase is to perform further scope definition of the selected alternative(s) and move towards the investment decision. However, after the FEL 3/Define (FID) gate, the risk quantification effort shifts to supporting implementation at the start of the project execution phase. The primary purpose of implementation is to establish a basis for Project Control during execution, and to do that, we need to allocate risk monies and time in budgets and control plans in a way that they can be effectively managed.

For investment decision analysis, risk quantification's main role is to provide 3-point estimates or distributions of overall CAPEX and schedule (presumably based on management's desired confidence levels of underrun) and the risk story behind them. The control concepts of contingency and escalation are relevant to early capital budgeting, but are not the main point of pre-sanction risk quantification. However, during the post-sanction execution phase, risk costs and time (in budgeting terms, contingency and escalation) become critical to the process of Project Control, and especially to a control sub-process called Change Control or Change Management. This chapter reviews the basics of Project Control and Change Management (or Control) at a high level and defines some key budgeting and control terms so that the risk analyst can better support control needs.

Project Control Explained

Up to the FEL 3/Define gate, the project system's emphasis is on creativity, optimization, and value. The owners want to obtain the most out of the alternative scope opportunities in terms of production, quality, operability, sustainability, and safety for the least investment of money and time, with an acceptable level of confidence. With incomplete project scope development before the FEL 3/Define gate, there is significant but decreasing uncertainty from phase to phase. At the FEL 3/Define gate, any significant, viable opportunities have been capitalized on.

After the FID, the emphasis shifts from creativity to discipline. *Change* shifts from being a potential source of value to a likely major risk driver. The scope is set and the purpose of the team is to deliver the defined asset at the cost and in the time agreed. The uncertainties and decisions ahead are mostly threats to be expeditiously and effectively responded to such as risk events, adverse conditions, poor supplier or labor performance, and late discovery of design errors.

In general, Project Control is a process to plan the project work activities, establish a performance baseline (e.g., cost budget and schedule), measure performance, and, if there is a variance from plan, study the variance causes and take corrective action as needed to restore performance to the baseline (and if not correctable, revise the plan baseline to best respond to the current situation). Because things change and unforeseen conditions and events happen over the course of the project duration, the team must regularly forecast how the project plan will perform going forward, i.e., is the plan still optimal given the foreseen performance and conditions and are there emerging risks on the horizon we did not anticipate?

All of these Project Control process steps help the Project Manager decide on timely and effective corrective actions. The PM is responsible for the project's success and to meet that responsibility, the PM needs timely, accurate information, ideas, and advice from their team. The PM gets this in various face-to-face daily and weekly progress status meetings and reports, but the Project Control function helps make this information meaningful and actionable in as close to real-time as possible.

As with the decision-making process, this Chapter cannot hope to do justice to the whole Project Control process. If the reader does not have at least a basic understanding of project execution and control, I recommend reading the previously referenced Total Cost Management Framework from AACE International.[1] As an introduction, the following paragraphs outline key concepts of planning, forecasting, and integrated change and risk management that the risk analyst needs to understand.

Planning

Planning involves decomposing the overall project scope into manageable elements of work in accordance with an execution strategy. The end result is a project or work breakdown structure (WBS) made up of work packages. The work packages (mini-projects if you will) each have their own allocated portion of scope, budget, resources, and schedule. Each work package will have a person within the owner, vendor, and/or contractor organization who is responsible for its execution and control. Hence, the work package is a control account.

Where risk quantification comes into play in planning is the question of whether and how to allocate money and time for uncertainty in these mini-projects. Each work package has possible risks and the person responsible for the work package has to respond appropriately to these risk events and impacts as they occur.

A key feature for the risk analyst to understand about a WBS is that is hierarchical. At the highest level, it comprises the entire project scope, At the lowest level it is a limited set of tasks within a particular discipline or trade to perform. In between, the work can be rolled up as appropriate at higher levels of management and contractual authority. For example, the lowest level of work package may be to install "Foundations in Area X," while at a higher level all the area foundation work packages roll up to a single "Foundations Subcontract" account. An account ID code will be assigned to each work package and the account structure will also be hierarchical. The WBS and account hierarchy from summary to detail may be something like: project, area, unit, system, discipline, task. Using a WBS, the cost and schedule plans are then integrated.

---

1   Hollmann, J, ed., *Total Cost Management Framework*, First Edition, AACE International, Morgantown, WV.

When it comes to money and time to cover the potential risks that could impact a work package, it could optionally be allocated to the work package budget, to the overall contract budget, or to some higher level. The selection of risk funding and time allocation depends on the planning concept of authority for work direction and for spending – who holds the risks monies and time in their budget and schedule to approve spending as needed to respond to risks or other occurrences that are not going as planned?

Budget and schedule are key planning deliverables developed for each work package; they are defined as follows:

♦ Budget: The quantities, hours, and costs for the work.

♦ Schedule: The activities and time to perform the work organized in a logical network.

Developing a budget is an extension of the estimating process. The cost estimate may originally have been prepared to come up with the numbers for NPV analysis. During FEL 1 and 2, the estimate is summarized in accordance with high level WBS accounts and has no control account detail except for work in the next phase. However at FEL 3, the estimate will be structured to the control level of the WBS to the extent it is known.

The account structure for how a project is controlled during execution may differ from the account structure of the estimate. Per the prior example, the estimator might estimate the quantity, hours, and cost to install the concrete for the "Foundations in Area X." However, when the control budget is established, the concrete and other discipline estimates may get rolled into a single "Foundations Subcontract" control budget account that covers all the disciplines and work areas. When we talk about contingency later, risk quantification will need to consider how the uncertainty element of this estimate and schedule gets allocated, i.e., risk allocation. Risk allocation is one focus of the practice of Contract Management – *Who is responsible for the risk? Where does the uncertainty reside in how we structure things?*

Forecasting

On a large project, many things will deviate from the original plan. Rather than the team being in a constant reactive (surprise) mode (which would be inefficient if not chaotic), the team must regularly and proactively forecast how they see the project performance going forward. If the plan is no longer optimal or consistent with the reality and the risks ahead, then they need to ask, *What should be changed?*

In effect, forecasting is re-planning with a small "p." However, if wholesale changes are needed, it may lead to re-baselining, which is re-planning with a big "P." Where risk quantification comes into play in forecasting depends on whether the money and time allocated for uncertainty in the existing plan is still adequate for the future. If things have changed significantly, the team may need to step back and reassess the whole scope and risk situation and perform risk quantification as if at a decision gate.

Change and Risk Management

As stated, large projects will experience many deviations from planned performance, changes will be made, and risk events will occur. Forecasting may also recommend improvements or modification of the plan to respond to anticipated conditions and performance. However, execution is about discipline more than creativity. The control motto is *"plan the work and work the plan."* Changes are not to be made on the fly. Change Control or Management then is the Project Control sub-process for (1) identifying actual or potential deviations, trends, and changes, (2) studying them, (3) recommending corrective actions to address them, and finally (4) deciding on an action. No change to the current plan, including the budget and schedule, is to be made without authorization, usually by the project manager or director. Risks that occur and any risk treatment and response actions that need to be taken are changes like any other during execution. Therefore, during execution, change and risk management are integrated as sub-processes within Project Control.

Change Management deals with deviations, trends, changes, and risk events. These are the manifestation of uncertainties becoming certain (i.e., actualization). At the start of the project, we establish allowances in the budget and schedule for uncertainty (contingency, escalation, and reserves) and as change actions are decided upon we use those allowances to pay for them. This takes place by the project manager or director authorizing the transfer of funds from the uncertainty allowances to the work control accounts as appropriate.

Risk quantification's first role in execution then is to establish the specific uncertainty allowances or provisions in the budget and schedule to meet control needs. It starts with but moves beyond the general CAPEX and completion milestone information used for decision analysis and NPV. If major changes or re-baselining require intermediate scope decisions, the risk quantification is applied as if at a project gate review.

It is not hard to see from this discussion of planning, forecasting, and change management that Project Control is a complex undertaking on a large project. There may be thousands of activities and control accounts and hundreds of procurements and contracts to manage. All of the activities and accounts are being measured, assessed, and managed in near real time using defined change management processes. Research has shown that the efficacy of Project Control is a key systemic risk. If planning, forecasting, change management, and other steps are not planned and done well in a competent, disciplined, and timely way, there will be increased cost growth and schedule slip. In the worst case, there will be loss of control, chaos, and cost and schedule blowouts.

The following sections describe the purpose, content, and funding or provision of the accounts established in the Project Control budgeting and scheduling process. In summary, these risk funding accounts and their definitions (aligned with the AACE approach) are as shown in Table 6.1.

Account/ Provision	Content Description	Responsibility/ Decision Authority
Base (Point)	Cost and duration that we are certain about	Work package lead
Allowances	Cost and duration for specific named items that we are certain are needed but are uncertain about their value	Work package lead
Contingency	Cost and duration for general uncertainties that we expect to incur based on analysis	Project Director/Manager
Escalation and Exchange	Cost for price uncertainty that we expect to incur resulting from external economic and monetary factors	Project Director/Manager
Management Reserves	Cost and duration for general uncertainties or specific items not expected to be incurred but provisioned at the funding authority's discretion	Owner/Business Sponsor(s)

Table 6:1: Risk Funding Account Descriptions and Responsibilities

Estimating and Scheduling Strategy Defines the Base

As part of Project Control planning, a first step is to establish the project's cost and schedule *strategy*. This defines what performance objective the *base* estimates of cost and duration will reflect. Here is an example strategy statement for clients who want to achieve or target competitive performance:

> The base cost and duration estimate values will reflect aggressive but reasonably achievable current pricing and performance. "Aggressive but reasonably achievable" means that the assumed performance will reflect the first quartile level (i.e., *p25*) of historical performance or equivalent for similar strategies and scope excluding the impact of identifiable changes and risks.

Explicit objectives and strategies are needed because contingency is an amount we assess relative to the base estimates and if we do not know what the base represents, we cannot effectively determine the contingency. Unfortunately, *I have rarely seen a clear cost and schedule strategy stated* in project execution plans or elsewhere to guide estimators and schedulers! Here is a statement of what most companies are doing whether they know it or not (i.e., the "historical norms" strategy):

> The base cost and duration estimate values reflect the historical norms of our past pricing and performance. "Historical norms" means the assumed [lacking a reliable historical database] average of historical performance, including the impact of changes and risk events and excluding only the worst outliers.

This is a strategy for mediocrity at best. Project Control works by flagging deviations from the base and if poor performance and risk event impacts are wired right into the base, little will ever be flagged. It is a state of blissful ignorance and a guarantee that you will rarely do better than the past average. I cannot imagine any capital manager making this their stated strategy, but by failing to communicate anything else, "historical norms" has become the de facto industry standard. This has opened the doors wide open to obfuscation that usually favors the purposes of the risk averse estimator, planner, and/or project manager. It hides fat, although in the team's defense, lacking historical data, nobody is really even aware that this is happening. This in turn has led to the not entirely unjustified belief that the project team would not really need any contingency if they did a good job (see Chapter 1 mistakes #2 and #4).

Some will argue that for procurement and contracting, pricing strategies are common such as *"pick the least cost technically ac-*

ceptable tender." This might lower cost if the bidders were ignorant of their customer's biases (or customer's cost ignorance), but they are not.

For example, in a research study that I facilitated, requests for quotations (RFQs) were sent out to suppliers by the study's participating companies. These RFQs all referenced identical equipment data sheets. The companies were somewhat surprised that suppliers quoted different prices to different companies for identical items. Vendor pricing is not impartial. Companies known to have an aggressive cost strategy got lower quotes (the identities of companies and vendors for each case were kept confidential; only general findings were shared).

One reason that many companies do not state an explicit cost and schedule planning strategy is that *they do not have any historical data or metrics* with which to assess and set quantitative objectives. Unfortunately, the state of project historical data or knowledge management at most owner companies is dismal (see Chapter 18).

Content of the Base in a Competitive or Cost-Effective Strategy

If you have a competitive cost strategy, the base (above-the-line) estimate of quantities, hours, and cost for control will be based on measurable, objective facts. At FEL 3/Define, quantities are facts taken off drawings or models (takeoffs). For materials and equipment cost, the base facts will generally be from quotations, or from recorded past experience. For labor hours, the base will reflect an analysis of past productivity or unit hours (e.g., hours/tonne) that are often captured in an estimating database of labor norms. Labor rates are often established by union contracts. Unit costs (e.g., costs/tonne) will also be based on analysis of historical experience and/or quotations. Indirects, mark-ups, and so on will also be based on historical experience. Pricing should also be as of the estimate basis date and not look forward in time (future price and exchange rate trends are covered by Escalation and Exchange, albeit with some exceptions). Done correctly, the base estimating at FEL 3/Define is rather mechanistic because it is deterministic and excludes the stochastic methods of quantifying risks. More information about base estimating and scheduling methods is provided in Chapter 9.

"Capital Strategy? What Strategy?"

Have your managers told you that your base estimating strategy should be predictable (on budget) or competitive (low cost) or both? If your answer is "No" or "I don't know," it is no surprise. Project guidelines are unclear because companies are unclear as to their *capital strategy*. When I start an engagement, I search my client's annual report or investor relation documents to find a CAPEX strategy in their mission statement so that I know what is expected of their project teams. Most have some sort of statement that requires an interpreter; here are some examples with my uncertain interpretation:

COMPANY	CAPITAL STRATEGY IN MISSION STATEMENTS	INTERPRETED CAPITAL FOCUS
Major Global Oil	"capital and cost discipline"	Predictability
Major European Chemical	"disciplined with regard to costs and expenditures"	Predictability
Major Global Oil	"enhance capital efficiency"	Competitiveness!
Major Global Pharmaceutical	"free up working capital"	Liquidity
Major European Utility	"organic expansion....combined with acquisitions"	Ambiguous
Major Global Mining	"project delivery" and "low cost over life of properties"	Ambiguous/ OPEX focus

These are fairly typical. Very few companies say they want their capital cost to be less than their peers for the same asset capability. This is strange because most have goals for high *return on capital employed* (ROCE) or similar: a ratio that can be achieved by less CAPEX for the same return. So, why not say they want their projects to be the least CAPEX without sacrificing other objectives?

Instead, most say they want predictability – the code words being "discipline" or "delivery" (often measured in terms of hitting CAPEX cash flow targets). The trouble with that is that the most effective way to assure predictability is to budget more than is needed and spread the overage around to cover any projects needing extra and/or to monkey with project progress. By targeting predictability, you may get predictable cash flow (making finance happy), but less project control discipline and higher overall capital spending for a given asset.

Allowances (Uncertainties Included in the Base)

In the base estimate, there will be specific items that we know will be required, but for which there is some residual uncertainty as to some aspect of these item's definition. For example, we may know that we need pump X while being uncertain as to whether we need 50 hp or 75 hp pending an engineering study. In this case, we will include "Allowance for Pump X" in the base estimate and price it at 50 hp or 75 hp, stating our reason for doing so. The word "allowance" flags us to update this cost item (and anything related to it) as soon as the uncertainty is cleared up. The phrase *"specific to an item"* limits the type of uncertainties, or allowances, that we include in the base.

The same thinking can apply to a *specific* class of items such as a "take-off allowance," which is a nominal addition to measured quantities to allow for an imperfect take-off process. Again, the allowance should be *specific to an item* type such as "concrete take-off allowance" and should also assume that best practices are applied for that item.

Inappropriate allowances (i.e., hidden contingency or fat) are general across-the-board allowances for some uncertainty in a general cost type such as "allowance for overtime," or "allowance for weather," or "design development allowance." While the words overtime, weather, and design may seem somewhat specific, they are being applied indiscriminately to broad classes of items such as hours, labor, or engineering. This is general uncertainty that should be addressed by contingency. For these examples, hours should be based on planned overtime, productivity should be based on stated weather assumptions, and engineering should be based on the stated scope.

Biased business behavior (see Chapter 1 mistakes #2 and #4) creates a strong incentive to overuse general allowances or excessive specific allowances. When decision makers or business sponsors do not allow adequate contingency (e.g., set an arbitrary limit of 10%), then allowances become the team's escape valve to ensure they have adequate funds or time to complete the work (and avoid punishment). This also tends to diminish Project Control discipline. Once a gaming mind set becomes operative, weak control becomes a risk in its own right.

Contingency

Contingency is a controversial topic in capital project management and control. Many of the reasons were outlined in Chapter 1. Each party in the project has different perception of its purpose, nature, and usage. Table 6.2 is a classic tongue-in-cheek summary of the how various project parties view cost contingency and the behaviors that these perceptions drive.[2]

Project Role	Contingency is Perceived as....	Contingency Perception Drives this Behavior:
Business Management	Money that will only be expended if the project is poorly managed	Cut it, then hold it; only disperse funds after an inquisition
Project Director or Manager	The max money we can get, but not so much that the project is killed	Convince management that *p*80 is a reasonable allow-ance
Engineers	Money to cover the things that got cut but we will add back later	Since contingency is also cut, include a big design al-lowance in the base
Procurement	A supplier problem after we shift the risk to them	Transfer risk to suppliers that they cannot effectively manage; then penalize
Fabrication/ Construction	Money spent by engineer-ing before the project ever gets to the field	Fight every contractor re-quest to the death

Table 6.2: Perceptions of Contingency and Resultant Behavioral Biases

In this book, the AACE definition of contingency applies:

> "An amount added to an estimate to allow for items, conditions, or events for which the state, occurrence, or effect is uncertain and that experience shows will likely result, in aggregate, in additional costs."[3]

This definition further clarifies that contingency specifically *excludes* the following (conversely it includes everything not in this list):

- ◆ Major scope changes,
- ◆ Extraordinary events such as major strikes and natural disasters,
- ◆ Management reserves, and
- ◆ Escalation and currency effects.

There are several important concepts in this definition that can be further defined in Table 6.3 as follows:

---

2   An early version is in an AACE Transactions article titled "Contingency" by the AACE New Jersey section in 1971.

3   AACE, Cost Engineering Terminology, RP10S-90.

Definition Says...	Definition Means...
"Experience shows"	Contingency is based on or validated by empiricism or historical data if at all possible.
"Will likely result"	The words "expected to be expended" are included later; it is a control account so it must be under project director/manager authority.
"In aggregate"	Contingency is only quantifiable to the bottom line; not to the accounts.
"Major scope changes"	For the owner: change to what is understood by decision makers (e.g., product X of quality Y on date Z). For the contractor: this is scope outside the contract.
"Extraordinary"	Contingency is *not* for low probability/high impact risks, black swans (see reserves for items "not expected to be expended").
"Management"	Contingency is expected to be expended; it is owned by the project director/manager and is not "reserved" by business management.

Table 6.3: The Meaning of the Words in the AACE's Definition of "Contingency"

In summary, to cost engineers, risk professionals, and informed management, contingency is:

♦ The difference between the mean (or $p50$ if one is a bit more aggressive) of our probabilistic, empirically valid risk quantification of the project cost and schedule outcomes (excluding extraordinary risks), and the base cost and duration considering their biases. The base estimate plus the contingency set at the mean is then (literally) the expected value.

♦ A Project Control administrative concept; a budget or time allocation that the project director/manager is authorized to use as needed to respond to non-extraordinary risks within the overall project scope.

Note that industry is of two minds about whether to apply the distribution mean or median ($p50$). For a distribution that is skewed to the high side, the mean will be greater than the median. The mean is more "risk weighted." For example, consider two projects below that each have four possible outcomes. Note that the median is the same for both, but the mean of the second more skewed alternative is double the first!

♦ Possible outcomes 5,10,15,30: median = 12.5, mean = 15
♦ Possible outcomes 5,10,15,90: median = 12.5, mean = 30

Admittedly, this is an exaggerated example. However, if you were the project manager of the second project, how would you feel if, with the risk of it being a career killer, you get no credit for that risk if it were funded at the $p50$? In a typical skewed analysis, the mean tends to be somewhere in the ballpark of $p55$ or so (the more skewed, the greater the p-value). It is usually a matter of a couple percent additional contingency, which may be a non-trivial sum on a large project. The choice of funding level is a matter of the company's risk attitude. However, another advantage of the mean over the median is that the means are additive in a program or portfolio view. The $p50$ of an analysis of a portfolio of projects will not be equal to the sum of the $p50$s of the analyses of its constituent projects. This can cause some communication confusion (which somehow seems to get blamed on the poor scapegoat: Monte Carlo Simulation).

Getting back to the definition of contingency, the formula for its calculation is then very simple:

Contingency = Mean (or $p50$) of Risk Quantification – Base Estimate

This formula is illustrated in Figure 6.1, where the curve is the probabilistic output of our risk quantification. The base estimate is from the cost estimating group. The contingency then is the amount between the $p50$ and the base. The low and high ranges at a $p80$ confidence interval are also shown.

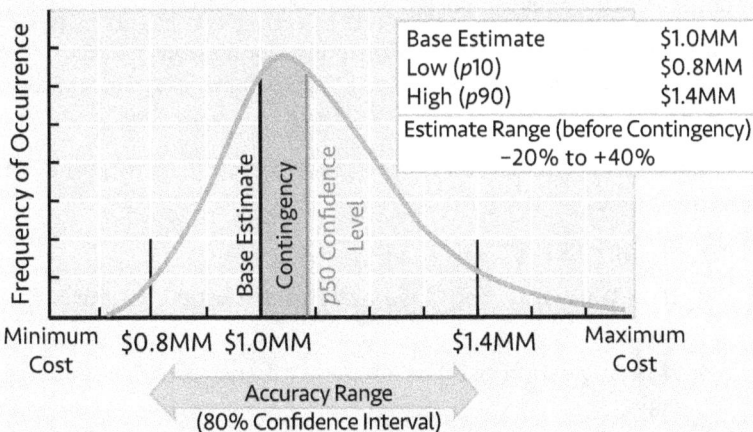

Figure 6.1: Example Contingency Calculation Using p50 of a Probabilistic Cost Risk Analysis

What if management has chosen to fund the investment at a $p70$ or $p80$ level? Would $p80$ minus the base estimate be treated as contingency? The answer is no. The question as to what confidence level to fund an investment is different from the question of how to administratively manage or control the funds during execution. The difference between the $p80$ and mean or $p50$ values should be treated as discretionary funds, which AACE defines as "management reserve," which I will discuss later in this Chapter.

Schedule Contingency

In best practice, cost and schedule risk are analyzed using an integrated approach. Hence the cost and schedule time distributions are based on the same inputs and will have considered trade-offs. Then, from a math perspective, the risk quantification of schedule uncertainty is the same as for cost except the unit of measure is time or duration. As shown in Chapter 3, execution phase slip (not considering startup) is commonly about 5% to 20% of the planned duration. The math is the easy part.

However, contingency is an administrative concept, so schedule contingency determination becomes problematic. There is more disagreement about what to do with schedule duration contingency than there is for cost. This is in part because schedule (e.g., float ownership) is at the center of the claims and disputes world, and legal departments tend to get involved. The experts in the AACE's Planning and Scheduling Committee (there were 30 contributors) took on the topic in 2012, and here is their consensus definition of schedule contingency:

> "An amount of time included in the project or program schedule to mitigate (dampen/buffer) the effects of risks or uncertainties identified or associated with specific elements of the project schedule."

They go on to define these attributes for schedule contingency (my emphasis):

- *It must be visible* in the schedule.
- It is time only and does not contain scope, resources, or costs.
- It is only established based upon an analysis of schedule risk.
- *It is not float* (i.e., neither project float nor total float).
- It is *not* lag/lead (relationship durations).

- It is *not* hidden artificial lengthening of schedule activities.
- It is *not* the improper use of what some term as "preferential logic."
- It is *not* a non-work period in the software calendar.
- It is *not* management reserve.

However, use of visible schedule contingency (i.e., a buffer activity) is not common practice. What is more common is:

- The schedule contingency is kept confidential (to avoid the perception by anyone that the completion date is other than sacrosanct) and then is only used in the NPV sensitivity analysis.
- The schedule contingency is considered in the negotiation of sale or supply contracts. The project team and construction contractor are held to the base duration by the business, but the business commits to a later first production or sale date with its customer. In a sense, it is a management reserve of time.

An exception is when a project has intermediate completion milestones or phases built into the schedule. An example is work in the sub-arctic, where excavation and site work must be done in the winter (a seasonal execution strategy). If the work is not done before the end of the season (or whatever the intermediate completion milestone is), the project overall completion will slip an entire year. In that case, a buffer activity prior to the intermediate milestone may be used to help assure that an early melt does not throw off the rest of the project.

If you believe the empirical reality of schedule slip and want to use the best practice recommended by the experts but also want to assure achievement of the stated completion milestone, there is only one rational action: include a buffer in the schedule, but find a way to complete the project by the stated completion date with the buffer included. With a fixed end date, you need to make the base plan (activities before the buffer) more aggressive in order to accommodate the buffer duration. This requires iterative cost and schedule planning, estimating, scheduling, and risk analysis effort considering that more aggressive schedules are risky, especially for megaprojects.

Escalation

As stated, AACE recommends budgeting escalation uncertainty costs separately from contingency. Historically, this was not always common practice, but after the start of the commodity super-cycle in 2003, many companies started to budget for escalation uniquely.

However, for small projects, particularly for those with less than 18 months or so execution duration (when the mid-point of spending is within the first year), escalation is still commonly applied as an allowance in estimates (i.e., added to each budget line as appropriate). The FEL/3 risk quantification question then is whether to budget for escalation as its own account or to allocate the cost as item allowances. This decision hinges on these questions:

♦ Degree of uncertainty: are current and forecast markets stable over the whole project duration?

♦ Project Control capability: can and will an added account be managed effectively as part of Change Management?

In answering these questions, here are some things to consider:

♦ If market uncertainty is significant and escalation allowances are buried within the control accounts, it will distort earned value (EV) calculations. For example, if budgets are inflated, early progress will be over-reported and performance trends masked (i.e., EV = budget x % complete, so an inflated budget means inflated EV). Also, management will lose sight of the fact that this cost is uncertain and can result in surprises.

♦ In a weak system, if the control task is made more complicated by creating separate contingency *and* escalation accounts, the team may take short cuts. The lost discipline in control creates its own systemic risk.

♦ To simplify accounting while still treating escalation as a risk, some include escalation in the contingency account. This is problematic when management believes contingency is fat; they will not be receptive to the increased values and may cut it.

♦ A separate escalation account may be seen as a slush fund. For example, during the super-cycle, many projects overran significantly due to poor practices but blamed the overruns on escalation. If one creates a separate escalation account, it should only be used for market-driven price changes and not used as a backup contingency.

♦ Escalation is not intended to fund market turns (e.g., 2009 and 2014 commodity price collapses). These are *extraordinary events* per the AACE definitions and best dealt with as management reserve in projects and scenarios in NPV sensitivity analysis.

Chapter 13 covers the probabilistic escalation quantification method in detail. In general, the base method involves estimating the cash flow and applying price indices to the spending by period. This applies whether the calculation is done by budget item, or on a more overall basis.

Exchange Rate

Base estimates are usually prepared in the currency with which the project will be funded (the base currency). However, some expenditures may be paid in other currencies. If the relative value of the base versus expended currencies changes from the basis of estimate, then more or less funds in the base currency will be required than originally estimated. A country's currency valuation is highly correlated with its general economic performance. Both are economically driven. If price escalation is volatile, exchange rates will be too.

However, exchange rate is also sensitive to a country's monetary policy. For example, in 2014, as the super-cycle ended, minor currency wars began as some countries lowered their discount rates (in some cases these rates went negative) to spur exports. Such an event, as with market turns, would be construed as *extraordinary* and are best dealt with as management reserve. In any case, per AACE definitions, the exchange rate uncertainty costs are excluded from contingency and from escalation.

As an example of exchange rate risks, as commodity prices increased in US dollar terms in 2003-2008, the US dollar was weakening relative to the currencies of countries where commodities were being extracted and projects were being constructed (for example, Canada). Prices within Canada in Canadian dollars were escalating due to regional market effects such as labor shortages; plus, if the project was funded in US dollars, the owner was also hit with the declining value of the US dollar versus the Canadian dollar. This reversed when commodities cooled off post-2012 and the US dollar strengthened (as I am writing this chapter, significant devaluation of developing country currencies is underway).

At many companies, the finance department owns large project exchange rate risk; the project team is instructed that they are not responsible for its impact. In that case, the finance function agrees to cover any significant overrun driven by exchange rate based on the assumption that they are best able to take treatment actions such as currency hedging. In order for finance to take such actions, they need the project team to forecast the project's cash flow by currency so they can plan for it.

If finance owns the currency risk, the cash flow by currency forecast (done at the project start and monthly thereafter) may be the project team's sole quantification effort required in respect to currency. Otherwise, Chapter 13 covers the probabilistic exchange risk quantification method in detail. In general, as with escalation, the base method involves estimating the cash flow by currency and applying exchange rate indices to the spending by period.

Management Reserves and Authority

AACE has defined Management Reserve as:

> "...an amount added to an estimate to allow for discretionary management purposes outside of the defined scope of the project, as otherwise estimated. May include amounts that are within the defined scope, but for which management does not want to fund as contingency or that cannot be effectively managed using contingency."[4]

The three purposes for management reserves are therefore:

1. Management choice: optional scope, "bells and whistles," contingent strategy, etc.,

2. Beyond contingency: *extraordinary* low probability/high impact risks, and/or

3. Lack of trust: management does not trust the project director/manager to effectively manage risks.

The first two instances make perfect sense; the third one not so much as discussed in numbered order per above:

1. Management choice: It is their decision – management can fund whatever they have delegation of authority from the owners/shareholders to do. Having a reserve for optional scope is logical.

---

4   AACE, Cost Engineering Terminology, RP10S-90.

2. Beyond contingency: Contingency is an administrative control concept that only works well for risks that can be quantified with a continuous distribution (design development, errors and omissions, poor labor productivity, union problems, soil conditions, weather impacts, etc.). These are likely to occur to some extent and Project Control is designed to detect and help come up with corrective action to respond to these. However, if the risk event is quantified as discrete or binary (yes/no risk or low probability/high impact risk such as a direct hit hurricane or typhoon) and its impact is extraordinary, it makes no sense to give the project manager some portion of the potential impact. Either fund all (management reserve) or nothing.

3. Lack of trust: This one is problematic. It is an admission that the project system is weak, there is lying or gaming going on, and/or there might be corruption. If any of these are a fact, it must be respected, but it also must be recognized for what it is.

Unfortunately, in the practices espoused by some companies and even professional organizations, item #3 is the default working assumption. In fact, the Project Management Institute (PMI) does not use the term "contingency" – its term is "contingency reserve."[5] The word "reserve" implies the cost is not expected to be spent. In PMI usage, contingency reserve is only to be used for risks identified in the risk register and for which a risk response (work around) has been pre-planned and presumably pre-approved.

This approach is faulty thinking and risky in its own right. It presumes that risk quantification is a deterministic practice rather than the purely stochastic exercise that it is. Those of us doing risk quantification must remain humble about what we know, which is that:

♦ Most of the risks in the risk register will not happen, and

♦ Most of the risks that happen will not be in the risk register, and certainly not pre-planned (but we do our best).

We know from research that risk impacts are driven more by systemic risks (or "Issues" in PMI parlance) than the risk events that

5   Parish, Roger, Contingency and Management Reserves in PMBOK® Guide 5th Edition, www.maxwideman.com/guests/project_reserves/cost.htm, 2013.

appear in the register. We know from experience that systemic risks (e.g., change committee delays) can cause otherwise nominal risk event impacts to compound into crises. Finally, we also know that projects tend to fail in insidious ways. PMs need funds to take immediate corrective action when deviations first appear (e.g., in their regular status meetings) and not wait until they become alarming enough to justify elevating the problem to a higher authority.

Further, the following are commonly true:

♦ Senior and business managers are not familiar with the project reality in the field and cannot make effective tactical decisions. At no time in the project process have they been informed or concerned with control level or risk register details of project execution. Making effective tactical decisions in near real time is the responsibility of the PM and his/her team.

♦ Elevating tactical decisions to business managers or committees is a guarantee of delay. Decision delay in a large project is a known risk impact multiplier (a compounding factor or tipping point risk). Change Management committees are a common characteristic of the blowouts.

Incompetency and/or weak skills in the project director and manager position and/or frequent turnover in these positions are not uncommon systemic risks. But that risk needs to be identified, managed, and quantified directly, not ignored as decision and control policy assumptions or issues. Elevating the decision authority for contingency funds to those above the project director or manager should be the exception, not the rule.

Hopefully, the preceding discussions will help you better understand the purposes and concerns of cost and schedule risk quantification to support budgeting for Project Control at the start of the project execution phase. Key issues in the execution phase are:

♦ Who has the responsibility and authority to make risk response decisions, and

♦ Do they have the budget for these responses?

The takeaway of context from Chapters 5 and 6 is that risk quantification is about making good investment decisions first and about administrative concerns (e.g., contingency) second.

In the first 6 chapters we have covered:

- ♦ The nature of project cost and schedule uncertainty with a focus on the importance of the level of scope development and other systemic risks.
- ♦ The concept of accuracy as a basic measure of uncertainty and what the actual accuracy is for various project types and programs.
- ♦ The practice of investment decision making and project funding and how cost and schedule risk quantification outputs and information are applied.
- ♦ The practice of Project Control and how cost and schedule risk quantification is applied for control purposes with a focus on risk response authority.

What we have not covered are the risk quantification methods themselves. Chapter 7 introduces the methods; the specifics of the methods are covered in Part 2.

Questions

1) How do the roles of value and risk, and the emphasis of risk quantification, change between the pre- and post-sanction project phases?

2) Describe the basic process of Project Control in a sentence.

3) Planning includes breaking down the work, developing a work breakdown structure, and then developing budgets and schedule for this work. Describe a main risk quantification role in this process.

4) Forecasting can be viewed as looking ahead during execution and re-planning as appropriate. Where does risk quantification come into play in these tasks?

5) What is the Project Control process for dealing with performance trends, deviations, changes, risk impacts, etc., and what role does RQ play in that process?

6) Why should project control and risk management be tightly aligned during execution?

7) Explain why having a "base" cost and schedule estimating strategy is critical to risk quantification.

8) How might you express a cost strategy to help assure the base estimate is not *fat*?

9) Describe the characteristics of "allowances" that are appropriate for inclusion in base estimates, and describe how might you assure that allowances are used appropriately.

10) For the owner, what uncertainties or risks should contingency funding cover? For the contractor?

11) What is the AACE recommended practice for applying schedule contingency in a CPM schedule?

12) Describe how applying visible schedule contingency determined through probabilistic methods (e.g., set at $p50$ duration) can complicate planning and risk quantification.

13) If your project's actual materials costs increased 20% over the budget estimate because the team decided late to sole source many items as a risk response to avoid potential construction delays, is that escalation or contingency risk?

14) What are some factors to consider as to whether to budget for Escalation as a separate cost account?

15) Describe an economic trend for an upstream commodity project (e.g., oil, mining) that would cause both escalation and exchange risks to increase for a project, and explain the correlation.

16) Describe some things that a business may wish to fund as Management Reserve.

17) Who should have the final authority to make decisions about the use of contingency and escalation and why?

"Imagination is the one weapon in the war against reality."
— Jules de Gaultier

7

Introduction to Risk Quantification Methods

For the first decade of my career, I was a practicing mining engineer in the underground coal mines of Pennsylvania. Mining engineering (at least for certain aspects of underground coal mining) is not a field of applied science so much as one of applied experience.

For example, as a mining student at Penn State, I was taught that a coal pillar at a certain depth and for an adjacent mine opening span should have a certain width. When I asked the instructor (who was confined to a wheel chair due to a mine accident) why, the rather unscientific answer was, "If it's smaller than that, it might collapse."

A century of hard-won industry experience had shown that with the condition of the coal and rock, being highly uncertain and immeasurable, and with people's lives at stake, it is best to go with what experience has proven rather than rely solely on geotechnical or rock mechanics calculations (although we did those as well). Maybe this experience is why the first question I ask about a practice or method is, *"Does it work?"*

Not too many years later I was introduced to cost and schedule risk quantification methods. When I asked, "Do they work?" I was told, "We don't know." Risk quantification practices have been accepted in industry without any objective empirical evidence that they work. However, the analyst's reputation could always be saved by invoking the "unknown-unknowns" gambit.

This book has a *methods that work* theme. That means that the risk quantification methods must be *empirically valid* as well as *practical*. The following sections describe methods that owners and contractors can apply to any project or program, at any phase, with any quality of inputs with in-house resources and modest software (i.e., spreadsheets with an MCS add-on) while producing reliable, fit-for-use results.

Risk Quantification First Principles: What is a Good Method?

As you might guess, my answer to the question in the section heading is, "*One that works.*" As discussed, decision makers depend on the reliability of our analyses to give them confidence that their decisions have a solid basis. Plus, they don't want methods that work only some of the time for some of their decisions. This leads to my 'what works' criteria as follows:

♦ The method is based on empirical research and is validated against actual data.

♦ The method is generally applicable to all projects in a company's capital portfolio – simple and complex, large and small, conceptual or detailed, and good or bad quality estimates and schedules.

♦ The method is simple enough that an owner firm is not dependent on consultants other than for their impartial view, particularly for strategic projects.

In 2008, I gained further insight into how others answer the question in the heading. In preparation for the AACE International *Decision and Risk Management Professional* (DRMP) certification product, a development team that I led also asked, "What is a good method?" Not surprisingly, each team member (mostly fellow consultants) answered with whatever specific method they were using at the time; there was no consensus. So we stepped back and asked, "What are the attributes or principles of a good method?" and to this question, consensus came quickly. Here is what the team came up with.[1]

♦ Meets client objectives, expectations, and requirements,

♦ Part of and facilitates an effective decision or risk management process (e.g., TCM),

♦ Fit-for-use,

♦ Starts with identifying the risk drivers with input from all appropriate parties,

♦ Methods clearly link risk drivers and cost/schedule outcomes,

♦ Avoids iatrogenic (self-inflicted) risks,

♦ Employs empiricism,

♦ Employs experience/competency, and

♦ Provides probabilistic estimating results in a way supports effective decision making and risk management

The purpose of this list was to give someone selecting a method a way to verify whether their chosen method aligned with principles of best practice in a technical sense. As for AACE, a method that did not align with these principles would likely not become a Recommended Practice. The following key principles are the most important ones:

1. Fit-for-use

2. Starts with identifying the risk drivers with input from all appropriate parties

3. Methods clearly link risk drivers and cost/schedule outcomes

4. Employs empiricism (i.e., it is *demonstrated to actually work!*)

In the methods discussed below, I will refer to these *first principles* of best practice.

---

1   AACE International, *Contingency Estimating-General Principles*, 40R-08 (despite the title, this relates to risk quantification in general).

Good Judgment, You Can't Live Without It...
and its Corollary, Be Humble

One of the principles above is *"employs experience/competency."* When I was employed in benchmarking research, I advised on a study of risk quantification practices.[2] One finding was that expert judgment in setting contingency was superior to risk analysis using line-item ranging (more on that method later). A useful question to ask an experienced person is, "Does this analysis feel right?" Many times I have seen a team go through a risk analysis and apply their risk quantification method and come up with results that make no sense and yet their results went unquestioned (maybe because they align with the decision maker's bias?).

For example, I once reviewed an estimate by a contractor for a large mining project located high in a remote mountain chain, with poorly developed infrastructure, labor shortages, environmental permitting risks, and a tight base estimate. It was given a *p*50 contingency of 7% by the contractor. This was an absurd outcome relative to industry experience, but nobody on the team or business spoke up to question it. Their owner's workaround rationalization was to fund the project at the *p*80 level (which was about 15% contingency), which left an equally absurd "worst case" range of about +20%. For a company that had recent projects overrun by much more than this, the worst case made no logical sense.

Just as decision makers are subject to bias, so are risk analysts. There are a number of sophisticated methods, models, and systems for risk quantification in use that are compelling in form. These include elaborate software, powerful graphics, links to other project management tools (e.g., CPM) and so on; however, they tend to cater to the expert user. For experts invested in an approach, *inertia, repetition bias,* and *anchoring biases* can be significant. To check this bias, the accounting world gives us a guiding concept called "substance over form," wherein the economic substance of a transaction should be preferred over its legal form. As with the accounting profession, we need to stay open minded to the evidence as to whether our selected method actually works and is practical.

Another effect of sophisticated methods is that they can contribute to an illusion of control, i.e., a tendency to see risk quantification as a quasi-deterministic method rather than the highly stochastic method that it is. This is evidenced in the PMI-advocated

---

2   Juntima, G. and S. Burroughs, "Exploring Techniques for Contingency Setting," AACE International Transactions, 2004.

Contingency and Judgment: A Work In Progress

In August 2015, Nalcor Energy, a Crown Corporation of Newfoundland and Labrador, Canada, revised the budget for its Muskrat Falls hydropower generation facility project from $6.99 billion to $7.65 billion. Construction progress was reported as 33.5 per cent complete versus 43.3 per cent planned. The Muskrat Falls Project Oversight Committee made the following observations in its report:

"Nalcor noted that the Contingency of $186.8 million is designed to cover these potential risks and has been estimated in accordance with the low range advised by the Association for the Advancement of Cost Engineering International (AACEI) standard. Nalcor further advises that the AACEI standard for the hydropower industry states that the accuracy of the capital cost at this stage of a project is between −3 to +3 per cent. Nalcor has used 4 per cent on the remaining scope of the project. Nalcor advises that it sets aggressive contingency amounts in order to drive costs as low as possible. The Committee notes that significant schedule pressures with respect to the Muskrat Falls Generating Facility remain."

- What are your thoughts on the report's reference to AACEI "standards?"
- How might the statement that "significant schedule pressures remain" influence your judgment on cost contingency?
- In your judgment, what might Nalcor have meant by "sets aggressive contingency amounts in order to drive costs as low as possible?"
- Without a quantitative analysis, and having only this information, what is your judgment of the contingency of 4 percent on the remaining scope?

control approach, wherein contingency is only intended for specific risks detailed in a register. At worst, teams start to believe that they can safely allocate contingency to items in the budget rather than deal with uncertainty "in aggregate" as per the AACE definition. We must keep in mind that our quantification is better than a guess (it does correlate with reality, but not by as much as we would like). To paraphrase Winston Churchill's statement about democracy, we must be humble and know that the *method we are using is the worst, except for all those other methods that we have tried from time to time.*

Recommended Risk Quantification Methods

So, what methods pass my personal "does it work" test as well as AACE's *first principles* checklist? They are:

- Empirically validated parametric modeling for systemic risks,

- ◆ Expected Value with MCS for project-specific risks (in a hybrid with above), and
- ◆ Escalation using CAPEX market adjusted price indices and MCS (in a hybrid with above).

The *hybrid* reference refers to the fact that these methods are applied in an integrated sequence, i.e., start with systemic risk, then project-specific, then escalation – accumulating their impacts along the way. This approach uniquely yields a "universal" CAPEX outcome distribution, which is optimal for use in decision analysis NPV models (e.g., escalation is not looked at separately for NPV).

For a program or group of related projects, these methods can be applied in an integrative analysis pass to quantify risks that are unique from a holistic perspective. Finally, the methods above explicitly address the impact of complexity, i.e., they can model non-linear or chaotic behavior that results in bimodal outcomes (i.e., potential blowout prediction). Here is how these three methods rate with respect to the first principles:

1. *Fit-for-use*: they can be applied to any project at any phase. One does not need a quality estimate or CPM schedule (deliverable quality is a systemic risk in its own right).

2. *Starts with identifying the risk drivers*: all are inherently risk driven and are an extension of traditional qualitative screening approaches (i.e., use the risk register).

3. *Methods clearly link risk drivers and cost/schedule outcomes*: all inherently integrate cost and schedule while explicitly considering potential risk responses.

4. *Employs empiricism*: the parametric method is explicitly empirically derived. The approach can forecast low-biased small, high-biased large and mega bimodal realities.

The following are summary descriptions of the methods; the details are covered in Part 2.

Project Historical Data (Prerequisite for Empiricism)

I include historical data analysis or knowledge management here as a risk quantification method because it is the foundation for the others. For risk quantification methods to be realistic or empirically valid, they must be based on, validated against, and/or supported by actual history. Unfortunately, historical project data collection and analysis tend to be the last capability that companies implement. Those that do have some historical data tend to focus on cost and schedule performance (e.g., estimate versus actual data) and not risk learnings which would allow them to study *why* cost and schedule outcomes were what they were; i.e., what is driving the outcomes? These drivers and learnings include the following:

- ♦ Cost, schedule, and systemic risk rating data with which to develop and/or calibrate parametric risk models.
- ♦ Learnings about critical risk events and conditions: their nature, occurrence, and impact to support risk checklists, lessons learned on responses, and so on to support expected value modeling.

Empirically Validated Parametric Modeling (for Systemic Risks)

This methodology is conceptually simple – just collect and clean quantitative historical data about past project cost growth and schedule slip (dependent variables) and quantitative ratings of project practices and attributes (independent variables, which are systemic risks). Then, using multivariate linear regression (MLR) analysis, look for correlations between the cost growth and schedule slip and the practices and attributes while keeping in mind to look for causal relationships. This is the path taken by Rand, CII, IPA, and others. The resulting risk model is a simple parametric equation of the general form:

Cost Growth or Schedule Slip % = C + (*a* x Risk A) + (*b* x Risk B) + ...
where C is a constant and *a, b*, etc. are coefficients

Each systemic risk (Risk A, etc.) will have a quantified rating. For example, the CII PDRI index may be used for the scope development rating. The equation provides a mean outcome. However, as we will cover in Part 2, we can also derive the accuracy range from the model. No Monte Carlo Simulation is required to get this mean outcome or distribution.

Most of the effort in applying the method is in assuring that the risk rating inputs reflect the real situation without bias. An independent facilitator/analyst is helpful for that. Some systemic risks can be rated objectively, such as the status of design deliverables determined through deliverable QA/QC reviews. Others are more subjective, such as the state of team development, which is obtained from interviewing the business sponsor, project manager, and other leaders.

Unfortunately, most companies do not have suitable historical data with which to develop parametric models. Most have the
sanctioned and final capitalized amounts, plus the start and end
dates, but that is about it. Very few companies have good data about
risk drivers. The good news is that there are publicly available industry sources that provide the basic relationships and functioning
models. The primary sources are Hackney, Rand, and CII. In fact,
AACE International has built the Hackney and Rand models into
functioning Excel spreadsheets.[3] You might ask if this information
is still applicable – the answer is *yes*. The good news is that decades
of research show that the industry cost growth and schedule slip
experience has remained essentially the same (though we have
learned more about complexity and megaprojects). The bad news is
that cost and schedule performance has not improved with respect
to uncertainty.

A challenge to accepting the parametric method is that many
people distrust things that are simple and cheap. Hopefully the
fact that these models are the industry's only empirically validated
method will balance out this aversion. Owners and contractors
usually start with a modified version of the Rand model with the
latest learnings from research added. Later, as they collect their
own project data (and historical database development is integral
to doing this well), they can calibrate the tool periodically (adjust
constant, coefficients, etc.) so it matches their experience.

In terms of implementation priority, this method is the most
important because systemic risks are almost always dominant in
terms of impact. While systemic risks speak to the *state of the system* (maturity, strength, bias, quality, complexity, etc.), they are
not "background" risk. They are what matters most and they need
to be emphasized in evaluation. Systemic risks also compound the
impact of and confound the responses to project-specific risks (e.g.,
risk events), which is why we quantify those in a second step.

Expected Value with MCS (for Project-Specific Risks)

Having addressed the systemic risks, the next risks to quantify are project-specific. These are risk events and conditions, i.e.,
things that may occur within the given project and project system
(in whatever state it is in). Note that for Class 5 (FEL1/Assess)
estimates, this step can be skipped because there are few project

---

3   These models are available from AACE International (www.aacei.org)
as part of RP 43R-08.

specifics to even consider, and systemic risk impacts (e.g., scope definition) prevail.

The calculations in the Expected Value method, like in parametric modeling, are quite simple. Here is the form of calculation for a single risk:

Cost or Schedule Impact = Probability of Occurrence x Impact if it Occurs

A nice feature of this method is that it is an extension of information and methods that almost everyone uses already – information from the risk register. If risk management is ongoing (as it should be), the team will already have identified the risks and ranked them using a traditional risk matrix or probability-impact matrix (i.e., the red-yellow-green chart). The risk matrix is a qualitative representation of the expected value calculation above. For example, a "red" risk will have high probability and/or high impact, depending on what high-low criteria the team set for this ranking.

Procedurally, there is more to the Expected Value method. Part 2 of the book will elaborate, but there are six basic steps:

1. **Identify Critical Risks**: Critical risk #1 is *systemic*, i.e., a risk with 100% chance of occurring and an impact equal to the parametric model outcome. The rest of the critical risks are the "red" (or near red) *project-specific* risks from the register. Lessor ranked risks tend to be noise covered by the range of the empirically based systemic model. Escalation and exchange risks are excluded at this point.

2. **Quantify the Probability of Occurrence**: The register will have a qualitative ranking. Get consensus from the team in a workshop as to a specific percent chance value or range.

3. **Consider Risk Response**: For each critical project-specific risk, answer the question, "How would we respond if this happened?" The answer will depend on your cost/schedule objective (*what outcome is important?*) and the response will guide the quantification of cost and schedule.

4. **Quantify the Impacts**: The register will have a qualitative ranking. Get consensus from the team in a workshop with expert planning guidance as to 3-point cost and schedule estimates of impact specific to and integrated by the assumed risk response(s). Direct, indirect, and time-dependent cost impacts are considered. Follow up with elaboration after the

workshop as needed before running Monte Carlo Simulations.

5. **Run the Monte Carlo Simulation**: The impacts will have been entered as distributions and if any risks are correlated, this will have been allowed for.

6. **Set Aside Reserve Risks and Iterate Analysis**: If, on reviewing the outcome, any of the risks are not amenable to contingency (e.g., low probability, high impact), they can be removed from the list and the MCS re-run. Reserve risks will be funded or not as decided by management.

The primary output of the above quantification will be integrated cost and schedule distributions. Because the systemic risk outcomes for cost and schedule were entered as risk #1, this Expected Value output includes *all* contingency risks, plus a list of potential reserve risks and their quantification. The next risks to address are escalation and exchange (if applicable).

Escalation/Exchange Using CAPEX Market Adjusted Price and Exchange Indices and MCS

Escalation and exchange were excluded from the above analyses. Escalation and exchange are quantified separately, although each uses similar quantification methods and inputs. Escalation is estimated by applying forecast price indices against a cash flow forecast by cost type. Exchange is estimated by applying exchange rate indices against a cash flow by expended currency. The indices of prices to the owner and rates are obtained with the input of economists familiar with capital projects. Part 2 will cover this in detail.

What is somewhat different in this recommended approach from traditional deterministic approaches (and is essential to best practice) is to do these estimates probabilistically while considering cost and schedule contingency analysis outputs as inputs to escalation. If done in this way, the escalation/exchange output is a single *universal CAPEX distribution* that can be used in an NPV model. It addresses all the cost and schedule risks – systemic, project-specific, and escalation and exchange.

Doing it probabilistically requires treating the price and exchange indices, cash flow spending pattern, and duration (schedule contingency), and cost contingency accounts as uncertain; i.e., they are entered in a MCS model as distributions. This is the largest model, but is still just a spreadsheet-based tool with MCS.

Unfortunately, most projects do not effectively consider systemic risks. Also, they estimate escalation deterministically (i.e., a point value). Risk quantification for these projects is pointless if not economically dangerous because systemic risks are dominant when a system is weak and escalation and exchange risks are dominant when the economy is volatile. If your projects suffer both of these, expect overruns.

Method Extensions

The methods above cover the typical project of low to moderate complexity. There are special situations that require extensions in how the above methods are applied. The situations include:

◆ Highly complex projects, including megaprojects,
◆ Programs (which may have megaproject features), and
◆ Portfolios (i.e., capital budgets and finance concerns).

Complexity and Megaprojects

Research has shown that if you plot the cost growth outcome distribution from a set of many large projects, the resulting graph will often be bimodal. This reflects two populations of projects: orderly and disorderly (chaotic).[4] Most risk quantification methods assume an orderly project regime, i.e., the project is under control. In an orderly regime, if variations from plan are noticed or a risk event occurs, corrective actions and risk responses are made, and order is restored or maintained (even if performance is not as good as planned).

However, when a project is complex and there is stress applied (e.g., harsh requirements, simultaneous risk events), then control can break down, and the regime becomes, *"I don't care what you do next, just make some progress!"*

While the road to failure via chaos is by definition impossible to map, its potential for happening can be foreseen by measuring complexity and stress factors (a tipping point indicator), and its final net result is evident (bimodality with blowouts) and hence can be modeled. In part 2, the tipping point indicator and model extensions will be described.

---

4   For taxpayer funded infrastructure projects, the extreme overruns may also represent strategic misrepresentation (greatly underestimating on purpose); however, that behavior, if present, is relatively subtle in process industry projects. See Chapter 15 for more detail.

Programs

Programs are made up of separate but related projects. Each project has a project manager and budget, and hence will require its own risk quantification and contingency. When evaluating each project's systemic risks, an initial consideration is to assure the risk ratings are similar for each project (to the extent the program is being executed under the same project system). Also, the risk registers of each project should be reviewed to look for commonalities to assure effective collective management of project-specific risks as appropriate.

Where programs differ from stand-alone projects is in the level of complexity. The projects are tied to some extent in a master schedule under a project director or equivalent. Often, the project execution plans are tied, physical processes have connections, and regulatory bodies may view some aspects of the program as a whole. This layering results in additional integrative risks. So, a second pass of risk quantification is needed to deal with this and to quantify a program level reserve for the director's use as appropriate.

In the program pass, the program leadership team should review the systemic risks for the program. For example, each project may feel confident in their team development, but at a program level, there may be coordination issues. For project-specific risks, new risks may emerge or existing ones become more critical at a program level, particularly where projects interact. For example, a nominal delay for one project may create a more significant delay for a later project (e.g., push it into another season). Or, the projects may find they are all competing for the same scarce resource. A program or super-mega project can create its own micro-economy that causes labor shortages and additional escalation.

The second pass risk quantification treats the program as a single project, starting with a program level systemic risk run. The project-specific run then quantifies the additional program interaction risks that have been identified. Finally, the added complexity may heighten the probability of chaotic behavior.

The program risk quantification mean cost outcome, including the added interaction risks, may exceed the sum of the project cost contingencies (using mean values facilitates program level analyses because they are additive). If so, a contingency or reserve for this overage may be established under project director authority. At a program level, the distribution of outcomes for the program as a whole provides not only an overall mean for program contingency determination, but an overall worst outcome, which is new information (i.e., the *p*90 values of the projects are *not* additive). This program level extension will be further described in Part 2.

Portfolios/Capital Budgets

From a risk quantification point of view, the portfolio or capital budget has quite a different flavor versus projects and programs. If a project or program overruns, the business is likely to be able to spend the extra funds, which we must quantify. The business's focus at any moment is project control of what is already funded and is in execution. In a portfolio, an active project that is overrunning will likely be funded (i.e., escalating commitment bias), but other projects or programs in the budget will be de-scoped and/or delayed or cancelled to balance it out. This is because capital is a constrained resource for a company (often set near its annual depreciation), depending on strategic initiatives underway. In summary, the portfolio focus is more on financial control and cash flow.

Portfolio risk analysis is a FEL 1/Assess process where investment alternatives with less defined scope are re-run through the collective NPV development process. Parametric analysis of systemic risks (particularly the level of project definition, technology, and complexity) is the primary risk quantification method used. However, there is one portfolio management risk that needs to be identified and quantified at the project and program level and that is the practice of *management-by-cash flow* (MBC).

Companies where management is dominated by finance (which is inherent with governments) often have a primary capital investment strategy of "capital discipline," which translates loosely to *achieve your monthly and annual capital spending plan exactly*. Given the uncertainty of capital projects, the *only* way to accomplish cash flow perfection in the short term (monthly or annual) is to accelerate and throttle back on project and program activities and/or manipulate payment schemes. However, MBC is destructive to project control discipline and value. Teams become obsessed (and stressed) with cash flow issues rather than effective cost and schedule performance. Perversely, finance's emphasis on certainty in spend rate causes increased uncertainty in total project costs as well as increased uncertainty in capital spending as a whole. To keep total capital spend within constraints in MBC, other projects are de-scoped, deferred, or cancelled, which results in a less productive asset base for the money. If MBC is the default or operative

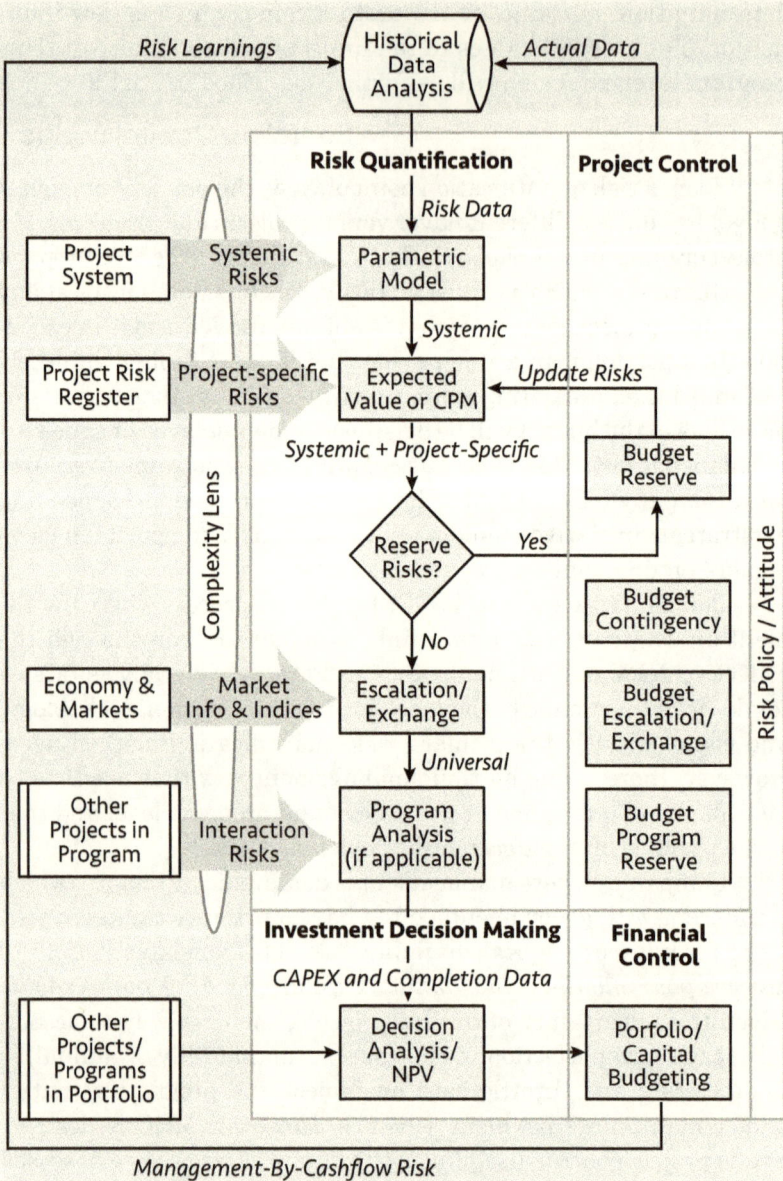

Figure 7.1: Risk Quantification Method Flowchart

project system strategy, the systemic risks on every project increase significantly.

Overall Risk Quantification Methodology

Figure 7.1 illustrates the methodological flow for risk quantification. The Figure is intended to show the well-structured logic behind the approach (and not to make it overly complicated). The figure highlights the following features:

- Start with historical data (empiricism),
- Best methods are applied for each risk type,
- Methods are cumulative (and can compound), building up to a universal CAPEX and completion date distribution for use in decision analysis and NPV models,
- Risk quantification must support both investment decision making and project control aligned with company policy and risk attitudes,
- Risk quantification must support projects, programs, and portfolios as appropriate, and
- Project behavior can be orderly or disorderly, with the difference being added complexity (the complexity lens).

For Programs, the chart in Figure 7.2 illustrates how the same methods are applied to assess the program as a whole. At the program level, the emphasis is on assessing commonalities and interactions, recognizing the added complexity of enterprise. Generally, the Program will benefit from having its own risk funding to deal with interaction risks and to assure that the enterprise is prepared to make interventions into its projects if required.

Alternative Methods: Recommended (and Otherwise)

CPM-Based Model Alternative if Applicable

I recommend companies implement and apply the *hybrid* approach discussed above, including Expected Value for their standard practice, because this is most broadly consistent with first-principles (risk-impact linkage, empiricism, fit-for-use, addresses systemic risks). It is also applicable on every project at any time without exception and it is also relatively inexpensive.

However, for strategically important projects where team and external resources can be utilized, I recommend that teams also apply the Cost-Loaded CPM with Risk Drivers method (it is in the AACE Recommended Practice toolbox). However, the emphasis should be on building a robust, risk-tolerant schedule; i.e., reduce the plan's uncertainty, as opposed to using it for risk quantification other than as a validation of the hybrid method outcomes.

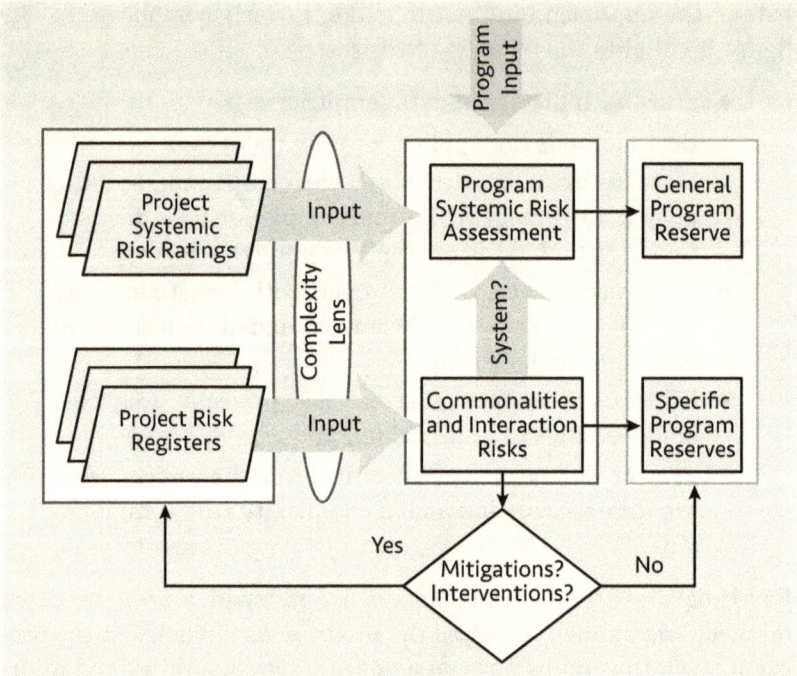

Figure 7.2: Risk Quantification Flowchart Extended to the Program Level

In short, the CPM with risk driver method involves:

♦ Linking critical risks to schedule activities in a CPM model,

♦ Cost loading the activities with time-dependent costs,

♦ Adding non-time dependent cost impacts separately, and

♦ Running a Monte Carlo simulation.

Systemic risks can be addressed objectively by using parametric modeling separately and then linking its cost and schedule impact to a systemic contingency activity just prior to the execution completion milestone. See Appendix A for how to apply that approach.

A major concern with the CPM approach is that it requires a high quality schedule model that is simply not available for many projects. One study of project schedules from major global companies at the time of project authorization showed that only 13% had CPM schedules with resource loading (a proxy indicator of a quality schedule).[5]

---

5   Griffith, Andrew, "Scheduling Practices and Project Success," Cost Engineering Journal, AACE International, Morgantown WV, 2006.

There are other shortcomings. As was discussed, risk responses often involve changing schedule to preserve the completion milestone, with significant cost/schedule trading. The only way to model this in CPM is probabilistic branching. Even then, trading means there may be no schedule impact, but significant knock-on effects on hours and cost. These are very difficult to include in a CPM model, but intuitively easy to handle with the expected value method. Table 7.1 describes the strengths and weaknesses of the alternative approaches.

METHOD	STRENGTHS	WEAKNESSES
COST LOADED CPM	• Explicit risk-impact linkage (but less for systemic risks) • Explicit cost/schedule integration for time dependent costs • Encourages use of quality planning & scheduling methods • Commercial software	• No empirical basis • Requires high quality CPM model, cost-loaded schedule, competent scheduler (consultant) • Not applicable to Class 5 • Static logic assumed and difficult to address cost/schedule trading • Weak for systemic risks without special provision
PARAMETRIC/ EXPECTED- VALUE	• Explicit risk-impact linkage • Empirical basis • Applicable to estimates and schedules of any quality • Applicable to all levels of scope definition (phase) • Address risk response	• No commercial software, fewer users • Schedule risks and cost/schedule integration require more intuitive assessment (more skill and knowledge) • Does not encourage use of quality planning & scheduling practice

Table 7.1: Strengths and Weaknesses of CPM and Expected Value Approaches

Not Recommended: Line-Item and Activity Ranging

In the 1980s, Monte Carlo Simulation became available as add-ons to spreadsheets. Cost estimators who had already made spreadsheets their tool of choice quickly grasped MCS's ability to address uncertainty in their cost estimates. It was amazingly easy. You only need replace the line-item cost estimates with 3-point estimates (where the old estimate is the most likely, and a high/low range is set for the other two points based on team input), run the MCS, and out comes a total cost distribution from which management can select a value depending on their risk appetite. I call this method *line-item ranging* (LIR). For schedulers, a similar capability was available to use 3-point estimates for activity durations in their CPM schedules. For those companies willing to try a more sophisticated method, this caught on quickly and became a common method of choice.

Unfortunately, line-item ranging is not effective in developing a realistic contingency. In 2004, an empirical research study found that, "...contingency estimates are, on average, getting further from the actual contingency required."[6] In particular, it found that LIR was a "disaster" for projects for which the scope was poorly defined (and presumably had other systemic risks). Other studies have found that the method came up with 9% contingency with a SD of +/- 4% – regardless of the systemic or other risks of the project.[7]

What LIR *is* good at is reliably generating the contingency and accuracy expected by management (see Chapter 4). Unfortunately, some have incorrectly blamed the failure of LIR on MCS. Granted, many practitioners use MCS inappropriately, but LIR fails because it is contrary to the first principles listed earlier. Despite the good intentions of analysts, the method simply captures the team's opinion about the quality of their estimates, and most estimators are biased about the quality of their own estimates. Arguably, LIR does not quantify risks at all, and it certainly does not stand scrutiny when compared to actual cost growth outcomes.

Activity ranging suffers the same problems as LIR. The only difference is that because of cost/schedule trading (due to pressure to hit the first production milestone), actual schedule slip tends to have a much tighter range than cost. Therefore the method's average forecast coincidentally looks like the average actual outcomes (and generally makes it difficult to correlate cost growth and schedule slip outcomes). However, keep in mind that for decision making, the *average* outcome usually does not allow business to discriminate between alternatives – the *worst* case does. And LIR and activity ranging produce more or less the same average *and* the same worst cases every time they are applied. In short, do not use these methods. Choose methods that explicitly link identified risks to estimates of their impacts.

---

6   Op. Sit., Juntima, G. and S. Burroughs.

7   Op. Sit., Merrow, E., *Industrial Megaprojects*.

Questions

1) The chapter theme is "methods that work." List the four key principles that guide practices that AACE International recommends for risk quantification and that are used in this book.

2) What question should one ask of experienced people about risk quantification outcomes, and why might decision makers and teams stick with a risk quantification method and outcome regardless of the question's answer?

3) Three main RQ methods are recommended as meeting the criteria for "methods that work." However, one foundational area of practice is described first; what is it, and why is it essential?

4) What method is recommended for quantifying Systemic risks? Briefly describe the method's development approach.

5) If a company does not have adequate data about its past project to build parametric models, how might it get started with applying the method?

6) What method is recommended for quantifying Project-Specific risks? Briefly describe the method's approach including how systemic risks are factored in.

7) What is a "critical" risk?

8) What method is recommended for quantifying Escalation and Exchange risks? Briefly describe the method's approach.

9) Using the various methods described for the various risk types, how would one answer the question "can you provide me with one overall project cost distribution?"

10) Name the three special types of projects or combinations of projects that risk quantification methods must address (if they are relevant to one's company) and a unique RQ consideration for each.

11) A methodology flowchart for project risk quantification was shown that has a recycle loop in it; what does that loop represent?

12) The Cost-Loaded CPM with Risk Drivers method is included among AACE Recommended Practices. How does this book suggest it be used and why?

13) Describe the probabilistic RQ methods that are perhaps the
   most common in use and why they are not recommended by
   AACE or in this book.

"We are approaching a new age of synthesis. Knowledge cannot be merely a degree or a skill... it demands a broader vision, capabilities in critical thinking and logical deduction without which we cannot have constructive progress."
– Li Ka-shing

8
Organizing for Risk Quantification

Competencies, Resources, and Organization for Risk Quantification

As part of my consulting practice, I advise firms on improving their cost engineering practices, including risk management and quantification. These engagements usually result in an action plan to put improvements into effect. The easy improvement tasks are developing and implementing methods and tools (Part 2 covers risk quantification in that regard). The difficult tasks are always the people part: finding qualified personnel, training them, and developing their careers – organizational development.

No algorithm alone will produce reliable risk quantification outcomes. The AACE first principles of risk quantification (RP 40R-08) include the importance of the methods being integral to the capital management and project processes (e.g., TCM and phase gating). Also, experience and competency are required for successful risk quantification. For example, the identity and nature of risks must be elicited from the team; team inputs must be validated as unbiased, and reliable range estimates of impacts must be made. So while this book is focused on methods that are within the reach of a typical small to medium sized organization, that does not mean just anyone can lead or perform the risk quantification.

Competencies Required

Competency development starts with identifying the competencies required to achieve the organization's objectives. While they will vary depending on the company and project portfolio, the following is a list of experience and competencies that an organization must have (at some level) to support the risk quantification methods:

1) Risk Management

♦ Be able to create and manage an overarching capital project risk management process, qualitative and quantitative, and to have the competencies in-house to manage and perform the process steps.

2) Historical Data/Knowledge Management

♦ Create and manage a historical database that includes the building blocks for developing and applying risk quantification methods and tools (e.g., risk checklists, lessons learned, data for model building).

3) Parametric Method/Systemic Risks

♦ In the risk organization, develop an understanding of the business in general (i.e., its commercial situation) as well as of the project system, portfolio, organization, objectives, and cost/schedule trading behavior.

♦ Develop the skills and knowledge to develop (e.g., Excel modeling, regression analysis), apply, and maintain (i.e., calibration) parametric models.

4) Expected Value Method/Project-Specific Risks

♦ Create and maintain risk registers (a key deliverable of Risk Management).

♦ Be able to facilitate workshops and conduct interviews to obtain inputs and elicit information, which requires a good understanding of biases.

♦ Understand estimating and scheduling practices well enough to assess the quality and bias of the base products and to assess risk impacts.

♦ Understand project control practices well enough to spot and track risks reported in control deliverables and to work with the control team in assessing and dealing with risk impacts.

♦ Understand project execution (engineering, procurement, fabrication, construction, and startup) well enough to assess risk behavior, how things interact, risk responses, and risk impacts.

5) Escalation/Exchange

♦ Understand economics and its effects on the project supply chain well enough to understand what is driving price escalation and exchange rate trends. Also, be able to communicate with economics consultants.

6) General

♦ Have good communication skills to assure that the team understands what is needed to support the process and to assure the decision makers understand the quantification findings and their implications to project success.

♦ Understand and be able to apply basic probability and statistics, including descriptive and inferential statistics (e.g., MCS and regression modeling).

7) External

♦ Identify expert resources to provide cold-eyes or outside view reviews and to conduct independent assessments and quantification for strategic projects. These can also help counter bias (e.g., avoid groupthink), provide fresh insights when elements of the scope are outside the company's experience, and support getting new processes, methods, and tools started and help improve them later.

A good reference to guide risk quantification competency development is the Body of Knowledge (BoK) outline of the AACE International Decision and Risk Management Professional (DRMP) certification examination.[1] This certification BoK, as with AACE Recommended Practices, has a strong quantitative emphasis.

Table 8.1, outlines the AACE DRMP Certification Body of Knowledge Outline (BoK), including Supporting Skills and Knowl-

---

1   Regan, Sean, ed., *Decision and Risk Management Professional (DRMP) Certification Study Guide*, AACE International, Morgantown, WV, 2013

edge (Part A), Risk Management Skills and Knowledge (Part B), Decision Making Skills and Knowledge (Part C), and Total Cost Management/Project Control (Part D). As can be seen, the breadth of skills and knowledge required is quite extensive. It covers not only risk management and quantification, but business and project management in general.

SUPPORTING SKILLS AND KNOWLEDGE	
Elements of Costs	
Cost definitions	Cost vs. pricing
Asset and project life cycles	Influence curve
Portfolio, program, project scope	Classifications: operating, capital, expense
Owner vs. contractor view of costs	Types: labor, material, equipment
Monetary vs. economic/opportunity costs	
Elements of Planning and Scheduling	
Schedule definitions	Cost/schedule integration and trade-off
Activities and durations	Integrated schedules
Logic: milestones, CPM, critical chain, PERT	Programs and portfolios
Delays	Resource planning
Acceleration, crashing	
Elements of Analysis	
Statistics and probability (descriptive and inferential)	
Economic and financial analysis (NPV/IRR/ROI, cash flow)	
Optimization & Modeling (regression, MCS, scenario, sensitivity)	
Enabling Knowledge	
Ethics	EH&S/sustainability
Organizational/leadership/teams	Legal
Culture/bias	Insurance (including bonding, etc.)
Performance/productivity/human factors	Contracting (including risk allocation)
Psychology/ sociology/ group dynamics/ elicitation/ bias	Finance (Forex, hedging, etc.)
Psychology of estimating and decision analysis	Markets, economics
Quality/cost of quality	Technology (R&D, complexity, etc.)
Value/VIPs	Stakeholder management

Table 8.1A: Supporting Skills and Knowledge
AACE's DRMP Certification Body of Knowledge Outline

RISK MANAGEMENT (RM) SKILLS AND KNOWLEDGE	
Overall Risk Management Terminology/Concepts	
Uncertainty	Empiricism
Risk	Causation
Accuracy	Roles and responsibility/organization
Range	Risk appetite/acceptance/tolerance/policy
Scope	Assurance
Allowances, contingency, reserves	Objectives
Risk taxonomy	Dependency, compounding
Processes and General Practices for Risk Management	
Risk management and Total Cost Management	
Risk management processes (COSO, ISO, BS 31000, ASNZ 4360, APM PRAM, MoR)	
Process alignment with objective	
Planning for risk management (policy, responsibility, available resources)	
Risk assessment: identification and causation	
Risk assessment: qualitative analysis	
Risk treatment (including risk response strategies)	
Specific Risk Management Practices	
Risk assessment: fault tree analysis, cause / effect analysis	
Risk treatment–contingency planning, fallback responses, and disrupter analysis	
Risk assessment: quantitative/contingency, management reserves, escalation, exchange	
Risk treatment (including contract risk allocation)	
Risk control: change management (integration with RM)	
Forecasting (integration with RM)	

Table 8.1B: Risk Management (RM) Skills and Knowledge
AACE's DRMP Certification Body of Knowledge Outline

DECISION MAKING (DM) SKILLS AND KNOWLEDGE	
Overall DM Terminology/Concepts	
Risk (see Risk Sections above)	Economic Costs
Valuation, monetary equivalent, trade-off, risk premium	Expected Monetary Value
Decision Criterion/Criteria	Utility Function
Objective Function	Modeling, Sensitivity, Scenarios
Economic/Financial Analysis	Expert Judgment

DECISION MAKING (DM) SKILLS AND KNOWLEDGE	
Processes and General Practices for Decision Management	
Decision Process and Practices	Decision and Risk Modeling
Decision Policy	Decision Basis (Business Case)
Decision Analysis	Decision Implementation (Communication, phase-gate, etc)
Specific Practices: Decision Modeling	
Decision Trees	
Influence Diagrams (Bayesian Decision Networks)	
Monte Carlo Simulation	

Table 8.1C: Decision Making Skills and Knowledge
AACE's DRMP Certification Body of Knowledge Outline

TOTAL COST MANAGEMENT(TCM)/PROJECT CONTROL (INFLUENCING PRACTICES)	
Planning	Performance measurement and assessment
Schedule planning and development	Change management
Estimating and budgeting	Forecasting
Resource planning	Historical database management
Value analysis, engineering & management	Forensic performance assessment
Procurement planning (including contract management)	

Table 8.1D: Total Cost Management/Project Control (Influencing Practices)
AACE's DRMP Certification Body of Knowledge Outline

Use a competency inventory such as in Table 8.1 to develop a competency development model for your staff by adding competency level performance statements such as the example for MCS in Table 8.2. Periodic staff reviews assess achievement of the planned level of performance.

Resources Required

Each competency above does not equate to an added staff member. Much of the expertise already exists within most organizations. Existing staff (PMs, estimators, schedulers, project controls staff, database coordinators, and project engineers) will need to be knowledgeable of their roles in risk quantification, but no new resources need to be obtained for those roles.

Competency: MCS	Develop and apply MCS risk quantification and decision support models that meet customer specific needs for the purpose at hand.
Junior	Applies MCS capability to a typical spreadsheet model. Needs some assistance.
Intermediate	Develops MCS models for any typical project need with occasional assistance.
Advanced	Proficiently develops MCS models for typical and unusual project needs.
Senior	Expert who develops novel MCS models for strategic and unique situations.

Table 8.2: Example Competency Performance Levels (for MCS)

Table 8.3 describes a minimal central organization for a small to mid-sized company. As the portfolio increases and becomes more diverse (e.g., upstream offshore, upstream onshore, midstream, downstream, chemicals), staff will need to increase accordingly.

Assumed Existing Staff:
Most companies have a lead Risk Manager plus analysts who perform qualitative risk assessments and coordinate the risk register. It is also assumed that the company has historical data management process and tools in place that will support risk needs.
Added Staff for Empirically-Valid Risk Quantification:
Risk Analyst (1-Advanced or Expert): data management, regression, modeling, and some model application.
Risk Analyst (2-Advanced or Expert): quantification workshop facilitation and application (in addition to typical qualitative facilitators or they could be cross trained).
Risk Associate (1-Intermediate): assists Risk Analysts; in development to become Risk Analyst.
Supplemental:
Consultant(s): experienced cold-eye or outside view provider for strategic projects as well as general advice or general analysis support.

Table 8.3: Minimal Organization, Small to Medium Sized Company

Beyond the staff, the main resource required is software. The methods recommended in this book can be implemented with standard spreadsheets and MCS add-ons. If you decide to apply the risk driven CPM-based approach in-house as well, specialized risk analysis software is required that integrates with the company's CPM software.

Table 8.4 summarizes the two most common spreadsheet add-on programs. Both offer similar features and capabilities for the average user. There are other programs, and they may offer more features for the expert, but their use is much less common.

@RISK FOR EXCEL®	PALISADE CORPORATION, WWW.PALISADE.COM
@RISK is listed first because I have found this add-on to be the most practical for the average user. A key step in MCS application is to replace spreadsheet model variables (e.g., cost impact) with distributions and @RISK stands out by implementing its distributions as true Excel® functions; i.e., if you can use Excel, you can apply @RISK with minimal learning curve. Palisade also offers a decision tree with MCS product called PrecisionTree®.	
CRYSTAL BALL®	ORACLE CORPORATION, WWW.ORACLE.COM
Crystal Ball® offers features that are similar to @RISK's. The main difference is that distributions are not implemented as true Excel functions but as functionality linked to the Excel variable cell. This makes housekeeping more difficult for the average user because you cannot see the distribution function at a glance. However, companies having Oracle enterprise applications tend to prefer Oracle products.	

Table 8.4: MCS Spreadsheet Add-ons (for the hybrid expected value method)

While this book does not recommend CPM-based risk quantification as a core method, Table 8.5 summarizes the two most common add-on programs for incorporating MCS capability in CPM models. These programs both support integrated cost and schedule analysis, linking risks to the impacts, probabilistic branching, and other key steps. Again, there are other programs, and they may offer more features for the expert, but their use is less common.

@RISK® FOR MS PROJECT®	PALISADE CORPORATION, WWW.PALISADE.COM
@RISK for Excel offers functionality to integrate its use with MS Project, which is a CPM scheduling program often applied on smaller or non-process industry projects. Excel becomes a front-end for the Microsoft Project schedule (i.e., the risk register is implemented in Excel.)	
PRIMAVERA RISK ANALYSIS®	ORACLE CORPORATION, WWW.ORACLE.COM
PRA (formerly PertMaster) provides direct integration with Primavera P6 CPM scheduling software, which is commonly applied on large process industry projects. PRA integrates in a risk register for risk management and linkage to the MCS simulation.	

Table 8.5: CPM Model MCS Add-ons (for the CPM-based method)

The Making of an Empiricist

Competency models are great guides for skills and knowledge development. But we usually do not get to pick when, where, or how we gain our experiences; career paths are not straight lines.

My path to empirical modeling started on February 16, 1984. That night the Pennsylvania Mines Corporation's Greenwich Collieries No. 1 Mine in Indiana County, Pennsylvania had a methane gas explosion. Three men were killed and ten others were injured. As the company's ventilation engineer, I was woken up. When I got to the site, a rescue crew had entered the mine to search for the three missing men in an area now without proper ventilation. The crew found methane buildups in explosive concentrations. Does the rescue command tell the crew to continue the search? Or, back off and reestablish ventilation first? And if so, how? I had recently begun running ventilation simulations on the company's first IBM PC; the recovery team hoped I had some answers. I didn't. The disaster was outside anything in my six years of experience and I had no PC or mental model for this chaos. The moment crystallized for me the difference between the abstract and the real. *Models are nice, but risks are real and experience is vital.*

I would go on to build many other models: estimating the cost of high level nuclear waste disposal for the DOE, the cost of film making machines for Kodak, the cost of major oil pipelines in North America, and others including project cost and schedule risk analysis. From the start of this crooked career path into modeling I was presented with a philosophical tug-of-war that one source describes as, "The dispute between rationalism and empiricism concerns the extent to which we are dependent upon sense experience in our effort to gain knowledge. Rationalists claim that there are significant ways in which our concepts and knowledge are gained independently of sense experience. Empiricists claim that sense experience is the ultimate source of all our concepts and knowledge."[1]

I learned that it takes a rationalist to build a model, but that cannot be all. It takes an empiricist to make a model or method that works.

---

1   Markie, Peter, "Rationalism versus Empiricism," Stanford Encyclopedia of Philosophy, 2013.

Organization Models

A risk quantification team must be designed to align with the business organization and project team organizations. Some examples include:

♦ At an EPC or other contracting or supplier company, the risk quantification effort may primarily support developing bid proposals, with primary input from and analysis by the cost estimating function.

♦ An owner company (one that owns and operates the assets created by projects) may apply risk quantification primarily to support analyzing investment alternatives by its business development department (engineering specialists who prepare conceptual cost estimates as well as risk analyses).

♦ In another company, the risk management function may have a staff that does risk quantification as a service for the Project Control function as needed; this may be embedded in a Project Management Office (PMO).

♦ Or, the methods may be dispersed to business units for their teams to apply in various ways depending on their business needs.

There is no right or wrong organizational model. However, the capital project risk quantification capability should reside in a core group to assure consistency and impartiality, to support ongoing improvement and empirical calibration, and to enhance competency development.

Many companies will also have an overarching Enterprise Risk Management (ERM) strategy and process that includes some level of integration of risk management processes within the various business and functional units of the company. The ERM function will likely have an organizational structure showing reporting and communication lines among risk management resources throughout the company. Some of the more important lines of communication with respect to CAPEX or Project Management risk quantification are with risk peers in business planning, finance, supply chain, and operations and maintenance (especially for planning shutdowns and turnarounds). Linkage is important to assuring consistent contributions of uncertainty risk information to investment NPV analysis considering common strategy. These groups may also be able to share competencies, resources and learnings, and career development planning.

Examples of Successful Approaches

The following summarizes two reference articles: one by an EPC contractor and one by an owner company. These articles describe applications of some of the methods aligned with those covered in this text. They provide some indication of the possibilities with the methods. I have worked with other companies in oil and gas, mining, power, and project financing to help implement these methods in their workplace and the experience has demonstrated the method's general applicability in the process industries.

An EPC Contractor

This first reference is from a risk conference presentation by a leading global engineering, procurement, and construction (EPC) and consulting company primarily in the infrastructure arena.[2] The company's cost and schedule risk quantification is largely in support of bid proposal estimating. The conference's abstract for the presentation described the company's situation in respect to risk quantification as follows:

> "Until 2009, Black & Veatch struggled with anticipating and reacting to potential risks and market influences, which tended to behave cyclically. As events such as weather, labor shortages, supplier interruptions and the like occurred, company management tended to increase contingency risk funding into project proposals. Over succeeding years, business was lost due to this increase and, as a result, the reserves were reduced to a point that losses increased from the impact of risk events and the cycle began again."[3]

The company sought to improve its methods and tools; the presentation summarized the improvement effort's statement and goal as follows:

♦ "Opportunity: Recent evaluations of active Engineering Procurement and Construction projects indicated the process for determining contingency rates significantly under-predicted the actual contingency risk."

♦ "Goal: Develop a more objective and quantitative approach for estimating contingency."

The method implemented, as illustrated in Figure 8.1 from the presentation, was a hybrid of parametric modeling of systemic risks and expected value modeling with MCS of project-specific risks. The presentation outlined the value proposition of the model as follows:

---

2   Hervert, Lyle, "Contingency Risk Estimating Model," Palisade @Risk Conference, Nov 16, 2011.

3   Palisade.com, "Black & Veatch Uses @RISK to Model Project Contingencies," http://www.palisade.com/news/2012/01_news.asp, 2012.

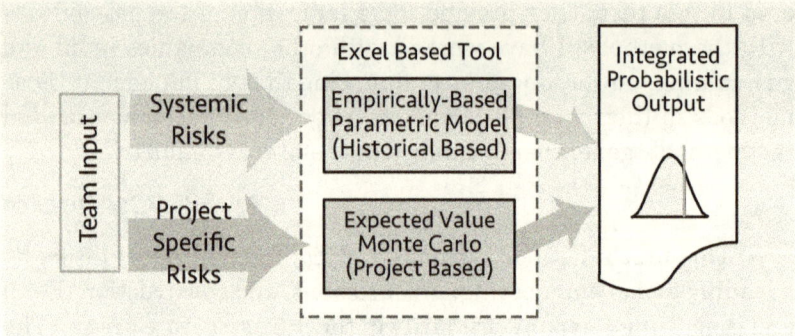

Figure 8.1: The Black & Veatch Contingency Risk Estimating Model (used with permission)

♦ "Reduces risk of significant variances and more predictable results"
♦ "Provides method for assessing status of current projects"
♦ "Helps team focus on risk items rather than risk percentage"
♦ "Provides a documented methodology and philosophy for contingency."

The conference abstract for the presentation summarized the improvement effort results as follows:

> "The increased accuracy and precision of the risk estimate has benefitted the company by improving the competitiveness of proposals while simultaneously protecting profits by appropriate reaction to identified risks. All major construction projects are now assessed using this model with senior executive review."

An Owner Company

This reference is from an AACE International transactions paper.[4] It described:

> "...the journey of a large North American pipeline company in improving internal cost estimating expertise and the development of a toolset and the processes to support cost estimating."

For this owner company, the risk quantification methods were largely in support of capital project investment decision making. The paper's abstract describes the company's objectives for improving its capabilities including risk quantification as follows:

---

4   Kitson, Brent, "Developing and Calibrating a Cost Estimating Toolset: An Owner's Experience," AACE International Transactions, 2011.

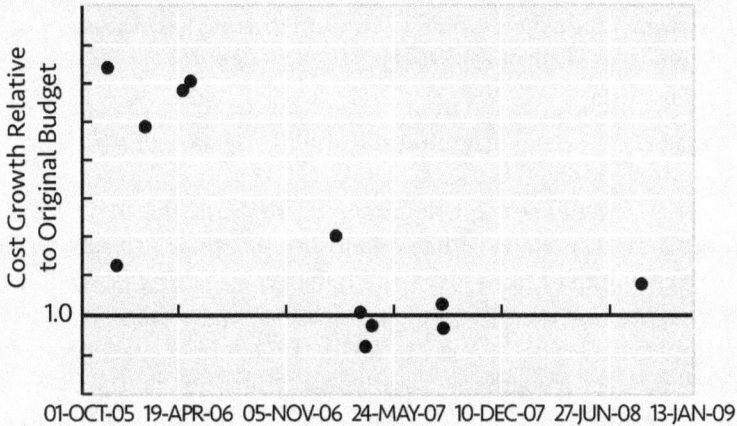

Figure 8.2: Owner Company Cost Growth Improvement
(used with permission, ©2011 by AACE International)[5]

"The ability to effectively complete a comprehensive screening of alternatives will support the identification of the optimized solution. It is
critical to assess the risk profile of a potential business opportunity. A
comprehensive cost estimating toolset will enable estimation of costs
complete with an assessment of the uncertainty and risk profile of the
estimate."

The paper describes the contingency risk quantification model (which
is consistent with the methods covered in this text) as follows:

"The [contingency] model is comprised of two models, which are integrated to provide a probabilistic cost outcome. The methodology is
based on categorizing risks as systemic or project-specific... Integrating
the systemic and project-specific models and completing a Monte Carlo
simulation produces a probability cost distribution."

The paper also describes an escalation model to cover market risk.
It also describes what they called a "historical project knowledge
management system" (PKMS). Their data analysis capability allows
them to better track performance as well as to provide means to
calibrate their systems. The paper summarized the improvement
effort results as follows:

"The results of the improved cost estimating processes have been significant. The ability to estimate accurately enables optimization of the
project screening process. Confidence in the estimating process enables
more efficient screening of potential project alternatives. The cost es-

---

5   Reprinted with the permission of AACE International, http://www.aacei.
     org, ©2011 by AACE International; all rights reserved.

timating process includes an evaluation of project risk and mitigation strategies. The project execution team effectiveness has increased due to the better planning achieved in the estimating process."

Figure 8.2 highlights the improvement in cost growth as measured by the ratio of actual/original estimate at the date of sanction.

This concludes the Chapter and Part 1 of the text. To summarize, Part 1 introduced basic concepts of capital project systems, scope development, and investment decision making as well as the risk analysis and quantification needed to support them. It reviewed the empirical research on cost growth, schedule slip, and accuracy, and what risks drive them. Finally, it outlined the methods for risk quantification and the organizational capabilities needed to put them into effect.

In Part 2, the details of practical, realistic risk quantification methods and models are addressed, including:

- ♦ "How-tos" for the practitioner,
- ♦ Considerations for non-process industries and contractors,
- ♦ Explanations concerning why the methods and models are needed,
- ♦ Ways to communicate risk findings, and
- ♦ Closing the loop on capturing learnings from projects and using the information to improve the process, methods, and capabilities going forward.

Questions

1) For the Parametric and Expected Value risk quantification methods, list at least two key in-house competencies (skills and knowledge areas) required for each.

2) To perform risk quantification in-house (assume they already do qualitative risk management), what minimum staff resources would be needed for a company with a limited range of asset types and small portfolio? What would you add in companies with a larger capital portfolio?

3) What organizational feature would be likely to promote staff consistency and impartiality and enhance competency development in risk quantification?

4) What are some suggested roles that external resources can play in a company's RQ practice?

"Facts are stubborn, but statistics are more pliable.."
— Attributed to Mark Twain

9

Base Cost Estimating and Scheduling

A main focus of the book so far has been on the empirical nature of project cost and schedule risk – its uncertainty (sometimes expressed as accuracy). So, is there anything *certain* in cost estimating and scheduling, i.e., pure facts?

Actually, there is very little that is certain. The cost and schedule duration that we choose (based on some capital decision analysis or project control strategy) are good starting points, i.e., a *base*. Risk quantification is therefore relative to this base, which itself is uncertain. Surprisingly perhaps, the base is a slippery thing, but in this chapter we will try to get a grasp on it before we move onto risk quantification methods *per se*.

A definition of *base estimates* and *schedules* is a good place to start this Chapter, but I had trouble finding a definition in the literature that aligned with this book's approach:

♦ Some sources define the base as an estimate or schedule *excluding risk*, but that is not true; there is always some uncertainty in base estimates and schedules.

♦ Others define the base as an estimate or schedule of what is *known*. That is also not true because some scope is assumed, particularly at early phases.

♦ Others define the base as that which is *realistic*; however, that is a loaded term that depends on biased judgments.

The base is really the cost and schedule that we *choose* as our starting point before quantifying risks, and that choice implies having a *base strategy*. Here is the definition of base estimate that will apply for the rest of the book:

> A *base estimate* is an estimate that excludes escalation, foreign currency exchange, contingency, and management reserves and is prepared in accordance with a documented base cost and duration strategy.

We will discuss base strategy later in this chapter.

While definitions of *base* in literature may be ambiguous, the work processes, practices, tools, and data to perform base estimating and scheduling are well documented. There are many good books covering scope quantification (e.g., material take-off), costing and pricing for cost estimating, and activity and logic planning and duration estimating for scheduling considering resources. Two good starting points are the AACE International *Total Cost Management Framework* and *Skills and Knowledge of Cost Engineering*. In the interest of completeness, this chapter will summarize the base method fundamentals before discussing risk quantification methods. What you should take away from this chapter is an understanding of:

♦ What the base cost estimating and scheduling methods are (generally speaking), and

♦ What is uncertain within these base methods that we must carry into risk quantification.

As to the second point, the base estimating and scheduling attributes (which we will quantify as systemic risk drivers) that I will discuss in this chapter include:

- Bias in estimating and scheduling,
- The level of scope definition captured by the base,
- Quality of estimating and scheduling practices,
- Quality of reference data used, and
- Allowances for risk (and exclusions from) within base estimates and schedules.

So, if the base is not certain, how uncertain is it? When I started out in cost estimating many years ago, I heard any number of experienced cost estimators say things such as, "My estimates are always within +/-3% accuracy." I also read estimating software advertisements with similar claims. On the other hand, it seemed that every project I read about came in late and was overrunning its budget by 10, 20, 30% or even much more. It was not until years later that I learned that the estimators and software vendors were not lying about their talents. They were simply failing to mention that they disclaim any and all responsibility for quantifying risk other than what they themselves controlled in their work.

This was touched on with respect to accuracy in Chapter 4. I call these inside risks. In other words, such stellar accuracy was presumably measured by comparing their base estimates to the final actual cost or duration after deducting the impacts of scope or design change or evolution, risk events, unexpected conditions, poor execution and so on – in short, all the things that really make a difference in the initial selection and ultimate success of a capital investment. Estimators and schedulers can be forgiven for their pride in the quality of their work; however, accuracy is not a measure of quality but of risk. A good estimator and scheduler will understand this and not try to hide from it.

I am frequently asked, "How would you describe a good estimator?" My answer is, "A good estimator is one who knows how wrong their estimate is." What I mean by that is, given that estimates and schedule duration are by definition *uncertain* forecasts, the end product of a good estimator's or scheduler's work must define ALL the uncertainty of that forecast, i.e., distributions of possible costs and duration. No risk should be disclaimed or disavowed because the real value of the product lies in understanding all its risks. Similarly, a risk analyst who is not cognizant of base estimating and scheduling practice (which requires knowledge of project execution practices) is not going to be highly effective either. In short, brush up on your knowledge of base estimating and scheduling practices if you are not familiar with them already.

So, to answer the original question of how uncertain the base is (without considering outside risks), the answer depends on our analysis of the base estimating and scheduling characteristics listed previously. The uncertainty resulting from the first two characteristics of bias (including allowances in the base for risk) and scope definition are dominant and can result in a very wide range-of-ranges for accuracy. The remaining uncertainties of the quality of the estimating and scheduling practices and data used are negligible if one employs defined base processes and procedures including reviews (i.e., the +/-3% quoted by the proud estimator). However, if your process and data are ad-hoc and/or the estimator and scheduler are unskilled, this does not apply.

The next section covers base cost estimating and scheduling method fundamentals – the starting point of risk quantification. This includes a discussion of the key uncertainties in base methods practice. Note that much of the general text on base estimating and scheduling that follows is derived from AACE International's Total Cost Management Framework, 1st edition (Sections 7.2 and 7.3) of which I was editor.[1]

Base Cost Estimating

Base Estimating Methods

Per the AACE International *Total Cost Management Framework* (Section 7.3), cost estimating, which includes risk quantification, is a predictive process used to quantify, cost, and price the resources required by the scope of a project. At its core, cost estimating involves the application of techniques that convert quantified technical and programmatic information about a project into financial and resource information (e.g., cost and hours).

The scope of a project is defined in various planning and technical deliverables. To start the estimating process, information in the source deliverables is quantified in a way that supports the applicable estimating algorithms being used. For example, a construction estimating algorithm may require pipe quantity in linear meters measured through the pipe centerline as a key input. The output of quantification is referred to as a "take-off" or "material take-off"

---

1   Hollmann, J. ed., *Total Cost Management Framework*, First Edition; excerpts with permission of AACE International, 1265 Suncrest Towne Centre Dr., Morgantown, WV 26505; http://www.aacei.org, Copyright © 2006 by AACE International; all rights reserved.

when the quantities are derived or developed from a drawing or, as most common today, a 3D model of the asset.

Next is the costing step to translate quantified scope information into cost, hours, or other resource information. The translation is done with a mathematical algorithm that is often referred to as *cost estimating relationship* (CER). In its simplest form, a CER will appear as:

Cost Resource = Factor x Parameter, where:

- ♦ Cost Resource = money (labor, material, etc.) or time (hours, etc.),
- ♦ Factor = a unit cost factor in terms of cost resource/parameter unit, and
- ♦ Parameter = quantification of a scope item.

In some CERs, the algorithm relationships are highly uncertain in nature, such as with parametric models (not unlike our systemic risk models). These models tend to aggregate a broad chunk of scope and cost into relatively simple algorithms. For example, a parametric model may estimate the total cost of a process plant as follows:

Total Process Plant Cost = (Gross Production Capacity) x (Capital Cost per Unit of Capacity)

Given the wide scope variation within a plant of a given type, an output of a CER such as this will be highly uncertain. However, it does *not* follow that all parametric models are highly uncertain. For example, if the scope of a certain plant type rarely varies (i.e., a clone), then the model could be reasonably reliable. Models can also be complex algorithms (usually a computer program) designed to replicate the performance of a process or system. Complex cost models are particularly well suited for simulation and optimization uses.

Other CERs tend to be more certain in nature and are often called definitive, detail unit cost, or line-item CERs. These CER types tend to disaggregate scope and cost into more clearly defined pieces. These pieces often but not necessarily align with scheduled activities. For example, a detailed CER may estimate the cost of one item as follows:

Valve type A installation hours = (Number of valves of type A) x (Hours per valve of type A)

An overall detailed estimate will then re-aggregate the results of a large number of these types of CERs, and taken together, these types

Pump and Dump

Part of my business is to review process industry project cost estimates for owners at the FEL3/Define gate ("Feasibility" in the mining industry). For large projects, the major EPC contractors doing the Front End Engineering and Design (FEED) prepare these estimates (other than owner's costs). EPC contractors have estimating departments and established methods, tools, and data. They are proud of their work and rightfully so. Preparing a Class 3 estimate is a major undertaking, integrating the work of all the disciplines, with much of the work coming together shortly before the owner's gate review. I am often asked of my general impression of the base estimate quality. My answer has two parts.

First, usually the EPC base estimate totals are suitable as a basis for investment decision making, albeit exhibiting bias and overly generous application of allowances (to be considered in my later risk quantification). Second, I usually find that the base estimate details are not suitable as a high quality basis for control. This is a systemic risk (also to be considered in risk quantification). The cause is as follows:

All major projects are now designed using 3D CAD modeling. However, at the end of FEED, the models are not complete. So cost estimate quantity take-off is a mix of automated and manual methods; this leads to duplication and missing items. The bigger problem is with the 3D model "dumps" of material quantities data. These quantities are then "pumped" into a cost estimating tool where the quantities are multiplied by unit hours and unit material costs. The volume of take-off data on a megaproject is massive, and sometimes, with time and resources being short, the design discipline's review of the quantities is poorly done.

Also problematic is semi-automatic application of the unit hours and material costs to the quantities. Every item of type *X* gets the same unit hours – it is rather mindless. The item (e.g., steel) could be installed on the top of a tower, on the ground, in the open or in a confined space – the tool does not know or care. The best estimators adjust the item hours for specific conditions. Some do this later when construction begins. But again, resource and time constraints lead to shortcuts. I call this semi-automated estimating practice "pump and dump." The project detailed engineering begins with a poor basis for change control and performance measurement. This is a common feature of blowout projects.

of estimates are usually less uncertain than parametric estimates or cost models. However, it does not follow that all estimates based on definitive CERs are highly certain. There may still be significant uncertainties in scope definition, in quantification, in cost database quality, or in other areas. Keep in mind that the above examples are somewhat simplistic. CERs can be as complex and varied as mathematics allows and most estimates will use a mix of CER types for various items.

Base estimating algorithms are often adjusted by the application of factors to make the result match the current estimate situation and conditions. The conditions that may vary include labor rates, labor productivity, jobsite conditions, material mark-ups, location factors, taxes, and so on. Quantity measures used reflect preliminary models that may not precisely match actual technical or programmatic conditions. The quantity conditions that may vary from the measurement basis include waste and spoilage allowance, accuracy of measurement (take-off) allowance, and specification, function, or item content differences.

Cost estimate resource outputs are inputs to schedule development; therefore, estimating and scheduling are integrated processes. For example, if the schedule model is changed to shorten duration to meet a milestone goal, this may require the labor productivity assumptions of the estimate to be changed (and this may also increase project risk).

Estimating is facilitated by software and databases. Software may be as simple as a spreadsheet or may be complex specialized line-item or parametric modeling systems, sometimes integrated with the scheduling software. Estimating is very much a data-driven process and requires reference data in the form of standard unit cost and hours, prices, factors, parameters, and other inputs to estimating algorithms.

At completion, a quality review process is applied to ensure that the estimate was done in accordance with the defined strategy and requirements. Prior to the review, a supporting *Basis of Estimate* (BoE) document describes how the estimate was developed and defines the information used. This includes the scope covered, methodologies used, references and defining deliverables used, assumptions and exclusions, adjustments, and, after risk quantification is done, an indication of the level of uncertainty.

In addition to quality reviews, the estimate should be benchmarked or validated against or compared to historical experience and/or past estimates to check its appropriateness and competitiveness, and to identify improvement opportunities. Independent validation examines the estimate from a different perspective and using different metrics than are used in estimate preparation. The review and/or validation may result in all or part of the estimate being recycled through any of the preceding steps.

Base Estimate Content: Capital Costs

When cost growth metrics are described in this book, the base estimate and actual costs are assumed to include capital cost from the perspective of the owner. This book assumes that capital costs exclude the cost of early definition up to the point where a single alternative project is decided upon (excludes costs prior to the FEL 2/Select gate and Class 4 estimate). It includes all costs after that up to the point that the asset is in stable operation (start-up); there is no meaningful revenue up to this point. However, capital cost excludes start-up costs during the time it takes to get the quality of the product up to specification and the capacity up to the nameplate production (if it is ever achieved); there may be revenue during this late effort.

Different companies have different capitalization rules. For example, some companies expense more front-end and start-up costs than others; this is a source of uncertainty in industry cost growth measures. The final arbiter as to what is CAPEX is often the local tax authority. Because of this accounting uncertainty, benchmarking (and parametric risk analysis) of front-end and start-up costs is problematic.

Base Planning and Scheduling

Base Planning and Scheduling Methods

Per the AACE International *Total Cost Management Framework* (Section 7.2),[2] schedule planning and development are the processes for planning work over time in consideration of the costs and resources required to complete that work. Schedule *planning* and schedule *development* are separate, but related, sub-processes that call for different skills and knowledge emphasis.

Schedule *planning* starts with translating work scope into manageable activities and determining the manner and sequence (i.e., logic) in which these activities are best performed. The means, methods, and resources used for accomplishing the activities are then identified. Schedule planning concludes with estimating the time duration of the sequenced activities based on adequate resources being available and planned means and methods.

The duration of planned activities is estimated to calculate start and finish dates based on the defined scope of work, estimates of required resources and their availability, and the expected

---

2   Ibid (Hollmann).

First Come, First Serve (EPc or Cep?)

In reviewing project schedule quality, one attribute stands out as contributing to significant cost overruns and schedule slips and that is the lack of schedule integration. In an integrated schedule, all of the owner and contractor engineering, procurement, fabrication, construction, and startup and commissioning phases and activities are included in a balanced way.

An IPA, Inc. study published in 2006 found that, *"Only 33 percent of the projects in the study sample had an integrated project schedule at the time of authorization. The phase that was most frequently missing was the final phase, commissioning and startup."*[1] For a process plant, it is critical that schedule logic is considered "back-to-front" because the completion milestone is so critical. Start with when the owner wants each unit and system to be started up, and plan backwards from there.

Similarly, engineering and procurement should be planned to facilitate efficient fabrication and construction. Ask when construction needs designs and materials to be ready, and then plan backwards from there. This sounds like common sense, but as the IPA study indicates, these practices are the exception. More often you find that engineering and procurement drive the schedule logic based on what is most efficient for them. Further, being first to the plate, engineers will plan in great detail while construction and start-up, being poorly represented on the initial team, will get summary level activities at best. For example, you might find 1,000 detailed engineering and procurement activities, 100 summary level construction activities and 10 activities for start-up (if it is included at all). (Note: if you use CPM based risk analysis, it is *not* OK to ignore this problem by creating a new summary CPM so you can run the risk. You are ignoring the risk that really matters, which is that the project does not have a good plan! This needs to be corrected.)

One company calls this unbalanced approach "EPc," where the small "c" represents the level of attention that construction receives in planning by engineering-dominated EPC firms. They were so frustrated by this dynamic that they tried a strategy they called Cep with a small "ep." They bid the work to major construction contractors who would then find engineering and procurement partners to work with them. How well that works is an open question.

However, the lesson learned is that when reviewing the quality of a base schedule, look for integration and balance. If integration and balance are missing, it is a significant systemic risk and contributor to the tipping point. This practice was a main cause in the "Anatomy of a Blowout" case in Chapter 14.

---

1   Griffith, Andrew, "Scheduling Practices and Project Success", Cost Engineering Journal, AACE International, Morgantown WV, 2006.

performance (or consumption) rate of those resources. Historical experience can assist in determining if the duration is reasonable or analogous. If the duration estimate of the plan does not achieve milestone objectives, the planned activity's means and methods and/ or preferential logic may be revised as needed (e.g., by adjusting the schedule). An output of this step is a schedule model to be used for schedule development. Schedule planning puts an emphasis on the practitioner's knowledge of the work, means and methods, and skills with tapping the knowledge and experience of those responsible for performance of that work. Shortage of these skills is a common systemic risk.

Starting with the initial schedule model, schedule *development* allocates the available resources (e.g., labor, material, equipment) to activities in the model in accordance with cost and resource planning and alternative allocation criteria (while respecting project strategy and constraints). That allocation is called "resource loading," which is a necessary precursor to integrated cost and schedule risk analysis using the CPM method. Schedule development is interactive with cost estimating (which quantifies resources) and generally includes iteratively refining the schedule planning and cost estimate in a way that achieves project objectives in consideration of risks.

For example, the schedule may have an activity "Install vessel A foundation" and the estimator says the labor required for this 10 m^3 foundation is 320 hours. That is 32 man-days for a work schedule with 10 hour shifts. If concrete crews have eight workers, then theoretically they could install it in four days (i.e., 4 x 8 = 32). If the initial plan allowed three days, we would have to make adjustments. This is overly simplistic but gives the idea. A related practice called "resource leveling" would have us adjusting the scheduled concrete activities so that there was always just enough work planned to keep that eight person crew busy (assuming a small job with one crew). A schedule that had concrete manpower levels jumping from two people to twelve every other day would not work. Development also includes the incorporation of schedule contingency and refinements in that respect. It should be clear from these examples that doing this well is a challenge. The primary outcome of the process is the schedule control baseline.

Planning and scheduling is facilitated by specialized software and databases. Usually the software employs the critical path method (CPM) of schedule modeling. CPM employs a logic scheme where each activity has a start and finish, a duration, and a sequence logic tie to other activities (e.g., finish-to-start). The longest chain of activities from project start to completion is called the *critical path*.

An alternate scheduling approach is the *critical chain* method, which seeks to optimize the use of limited resources. The critical chain is the longest sequence of resource-leveled activities from the beginning to end of the project. Critical chain also removes slack duration from each activity in the chain and aggregates this time in buffers at the end of the chain. During execution the consumption of these buffers is monitored.

The CPM systems may be integrated with cost estimating systems to share resource information. Scheduling is a logic-driven process and hence uses less in the way of reference databases than estimating. Scheduling requires more interaction with the team, judgment, and subjective input to define activities, logic, and durations. However, schedule data may be contained in a historical database system and analogous past schedules are often a good starting point or reference.

Schedule models are representations based upon initial assumptions and interpretations of scope and plans. Stakeholders are prone to misunderstanding what a schedule represents, so a *Basis of Schedule* (BoS; similar to a BoE) document must be developed and communicated to the project team. Schedule quality reviews seek to assure that the schedule is in accordance with the defined strategy and requirements. Finally, the schedule should be benchmarked and independently validated against or compared to internal and external schedule metrics to assess its appropriateness, its competitiveness in terms of duration, and to identify improvement opportunities.

Base Schedule Duration Estimate Content: Execution

When schedule slip metrics are described in this book, the base duration estimate and actual duration are assumed to include the execution phase from the perspective of the owner. The definition of these phases is fairly consistent in industry, extending from the sanction or financial investment decision (FID) milestone to the mechanical completion milestone when the asset is turned over from construction to operations management. Note that this definition excludes the FEED or Basic Engineering phase and the start-up phases in their entireties. As with cost, the practices can be unclear in what projects count as the beginning and end milestones. At the start, many companies sanction too early, based on poor definition (often chasing revenue) that is closer to FEL2/Select /Class 4 than the desired FEL 3/Define/Class 3 level. Also, at the end of large project execution there is often overlap between construction and start-up phases; some units of a plant may become operational before others.

It is difficult to separate the causes of uncertainty in the front-end and start-up phase durations because there is significant measurement noise. Again, the final arbiter is sometimes the local tax authority as to when a company can start capitalizing its assets. This is an accounting bias. As with costs, research of non-execution phase durations tends to identify only dominant risk drivers such as start-up durations correlation with the level of definition and new technology.

Sources and Measurements of Uncertainty or Variability in the Base Methods

Bias and Strategy

When I am asked to review a cost estimate or schedule, or to conduct a risk analysis associated with the estimate, I always ask the team, "What costing or scheduling strategy does this estimate or schedule represent?" The usual answer is something along the lines of, "What do you mean? It's our estimate of what it will take to do the work." Or, "It represents the way we do things around here." Or, "I use costs (or durations) that I think are realistic." As discussed in Chapter 6, teams rarely can clearly articulate what strategy the base estimate and schedule represent in a way that is useful for starting risk quantification (which may relate to lack of a good industry definition of *base*).

For risk quantification, you need to know how aggressive or conservative (i.e., biased) the base is. This is because risk quantification (e.g., contingency) is relative to the base and is influenced by it. In Figure 9.1, the curve represents the distribution of possible costs for a project derived through risk analysis and the $p50$ confidence level line represents the value at which the company will fund the project based on their risk policy. The amount of contingency then is the difference between the $p50$ level and the base estimate. An aggressive base (the heavy line on the left) will require more contingency than a conservative base (the heavy line on the right.)

A base schedule strategy may be noted when the execution strategy is exceptional (e.g., fast-track), but otherwise both estimat-

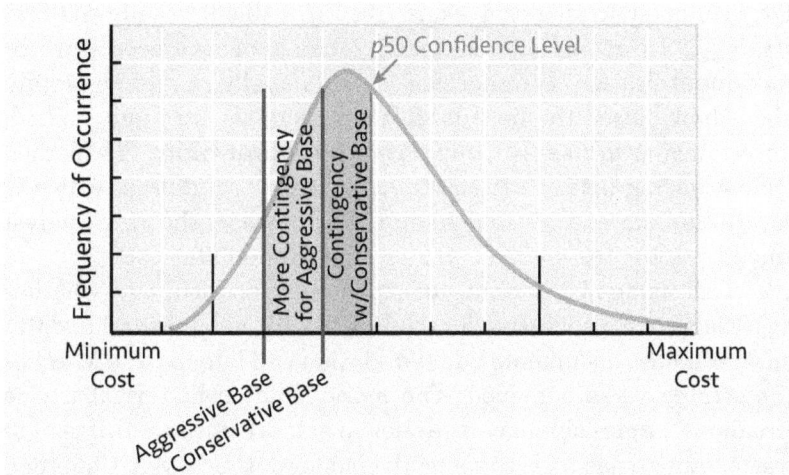

Figure 9.1: How Base Estimate Bias Relates to Contingency Determination

ing and scheduling approaches tend to be silent as to bias. Everyone
needs to be aware that there is no standard for base estimate or
schedule bias. As mentioned in Chapter 6, rather than leave the bias
as a question mark at the start for the estimator or scheduler to
decide, the estimate and schedule should start by explicitly defining
a cost and schedule strategy.

STRATEGY (Stated or Otherwise)	TYPICAL BASIS OF THE BASE (AND RISK IMPLICATION)
Targeted	An articulated strategy that the base represents a defined level of performance relative to past known performance, presumably based on analysis. The base may be aggressive or conservative relative to the known past as defined.
Historical Norms (or Analogy)	More or less the average performance of past projects of this type. Often referred to as "realistic" costs or durations. The base includes the impact of nominal risk events and mediocre performance of past projects; a conservative approach.
Ad-Hoc	Leave it up to the estimator or scheduler. Usually they will use a defacto Historical Norms approach, but you cannot be sure (little idea what the base represents; could be wildly aggressive or conservative).
Database Reference	Most reference databases (e.g., unit hours) represent a defined basis, which could be any of the three above. However, the source of many databases is unclear, inconsistent from category to category, and users apply "database markups" that render this the same as "Historical Norms" (may or may not know what the base represents, but less wildly inconsistent than Ad-Hoc).

Table 9.1: Common Base Estimating and Scheduling Strategies

Four common strategies are described in Table 9.1. Only the first strategy, "Targeted," can be clearly relied upon as a good start for risk quantification. In other words, you usually cannot be certain about how biased the base is. Regardless of the strategy applied, uncertainty as to bias is an initial risk driver to quantify. The method for measuring bias is estimate and schedule *validation*, which is covered at the end of this chapter. In any case, the risk analyst should ask the team which strategy description fits best.

I recommend describing an explicit targeted strategy (whether aggressive or conservative) in the BoE/BoS documents and in database reference documentation. Validation will later assess whether the strategy was achieved. The more common historical norms ("realistic") approach may be easier to achieve but can also lead to waste; human nature is to spend the money or time given. Chapter 6 provided the following good example of a cost strategy statement:

> "The base cost and duration estimate values will reflect aggressive but reasonably achievable current pricing and performance. 'Aggressive but reasonably achievable' means that the assumed performance will reflect the first quartile level (i.e., p25) of historical performance or equivalent for similar strategies and scope excluding the impact of identifiable changes and risks."

Similar strategy approaches apply for base schedule duration estimates. AACE has an RP 32R-04 that addresses "Determining Activity Durations." This and most other literature on schedule practice (at least for CPM) recommends that schedule *base* durations be set at p50 or equivalent. This is a historical norms approach. It is often referred to as analogy estimating, which may be purely subjective or more or less based on historical data. Some schedulers use the 3-point PERT (program evaluation and review technique) approach that helps provide some clarity, but is still subjective. With PERT the estimated duration is:

> PERT Duration = (Optimistic Duration + 4 x Most Likely Duration + Pessimistic Duration)/6

Note that the above schedule duration estimating approach is *inherently conservative*. The most likely or p50, being the norm of past experience, is already assuming less than ideal performance. This has come about in part because the explicit treatment and allowance for risk in scheduling is less "settled science" than for cost; risk allowances tend to be hidden in the activities. Increasingly, lean planning and scheduling approaches are being considered, such as critical chain, which is a targeted approach. In critical chain, one consciously removes any hidden slack from activity duration estimates and aggregates it in visible buffers at the end of a chain of activities.

Note that there are no standards for what base cost or duration estimates should represent in terms of bias or competitiveness. Some mistakenly refer to AACE International's RPs for "Estimate or Schedule Classification." This is inappropriate because the RPs only define what level of scope definition the estimate or schedule is based upon and say nothing about bias. Finally, as was discussed previously, there is accounting bias in cost and schedule duration estimates. The rules that the planners live by vary with respect to what is capitalized and when capitalization starts and ends. The rules are largely consistent within a given company and region only; accounting bias must be considered when comparing one's outcomes with industry metrics.

The Level of Scope Definition

As previously described, the cost estimating process at its core includes the main steps of quantifying the scope (take-off) and costing. For scheduling, the planning step must translate the work scope into activities and logic before activity duration is estimated. So the first uncertainty in the processes is that of the scope. There are two main elements of scope uncertainty:

♦ The level of scope definition (what is "known" about the scope), and

♦ The uncertainty or variability of our quantification and work and of the activity breakdown (how well did we quantify or capture that which is known about the scope).

The first item was discussed in Chapter 3 (and Part 1 in general). The level of scope definition is often the greatest source of uncertainty, which is why the industry evolved the now ubiquitous Phase gate scope development systems. The less we know about the scope, the more the base cost or duration tends to be underestimated. The estimator and scheduler have *no* real control about how well the scope is defined at any time. They must deal with the scope as it is provided to them in technical and planning deliverables. All they can control is how well they translate that scope into quantities, activities, cost, and time.

As previously discussed, the practices of Estimate and Schedule Classification as documented in AACE International RPs provide a means of objectively rating the level of scope definition. We can use these ratings in parametric quantification of systemic risk (which will be discussed later). Once the level of scope definition is understood, uncertainty as to planning quality remains.

For example:

♦ Are there uncertainties as to whether the quantity take-off method is reliable?

♦ Was the quantification model a good fit for the asset type?

These estimating and scheduling process quality questions are covered in the next section.

Quality of Estimating Practices and Data

General Methods Variability

After bias and level of scope definition, the first base estimate uncertainty that the estimator can control is in the quality of the methods applied, the requirements for which must be defined upfront. If there are no requirements defined (i.e., ad-hoc estimating or scheduling approaches), quality will be poor and uncertainty or variability is likely to be significant.

Often, the main (if not the only) methodological requirement stated in procedures and contracts is that cost estimate preparation be done in accordance with AACE Classification RPs (i.e., "… the estimate shall be AACE Class 3 per RP 18R-97"). This means little because these RPs provide little in the way of preparation guidelines.

For example, Table 9.2 from AACE's RP 47R-11 for Mining Estimate Classification states, "Class 3 estimates are generally based on detail take-offs and estimates for significant cost items." Such general statements do not relieve the owner of the need to define their own *specific* estimating practice requirements in procedures and contracts, starting with establishing the cost and schedule strategy.

Specific Methods, Cost Data, and Pricing Variability

Some specific sources of methodological uncertainty or variability are described in Table 9.3 (it is not all inclusive). These should be assessed in estimate reviews and quantified as allowances provided for within the base estimate, or as systemic risks in contingency.

CLASS 3 ESTIMATE	
Description: A Class 3 estimate is prepared using probable or proven ore reserves as defined within acceptable confidence limits as per the securities codes. A detailed mine plan is required (pre-stripping may begin upon project approval). Metallurgical test work is sufficient to expand the detail in equipment lists and specifications. Engineering is expected to provide general arrangement drawings (GAs), preliminary piping and instrument diagrams (P&ID's) and single line electrical drawings. Also, plot plans and layout drawings are better defined. **Degree of Project Definition Deliverables Required:** Key Deliverable and Target Status: Piping and Instrumentation Diagrams (P&IDs) issued for design for plant and detailed Mine Plan for the mine. 10% to 40% of full project definition. **End Usage:** Class 3 estimates are typically prepared to support full project funding requests for internal and/or external investment. By default, the Class 3 estimate is the initial baseline for project and change control until superseded by the updated project control estimate (Class 2).	**Estimating Methods Used:** Class 3 estimates are generally based on detail take-offs and estimates for significant cost items for direct and indirect costs where detailing can be done (e.g., pipe fittings not detailed). Major equipment and contracts are priced based on supplier quotations. Construction (bulks, labour and equipment) are estimated based on local pricing and trade agreements covering the available quantity take-offs. Mass earthwork and infrastructure such as transport pipelines and power transmission lines are based on take-off from preliminary contours and routing. Less significant costs may be factored such as small bore pipe as a % of large bore. **Expected Accuracy Range:** Typical accuracy ranges for Class 3 estimates are -10% to -20% on the low side, and +10% to +30% on the high side, depending on the technological, geographical and geological complexity of the project, appropriate reference information, and other risks (after inclusion of an appropriate contingency determination). The uncertainty varies by work type with moderate ranges applying to structures and plant commodities, wider ranges applying to earthworks and infrastructure and narrower ranges applying to equipment installation.

Table 9.2: Example Estimate Characteristics list from AACE RP 47R-11 (Mining)

QUANTIFICATION OF SCOPE (TAKE-OFF) VARIABILITY	
Manual take-off (MTO)	• Errors may occur due to missing or double counting items, using the wrong drawing scale, incorrect recording of items, etc.
Automated take-off (CAD Models and Building Information Modeling (BIM))	• Models are often incomplete and require manual take-off for some items with the chance for missing items or double counting. • Can be very difficult to review massive data dumps.
Stochastic Estimating	• Parametric models may poorly represent the asset or miss scope.
COSTING AND PRICING VARIABILITY	
Data Availability	• No database or no analogous data are available.
Data Applicability	• Data is available but not well matched to the current scope. • Data is poorly documented so applicability is unsure.
Data Bias	• Data reflects a different cost strategy than the project's. • Data is out of date. • Prices from external sources are biased (particularly if sole sourced).
Factors and Markups	• Factors and markups used to adjust base cost data may not be available or applicable.
Automation	• "Pump & Dump:" Systems may multiply the quantity times generic unit costs or hours without considering the item's attributes.
Stochastic Estimating	• Parametric model may poorly represent the cost relationship.

Table 9.3: Typical Sources of Methodological Uncertainty or Variability

Allowances for Risk within Base Estimates

In Chapter 7, the concept of allowances was introduced. As a reminder, in cost estimating, allowances are quantities and costs included in base estimates to cover *specific* known but not clearly defined requirements. Unlike contingency for general uncertainty that you will address through risk quantification, allowances are more certain. We know we will need the item or similar item, but are just a bit uncertain about some element of its definition.

These should be used sparingly and only for specific items that one can name as opposed to general uncertainties. In project controls, one can progress an allowance item. We flag them in estimates as allowances and spell them out in the BoE document as reminders to update the cost as better information is obtained. However, allowances are often misused as "above-the-line" contingency. When management is resistant to the use of contingency, estimators tend to pad their estimates to cover the cost they know will be needed.

Equipment Items	Class 4	Class 3
	Equipment Design Allowance	
Field Fabricated Vessels	3-5%	2-3%
Shop Fabricated Vessels	4-8%	3-5%
Exchangers	3-6%	2-4%
Compressors	3-5%	2-3%
Heaters/Boilers	4-8%	3-5%
Pumps	5-8%	4-6%
Material Processing Equipment	5-8%	4-6%
Material Handling Equipment	3-6%	2-4%

Bulk Material Items	Class 4		Class 3	
	MTO	Overbuy	MTO	Overbuy
Concrete	4-6%	7-15%	3-5%	5-10%
Structural Steel	4-8%	4-10%	3-5%	3-5%
Architectural	3-8%	4-10%	2-5%	3-5%
Carbon Steel Piping (above ground)	5-10%	4-10%	4-5%	3-5%
Alloy Piping (above ground)	4-8%	4-8%	2-4%	2-4%
Screwed/Socketweld Piping	5-15%	5-15%	4-10%	4-10%
Underground Piping	5-10%	5-15%	4-6%	4-8%
Electrical	5-8%	5-10%	4-6%	4-6%
Instrumentation	3-6%	4-10%	2-4%	3-5%
Painting/Insulation	4-8%	4-10%	3-5%	3-5%

Table 9.4: Typical Cost Estimate Allowances

There are generally two types of allowances found in a base estimate. The first is for a specific item or activity (e.g., allowance for sump pump), which will be self-explanatory. The second is for uncertainties in specific base estimating quantification or costing practices. Table 9.4 lists some typical allowances for large process industry projects (note that Class 5 estimates usually do not have item breakouts). The allowances are:

- ◆ Equipment Design (for minor items often not in equipment quote),
- ◆ MTO (for variabilities in material take-off practice), and
- ◆ Overbuy (for damages, loss, theft, and so on)

The equipment design and material overbuy allowances are markups to cost. MTO allowances are markups to quantities. These are not separate items in the base estimate but are included in the items themselves.

Note that cost for labor due to assumed overtime strategy or weather conditions are always project-specific and should be spelled out in the execution strategy and included in backup labor rate buildups and productivity markups as appropriate. These are not allowances and there should be no separate overtime cost account. The impact of risks on labor productivity is one of the greatest uncertainties on most projects (i.e., blowouts often experience a doubling of labor hours or more).

Exclusions from the Base Estimate

The flip-side of allowances are *exclusions* from the base estimate.

> An *exclusion* is an item, activity, or cost that would normally be a part of the project scope, but management has instructed the team to exclude it from plans, estimates, and schedules.

Often it is excluded because a separate and/or later project is supposed to pay for the excluded scope. Sometimes the plan is to aggressively expense some costs that are typically capitalized. Other times it is the result of cost saving initiatives that may be more or less arbitrary.

The problem is that often these items and costs are truly needed: the separate project does not get approved, the tax authorities push back on accounting practices, or the "savings" scope gets added back into the capital scope as late changes. In the end, the more exclusions there are, the more uncertain the base estimate becomes. Other exclusions can include land, costs for the operation organization's participation in the project (and various other owner's costs), site and facility clean-up and remediation, and anything optional such as painting pipes and tanks (which the surrounding community stakeholders may view differently than the owner).

Quality of Scheduling Practices and Data

General Methods Variability

Because most claims and disputes (and legal involvement in the project) revolve around schedule delays, the methods used for scheduling tend to be better defined in procedures and contracts than the methods for estimating. In fact, there may be a schedule specification prepared for a contract. Despite this, there is tremendous variability in planning and scheduling practices in industry. As was mentioned in Chapter 7, an empirical study found that only 13% of large projects had high quality (from a simply mechanistic view, without even considering whether the logic made sense) CPM schedules.[3] Some sources of scheduling practice variability derived from AACE RP 57R-09 include:

♦ All work needed to complete the project must be represented in the schedule.

♦ There should be no open ends: each activity needs a predecessor to its start date and a successor from its finish date.

♦ The schedule should not rely on date constraints; these make the network into a calendar, not a schedule.

♦ Lags and leads (negative lags) are generally to be avoided.

♦ The schedule should be resource loaded as needed to assure it is consistent with resource plans and cost estimates.

Shortages of planners – planners who know how work is actually performed (the logic) and who are skilled in communicating with those responsible for the work – is a common systemic team development risk for projects.

Allowances for Risk within Base Schedules

The use of allowances and contingency for schedule is a much less settled area of practice than for cost estimating. Per AACE 10S-90 definitions:

> Schedule allowances are "... dummy activities and/or time included in existing activities in a schedule to cover the time for known, but undefined requirements."

---

3   Griffith, Andrew, "Scheduling Practices and Project Success," AACE International Transactions, 2005.

Dummy activities explicitly labeled as an allowance in CPM schedules are very rare. Almost always the other activities have hidden slack in them; i.e., the durations represent the scheduler's and/or team's estimate of what is "realistic" (be it a guess or the *p*50 as in PERT). It is an approach that invites less than ideal work performance. However, using dummy activities or buffers is a specific feature of Critical Chain scheduling, which, from a risk management perspective, makes it a better approach.

Exclusions from the Base Schedule

As with costs, there may be work activities excluded from the plan, and as with cost exclusions, these activities are often truly needed. They tend to get added back into the capital scope as late changes. In the end, the more exclusions there are, the more uncertain the schedule duration becomes.

Review and Validation: Assessing Quality and Bias

At the start of this chapter, I listed the attributes of the base estimate and schedule process and deliverables that drive uncertainty, irrespective of any attributes of the project scope, risk events, or conditions. I labeled these risks as "inside risks" because they are largely within the control of or can be readily assured by the estimating and scheduling functions. Measurement of these attributes, which are systemic risks, is the starting point of the risk quantification methods in this book. There are two assurance/measurement practices that are used to assess these inside risks: *quality reviews* and *validation*. The inside risks that they cover include:

1) Quality Review

- ♦ Quality of estimating and scheduling practices,
- ♦ Quality of reference data used,
- ♦ The level of scope definition captured by the base, and
- ♦ Allowances and exclusions.

2) Validation

- ♦ Bias in estimating and scheduling, and
- ♦ Allowances and exclusions (as contributors to bias).

Quality review practices are generally well covered in books on cost estimating and planning and scheduling. Also, because large projects are generally planned by experienced organizations with established methods, I have not found general quality (e.g., error, deviation from procedure) to be a major source of variability in the big picture. However, validation is less well covered in the literature, and less well done (if at all). Therefore, given the hidden, pervasive, and sometimes political nature of bias, validation is covered in some depth here.

Estimate and Schedule Quality Reviews

As introduced in Chapter 4, quality is defined as conformance to requirements. Therefore, the road to quality starts with establishing requirements that address the company and project needs and that tie back to company strategy. If these are defined, simply assure that the practices used and the deliverables produced meet these requirements.

Quality reviews are generally performed at multiple levels: first by the practitioners themselves and then, depending on the complexity, size, and importance of the estimate or schedule, by successive levels of stakeholders. The practitioners will usually focus on the mechanics such as the math, logic, diagnostics (e.g., CPM systems can check for constraints) and so on. Next, those who contributed information and source deliverables such as engineering, procurement, and construction will review their parts to assure that the estimate items and quantities, pricing, activities, and logic reflect their expectations. The project manager, along with team leads, will then review the products at a more summary level. Finally, senior managers will perform their overall reviews.

I recommend that reviews start with the BoE/BoS deliverables. If these documents are unavailable, poorly prepared, incomplete, or ambiguous, the quality of the end products is suspect. In this case, postpone full reviews until the BoE/BoS are complete. Key sections in the BoE/BoS are the description of allowances (additions) and exclusions (subtractions) from the base estimate or schedule. These should be carefully considered as to their appropriateness, with a particular eye out for bias: hiding of contingency above the line (add fat) and/or overly aggressive cost and duration savings initiatives (cutting too far).

Quality reviews should be planned and should follow an established procedure. To help ensure objectivity, a checklist of requirements and a measure of their attainment can support the review. For example, conformance with each requirement can be rated on a scale (see below) and an overall view can be obtained. These ratings, objective or otherwise, will be inputs to systemic risk quantification.

The example ratings are:

0 - Significant deficiency,
1 - Some deficiency,
2 - Minor deficiency, and
3 - Full conformance.

A key section of the BoE/BoS is a description of what deliverables the estimate or schedule was based upon and their status. A recommended approach, if it is not already a requirement of one's phase gate project system, is to rate the level of scope definition using one of the following indices (or equivalent; see Chapter 3). These ratings will also be inputs to systemic risk quantification:

♦ AACE Classification (e.g., Class 5, 4 or 3, with or without exceptions),

♦ IPA FEL (e.g., 1, 2 or 3, with or without exceptions), or

♦ CII PDRI (e.g., number from 200 to 1000).

The level of scope definition is an inside risk because it can be within the estimating and scheduling group's responsibility to assure the phase gate system requirements are achieved. Nobody knows better than these professionals what a good technical product looks like. If they do not think they have a good basis for cost or schedule, which in turn are the basis of decisions and control, then the scope definition needs to be revisited.

Estimate and Schedule Validation (Assess Bias)

Validation is a step in the estimate and schedule review processes whereby the end result is evaluated for its conformance with the business's cost and schedule strategy. If there is no explicit strategy, validation loses much of its value. Validation is by definition quantitative in nature. It checks for competitiveness and bias relative to company and industry historical experience and project and business expectations and targets. Validation is contingent upon having an appropriate reference database of historical metrics and comparison project records, and may involve the preparation of independent check estimates or schedules.

Figure 9.2 provides an example process map for validation. Each company will need to develop its own process that ties to their estimating and scheduling processes. At its heart the process involves the calculation of quantitative metrics and comparison of them to reference benchmarks.

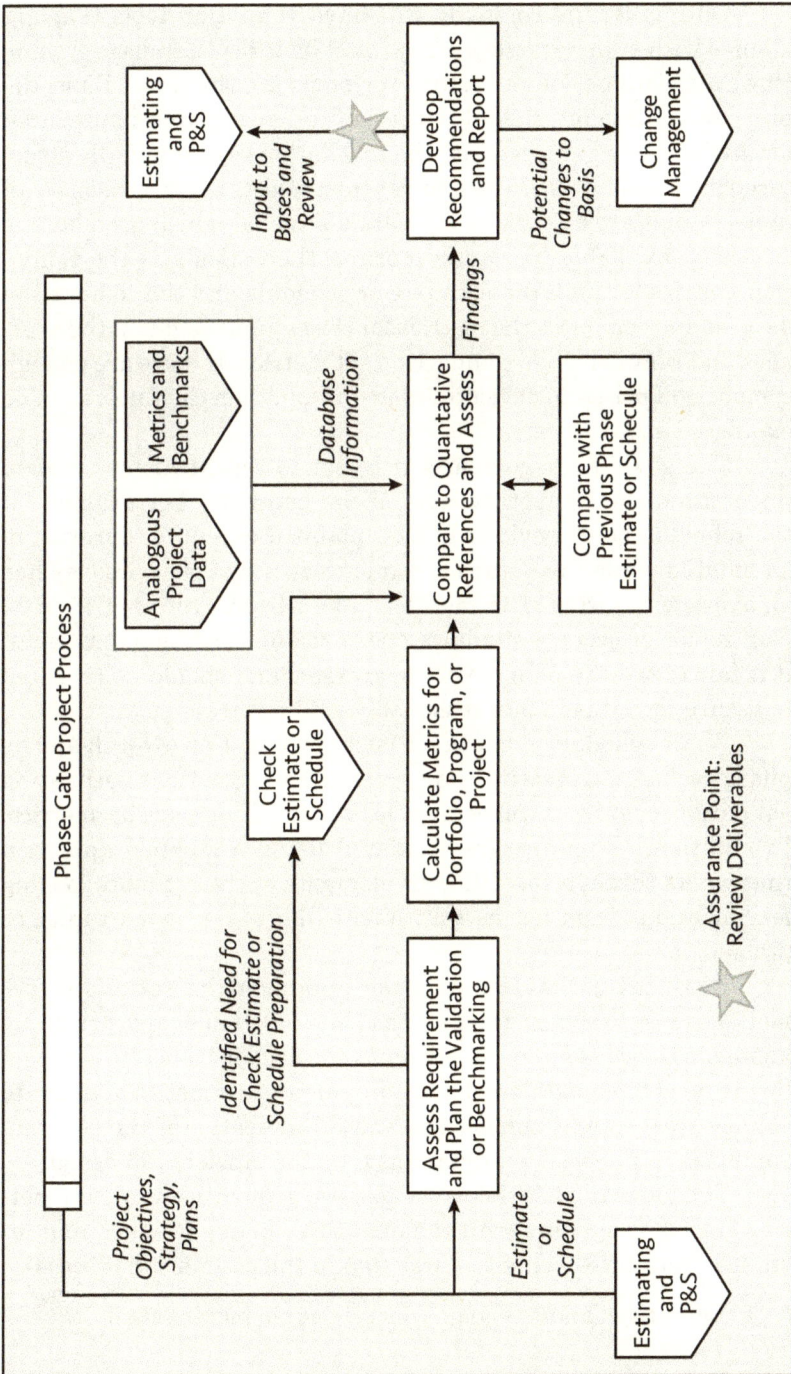

Figure 9.2: Typical Validation Process Map

Optimally, the company will have validation tools that are aligned with or integrated with a project historical database system. However, with or without a tool, the steps are the same. First, the project estimate or schedule duration to be validated is prepared for analysis (e.g., entered into the tool database or manually structured as needed if not). The analyst then selects a comparison set of projects that are already in the database or for which good data is otherwise available. The analyst or tool then calculates the validation metrics for both the estimate or schedule and the comparison dataset and compares the metrics for the estimate against the averages and ranges for the comparison set metrics. If there are enough comparison points to develop a distribution, then the ranges can be expressed as p-values.

The goal of the comparison is not to repeat history, but to understand the competitiveness of the estimate. For example, if the schedule being reviewed has a planned execution duration of 14 months while the database comparison set of past projects has an average duration of 18 months and a $p10$-$p90$ range of 15 to 24 months for projects of similar scope, size and execution strategies, it is fair to say the plan is very aggressive and should be revisited to assure that it is in fact reasonably achievable.

While schedule validation focuses on duration (overall and by phase such as engineering, procurement, construction), estimating validation usually involves a wider array of comparison metrics. In addition, estimates are validated using a stepped approach that walks through the different elements of the estimate looking for variations from norms that might indicate an opportunity or problem.

I call my estimate validation approach the *ratio-to-driver* method. It is based on the fact that one cost is usually driven by another cost or resource. For example, the need for concrete is driven by the need to support steel and equipment, so a metric of concrete volume/steel weight should give you an indication if the concrete volume is in line with expectations (i.e., the efficiency of design).

The following list shows the general sequence or order of metrics to look at starting with the quantities being designed and installed (quantities being the first step in the estimating process):

1. Quantity/Quantity (e.g., concrete cubic meters/steel tonnes)
2. Bulk Materials/Equipment ($/$)
3. Direct Field Labor/Bulk Materials ($/$)

4. Field Indirects/Directs ($/$)
5. Engineering Hours/Quantities (e.g., structural engineering hours/steel tonnes)
6. Engineering Hours/Direct Field Hours (hours/hours)
7. PM and Owner's Costs/Field and Engineering Labor ($/$)

Costs can become biased at any level in this chain of ratios. For example, the cost of concrete may seem high relative to the cost of equipment, but this may be due to a high quantity of concrete (over design or poor soils) or high unit hours or high material cost for concrete. One should seek the specific source of any deviations from expectations. If it is justifiable, then move on to the next item.

The above approach helps you to find the source of bias and cost variations. However, bottom-line cost metrics will always be of critical interest to management and can give an indication of bias at a glance. Two common bottom line cost effectiveness metrics are:

♦ Cost/Capacity; e.g., cost per barrel/day throughput, and
♦ Lang factor; e.g., ratio of total cost/equipment (or total cost/materials if project is not equipment-centric).

Both of these metrics are reliable only for projects of very similar scope. They work best for large greenfield projects and are generally not reliable for revamp projects. For smaller, non-greenfield projects, one can assess the more detailed discipline level metrics and from a weighted point of view, make an assessment about general bias if it is apparent.

A practice to be avoided is using metrics that include a given cost in both the numerator and denominator (including Lang factors). These types of metrics obscure cause and effect and variations are buffered or hidden. In the worst case they drive uncompetitive behaviors. One of the most egregious cases of poor validation metrics is the all too common use of Engineering/Total Project Cost. This is dangerous because the easiest way to lower this ratio value (or similarly with PM) is to arbitrarily cut engineering. This usually results in increased total project costs due to rework and poor quality. Better metrics are those shown in the list on the previous page that focus on inputs/outputs or ratio-to-driver such as hours of engineering per a given quantity of output.

The validation assessment outcomes should be reported in the BoE/BoS as appropriate. As with quality reviews, key sections in the BoE/BoS as regards bias are the description of allowances (additions) and exclusions (subtractions) from the base estimate or schedule. As stated previously, these should be carefully considered as to their appropriateness, with a particular eye out for bias: hiding of contingency above the line ("adding fat") and/or overly aggressive cost and duration savings initiatives. An independent validator must make sure that management is made aware of bias when it is found.

Overall ratings for the estimate and for the schedule can also be developed. These can be used as inputs to systemic risk quantification. The following are some example ratings (the p-values reflect the project's level in a distribution of reference metrics):

1 - Very Conservative (greater than the $p80$)
2 - Somewhat Conservative ($p60$ to $p80$)
3 - Average (i.e., Historical Norm or $p40$ to $p60$)
4 - Somewhat Aggressive ($p20$ to $p40$)
5 - Very Aggressive (less than the $p20$).

If there are any specific allowances or exclusions driving the bias, they should be noted. For exclusions, the inclusiveness of the estimate may be rated as a separate systemic risk rating.

Summary

This chapter described the starting point of risk quantification methods – the base estimating and planning and scheduling methods and practices. These base methods and their outcomes have variability and bias even before project attributes (e.g., complexity), risk events, and conditions are considered. These are inside risks because they are generally in control of or subject to assurance by the estimator or scheduler.

The chapter closed by providing some measures of the inside risks (quality, level of scope definition, and bias) that can be used for systemic risk quantification methods. It is not unusual to find some risks analysts only quantifying these inside risks and no other; this is particularly true for contractors when they are not liable for design changes, risk events, and so on because of the reimbursable nature of the contract.

Base estimating and scheduling at the funding gate is largely deterministic. However, before we get further into more risk quantification (which is more stochastic), we need to make sure that we understand some risk quantification fundamentals used by all the methods starting with a topic many of us have dreaded since in our college days: probability and statistics.

Questions

1) What does the book propose as a definition for what a "Base" estimate or schedule is?

2) What are the four base strategies and which is suggested as a best practice and why?

3) What is a Cost Estimating Relationship (CER)?

4) Describe how the roles of Schedule Planning (i.e., or just Planning) differ from Schedule Development (i.e., or just Scheduling).

5) What is the difference between Critical Path Method (CPM) and Critical Chain methods of schedule modeling, and how might the later better facilitate risk quantification and management?

6) What is the key deliverable defining an estimate or schedule called, and what is its main role?

7) How does bias in base estimated cost or schedule duration relate to contingency?

8) AACE Recommended Practices for Cost and Schedule "Classification" are commonly referenced guidelines relating to estimate and schedule development. What do they recommend?

9) In terms of contribution to overall uncertainty in estimates and schedules, roughly where would "quality of base practices" typically rank with other key risk drivers?

10) List three common types of estimating practice allowances that are appropriate in base estimates.

11) How should uncertainties as to cost for "overtime" be handled?

12) How do the purposes of "Quality Review" and "Validation" differ in respect to the base?

"I'm afraid I can't put it more clearly," Alice replied, very politely,
"for I can't understand it myself, to begin with; and being so many
different sizes in a day is very confusing."
– Lewis Carroll, Alice in Wonderland

10
Statistics and Models

I related the story in Chapter 5 of the somewhat embarrassed senior manager (his department included the risk management function) who took me aside in the hallway after a presentation on risk management and said, "John, I have no idea what was just said in there." The root cause of the confusion was the presentation's emphasis on somewhat arcane aspects of probability and statistics rather than plain English. That was a story about a failure of communication, not of methodology. To perform risk quantification effectively, we have to rely heavily on probability and statistics and that means understanding it and being able to describe its workings and outcomes clearly.

Before starting, I must warn the reader that I am *not* an expert in statistics. This chapter is my take on what an analyst needs to know in order to apply the risk quantification methods in this book, to draw meaningful conclusions from them, and to speak about them clearly. Like most, I learned about probability and statistics in a basic university course or two and after that I used it very little in my work. As my career migrated from engineering into cost estimating, I found the topic of *accuracy range* at the front and center of conversation (as it is in this book way back in Chapter 4). I found a lot of "range-speak" going on, i.e., when someone said their estimate was +/–10%, everyone seemed to nod their heads knowingly. But when I pressed them on the topic, not many of these people were able to explain this range thing very well. Later, when I joined a benchmarking firm, I was thrown into the deep end of the "statistics pool" and learned a bit about how things really worked with cost and schedule – and the real statistics often had little similarity to accepted knowledge. So, this chapter discusses what we need to know as entry level to the risk quantification business. The words in italics are terms you will want to understand going forward (but try to find simple synonyms for your business presentation if you can).

Statistics Basics

Statistics is about describing data and then drawing useful conclusions from it. At the heart of statistics is data, real or imagined. We call real data (historical data) *empirical data.* In our world, historical data includes measures of actual cost growth and schedule duration slip outcomes as well as data about project and system attributes that might drive the outcomes. The opposite of empirical data is *theoretical* or *conjectural* data, which includes expert judgments of the likelihood of a risk occurring and the risk's impact in cost or time if it happens.

From this point on I will refer to the theoretical or conjectural data as "assumed" (a synonym for conjectural). I do so because as a practical matter the source or derivation of data used will vary widely from expert guesses to extensive study. Arguably a term such as "assessed" is better to reflect a preference for rigor; however, as often as not, given the exigencies of interviews and risk workshops, the input data (in most cases ranges) will be from an expert or two in their "considered opinion" with a strong amount of subjectivity. So, read "assumed" as *"the best one can practically get or come up with in the circumstances."*

This does *not* mean we accept inputs as-is (i.e., don't assume data is correct as first stated); as analysts, we must probe and push the team (particularly as regards worst cases), but in the end the lows and highs are subjective opinions.

I Don't Believe It Either

I have many years of statistical model building experience – not enough to be a true expert, but enough to have developed a healthy skepticism of statistical research. Is coffee good or bad for you?

The same type of question arises with statistical modeling for project risk, cost, and schedule. As an example, from 1999 to 2001, I led research at IPA, Inc. that found that strong owner project control does reduce cost growth on projects; prior to that study there was only anecdotal evidence.[1] However, it was a surprise (maybe it should not have been) that the practices that mattered were core fundamentals:

♦ Assign an owner project control person,

♦ Estimate in-house,

♦ Do physical progressing,

♦ Report more frequently than monthly, and

♦ Collect historical data.

To paraphrase Woody Allen, "80 percent of control is showing up."

How this relates to belief in statistical modeling is that this study "controlled" for practices already known to drive better outcomes such as better scope definition. After controlling for known drivers, there was little room for other practices to improve outcomes even more. Before my study, I had not given much attention to other studies, but I did afterwards. Article after article claimed that this practice saves X% and that this tool saves Y%. The myriad of savings quickly added up to more than 100% – get your projects for free!

What I learned was very few studies adequately control for known risk drivers. They are continually re-discovering the same fundamental drivers. For example, a company with the wherewithal to apply a fancy practice X probably also employs good FEL (scope definition). If you include (control for) "FEL rating" in your regression model along with "used practice X," that "new" practice no longer matters.

The difficulty is that control requires a very large sample size. Each variable controlled for requires many observations, a good range of values, and clean data. Few studies have this. So, if you are asking why this book builds on studies such as those by Rand, it is because they were *controlled*.

So, until I see a study that controls for everything else in our lives, I will continue to drink coffee every morning!

---

1   Hollmann, J., "Best Owner Practices for Project Control", AACE Transactions, AACE International, 2002.

For example, if the permitting lead says a permit may be as much as three months late, ask why they say that; but if the answer is rational and there is no sign of disagreement in the room, we move on. Lean to more rigor and do assess things off-line when it is called for (e.g., the experts widely disagree or lack confidence, the risk, response or impact is too unique or complicated to make quick conclusions, the assumption implies a show-stopper).

The risk quantification methods in this book combine the analysis of historical data and assumed data, using statistical approaches to do so. The word "realistic" in this book's title reflects the application of historical data and assumptions with minimal conjecture (i.e., minimal guessing or luck).

Statistics about data fall into two categories: *descriptive* and *inferential*. Most of us are familiar with descriptive statistics, which, as the term implies, simply describe the data. In particular they describe the central tendency or how the data groups (mean, median, mode) and how the data spreads (range or standard deviation). Grouping and spread are parameters defining how data is distributed, as in a plot of the data values in a *histogram* (a graph with bars showing the frequency that a variable has certain defined values). The mean and standard deviation or range provide a rough idea about the general outline of the data *distribution*.

Unfortunately, descriptive statistics do not always help us make useful conclusions about what we have learned. For example, if the range of concrete unit hour data we collected from 17 actual projects was 6 to 18 hours/cubic meter, that range tells us nothing about *why* the range is what it is.

To answer why, we turn to inferential statistics, which help us draw generalizations about the data and how it might relate to our current project or group of projects. Inferential statistics compares several *samples* of data observations and give us information as to whether these samples might be *correlated*. For example, if we have data on centimeters of rain that fell during the 17 concrete projects in our data set, we can use inferential statistics (e.g., regression) to test whether the concrete unit hours are correlated with the amount of rain. If so (e.g., more rain is correlated with higher unit hours), then the inference is that rain adversely affects productivity – rain is a risk driver.

Descriptive Statistics

Probability Distributions

The first characteristic of a sample of data is its pattern of occurrence or distribution, often plotted on a histogram chart. For example, we could break our 17 example observations of concrete

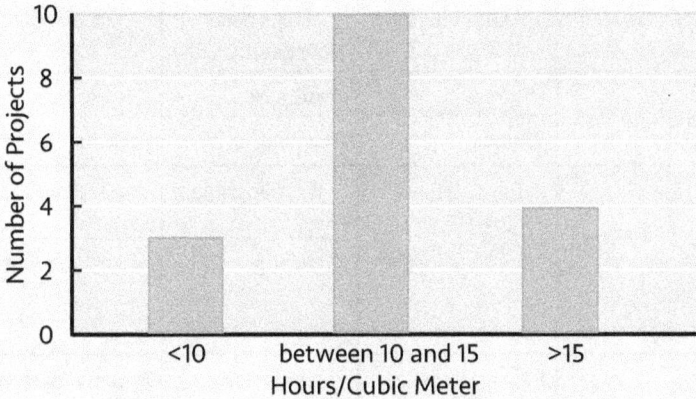

Figure 10.1: Histogram, Concrete Hour Data

unit hour data into three ranges of values to observe the pattern of occurrence:

♦ Less than 10 hours/cubic meter (m^3) = 3 projects
♦ Between 10 and 15 hours/m^3 (inclusive) = 10 projects
♦ Greater than 15 hours/m^3 = 4 projects

Figure 10.1 is a histogram of this data.

For this distribution we can calculate that 76% of the observations had less than or equal to 15 hours/m^3 (13/17 = 0.76). If we could infer that this past distribution applies to our project, we could say there is a 76% probability of the concrete unit hours for our project being less than or equal to 15 hours/m^3. In that sense, we are referring to the distribution as a *probability distribution* (in this example, it is historically based rather than an assumed distribution).

Distributions are *continuous* (any value in a range) or *discrete* (only certain values in a range) and they may or may not be *bounded* or limited on the low and/or high ends. We call mathematical descriptions of the distributions *Probability Distribution Functions* (PDFs, which are also sometimes referred to as *Probability Density Functions*). An excellent description of PDFs can be found in AACE International's RP 66R-11, which outlines the more useful PDFs for cost and schedule risk analysis. A portion of the PDF selection table from that RP is provided in Table 10.1.[1]

---

1   "Selecting Probability Distribution Functions for Use In Cost and Schedule Risk Simulation Models," Recommended Practice 66R-11, AACE International.

PDF Name	DISCRETE	UNIFORM (RECTANGULAR)	TRIANGLE
CHARACTERISTICS	Discrete	Continuous	Continuous
	Bounded	Bounded	Bounded
PARAMETERS	Discrete values with assigned probabilities.	Lowest possible value	Lowest possible value
		Highest possible value	Most likely value
			Highest possible value
TYPICAL APPLICATION	For variables that have only discrete values.	For variables where a mode does not occur and/or the distribution shape is unknown or disputed.	Broadly used where a most likely value is clearly discerned, but the shape of the distribution is not highly skewed.
ADVANTAGES	Well known and generally understood. Simple to use.	Well known and generally understood. Simple to use. Can be easy for users to provide parameters.	Well known and generally understood. Can be easy for users to provide parameters. Its low central tendency can compensate for users that set low/high ranges that are too narrow.
DISADVANTAGES	Estimates of the discrete values may have some uncertainty that is not captured.	Can overstate the probability of values at the extremes if the probabilities are indeed lesser in these ranges.	Can overstate the probability of values on the skewed side of ranges when users set extreme low/high values but the actual distribution has a strong central tendency.

Table 10.1: Typical PDFs Used in Risk Analysis
Based on Recommended Practice 66R-11, "Selecting Probability Distribution Functions for Use in Cost and Schedule Risk Simulation Models," AACE International (latest revision).

NORMAL	LOGNORMAL	PERT OR BETA-PERT	BINOMIAL
Continuous	Continuous	Continuous	Discrete
Unbounded	Bounded on the low side at zero	Bounded	Bounded
Mean	Mean of the variable's natural logarithm	Lowest possible value	Represented by values of zero and one and probability of it being one
Standard deviation	Standard deviation of the variable's natural logarithm	Most likely value	
		Highest possible value	
Used to describe values that have symmetrical distributions and there is some empirical basis to define parameters.	Used to describe values that have asymmetrical distributions and there is some empirical basis to define parameters.	Used where a most likely value is clearly discerned, and the shape of the distribution is highly skewed.	Used to represent the probability of occurrence of a yes/no risk event.
Well known and generally understood. Works well for items with unskewed ranges.	Well known and generally understood. Works well for items with either skewed or unskewed ranges.	Can be easy for users to provide parameters. Less overweighting of skewed ranges than Triangle.	Simple to use for yes/no risk event probability. If the yes probability is uncertain, a PDF can be embedded for that value.
Difficult for users to objectively express a standard deviation. Most time and cost estimates are skewed. Being unbounded, can result in inappropriate negative values on the low end.	Difficult for users to objectively express a standard deviation.	Less well known. If the team exhibits optimism bias, may underweight the skewed sides.	Simple application treats the probability of occurrence as deterministic.

Table 10.1: Typical PDFs Used in Risk Analysis (continued)

When we do not have a known historical distribution, we usually try to select a PDF that best fits our assumptions. The most common PDF that people are familiar with is the *normal* distribution, which is symmetrical. Unfortunately, project cost growth and schedule slip data expressed as percentages are almost always *skewed* (unsymmetrical) towards more overruns than underruns. Because of that, the *lognormal* distribution is often a good fit for actual data; however, that PDF's definitional parameters require offline analysis to define. Therefore, most analysts use the triangular or PERT distributions because they can be practically defined with 3-point estimates.

Measures of Central Tendency

These statistical descriptors are most familiar:

Mean (Expected Value): The mathematical average of the sample data.

Median (*p*50): Half the data points in the sample are more and half are less than this value.

Mode (Most Likely): The most frequently occurring value in the sample (there can be more than one mode such as with orderly versus blowout project costs).

The mean, median, and mode will be the same for symmetrically distributed data (e.g., a normal distribution). Note that the mean is the only value that is additive for multiple groups of projects that have skewed data, which is almost always the case (the modes and medians are not additive for skewed distributions). This is important to remember because many companies use the *p*50 confidence level cost or duration (the median) to fund and plan their projects and are surprised to find that the *p*50 for a portfolio made up of groups of projects does not equal the sum of the project *p*50s. This can cause a bit of confusion for portfolio managers. The difference is that the median is not risk weighted – it ignores *how high* the highest value is. It only describes *how many* data points are on the left and right of the median. Arguably, using the *mean* as the point of funding better addresses the magnitude of risk and avoids the problem of other measures that do not add up.

The most likely value or mode is important to remember because this is the value that estimators and schedulers sometimes use as their base estimate (i.e., what they might call realistic values or historical norms). On a histogram, it is the highest frequency or tallest bar (or two bars if bimodal). However, for data that is skewed

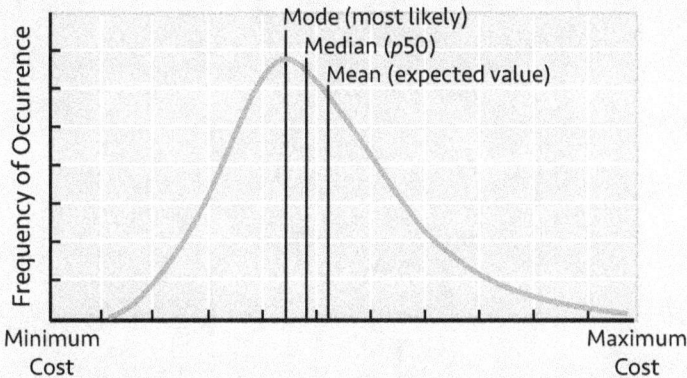

Figure 10.2: Mean (Expected Value), Median (p50) and Mode (Most Likely)

to the high side, the mode tends to be less than both the mean and the median as shown for the skewed distribution in Figure 10.2. This difference between the mode (our base) and the median or mean (where we fund the project) is the fundamental principle of probabilistic-based contingency determination.

Measures of Spread

In Chapter 4, the topic of project estimate and schedule accuracy range was covered in some detail. Statistically speaking, accuracy is a shorthand way of describing the spread or dispersion of data in a cost or schedule distribution (either historical or assumed). Spread deals with the question, "*How far could the eventual outcome be from our base or reference estimate?*" This question is most important to investment and other decision making because investors and stakeholders need to have a good idea about how good or bad things could be economically in the best and worst cases. In probability and statistics, the spread is usually described using one of the following metrics:

- ◆ Standard Deviation (σ),
- ◆ Confidence Levels and Confidence Intervals (see Chapter 4), and/or
- ◆ Range (see Chapter 4).

Standard deviation is a mathematical measure of the spread. I am not going to go into the math as you can find that easily online. However, there are three important things to know about this measure in terms of practical risk quantification:

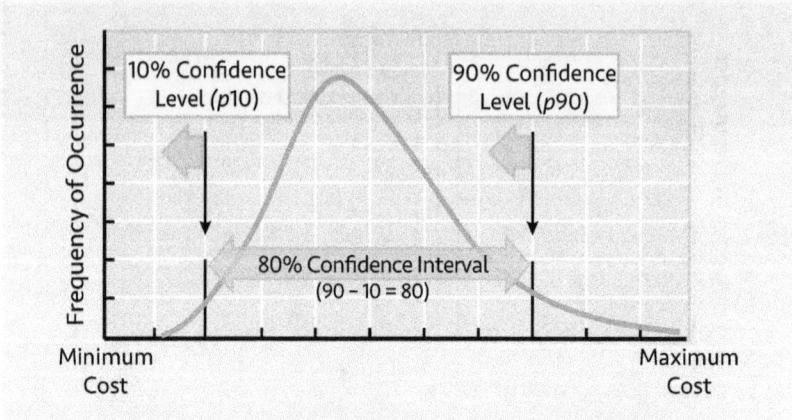

Figure 10.3: Confidence Level versus Confidence Interval

♦ It is expressed in the same units as the data, making it easy to relate to. For example, if the mean of a data sample is 18 hours/tonne with a standard deviation of 9 hours/tonne, we can see that plus one standard deviation is about +50% of the mean (9/18).

♦ The standard deviation tells us how likely data is to be within the plus/minus standard deviation value (or multiples of it). In particular, for a normal distribution, about 68% of data will be within plus or minus one standard deviation, 95% within two, and 99% within three. Standard deviation is a good relative indicator of confidence for any distribution.

♦ While being a good relative indicator, the standard deviation tells us *nothing* about how skewed the data is, and because most project data is skewed, the standard deviation is not a very useful measure for communication. It is in skewness (the tail) that disaster resides. *It is better to use confidence levels and intervals* to communicate risks because these concepts show skewness.

The *confidence level* was described in Chapter 4 and is also illustrated in Figure 10.3. The level is the probability (*p*) that a value will be less than the selected value. For example, if we say the *p*90 value for steel construction unit hours is 30 hours/tonne, that means we can have 90% confidence that the actual hours/tonne will be less than 30.

The *confidence interval* expresses a bounded confidence; i.e., confidence that a value will fall *within* or *between* two values. Note that there are *confidence intervals* and *confidence levels* – make sure you are clear as to which you are referring to. For example, if the $p10$ value of our steel unit hours was 10 hours/tonne, we can have 80 percent confidence that the actual hours/tonne will be between 10 and 30 (between the $p10$ and $p90$ values). Skewness will be evident when the higher ($p90$) confidence level bound is much further from the mean than the corresponding lower bound ($p10$).

For example, if the mean of our steel unit hours was 15 hours/tonne, then 30 hours/tonne at the $p90$ level is much further from the mean than 10 hours/tonne at the $p10$ level. AACE's RPs for Estimate Classification (e.g., RP 18R-97) uses the $p80$ confidence interval (i.e., the plus percentage is the $p90$ level and the minus percentage is the $p10$ level) for its range-of-range accuracy values.

Life is Lognormal

I borrowed the phrase "Life is Lognormal"[2] because it perfectly captures the reality for the project world (it would make a great slogan for a risk quantification t-shirt). The lognormal distribution is usually a good fit for cost and schedule outcome data distribution. The name of the distribution reflects that the logarithms of the data values are normally distributed and symmetrical. For project risk quantification purposes, this is most useful for parametric modeling based on regression.

As we will discuss in the next section, linear regression works best for normally distributed data (or more properly stated, when errors of the prediction are normally distributed). Therefore, analysts will often *transform* their cost growth (e.g., actual cost/estimated cost) and schedule slip (actual duration/estimate duration) historical data by first calculating the logarithms of it and then performing the linear regression.

Another transformation trick is to use the inverse of the usual cost growth or slip ratios. This is done because while actual/estimate data is skewed to the high side, its inverse, estimate/actual, is usually close to normally distributed and therefore more amenable to linear regression analysis without resorting to logarithms. The use of the inverse is shown in a later example.

---

2   Limpert, E. and W. Stahel, Seminar for Statistics, Swiss Federal Institute of Technology Zurich.

Inferential Statistics:
Multiple Linear Regression Models

When dealing with historical data and statistics (e.g., averages), what we really want to know is whether the statistics apply to our current project. In other words, what can we infer from the statistics? The most useful inferential statistics approach for risk quantification using historical data is called *regression analysis*, which estimates the relationship between a dependent variable (e.g., cost growth or *Y*) and any number of independent variables (e.g., risk drivers X_1, X_2) for a sample of observations from a population (a *data set* or group of data points).

The *regression function* or parametric formula that we derive allows one to predict the mean value of the dependent variable for any combination of the independent variables. Also, because the analysis tells us about how far the actual data differed from the mean prediction (standard error of the regression), it allows us to infer confidence (e.g., 68% of observations will be within plus/minus one standard error).

Multiple Linear Regression (MLR)

There are many techniques for regression analysis, but the most practical one is *multiple linear regression* (MLR) where there is more than one independent variable or parameter. Mathematically, the analysis develops parameters that minimize the error between the data contained in the data set and a parametric formula that predicts comparable dependent values. MLR analysis capability is available in Microsoft Excel (in its Analysis ToolPak, which must be activated). MLR analysis using the Excel functionality is relatively simple.

As an example, Table 10.2 illustrates data developed for an MLR analysis of historical percent cost growth. We start by creating a table with the project cost outcome variable of interest (percent cost growth) in the first column (in the example, this ranges from –4% to +31% with an average of 11%). This percent was calculated from the ratio of actual cost/estimated cost, which is shown in the second column. However, for the dependent variable (or *Y* value) of the regression analysis, I will use the inverse of this (estimate/actual), which is shown in the third column. I did this because estimate/actual values tend to be more or less normally distributed, which facilitates better regression.

DEPENDENT VARIABLE			INDEPENDENT VARIABLES	
COST GROWTH			COMPLEXITY	TEAM
AS A %	AS ACT/EST	AS EST/ACT	RATING (1 TO 5)*	
2%	1.02	0.98	2	1
15%	1.15	0.87	3	2
31%	1.31	0.76	5	5
12%	1.12	0.89	3	4
8%	1.08	0.93	3	2
-4%	0.96	1.04	1	2
6%	1.06	0.94	2	1
21%	1.21	0.83	5	4
16%	1.16	0.86	3	2
5%	1.05	0.95	2	3
* Complexity: 5 = most complex; Team: 5 = best developed.				

Table 10.2: Example Data Input for a Regression Analysis

In considering what was driving the cost growth, I hypothesized that the greater the *complexity* of the project work breakdown and the weaker the *team development* (roles filled, skills, etc.), the greater the cost growth would be. Therefore I gathered ratings data on these two independent variables (X_1 and X_2) and entered them in the adjacent columns.

Once the data table is complete, we have Excel run the regression calculations using dependent variable Y and independent variables X_1 and X_2. The Excel regression output is shown in Table 10.3.

A regression-based parametric model will have the following general format.

Y (the mean prediction) = constant + a x X_1 + b x X_2 + c x X_3 + etc.

From our example output in Table 10.3, the model constant is the "intercept" coefficient and below the intercept we also find the "X-variable" coefficients (for complexity and team). Therefore, the resulting model is:

Cost Growth (est/act) = 1.076 – 0.059 x Complex + 0.0004 x Team.

Figure 10.4 is a graph of the actual versus predicted cost growth (estimated/actual) values:

SUMMARY OUTPUT					
Regression Statistics					
Multiple R	0.940				
R Square	0.884				
Adjusted R Square	0.851				
Standard Error	0.031				
Observations	10				
ANOVA					
	df	*SS*	*MS*	*F*	*Significance F*
Regression	2	0.051	0.026	26.7	0.0005
Residual	7	0.007	0.001		
Total	9	0.058			
	Coefficients	*Standard Error*	*t Stat*	*P-value*	
Intercept	1.0758	0.0255	42.1165	0.0000	
(X1)	-0.0590	0.0120	-4.9274	0.0017	
(X2)	0.0004	0.0114	0.0349	0.9731	

Table 10.3: Excel Output for the Example MLR Analysis

MLR Model Diagnostics and Interpretation

Two questions need to be asked about our first pass regression model:

♦ Does it make sense, and

♦ Does it work?

The first question addresses whether the variables are drivers of the outcome. Are they causal? Most of us have heard the phrase "*cor-*

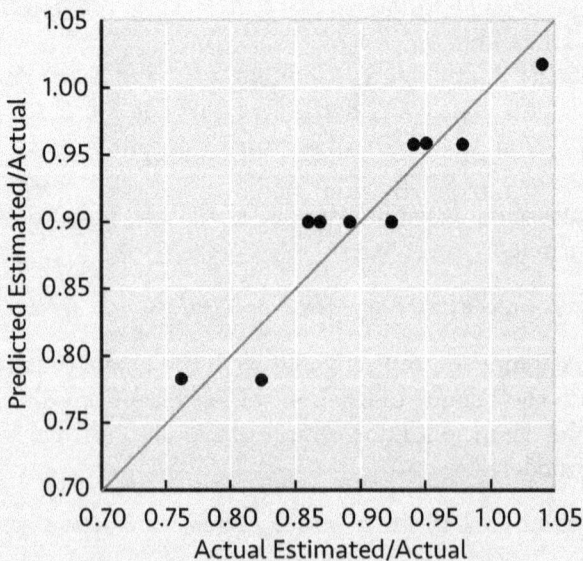

Figure 10.4: Actual Versus Predicted Cost Growth (Est/Act) From Example

relation is not the same as causation." This means that we need to assure ourselves that the correlations can be rationally explained. For example, in Table 10.3, it makes some sense (indeed it was our hypothesis going in) that projects with more complexity (5 in a scale of 0 to 5) would have greater percentage cost growth.

The second question we ask ourselves has to do with assuring that the relationships (i.e., the coefficients) are significant and are not random chance. To check this, the Excel output in Table 10.3 provides *p*-values for each independent variable. These should be less than 0.05 (which means there is less than a 5 percent chance that the relationship is random or luck). Similarly, the whole model has a *Significance F* value (which should also be less than 0.05).

At a summary level, there are also diagnostics for fit. One is the R-square (R^2) value; the closer this is to 1.00 the better the fit.

The *standard error*, which is in the same units as the predicted value, is also insightful. In our example, the R-square of 0.88 is reasonably close to 1.00. The standard error of about 0.03 is small (this standard error is about 3% of the mean value of 0.91). The Significance F value is less than 0.05, which is good. Also, the *p*-values for the intercept (constant) and the independent variable "complexity" (X_1) are also less than 0.05.

However, the "team rating" (X_2) *p*-value is greater than 0.05. My working hypothesis had been that a better team (e.g., 5 on a scale of 0 to 5) would correlate with less cost growth. However, this is not confirmed by the regression. It is possible that the team data has some error and/or is correlated with complexity. In any case, the lack of a significant coefficient on team does not make much sense at face value. On reflection, an alternate hypothesis may be that this company put its best teams on the complex projects, which would be a reasonable thing to do. (If so, however, the model indicates that the practice did not help the company much.)

The analyst seeing results such as these should:

♦ Double check the team input data (did we reverse the rating?).

♦ Obtain more observations if possible (ten points for two variables is barely adequate; can we find additional observations?).

♦ Check for correlation.

♦ Try to get a better fit by transforming the cost growth data using a nonlinear value such as the log of actual/ estimate instead of estimate/actual.

◆ Check for variable interaction by including an interaction variable (e.g., $X_3 = X_1 \times X_2$) and see if that changes the relationships.

However, watch out for over-fitting. With enough manipulation of data, an analyst can always improve the diagnostics, but, in the end, the model must make sense and all relationships must be rationally explainable. In the example, if data improvements don't work out, be prepared to conclude that "team" is not a significant driver, run the regression with just "complex," and see if the diagnostics are acceptable with that alone.

The following are a few statistical pre-conditions that need to be met for MLR modeling to work well. The example questions above are based on understanding these pre-conditions:

◆ Data is "clean," i.e., the variables are free from error.

◆ There are no dominant Y-drivers that are not captured in an X value driver (for example, if cost growth was not normalized for escalation, you should include "year" as an independent variable X_3).

◆ The independent variables are not correlated (e.g., data do not go up and down together). Less than 0.7 correlation is desirable, otherwise there is an unstable analysis outcome.

◆ Residuals (these are called "errors" of the predication but error implies a mistake to some people, hence the term "residuals") are more or less normally distributed and *homoscedastic* (balanced such that the residuals for low values of the independent variable are similar to the residuals for high values). This can often be addressed by transforming asymmetrical data to logarithms.

◆ There should be at least five observations per independent variable (ten or more observations per variable is better).

◆ Sample observations should cover the full range of possible independent variable values that one is likely to experience (for example, not all the complexity values can be three; we need to have some low values and some high values).

For correlation (being in synchronization), Excel provides a "Correlation Analysis" in its ToolPak. For the example above, "complex" and "team" have a 0.74 correlation coefficient, which is greater than our 0.7 threshold, suggesting this regression model may be unstable (correlated variables battling each other for dominance). The correlation may have just been bad luck in the sampling (which can be addressed by using more observations). With a better statistical software package than Excel (there are good affordable add-ons available), homoscedasticity (dependent variable has similar variability across the range of independent variable values) can be tested by reviewing a plot of the residuals for the ten data points; the residual scatter should look random (no pattern).

The description and example above represent beginner level regression analysis and modeling but illustrate the principles of risk quantification methods that require empiricism. Regression modeling requires a good understanding of what is being modeled, good judgment (i.e., the ability to logically hypothesize relationships), and good quality input data. Note that finding simple words to describe what you are doing can also be a challenge (you won't help your case by telling a manager "the model output is homoscedastic").

Distribution Outcome from a MLR Model

The MLR-based parametric model will generate a mean result value (e.g., the average cost growth or schedule slip metric) as a function of the independent variables. However, to support decision making, we need to produce a distribution of possible outcomes, not just a point value. The regression results provide some evidence of spread in the distribution of the residuals, i.e., the standard error of the estimate (0.031 in the example Excel output). You can also calculate the standard deviation for the raw cost growth data (it is 0.08 for the example estimated/actutal data).

However, these general indicators of spread are not indicative of the spread of any particular sub-group of the modeled data. For example, if we enter a high complexity (X_1) rating (five) into our model (and team is set to its average), it predicts 28% cost growth. This high outcome value intuitively implies there must be a wide distribution of outcomes for a population of complex projects. Conversely, the model predicts –2% cost growth for a low complexity project (rating of one), which implies a narrow distribution for that group. We need a way to model the *spread* as well as the central tendency.

Fortunately, there is a fairly simple method to model spread that is consistent with observed industry data. The observation from my own benchmarking experience and from others is that for typical base estimating practices, the standard deviation of the distribution of outcomes is roughly equal to the contingency, where the contingency is the mean cost growth or schedule slip as predicted by the regression analysis.[3] This assumes that the *typical base estimate is not strongly biased*, i.e., it is what a professional independent estimator would call "reasonable."

The second observation that we can use is that cost growth *and* schedule duration slip data reported as estimate/actual ratios are usually normally distributed. This is helpful because the known attributes of a normal distribution allow us to more confidently draw statistical inferences. Figure 10.5 shows how the *actual/estimate* data from our example Table is skewed but it is more or less normally distributed after transforming the data to *estimate/actual* form.

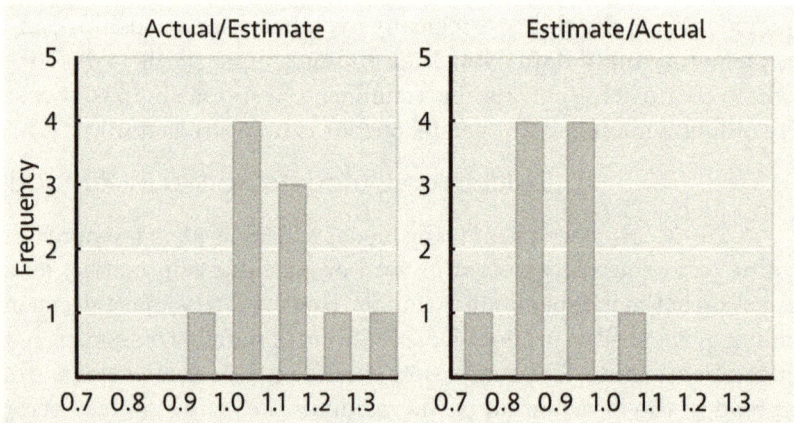

Figure 10.5: Example of Transforming a Variable to One That Is Normally Distributed

So, how do we use these two observations (i.e., that contingency can be used as the standard deviation in a normal distribution and estimate/actual ratios are normally distributed) to create a distribution from an MLR outcome? We can describe a normal distribution with two properties: the mean and the standard deviation. And, per our observation for typical base estimates, the contingency can be used as the standard deviation in order to describe the normal distribution.

Microsoft Excel provides us with a formula to generate a normal distribution from the mean and standard deviation called

---

3   Rothwell, Geoffrey, "Cost Contingency as the Standard Deviation of the Cost Estimate," Cost Engineering Journal, AACE International, Morgantown, WV, July 2005.

the *inverse normal function*. Its syntax is NORMINV (probability, mean, standard deviation), where probability is the confidence level (*p*-value). Below is an example of how to create a distribution that corresponds to a group of projects that all happened to have a complexity rating of 5:

Base Estimate (the point of no cost growth when act = est)   = 1.00

Output of the est/act regression model with complex is 5   = 0.78
(this is the mean of the predicted estimate/actual ratio when complexity is 5)

Contingency in estimate/actual terms (1 – 0.780)   = 0.22
(contingency is base minus predicted actual/estimate ratio)

Using NORMINV, a Cumulative Probability Distribution table can be created (Table 10.5):

P	NORMINV (P,0.22,0.22)A	EST/ACT (1-A)B	ACT/EST (1/B)C	% COST GROWTH [(C-1) AS %]
10%	(0.06)	1.06	0.94	–6%
20%	0.03	0.97	1.04	4%
30%	0.10	0.90	1.12	12%
40%	0.16	0.84	1.20	20%
50%	0.22	0.78	1.28	28%
60%	0.28	0.72	1.38	38%
70%	0.34	0.66	1.50	50%
80%	0.41	0.59	1.68	68%
90%	0.50	0.50	2.01	101%

Table 10.5: A Cumulative Probability Distribution Table Using the NORMINV Function

Note that the transformation from est/act to act/est restored skewness to the outcome cost growth distribution – the accuracy range around the total cost including contingency of 1.28 is plus +57% and minus 27%. Also note that the *p*-value at which act/est is equal to 1.00 (the base estimate) is about *p*15. This is consistent with my observation that the typical base estimate for large projects is in the ballpark of the *p*20 confidence level of actual cost outcomes. In the Table 10.5 example the model outcome is for the worst complexity rating (5). Figure 10.6 shows how the distribution narrows with lower complexity ratings (1.5 and 3.25). In applying a model,

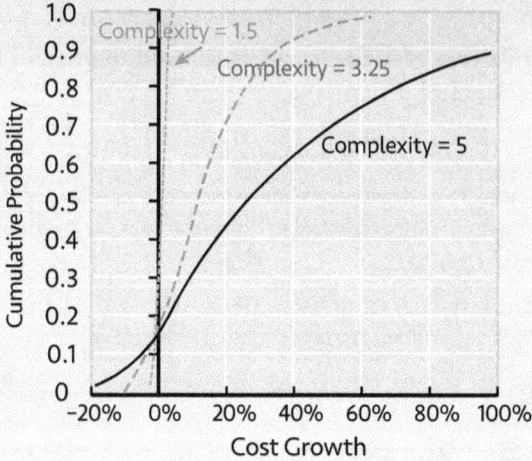

Variability of Cost Growth for Three Levels of Complexity

Figure 10.6: Cumulative Probability Distributions for Various Complexity Ratings

do not extrapolate beyond the bounds of the independent variables in the sample data.

In summary, we have seen how to perform an MLR analysis using transformed inputs, interpret its findings, convert it to a parametric model, and then generate a distribution based on the model mean outcome and the empirical observation of cost growth and schedule slip behavior relative to typical base estimating practice. Chapter 11 will show how these statistical practices translate into a working model to quantify Systemic risks. We will also show that there are valid starter models to work with. It takes time and practice to become proficient with these techniques.

Inferential Statistics: Monte Carlo Simulation Models

In the preceding section, we described how to use multiple linear regression of historical data to infer relationships between a dependent variable (e.g., cost growth or schedule slip) and independent variables (e.g., risk drivers such as complexity). These relationships are then used in a parametric risk model that, depending on size of the sample and quality of the observations, we can reasonably assume represents how a group of similar projects would behave. The model outcome also has useful statistical properties that we can make inferences from (i.e., a predicted outcome distribution). This is by nature "realistic."

However, what if we do not have historical data? How do we develop a risk model that generates an outcome distribution when we only have *assumptions* about how a group of projects behaves? In making assumptions we need some rational basis, backed by assessment as is appropriate, and may have some supporting anecdotal evidence, but assumptions or assessments are not equivalent to measurements of real data.

The solution is that we can "invent" a model of how the projects will behave and then repeatedly and randomly sample from that pseudo population to obtain a distribution of outcomes. The random sampling from the *invented* model is what is called Monte Carlo Simulation (MCS).

If you read the above paragraph and asked yourself how an invented model can be called "realistic," you are asking a very astute question. We need to answer that up front because Monte Carlo Simulation has obtained a bad reputation among many managers and decision makers. This unfortunate reputation came about because the most prevalent invented models in use, *Line-Item Ranging* (LIR) and its schedule counterpart, *Activity Ranging*, do not model the relationships of risks to project outcomes. LIR only models the team's opinion about general uncertainty (inside risk). As we have discussed, that approach does not correctly account for a project's risk.

Others have said MCS cannot model the complexity of project behavior (e.g., bimodality); that is also not true as we will show later.

The key to correct MCS application is starting with a *realistic* model. A realistic model *must:*

♦ Explicitly link identified risks to outcomes, and
♦ Remove as much conjecture as possible.

If models are indeed realistic, there would be no debate as to MCS efficacy for risk quantification. These are *risk-driven* modeling approaches.

Creating a Risk-Driven Model

We first need to devise a model of theorized project risk behavior to apply MCS. Performing this step is not much different than how we approach historically based regression modeling. In our MLR example, we started with a hypothesis that cost growth was correlated with or driven by complexity and team development. A hypothetical model then would be:

Cost growth = constant + *a* x (complexity) + *b* x (team)

With MLR we would gather actual measurements of growth, complexity, and team development and use MLR to calculate values for the constant, *a*, and *b*. However, in MCS we have no data, only our assumptions. The best we can do is make assumptions based on some degree of assessment as to the constant, *a*, and *b* values. Often, the assumed values are based on the consideration of opinion from experts. We can capture their range of opinion in representative distributions such as triangular or PERT, which are easy to use with their 3-point basis (low, most likely, high). By replacing the fixed values with distributions, we now have a model that represents how our pseudo portfolio of projects will behave:

Cost Growth = (constant distribution) + (*a* distribution) x (complexity)
+ (*b* distribution) x (team)

It should be noted that an MCS model can include a mixture of assumed and historically based distributions: a hybrid model. In fact, that is the basis of the methods that will be covered later in the book.

Also, note that when eliciting input from experts, you must stay within the context of how the *expert* sees the world and translate it to your model needs later. It is very unlikely that an expert will be able to give you a meaningful opinion on parameters *a* and *b* above directly. However, the expert *can* give you opinions on cost and schedule growth with increasing complexity and/or team capability. To illustrate this point, if you live in the US and I ask you what mileage your car gets, if I want the result in kilometers per liter, it will be necessary for me to translate from miles per gallon into kilometers per liter. When the input is generally well understood, such as the duration of a delay, the translation is easier.

Running a Simulation

Now we can run the MCS simulation. For most practitioners, MCS functionality (incorporating distributions in a model and performing sampling) is obtained through the use of spreadsheet add-ons (e.g., @Risk or Crystal Ball for Excel) or software extensions for scheduling systems (e.g., Primavera Risk Analysis (PRA) for Primavera scheduling; see Tables 8.4 and 8.5 for more information). There are also third party risk analysis systems that often offer more powerful analytical abilities for experts. I do all my cost and schedule risk quantification with Excel and @Risk, which is a practical, effective, and affordable approach.

In the simulation, we enter the known values (e.g., *complex* and *team*) in the model and run the MCS. The MCS routine will randomly sample from the distributions that we defined for the uncertain risk driver parameters (constant, *a*, and *b*), and calculate predicted cost growth for the entered complex and team ratings. It will repeat this sampling and calculate pseudo observations thousands of times (iterations), just as if we were gathering observational data from a real group of thousands of projects. It captures each of these thousands of observations and from that data set of outcomes it generates a distribution of possible outcomes.

Just as with MLR, there are statistical pre-conditions of MCS. In particular, MCS assumes the uncertain variables are independent. If they are dependent or correlated, MCS can deal with this by defining how they are correlated. We do this by estimating correlation coefficients between the related variables. A correlation coefficient can be between –1 and +1, where –1 is perfectly inversely correlated (mutually exclusive), 0 is no correlation, and +1 is perfectly correlated.

For example, if there is a +1 correlation coefficient between *x* and *y*, and the sampling routine picks a high value for *x* from its distribution, it will next pick a high value for *y* from its distribution. Strong correlations yield wider ranges in outcomes because each iteration is more likely to have extreme outcomes (lots of high-highs and lots of low-lows and not so many high-low balancing combinations). The degree of correlation is another uncertainty; my approach is to focus on what is important (which is having a realistic model to start with), and then just use a "low, moderate, high" approach to the correlations (e.g., 0.25, 0.5, 0.75).

Validating an MCS Model

Is such an invented model any good? To answer this question, benchmark the model outcome distribution against real outcome distributions. As we saw in Chapter 3, the outcome of LIR failed this test in industry research (except when the projects had no real risks) because the LIR model includes no risk drivers. As you can see in the LIR risk model structure below, the absence of risk drivers is self-evident:

Total Cost = Fixed Cost + (distribution of cost *a*) + (distribution of cost *b*)

If a model fails a benchmarking test, one must revisit the assumptions and inputs. Three main questions are:

- ♦ Are the chosen variables or risk drivers valid,
- ♦ Are the 3-point estimates and chosen distributions realistic, and
- ♦ Are there dependencies between the risks?

For example, in our MLR example, we found that "team" was not correlated with cost growth, but if we had used MCS it would have been very difficult to learn this because we have no real data – just assumptions. Validity of the model in MCS is hard to demonstrate. Therefore, MCS use should always be limited to models with minimal conjecture. The linkage of complexity, team, and other systemic risks to cost growth and schedule slip are all highly conjectural and therefore we should not use MCS as the initial model of *systemic* risks. We will look at more specific examples of the use of MCS for *project-specific* risks in Chapter 12.

Aligning Risk Types with the Risk Models

We have already introduced the three main risk types with respect to risk quantification: systemic, project-specific, and escalation/exchange. This section furthers explains why this categorization works with respect to the statistical modeling methods that are the foundation of risk quantification.

There are many reasons to categorize risks for risk management. For example, it helps to know where in the organization a risk originated (such as engineering or construction) so that we can better assign a risk to an owner and get a sense of where to focus management attention. Similarly, it helps to identify candidate opportunities for value improving practices. These categories are generally referred to as Risk Breakdown Structures (RBS) in risk management. In the literature, RBS discussions are primarily focused on managing the risks, i.e., sorting them out to address and control them. However, what is often missing is categorization for the purpose of how to best *quantify* them.

One reason projects do not have a quantification RBS category in their risk registers is that we do not quantify risks very often, usually only at decision gates. Another reason is that, as discussed, the most prevalent risk quantification models (i.e., Line Item and Activity Ranging) do not include the risks in their model. In that case, there is simply no need for such a classification (those methods assume the team somehow internalized all of the risk register information and all the risk implications, which will result in range prognostications; that is not a reasonable assumption). This book includes only risk-driven models. This approach recognizes that risk drivers do have different attributes that affect the choice and application of the most *realistic* risk quantification methods.

Inferential Statistical Method for Quantification (MLR versus MCS)

As discussed, there are only two root statistical methods available for risk quantification: MLR and MCS. Note that each can be manifested in different modeling applications (e.g., MCS can be applied to spreadsheets or CPM schedules while MLR outputs can be used as elements in a MCS). Each method has strengths and weakness. Table 10.5 summarizes the characteristics of risk knowledge that best align with each modeling method in terms of being *realistic*.

CHARACTERISTIC	MLR-BASED (PARA-METRIC) METHOD	MCS-BASED METHOD
SOURCE OF INFORMATION	Historical	Assumed/Assessment
RISK-TO-IMPACT RELATIONSHIP	High Conjecture (Stochastic)	Low Conjecture (Deterministic)

Table 10.5: Model Characteristics

The MLR method is inherently the most realistic because it is based on history. It can infer relationships that are not otherwise readily apparent, such as how a capital project or an economic system's attributes such as team competency impact cost growth.

On the other hand, MCS is based on theory, assessment, and/or assumptions. It is useful when the risk-to-impact relationship is hard to extract from history, but can easily be hypothesized or when expert assessment can be codified. For example, we cannot do MLR of how poor soil conditions may impact cost because the risk-to-impact relationship depends on too many possible permutations of soil-to-foundation interaction. However, if we ask the structural engineer, he or she can estimate with some confidence how a range of poor soils will affect their project's specific foundation design (e.g., "We'd have to shift from spread footers to piles."). It is these method characteristics that led to the key risk categories specified in this book; systemic, project-specific and escalation/exchange. These risk types each have a realistic quantification method that best aligns with them.

Armed with this statistical background, and understanding how the general statistical methods apply to various risk types, we are ready to describe specific working models of the types in Table 10.6. These are covered in Chapters 11, 12, and 13.

RISK CATEGORY	BEST INFERENTIAL MODEL TYPE
Company and Project System and Interaction with External Systems (*Systemic*); Chapter 11	MLR: 50+ years of industry research on the relationship of system attributes to outcomes. Otherwise known as *parametric modeling*.
Project Scope Dependent (*Project-Specific*); Chapter 12	MCS: quasi-deterministic, case-by-case modeling of risk-to-impact relationship. Recommended method is expected value models. Can use MLR outputs as MCS inputs where there is history for a variable.
Economic Systems (*Escalation/Exchange*); Chapter 13	MLR: well established research of economic drivers and their outcomes. Otherwise known as *econometric modeling* (which in this book we will leave to the economists but use their output).

Table 10.6: Model Characteristics That Define When Methods are Most Realistic and Practical

Questions

1) What are the two types of data we can use in modeling risk?

2) What are the two types of statistics and how do they differ?

3) Describe what correlation means and how does that relate to causation?

4) What are the three most common descriptive statistics and what do they describe?

5) What are the most common descriptors of the spread of a distribution?

6) Why might standard deviation not be a good spread descriptor to use for risk data?

7) Describe what a Distribution of data is in general, and name four probability distribution functions (PDFs) mentioned as commonly used in risk quantification.

8) What two distributions are commonly used because they can be defined with 3-point estimates and what are the three estimated points?

9) What key attribute of the normal distribution makes it uncommon as a way to represent cost and schedule outcome data?

10) What is a lognormal distribution and why is it a useful PDF in respect to risk modeling?

11) What does Regression analysis do in narrative terms (no math)?

12) What diagnostic measure of regression modeling allows one to approximate a distribution for model outcomes?

13) What does the term Transformation mean in respect to modeling, and why is it useful?

14) What method can be used to model probabilistic outcomes when the availability of useful historical data is limited?

15) What do we need to know about risk variable relationships for MCS application to be realistic? Give an example.

16) List the three main risk types and the statistical modeling approach that is most practical and realistic for each and why.

"I often say that when you can measure something that you are speaking about, express it in numbers, you know something about it; but when you cannot measure it, when you cannot express it in numbers, your knowledge is of the meagre and unsatisfactory kind."
— Lord Kelvin (Sir William Thomson)

11

Systemic Risks and the Parametric Method

By now, you should have a pretty good idea about what systems and systemic risks are about. The method for quantifying systemic risk, parametric models, was introduced in Chapter 7 and the statistical basis for parametric model development was covered in Chapter 10. That just leaves the practical details of how to create, apply, and maintain parametric methods to realistically quantify systemic risks.

The first question I usually get from new clients or training class attendees regarding parametric modeling is, "We don't have much historical data to use for creating a parametric model, so how can we do this?" The good news is that researchers have done much of the research for you. Introductory models are available for free (well almost — you must belong to AACE International to get the free versions) and all you have to do is adjust the reference models to bring them up to date with the latest research, improve their outputs to include distributions, and perform test calibrations (checks for bias) with your own high level cost growth and schedule slip data (that most companies can obtain from basic accounting records). This is what I did twenty years ago when I got started with these methods and it is what I help companies do now. To move beyond the "starter" mode, a company must improve its historical project data management to obtain the raw material for model calibration and model development. This is covered in Chapter 18. For those considering developing their own parametric models, be assured that you are not alone; besides for this book and its Hackney and Rand references, there is at least one other example of model development by a company in the literature – and hopefully more to come![1]

It is amazing to me that such powerful methods and working models are so freely and readily available and dismaying they are so rarely used. However, being able to develop and implement your own tools does not mean you can cut yourself off from the IPAs and CIIs of the world. Research continues to discover new insights into systemic risk drivers, and it is always recommended to get an independent outside review or benchmarking of project risks and in-house analyses. It is too easy to be influenced by internal pressures, become biased, and/or fall into poor, repetitive application habits.

Start with the John Hackney and Rand Corporation Models

The 1965 research by John Hackney on cost growth, the 1981 Department of Energy sponsored Rand Corporation research on cost growth, and Rand's later 1986 research on execution schedule duration slip were introduced in Chapter 3. AACE International released published functional versions of these models in Excel as educational examples of parametric models for systemic risk quantification. The relevant AACE RP series includes:

♦ RP 42R-08: Risk Analysis and Contingency Determination Using Parametric Estimating, and

♦ RP 43R-08: Example Models as Applied for the Process Industries (the Excel models are appendices to this RP).

---

1 Schoenhardt, Matthew, "Parametric Contingency Estimating on Small Projects," AACE International Transactions, AACE International, Morgantown, WV, 2016.

These are the starting points for implementing your own parametric models for systemic risk quantification.

John Hackney Model

John Hackney first published his parametric cost growth model in his book entitled *Control and Management of Capital Projects* in 1965. Mr. Hackney, one of AACE International's founders and a past president, had been a manager at several major owner companies, and had developed his own database of project cost outcomes as well as his own assessment of the projects' attributes and practices. He was not a statistician, but an engineer and a seasoned practitioner. As described in Chapter 3, he measured project cost growth as a percentage from the base estimate without contingency after normalizing for escalation (normalized actual/base estimate). He then developed a scope definition rating scheme of what we now call systemic risks that he based on his own experience. The ratings included 117 elements, in 29 groups and six broad categories. He then rated the projects in his data set and found a strong correlation with the cost growth.

If nothing else, his rating scheme provides an excellent review checklist of project definitional attributes to consider for estimating and scheduling. One weakness, however, is that the model violates "Occam's Razor" principle which means (as Albert Einstein is credited with saying), "Everything should be made as simple as possible, but not simpler." He provided no empirical evidence that any one of his 117 elements drove cost uncertainty, and by including so many elements, he may have under weighted some (such as new technology). For that reason, I recommend study of his ratings, model, and the associated AACE working tool as educational material rather than as the starting point of in-house modeling efforts; the Rand model is better suited for that.

Base Rand Model: Cost Growth

The 1981 and 1986 Rand models are the recommended starting point for building your in-house cost growth and schedule slip tools. They have a solid foundation and, because industry cost and schedule uncertainty have not improved much over the last 50 years (other than perhaps the increasing complexity and prevalence of megaprojects), they are still credible as a starting point. I will start by describing the Rand cost growth and schedule models "as-is." Later I will describe how to convert these into a workable toolset.

As described in Chapter 3, the 1981 Rand study examined cost growth data provided by a group of major US-based process industry companies. The cost growth data is relative to the total estimate including contingency after normalization for escalation, capacity or product changes, regulatory changes, and unforeseeable risk events. It looked at only risk factors *"internal to the nature of the project"* (i.e., what we call systemic risks).[2]

The cost growth metric was the ratio of total sanction estimate to normalized actual project cost. As discussed in Chapter 10, the estimate/actual ratio is roughly normally distributed and is amenable to MLR. Unlike the Hackney model, the Rand model only included statistically significant cost growth drivers (overall R^2 of 0.83). This is consistent with the Occam's Razor principle of keeping things as simple as possible, but not simpler. And it is very simple – the five key systemic risk drivers are summarized in Table 11.1:

Risk Driver	Description	Range of Values
Percent New (Pctnew)	Percentage of capital cost in technology unproven in commercial use	0 to 100%
Impurity	The extent to which impurity buildup was a source of development and design problems	0 to 5: 5 is greatest extent
Complexity	Block count of continuously linked process steps in the plant block flow diagram	1 or more
Inclusiveness	The percentage of three items included in the estimate: ♦ Land purchase/leases/property rentals ♦ Initial plant inventory/warehouse parts/catalysts ♦ Pre-operating personnel costs	0 to 100%
Scope Definition	The level of Scope Definition (see explanation in Table 11.2)	2 to 8; 8 is least defined

Table 11.1: Rand Cost Growth Model - Risk Driver Variables

The Level of Scope Definition variable includes several sub-elements. Its basis is shown in Table 11.2.

---

2   Merrow, E., et al., "Understanding Cost Growth and Performance Short-falls in Pioneer Process Plants," R-2569-DOE Rand Corporation, 1981.

DEFINITION = LEVEL OF ENGINEERING (1 TO 4) + AVERAGE DEFINITION OF KEY ITEMS (1 TO 4) = 2 TO 8	
Level of Engineering	*Select Rating:* 1 Design Specifications (Class 2/1) 2 Study Design (Class 3) 3 Study Design (Class 4) 4 Screening Study (Class 5)
Average of these four Key Definitional Elements: 1) Onsite/offsite unit configuration (Plot Plan) 2) Soil/hydrology 3) HSE requirements 4) Environmental requirements	*Select Rating for each, then take average:* 1 Definitive/Completed Work 2 Preliminary/Limited Work 3 Assumed/Implicit Analysis 4 Not Used in Cost Estimate At All

Table 11.2: Rand Level of Scope Definition Rating Buildup

Table 11.3 displays the base Rand model in spreadsheet row and column format and includes the coefficients for each parameter that the Rand study team derived through MLR. To implement this in a spreadsheet, you multiply the entered parameter values by the given coefficients, and then sum the results for each parameter (including the constant) to obtain the mean cost growth from the sanction estimate metric in estimate/actual terms.

RISK DRIVER	ENTER PARAMETER (a)	COEFFICIENT (b)	$a \times b$
CONSTANT			+ 1.12196
PCTNEW	0 to 100?	−0.00297	product
IMPURITY	0 to 5?	−0.02125	product
COMPLEXITY	>=1?	−0.01137	product
INCLUSIVENESS	0 to 100?	+0.00111	product
DEFINITION	2 to 8?	−0.04011	product
DEFINITION (IF IN R&D)	2 to 8?	−0.06361	product
TOTAL (SUM PRODUCTS)			Sum

Table 11.3: Rand Cost Growth Model in Spreadsheet Form

Table 11.4 shows an example of a model run for a moderately complex chemical plant project with some new technology (but not in R&D), some minor impurity/corrosion issues, and scope definition at AACE Class 4 equivalent. At the bottom of the worksheet, the model outcome is transformed to more recognizable percent cost growth format. Because the Rand study modeled cost growth from the sanction amount including contingency, and we desire cost growth from the base estimate excluding contingency, an allowance is added of 10% which has long been the industry rule-of-thumb or de facto standard for contingency (that has not been based on empirically valid methods such as this).

Risk Driver	Parameter (*a*)	Coefficient (*b*)	*a* x *b*
Constant			+ 1.12196
PctNew	5%	–0.00297	–0.015
Impurity	1	–0.02125	–0.021
Complexity	5	–0.01137	–0.057
Inclusiveness	33%	+0.00111	+0.037
Definition	4	–0.04011	–0.160
Definition (if in R&D)	N/A	–0.06361	0
TOTAL (sum products)			0.904
Calculate Inverse (actual/sanction estimate)			1.11
Convert to % Cost Growth from sanction [(1.11-1) as percent]			11%
Add for contingency assumed to have been included in sanction			10%
Contingency Required (mean amount to add to the base estimate)			21%

Table 11.4: Example Application of the Rand Cost Growth Model

This is the starting point for implementing your own model. We will describe new research learnings and other improvements later in this Chapter. However, I do recommend reading the Rand study report itself. You will find that while the above was the best-fit model, its variable terms are not as black and white as Table 11.4 might make them appear. (Later, when I describe implementation, I will elaborate on this point.)

Some specific observations of variations and interpretations of the model in the Rand report include the following:

PctNew: While the parameter is for "technology unproven in commercial use," other measures (such as new integrations of proven steps, use of new equipment, or newness of the technology to the company) were also correlated with growth; PCTNEW was just the strongest.

Impurity: While the extent of impurity buildup problems had the strongest correlation, corrosion problems were almost as significantly correlated, and these also relate to process pressure and temperature problems.

INCLUSIVENESS: The study report indicated that the three items in the measure are not unique but are likely proxies for inclusiveness (or treatment of exclusions) in general.

DEFINITION: The report indicates that its four key definitional elements represent the breadth of information, but other categories of items in a composite measure work almost as well.

Base Rand Model: Construction Schedule Duration Slip

Using the same database as for cost growth, Rand later examined construction schedule slip in 1986. Fewer drivers were significantly correlated with schedule duration than for cost growth and the model fit was not as good (R^2=0.65). As was discussed in Chapter 3, this is probably because trading of cost for schedule sometimes occurs – schedule achievement can be bought, so the connection of risk drivers to schedule is masked. Another way to say this is that risk impacts almost always cost money, but not always time.

The study looked at construction slip (the start of first foundations through mechanical completion) in absolute months for large projects. As with cost, the time impacts of strikes, severe weather, major regulatory changes, and so on (i.e., non-contingency items) were removed. However, the report notes that the impact of these types of risks was minimal in the study dataset. Again, it is likely that these risks impacts were somewhat mitigated by the projects, although at some cost.

The study's three statistically significant systemic risk drivers are summarized in Table 11.5.

RISK DRIVER	DESCRIPTION	RANGE OF VALUES
OVERLAP	Months of planned overlap (concurrency) between detailed engineering and construction (applied only if plant used technology unproven in commercial use)	Number of months
SOLIDS	Plant uses raw solid feedstock (e.g., mining, tars)	Yes (1) or No (0)
DEFINITION	The level of Scope Definition (See Cost Growth)	2 to 8; 8 is least defined

Table 11.5: Rand Construction Duration Slip Model - Risk Driver Variables

Table 11.6 displays the base construction schedule model in spreadsheet row and column format and includes the coefficients for each parameter as derived through MLR. To implement this in a spreadsheet, simply multiply the entered parameter values by the given coefficients, and then sum the results for each parameter (including the constant) to obtain the mean cost growth metric in months of slip duration terms.

RISK DRIVER	PARAMETER (*a*)	COEFFICIENT (*b*)	*a* x *b*
CONSTANT			−3.147
OVERLAP (only if new)	Months?	+0.419	product
SOLIDS	Yes (1) or No (0)?	+2.212	product
DEFINITION	2 to 8?	+0.969	product
TOTAL (SUM PRODUCTS)			Sum

Table 11.6: Rand Construction Slip Model in Spreadsheet Form

Table 11.7 is an example of a model run for a chemical plant project with some new technology, no solids feeds, eight months overlap between engineering and construction, and equivalent AACE Class 4 definition. At the bottom of the worksheet, the model's absolute months outcome is converted to a (more useful) percentage slip value.

RISK DRIVER	PARAMETER (*a*)	COEFFICIENT (*b*)	*a* x *b*
CONSTANT			−3.147
OVERLAP (only if new)	8	+0.419	+3.35
SOLIDS	No (0)	+2.212	0
DEFINITION	4	+0.969	+3.88
TOTAL (SUM PRODUCTS)			4.1
Construction Slip as % (convert to % by dividing by 18.4 months)			22%

Table 11.7: Example Application of Rand Construction Slip Model

The study reported that the schedule slip in months and as a percent of planned duration was closely related (correlation coefficient of 0.88) with a mean of 18.4 months planned construction duration. Based on this observation, you can reasonably express the outcome in percent slip terms (% Slip = model outcome in months/18.4 months). The percent can then be applied to large projects of different durations (this would not apply to small projects).

As with the cost growth model, while the above was the best-fit model, the Rand team found other variables that correlated with schedule slip. For example, the overlap was correlated with slip even for regular technology projects, especially those with overlap of eight months or more, but not as strongly as for projects with new technology. One could interpret this overlap as representing a fast track, accelerated, or at least schedule-driven strategy. Note that complexity also had some correlation with slip.

Also, while the study was focused on construction duration, it noted that this encompassed much of the detailed engineering duration as well. The study further reported a strong correlation of engineering and construction durations (correlation coefficient = 0.72). Therefore, it would seem to be a reasonable assumption that the schedule slip for construction, expressed as a percent of planned duration, will also apply to the slip for the execution phase (start of detailed engineering through mechanical completion).

Implementing Customized Parametric Models

If you lack your own robust historical database, the Rand models provide a realistic, credible starting point. However, in the thirty plus years since their publication, there has been considerable research and development (particularly by IPA and CII). This work identified new systemic risk drivers (e.g., team development), better measurements (e.g., scope definition ratings), and enhanced findings with respect to megaprojects and complexity. Also, full distributions need to be generated and added to the model outputs (the models as published only generate mean values). The remainder of this Chapter describes these enhancements and provides an updated set of parametric models for cost growth and execution schedule slip.

What has not changed much since the time of the Rand studies is the basic distribution of project outcomes. For example, the cost growth or accuracy ranges found by John Hackney and described in his 1965 book look much like the ranges found in my study of accuracy published in the AACE Cost Engineering Journal in 2012. Visualize the amount of cost growth as an impact pie; its size is fixed. Each piece of pie is the impact of a given risk. We always used to cut the pie into four impact pieces for four risks, but now we have a new fifth risk visitor and we have to share; those five impact pieces will be smaller.

For example, adding team development or project control maturity risk to the model does not add more risk or wider range, but gives us a better understanding of what the dominant definition driver was telling us in 1981 (e.g., adds an element of system strength or integrity to the original measures). In short, the enhanced models described in this Chapter improve the model fit, but do not change the mean cost growth and execution schedule slip outcomes much for a project with average attributes and practices.

Selecting a Scope Definition Rating

The first enhancement of Rand models has to do with the availability of new industry measures of the level of scope definition. There are now three metric schemes in regular use from IPA (FEL), CII (PDRI) and AACE (Class). These are described in some detail in Chapter 3. Table 11.8 is my key (my "Rosetta Stone") for approximately translating the current measures to the Rand measure.

Rating	Best Practical	<---- Better Definition							Worst
RAND	3	3.6	4.2	4.8	5.5	6.1	6.7	7.3	8
FEL	3.2	2.9	2.6	2.3	2	1.75	1.5	1.25	1
CLASS	3	3.25	3.5	3.75	4	4.25	4.5	4.75	5
PDRI	300	350	410	480	560	670	790	920	1000

Table 11.8: Definition Rating Translation Matrix

The "Best Practical" level is the point at which additional definition no longer causes significant reduction in systemic risk impacts (i.e., the point of diminishing returns and the point at which projects can be sanctioned with confidence). The absolute best scores imply that detailed engineering is complete, which is too late in scope development to be relevant to investment decision making. Some other notes with respect to Table 11.8 include:

♦ As discussed in Chapter 3, the Class and FEL metrics were designed as threshold measures to define distinct gate expectations. They are not continuous (i.e., there is no such thing as the Class 3.5 in the AACE RPs). However, you can treat them as continuous for risk quantification purposes.

♦ The relationship of CII's Industrial PDRI to AACE Class and IPA FEL are non-linear.[3]

♦ The CII PDRI Industrial report suggests a score of 200 as desirable as a funding basis. My experience is that an impartial PDRI score of 300 is a more reasonable best practical at sanction (teams overrate their PDRI level as was described earlier with respect to "class-creep").

---

3 Zaheer, S. and C. Fallows, "Document Project Readiness by Estimate Class Using PDRI," AACE Transactions, 2011.

Updating the Rand Models

The 1981 Rand model included scope definition, process measures (technology, complexity, and severity), and estimate inclusiveness. It is a parsimonious systemic risk model in keeping with the Occam's razor principle, but perhaps too simple. The Rand elements focused on technological and physical attributes of the defined project system. Later empirical research identified other systemic elements correlated with better cost and schedule outcomes. Most of these were related to project system organizational and methodological capability. In the following sections, I will discuss key empirical studies and summarize the best practices that were identified.

Keep in mind that each study's reported benefits cannot simply be added to the 1981 Rand findings. There is no single publicly available MLR-based study that includes all the risk drivers in a way that addresses correlation (e.g., projects with strong controls and strong team development). However, we *can* use these learnings to develop an enhanced Rand model with the expectation that these new practices better explain the original Rand parameters. We also need to keep simplicity in mind. For example, the CII PDRI Industrial rating has 70 elements and, as with Hackney's 117 elements, there is limited empirical evidence as to which elements are significant.

The following are summaries of the additional reliable research findings on system practices or elements (i.e., if not done well, they are systemic risks) for consideration in updated models. I have grouped them into several system elements:

♦ Project Control
♦ Project Execution Planning and Schedule
♦ Team Development, and
♦ New Data (this is not about practices, but updated cost growth data).

Project Control

A paper I authored in 2002 presented research by IPA, Inc. on best owner control practices.[4] This controlled empirical study identified the following practices with statistically significant correlation with better project cost and/or schedule outcomes:

---

4   Hollmann, John, "Best Owner Practices for Project Control," AACE Transactions, 2002.

- The owner has in-house cost estimating and validation competency,
- Estimating is free of undue bias,
- An owner control lead is assigned to teams,
- Physical progressing is used,
- Reporting is frequent (more often than monthly) and in detail, and
- History is captured and used in front-end planning (i.e., empiricism).

These practices do not define the sum total of best practice; they are proxies for strong capability in general. The last bullet is critical – if a company has strong historical data capability, it usually has strong control capabilities across the board. Another key point is that monthly reports add no value; monthly reporting is too late to make any difference.

In addition, CII research on its development of the Project Definition Rating Index (PDRI) included project control practices.[5] PDRI elements were added based on input from the study participants; i.e., individual practices were not studied statistically although bottom line results (PDRI correlation with cost growth) were.

Project Execution Planning and Scheduling

A 2005 paper by Dr. Andrew Griffith addressed best *planning and scheduling* practices based on IPA's empirical database.[6] That study reported the following scheduling practices as being correlated with better project outcomes:

- Integrate all project phases into a single project schedule,
- Apply Critical Path Method (CPM) techniques,
- Resource load *critical* (not necessarily all) resources into the CPM schedule, and
- Hold project team reviews of the schedule.

Again, these practices do not define the sum total of best practice. For example, resource loading just to create a man-loading chart is not the point; success comes from using the resource information

---

5   CII, *Project Definition Rating Index-Industrial*, 2008.

6   Griffith, Andrew, "Scheduling Practices and Project Success," AACE Transactions, 2005.

to improve the schedule. Only 13% of the hundreds of schedules studied had these four elements.

In addition, as with project control, CII research on its development of the PDRI included planning and scheduling practices. Another CII sponsored study reported the following *project execution planning* practices as being important to project success:[7]

♦ Pre-project planning,
♦ Project change management,
♦ Design/information technology, and
♦ Team building.

Team Development

Everyone seems to recognize the importance of strong teams to project success. Studies by IPA and CII have confirmed that. In Edward Merrow's text (IPA) on Industrial Megaprojects, the following team attributes were reported to be correlated with better outcomes:[8]

♦ Clarity of business objectives,
♦ All needed functions on the team,
♦ Roles and responsibilities defined,
♦ Common work processes,
♦ Business sponsor involvement,
♦ Stakeholder management,
♦ Leadership, and
♦ Continuity (low turnover).

Again, CII's PDRI study includes many of these elements. The CII report by Lee mentioned previously also identified team building as important. A thesis by Williams using CII data covered team building as well (i.e., approaches to bring the team together and promote positive relationships).[9]

New Data

It was mentioned earlier that the project cost growth "pie" was not growing – cost growth is about the same now as it was 50 years

---

7   Lee, et. al, "The Relative Impacts of Selected Practices on Project Cost and Schedule," Construction Management and Economics, 2005.

8   Merrow, Edward, *Industrial Megaprojects*, Wiley, 2011.

9   Williams, T., "Use of Team Building on Construction Projects to Reduce Cost Growth and Schedule Growth," Virginia Tech Thesis, September 1998.

ago (and unfortunately, so are the outcomes of our risk quantification). Several recent studies confirm this. A meta-analysis (statistics on findings by others, excluding IPA) I conducted showed that cost growth outcomes have not changed.[10]

A paper by IPA at the same time, based on their high quality database, confirmed that accuracy has been resistant to improvement.[11] The IPA study went further and showed how estimate accuracy does improve phase-to-phase, confirming the primacy of the level of scope definition to risk quantification (and begging the question as to why companies still seem to treat phase-gate processes cavalierly). It also included distribution diagrams that displayed bimodality, which will be discussed further in Chapter 14.

Updated Model Adjustments

In addition to the systemic risk driver studies above, there have been additional refinements identified that might be termed "data housekeeping" or "adjustments." Most industry empirical studies suffer from not knowing the quality or content of the base estimate and schedule, which is the starting point for risk quantification. For example, the "estimate" in Rand's cost growth metric was the funded amount because the data was not complete enough to identify what contingency and reserves (or profit for contractors) were included in the budget so they could be taken out. The same was true for schedule, which may or may not have included buffers and sometimes had fuzzily defined beginning and/or completion milestones.

However, when we quantify risks, we have the benefit of knowing the quality and content of our own estimates and schedules. We can adjust for attributes that we know relate to cost and schedule uncertainty. Table 11.9 discusses the adjustments we can objectively make to any systemic risk model.

---

10 Hollmann, J., "Estimate Accuracy: Dealing with Reality," Cost Engineering Journal, AACE International, Nov/Dec 2012.

11 Ogilvie, A., et al., "Quantifying Estimate Accuracy and Precision for the Process Industries: A Review of Industry Data," Cost Engineering Journal, AACE International, Nov/Dec 2012.

Attribute	Adjustments
Reference to the Base Estimate	IPA (Merrow) reports that budgets include 9% contingency with a standard deviation of 4%. This translates to about 5% for Class 3, 10% for Class 4, and 15% for Class 5. These adjustments can be added to the Rand cost growth outcome to make it reflect cost growth from the base estimate.
Reference to the Base Schedule	The 1986 Rand study focused on the construction phase, and its slip model was in absolute terms (months). However, the study indicated that conversion to percentage slip for the execution phase was reasonable.
Estimate Bias	Research (contingency = standard deviation of cost growth distribution) and my experience indicate that the base estimate for large projects is about $p15$–$p20$ (i.e., 20% chance of under-running the base). Any more aggressive or conservative bias than this (as determined through validation) must be added or subtracted respectively from contingency predictions (e.g., small projects have a conservative bias). See "Fixed Price," which is a manifestation of bias in the bid.
Schedule Bias	Typical schedule duration estimates are designed to be "realistic" (de facto $p50$) relative to the scheduler's experience or database. Any more aggressive or conservative bias than this (as determined through validation) must be added or subtracted respectively from contingency predictions.
Equipment Content	Research indicates that estimates for major process equipment or machinery of a given capacity tend to be relatively accurate (as compared to bulk materials or labor), even at early scope definition phases. The typical large process plant project in industry studies includes about 20% equipment. Contingency predictions can be adjusted for more or less than this percent (i.e., assume equipment has half the uncertainty of other items).
Fixed Price	Project Control research (Hollmann) found that EPC lump sum projects had less cost growth than reimbursable because the base estimate (the lump sum) was biased upward to cover the contractor's risk. The research indicated that the portion of a base estimate that represents a firm, fixed price quote can be assumed to be "conservative" and requires 10% less contingency.

Table 11.9: Adjustments to Models for Known Estimate and Schedule Attributes

Adjusted Rand Model: Cost Growth

Tables 11.10 and 11.11 show a suggested practical and realistic parametric model for systemic risk quantification of cost growth (actual/base estimate). It is my greatest hope for this text that this or similar models will find their way into industry mainstream risk quantification practice. The tables were designed to facilitate transferring the model into spreadsheets for application.

Risk Driver	Enter Parameter (*a*)	Coefficient (*b*)	*a x b*
Constant			−30.5
Scope	3 to 5		
Planning	3 to 5		
Engineering	3 to 5		
Scope Definition	Average of Above	9.8	product
New Technology	0 to 100?	0.12	product
Process Severity	0 to 10?	1.0	product
Complexity	0 to 10?	1.2	product
TOTAL (sum the products); Result is the Mean of Actual/Base Estimate			Sum

Table 11.10: Base Cost Growth Model in Spreadsheet Form

This approach is not MLR-based other than being built on the Rand studies. It starts with the 1981 Rand results, but includes my allowances for later research findings (the adjustments are my interpretation of the various piecemeal studies).

Adjustments (Add or Subtract Percentages from the Base)					
Team Development	*Best*	*Good*	*Fair*	*Poor*	*Deficient*
w/Typical Strategy	−2	−1	0	+3	+6
w/Complex Strategy	−2	0	+3	+6	+9
Project Control	*Best*	*Good*	*Fair*	*Poor*	*Deficient*
w/Typical Strategy	−2	−1	0	+3	+6
w/Complex Strategy	−2	0	+3	+6	+9
Estimate Basis	*Best*	*Good*	*Fair*	*Poor*	*Deficient*
	−2	−1	0	+3	+6
Equipment	*Major process and electrical equipment only*				
percent of total base $	>40%	30-40%	20-30%	10-20%	<10%
adjustment	−4	−2	0	+2	+4
Fixed Price (non-equipment)	*Only if sanction is planned prior to expiration of the agreed price*				
percent of non-equip $	>40%	30-40%	20-30%	10-20%	<10%
adjustment	−4	−3	−2	−1	0
Estimate Bias	*See Distribution: Bias shifts the distribution*				

Table 11.11: Adjustments to Base Cost Growth Model

The mean outcomes (and distributions suggested in the next section) were checked against and are consistent with industry empirical studies of overall outcomes. However, users must confirm that the results are consistent with their own experience (these numbers should be used as starting points for your own analysis). These models are based on process industry research and data.

For those in other industries refer to Chapter 15, which contains an assessment that indicates that the model is applicable to any industry projects involving engineering and construction. See the "Applying the Parametric Model" section for an example of how to interpret and apply the ratings and adjustments.

Adjusted Rand Model: Execution Schedule Slip

Tables 11.12 and 11.13 show a suggested practical and realistic parametric model for systemic risk quantification of execution schedule slip (expressed as actual/base duration). The execution phase for process projects is from the start of detailed engineering (usually sanction if done using best practices) to mechanical completion. This model is not MLR-based other than being built on the Rand study.

It starts with the 1986 Rand results; however, the allowances for later research findings and adjustments are my interpretation of the various piecemeal studies. The mean outcomes (and distributions suggested in the next section) were checked against and are consistent with industry empirical studies of overall outcomes. However, users must confirm that the results are consistent with their own experience. See the "Applying the Parametric Model" section for an example of how to interpret and apply the ratings and adjustments.

RISK DRIVER	PARAMETER (*a*)	COEFFICIENT (*b*)	*a* × *b*
CONSTANT			−23.5
SCOPE	3 to 5		
PLANNING	3 to 5		
ENGINEERING	3 to 5		
SCOPE DEFINITION	Average of Above	9.6	product
NEW TECHNOLOGY	0 to 100?	0.10	product
PROCESS SEVERITY	0 to 10?	0.50	product
COMPLEXITY	0 to 10?	0.50	product
TOTAL (sum the products); Result is the Mean of Actual/Base Estimate			Sum

Table 11.12: Base Execution Schedule Slip Model in Spreadsheet Form

ADJUSTMENTS (ADD OR SUBTRACT PERCENTAGES FROM THE BASE)					
SCHEDULE BASIS	*Best*	*Good*	*Fair*	*Poor*	*Deficient*
	–2	–1	0	+2	+4
SCHEDULE BIAS	*See Distribution: Bias shifts the distribution*				

Table 11.13: Adjustments to Base Execution Schedule Slip Model

Deriving Distributions from the Base Output

The prior tables result in *mean* systemic contingency values and assume that the base estimate has typical bias (only between 20% and 30% of projects underrun the base cost or duration). Table 11.14 and Table 11.15 provide a method to derive an approximate distribution from the mean contingency value. The distribution is defined by probability (confidence) levels that the actual outcome will be less than the base estimate.

BASE DISTRIBUTION (TYPICAL BIAS)						
	MULTIPLIER OF BASE					
PROBABIL-ITY OF UNDERRUN	COST				EXECUTION SCHEDULE	
	For Mean % Growth				For Mean % Slip	
	>12.5%	7.5% to 12.5%	5% to 7.5%	2% to 5%	>10%	0 to 10%
10%	-0.47	-0.9	-1.69	-2.59	-0.18	-0.42
20%	-0.06	-0.33	-0.88	-1.51	0.15	0.01
30%	0.26	0.09	-0.28	-0.71	0.41	0.33
40%	0.56	0.46	0.25	-0.01	0.65	0.61
50%	0.85	0.82	0.75	0.66	0.88	0.87
60%	1.16	1.19	1.26	1.35	1.14	1.14
70%	1.51	1.70	1.82	2.09	1.43	1.43
80%	1.95	2.30	2.49	2.98	1.77	1.77
90%	2.62	3.20	3.46	4.26	2.26	2.26

Table 11.14: Multipliers of the Mean Cost Growth or Execution Schedule Slip

Table 11.14 provides multipliers of the mean cost growth or execution schedule slip. As the mean changes, so will the width of the spread.

Table 11.15 is an adjustment to the distribution for base estimate bias. As adders, the bias adjustment shifts all values of the distribution up or down while retaining the same absolute spread or bandwidth. Note that schedule slip uncertainty (spread) is less than for cost growth.

DISTRIBUTION ADJUSTMENT FOR BIAS		
Where in the Benchmark Range?	Add at Each Level	
	COST	EXECUTION SCHEDULE
VERY HIGH	−10	−5
HIGH	−5	−2
TYPICAL	0	0
LOW	+5	+3
VERY LOW	+10	+6

Table 11.15: Bias Adjustment Table for Cost Growth and Schedule Slip Distributions

These tables are based on models used by the author that generate lognormal estimates that are reasonably consistent with the referenced empirical research. Observe that the mean values (1.0 multipliers) are not the *p*50s. This is because the distribution is somewhat skewed to the high side, which shifts the mean to something more than *p*50. Also note that as the mean values of cost growth or schedule slip approach zero, the multipliers increase. Compare the model's outcomes with the study results shared in Chapter 3. The cost outcomes *exclude* blowouts (which will be covered in the methods of Chapter 14). A few blowouts in a sample will stretch the high range further to the right (as noted in some research studies; see Chapter 15). Again, users must confirm that the results are consistent with their own experience (these numbers should be used as starting points for your own analysis).

The following example shows how a mean contingency and multipliers are used to obtain *p*-values for estimates with typical bias. The first example derives initial *p*-values and the second example adjusts them for bias.

Example

The following example shows how a mean contingency (i.e., cost growth) and multipliers are used to obtain *p*-values for estimates with typical bias. The first example derives initial *p*-values and the second example adjusts them for bias.

Initial P-Values: For mean systemic cost contingency = 20%, the range (rounded) is calculated using the multipliers in Table 11.14 as follows:

♦ *p*10 would be −9% (20% x −0.47)
♦ *p*90 would be +52% (20% x 2.62)

Bias Example: Reviewer finds that the base estimate is "very high" relative to expectations (as is common for small project estimates). From Table 11.15, the adjustment = −10% (an over-estimated base requires less contingency):

It Is Personal

There are many numbers in this chapter, but don't think that historical data analysis and parametric modeling are "all about the math." One modeling task is very personal, and in one case I recall, very emotional. That task is obtaining the raw information from the experts who have it. Parametric models are driven by the inputs – the attributes, designs, and quantities that make up a capital asset. Useful information about these inputs is rarely in company databases (unless you design the database yourself – see Chapter 18). It is hidden in the drawers, boxes, personal files, and minds of those who designed, planned, and managed the projects.

When you spend several years on a single project, you learn a lot, but at the end of the project, usually nobody is interested in what you learned. It is an empty feeling when you are told the company policy is to shred and erase all your recorded knowledge by next Tuesday. So people don't; they keep it. Later, they refer to it occasionally as a "go-by," but not being modelers, they don't have a better way to leverage what they learned or to share it with others (especially if they are not supposed to have kept it).

This is where the modeler steps in. I recall at Eastman Kodak I conceptualized an estimating model of their complex film making machines. The business, which had to evaluate all kinds of machine concepts, thought it was a great idea, but had no useful database. So they said, go talk to Bob (name changed) to see if he has any ideas, so I did.

Bob told me that he had been with the company 40 years. He had worked on dozens of projects over that time, many as lead engineer or project manager. He had helped create many of Kodak's main manufacturing assets. He was obviously very proud of them. When I told him that I was looking for data and explained the parametric model concept, his look of joy was intense. He jumped up and said, "Well, let me show you something." For the next month, Bob and I gleefully mined his treasure. Designs, quantities, cost reports, and schedules were all neatly organized and analyzed. He told me how happy he was that his life work would be of use. He retired shortly after that and I like to think he left a little happier than he would have otherwise.

This was not the only such situation I experienced. Over the years I have been fortunate to work with a number of such experts and the treasure troves they had in their basements and garages. In short, don't think the analysis and modeling path is a lonely one – it can be rewarding in surprising ways.

- ♦ Mean systemic cost contingency = 20% (from above) –10% = 10%
- ♦ *p*10 would be –9% –10% = –19%
- ♦ *p*90 would be +52% –10% = +42%

More specific and objective bias adjustments could be developed and applied if best practice validation and/or benchmarking information is available. These base and bias ranges are considered typical for most process industry companies where there is no significant strategic misrepresentation, corruption, gross negligence, or other egregious violations of professional practice and ethics. See Chapter 15 for more information about other industries and outlier situations.

Calibrating the Output

The simplified models above represent typical large process industry projects and project systems without allowance for escalation or blowouts (i.e., orderly projects). As was discussed, company accounting practices (e.g., consistency in capitalization, FID timing) can result in more or less uncertainty. Also, while the base models are considered to be largely self-correcting for differences in scope technology and complexity (e.g., pipeline projects may have less uncertainty than specialty chemical plant projects, but they are also usually less complex), a company may have assets of unique scope or that require unusual project execution practices that additionally affect uncertainty.

For this reason, each company should collect its own cost, schedule, and risk history and use the data to calibrate risk quantification models and to spot trends over time (i.e., conduct process assurance). In addition, benchmarking with peer companies can help spot whether one's practices are competitive. Chapter 18 provides more information on developing historically based metrics for calibration. Chapter 15 provides more information on accuracy in various industries.

Case Example of Model Implementation

Consider an example of how to use the approach described above. A company's current situation is as follows:

♦ The project is a moderately complex chemical plant with five block steps, about 5% new technology, and some moderate corrosion issues.

♦ The schedule has reached Class 3 definition in engineering, but some planning deliverables are still in progress. Planning is a bit rushed to get ready for a FID Board meeting in 3 weeks.

♦ About 15% of its capital costs are for major equipment (lots of piping) and prices are based on budget quotes.

♦ The company's project system was initiated the prior year and is relatively immature with in-house organizational development underway. The owner's project control department is focused primarily on cost accounting and cash flow (highly dependent on contractors).

♦ The estimate and schedule were reviewed by consultants who reported reasonable deliverable and practice quality (with a few exceptions), but with aggressive assumptions for unit hours, indirect costs, and construction duration.

♦ The company policy is to fund projects at a *p70* confidence level, and allow for schedule contingency at the *p50* level.

Based on the case situation, the model parameters were rated and entered into the base cost and schedule spreadsheets as shown in Tables 11.16 and 11.17.

Risk Driver	Enter Parameter (*a*)	Coefficient (*b*)	*a* x *b*
Constant			−30.5
Scope	3		
Planning	4		
Engineering	3		
Scope Definition	3.3	9.8	32.3
New Technology	5%	0.12	0.60
Process Severity	3	1.0	3.0
Complexity	5	1.2	6.0
Subtotal Base (prior to adjustments)			**11.4**
Adjustments			
Team Development	Poor	(assume complex)	+6
Project Control	Poor	(assume complex)	+6
Estimate Basis	Fair		0
Equipment	15%		+2
Fixed Price	<10%		0
Total Base (prior to basis adjustment; rounded to whole number)			**25**
Bias	Low		+5
Systemic Cost Contingency			
Mean	25 + 5		**30%**
*p*10	25 x (−0.5) + 5		**−7%**
*p*70 (indicated funding)	25 x 1.5 + 5		**43%**
*p*90	25 x 2.6 + 5		**72%**

Table 11.16: Case Example Parametric Model Applications for Cost Growth (incorporate this as the impact of systemic risk in the expected value model)

RISK DRIVER	PARAMETER (*a*)	COEFFICIENT (*b*)	*a* x *b*
CONSTANT			−23.5
SCOPE DEFINITION	Average 3.3	9.6	31.7
NEW TECHNOLOGY	5%	0.10	0.5
PROCESS SEVERITY	3	0.50	1.5
COMPLEXITY	5	0.50	2.5
Subtotal Base (prior to adjustments)			**12.7**
ADJUSTMENTS			
Schedule Basis	Fair		0
TOTAL BASE (prior to bias adjustment; rounded to whole number)			**13**
Bias	Low		+3
SYSTEMIC EXECUTION *SCHEDULE DURATION* CONTINGENCY			
Mean	13 + 3		**16%**
p10	13 x (−0.2) + 3		**0%**
p50 completion	13 x 0.9 + 3		**15%**
p90	13 x 2.3 + 3		**33%**

Table 11.17: Case Example Parametric Model Applications for Schedule Slip (incorporate this as the impact of systemic risk in the expected value model)

Applying the Parametric Models

The case above illustrates that once the model is implemented in a spreadsheet, the application effort consists mainly of entering the parameter values. Experienced spreadsheet developers can improve this model using drop-down lists (i.e., pick from a list of ratings as opposed to entering rating values), providing guidance notations in the tool, and so forth. Outputs can be tabular and graphical as desired. The main challenge in application is not the tool, but the elicitation of information from the project stakeholders and team, and deciding on the parameter rating values. Some parameters are more subjective than others. Once the systemic risks are quantified, the outputs of this method are carried over to the Expected Value tool with MCS as covered in Chapter 12.

Eliciting Systemic Risk Rating Information

This Section discusses guidelines for:

♦ Eliciting risk rating information, and
♦ Quantifying or rating the parameters in the cost growth and schedule models (the intent is to expand on what was presented earlier and to gather the information into a useful reference format).

A fully enabled risk quantification system or tool will strive to reduce the subjectivity of and bias in the ratings. In particular, the scope definition ratings should be based on a comprehensive company phase-gate system with fully defined definition levels using or referring to the company's terminology, systems, tools, and procedures.

Facilitator/Risk Analyst

Unlike traditional risk identification workshops, systemic risk analysis focuses not on impersonal and technical risk conditions and events, but on how organizations are being managed (the system). This can be a very sensitive topic if that management falls short of excellence. Therefore, the analyst must be an experienced person with excellent communication skills who is comfortable speaking with senior managers about difficult topics and issues. A challenge is understanding what is not always stated because managers will often be in "sell" mode (they may also be prepping for a coming FID Board meeting). This is not a "check-the-box" practice, nor is it appropriate to allow the managers and teams to make self-ratings. The analyst must have some degree of independence (assurance that career is not affected by making tough rating judgments).

Information Needs and Sources

Business and program sponsors and project managers need to provide input on:

◆ Business ownership,
◆ Team development,
◆ Project general scope, and
◆ Cost and Schedule Strategy.

The project manager(s) and team leaders (engineering, procurement, contracts, construction, operations, and project controls) need to provide input on:

◆ Project planning,
◆ Project control, and
◆ Execution complexity.

The project manager(s), the engineering manager, and the R&D manager (if applicable) need to provide input on:

◆ Engineering definition,
◆ Process technology, and
◆ Complexity.

Finally, the project manager(s), project control manager, and estimating and scheduling leads need to provide input on:

♦ Estimate and schedule basis, and
♦ Bias.

If possible, bias determination should be supported by off-line validation and/or benchmarking studies. Also, any benchmarking and performance audit reports by others should be reviewed for insights.

Venue

Systemic risk information is best elicited in small group interviews between the analyst and the information providers noted above. This is because of the sensitivity of the information (particularly in regards to business ownership/team development) and difficulty of getting senior people in one room for more than an hour or two. For a program, each sub-project may require separate interview sessions.

Timing

This work should precede project-specific risk elicitation workshops. Assure that there is time to resolve conflicts prior to any decision that is to be based on the risk analysis. Systemic deficiencies are generally not amenable to quick resolution, so this is best aligned with the capital management organization's continuous improvement program or equivalent. Each interview with the subgroups above may be an hour or two. On a single project, these can all be done in one day.

Agenda

Each interview starts with introductions and review of the purpose and objectives. Each group will review their general scope and status of their respective topics. The analyst then takes the lead to probe into the specific rating issues. Avoid snap judgments on difficult ratings. While impressions may be shared in the meeting, do not report results until all the input has been given some thought off-line.

Actions / Follow-up

Each interview should conclude by summarizing open questions and issues with actions to close them. As most of these risks are weaknesses in general company organization and practices, the actions should preferably extend to long-term improvement efforts at a general level.

Systemic Risk Parameter Rating Guidelines

1. *Scope Definition*, AACE Class 3 to 5 (see conversions from FEL or PDRI, Table 11.8). This is the average of scope, planning, and engineering deliverable definition completeness and quality status ratings. The applicable reference is *AACE International Classification Recommended Practices* (e.g., RP 18R-97 for process plants).

2. *Process Technology*, 0 to 100% of capital cost. This is the percent of total capital project cost associated with units employing technology unproven in commercial use, significant new integrations of proven steps, and/or first of a kind or scale in use of equipment. Cost includes allowance for EPC of the block area with the subject technology. If R&D and/or process engineering has significant concerns, this is the rating to capture that.

3. *Process Severity*, 0 to 10 relative ranking:
   ♦ 0 = No concerns with impurities, corrosion, temperatures, pressures, or other process conditions,
   ♦ 5 = Moderate concerns resolvable with significant impact, and
   ♦ 10 = Major concerns with major impacts; not certain of resolvability with selected technology.

4. *Process and Execution Complexity*, 0 to 10 relative ranking:
   ♦ 0 = No continuous process steps (e.g., infrastructure) and simple execution strategy,
   ♦ 5 = Count of continuous steps with simple execution strategy, or lesser count w/moderate strategy complexity, and
   ♦ 10 = 10 or more continuous process steps or lesser count with very complex execution strategy and organization

5. *Team Development*: "Good" is the industry norm. A "Best" rating includes:
   ♦ Business sponsor engagement,
   ♦ Clear and well-communicated business and project objectives (including cost and schedule trade-off and risk policy),

- All needed functions are on the team,
- Well defined roles and responsibilities,
- Common, reliable project system and work processes,
- Robust stakeholder management,
- Strong, evident leadership with team building practices,
- Experience and competency in all key roles, and
- Organizational continuity.

Note that the Team Development is usually no better than the lowest of Estimate and Schedule Basis ratings. For Team Development and items six, seven, and eight below, a "Deficient" rating reflects gaps in most or all areas and a "Good" rating reflects *some* gaps relative to "Best."

6. *Project Control*: "Good" is the industry norm. A "Best" rating includes:
   - Well documented and followed owner control strategy and requirements,
   - Full Execution Strategy and integrated Project Control Plan including all functions,
   - Reliable, proven, and integrated cost, schedule, physical progressing and reporting systems, and earned value methods,
   - Weekly reporting,
   - Disciplined Change Management integrated with Risk Management,
   - Budget aligned with WBS and supported by quality estimate and schedule, and
   - Experienced owner and contractor control leads.

Like Team Development, Project Control is usually no better than the lowest of Estimate and Schedule Basis ratings.

7. *Estimate Basis*: "Good" is the industry norm. A "Best" rating includes:
   - Well documented and followed owner cost strategy and requirements,
   - Full execution strategy,
   - Excellent Basis of Estimate document,
   - Fully applicable and historically validated reference data (owner has historical database),
   - Reliable, proven methods,

- Full studies of rates, markups, and allowances for specific conditions,
- Well-planned and timely, stepped preparation with WBS integrated with schedule and documented code of accounts,
- Quantifications confirmed in all areas,
- Documented quality review with all values traceable, and
- Experienced estimators in all areas.

8. *Schedule Basis*: "Good" is the industry norm. A "Best" rating includes:

- Well documented and followed owner schedule strategy and requirements,
- Excellent Basis of Schedule document,
- Full execution strategy,
- Fully applicable and historically validated reference data (owner has historical database),
- Reliable, proven methods (CPM),
- Full studies of allowances for specific conditions,
- Well-planned and timely, stepped preparation with WBS integrated with estimate,
- Resource loading of critical resources,
- Schedule addresses all phases in a balanced way,
- Documented quality review with CPM diagnostics,
- Experienced team supported planning facilitated by experienced planner and implemented by experienced scheduler.

Bias and team development ratings are particularly subject to the bias of the analyst or the manager and/or team influencing the analyst. Self-rating by individuals or teams who have a personal stake in proceeding with the project is inherently a suspect process. Cost and schedule bias ratings should be based on a robust validation process using historically-based metrics, and/or independent check estimates. In all cases, no tool can replace the competency and judgment of the subject matter experts and risk analysts necessary to apply these methods.

Early Definition and Start-up Systemic Risks

The book so far has focused on the capitalized costs and the execution phase schedule of a process industry project. However, capitalized cost usually includes spending from the time a single project alternative is selected for Front-End Engineering and Design (FEED), (usually at the FEL 2/Select gate) through the point that stable operation is achieved and operations has full control of the asset (less standard costs of operating the plant during startup such as consumed feedstocks). The execution schedule extends from the time of sanction (usually the FEL 3/Define gate) through mechanical completion excluding start-up. Therefore, the cost and cost growth exclude scope definition during the FEL 1/Assess and FEL 2/Select phases (up to the FEL 2 gate) and costs to transition the asset from steady state operations to achieving the project's operational goals. Similarly, the execution duration excludes the FEL 1, 2, and 3 phases and all start-up.

The main reason that these costs and durations have been excluded is that these phases are not "projects" per se. They do not have clearly defined scopes and clearly defined beginning and end dates. In industry practice, there is high variability in cost and schedule duration of these phases (as described below). However, for start-up, a simple set of risk models is provided to at least frame the issue.

Early Definition

As noted above, this refers to the FEL 1/Assess and FEL 2/Select phases prior to the start of formal FEED. For large projects, these phases may go on for years as the business studies and recycles various concepts and alternatives as the market and the company's strategies change. Even after an alternative is selected and FEED is funded, FEED duration can take a relatively long time with relatively minor cost impact (assuming any early commitments allow for cancellation). For example, for large projects, the sanction or FID gate is often delayed for months or even years (during which the design work is suspended and the engineers are demobilized) while the business closes negotiations with various stakeholders, regulators, and financiers as to details of the deal. If the economy is weakening, this also often adds to the delay. Post-FID, once a significant amount of money is being spent and contracts are issued, the emphasis shifts to getting the work done expeditiously.

In short, for the early phases the expensed cost is relatively small and the duration is highly variable. It is not until after a single alternative is selected that cost risk models start to make sense (correlation from project to project) and after the FID gate that schedule risk models add value. Therefore, I have not provided any models for early definitional phase risk quantification.

Start-up: Background

Start-up follows mechanical completion with the introduction of feedstock and ends with attaining reasonably stable operation. For some companies or projects it may end later, such as when a certain product quality and/or percent of nameplate capacity are attained (accounting differences are a major problem with studying start-up costs).

Usually, the owner's operations staff manages the work after mechanical completion with limited assistance from the contractor. In process plants, getting process control systems (which are integrated with electrical systems) physically checked out (e.g., calibration, loop checks) and modifying the control software to optimize safe operations are late activities that take place during start-up. Operations may have a devilish time getting the control system to function correctly, which adds delay. Control problems can also lead to damage. I recall a case where a polymer hardened in a reactor because of incorrect temperature control set-points and the vessel had to be replaced at significant cost and time delay. For revamp projects, the plant engineers are often the only ones who really know how the software works, which can create a resource constraint. The operations people may or may not charge their time to the project (they charge to operations expense as usual); that is another source of estimating uncertainty.

Detailed start-up planning is usually done during the project's execution phase (at the FEL 3/Define gate the start-up plans are preliminary). Start-up plans by nature almost always assume that things will go well for all systems and units in the plant and as such the planned time to get to stable operations is usually limited to several weeks up to a few (three or four) months. During start-up, limited construction resources need to be available and the startup costs, less typical operating costs, are usually capitalized. If all goes well, as is typically assumed, start-up may only cost about one or two percent of the total project cost.

However, start-up, particularly for projects that are complex, have new technology, and/or have solid or problematic feeds, are particularly prone to significant uncertainties that make risk quantification difficult. For example, for new technology projects, actual start-up cost and duration may be ten times the optimistic base estimates for start-up. Compare that to the execution phase where the worst-case outcomes are perhaps twice the base cost estimate for execution.

The startup challenges start with simply achieving stable operation in the first place (but finance will want to close the books on the capital, stable production or not). Once stable, many plants struggle to achieve their nameplate capacity and/or product quality. The struggle to attain 80 or 90% nameplate capacity may go on for months or even years. Statistically speaking, the time to get to full capacity is unbounded as it transitions into the asset's operational life.

In some cases, the business may discover process or equipment technology or design deficiencies during start-up that trigger initiation of a new capital project to "debottleneck" or to fix the operability constraint. In short, the historical cost and schedule data on start-up is highly uncertain due to both accounting (when are the capital books closed?) and operational outcome (when does it end?) considerations. However, *risk quantification for start-up is possible*. Since we plan it and profitability depends on revenue starting, we owe the business some understanding of its cost and schedule risks.

For the start-up phase, the 1986 Rand study by Myers, et al. provides a very good summary of the situation and references several past studies.[12] The Rand study's focus was on developing (1) a start-up duration estimating model in months, and (2) a start-up cost estimating model. The study was not focused on cost growth and schedule slip *per se* because that requires industry to have reasonable base start-up estimates to begin with which, as the study states, is *not* a good assumption. To quote the study, "Estimates of start-up time and cost are exceptionally varied... and usually extremely optimistic... In part this stems from a lack of attention paid to this phase."

Therefore, for this book, we will assume the readers are using start-up base estimating and schedule practices that align with the 1986 Rand model benchmark and appropriately allow for process complexity and technology. In that case, we can use the 1986 study's statistics from its MLR analysis to derive risk quantification guidelines, if not a model.

12 Myers, C. W. et al., *Understanding Process Plant Schedule Slippage and Startup Costs*, Publication R-3215-PSSP/RC, Rand, 1986.

Start-up Systemic Risk Quantification Guideline

A key observation of the 1986 Rand study was that both the start-up duration and cost were driven by operational problems that arose. These in turn were driven by process complexity and technology issues. The 1986 study then is tied back to the 1981 Rand study, which covered these operational shortfalls. Without repeating the various Rand models here, the main risk drivers for both start-up cost and duration included:

♦ Level of *new technology* in the process, and
♦ The *severity* of process conditions, particularly with raw solids in the feeds.

As discussed for the Rand model for execution phase costs, these variables are proxies. While *solid feeds* correlated strongly with worse outcomes, other problematic feeds or recycled products (e.g., our sensitive polymer case) are also risk drivers.

If your base start-up cost and duration estimating methods address the process technology and complexity issues above, then the Rand regression analyses indicate that the distribution of start-up cost and schedule outcomes in Table 11.18 should apply. This distribution was derived using the Rand dataset means and their regression standard errors of prediction to generate a normal distribution. The Table assumes that the base estimating and scheduling bias puts your estimates at about the $p30$ level of actual outcomes.

Probability of Underrun	Multiplier of Base Start-up Cost or Duration
10%	0.30
20%	0.70
30%	1.00
40%	1.25
50%	1.50
60%	1.75
70%	2.00
80%	2.30
90%	2.70

Table 11.18: Start-up Cost and Duration Range

The following provides an example of how to apply Table 11.18:

Base estimate of start-up cost = 5% of CAPEX (a process plant with some new technology; for example, $5M of $100M CAPEX)

- The $p10$ confidence level would be 1.5% of CAPEX (5% x 0.30),
- The $p90$ confidence level would be 13.5% of CAPEX (5% x 2.70),
- The $p50$ confidence level would be 7.5% of CAPEX. If the confidence level that contingency was set at was $p50$, the contingency on start-up would be 2.5% (7.5% – 5% base, e.g., $2.5M contingency on $5M base start-up costs).

Note that the wide range of the table above will likely be much more of a concern to business for its implication to the start of the revenue cash flow stream than it will be for its direct capital cost impact.

Considering Programs and Integrative Systemic Risks

Programs are made up of a set of related projects. Their management is integrated to some extent (which can vary widely). Some megaprojects could be considered a type of program because they are often made up of sub-projects such as utilities, refining, storage, and infrastructure elements that are highly integrated, but likely to each have their own project manager, teams, and contingency (reporting to a project or program director or executive). Risk quantification for the program is likely going to be performed for each sub-project to derive their respective contingencies. However, because the projects are related and integrated, their interaction can lead to additional risks that have not been identified or quantified at the project level.

The recommended approach for program level risk quantification was shown in Figure 7.2. As with projects, the method involves separate but cumulative analysis of systemic and project specific risk analyses. For systemic risks, the parametric model is applied to the program the same way as described earlier for a project. However, in the "program pass" you will rate the level of definition, team, control, and estimate and schedule basis for the program assuming the program is only as strong as the weakest project link (enter the worst ratings found in any of the program's projects).

For example, if the refinery area was at Class 3 definition, but the utilities were only Class 4 (less defined), the whole program definition would be rated Class 4. Also, the complexity of the program will usually be greater than for any one of its constituent projects;

the extent of complexity depends on the degree and manner of integration. Usually, the program level systemic risk quantification will result in a mean cost outcome for the program that is greater than the sum of the means for the individual projects. This additional contingency can be funded as a general program level management reserve. A program reserve gives the program director (or committee, board, or other entity) the financial means to respond to integrative risk events or conditions in a timely manner.

For the program schedule, the treatment options are more varied because schedule contingency practice is less settled practice. The program analysis would be the same as for cost if the projects were sequential (i.e., finish-to-start relationship). For example, the runs for two constituent projects of 10 months each may result in 10% slip for one and 15% for the other (1 and 1.5 months), but the program level "weakest-link" run results in 20% or 4 months on the 20-month total duration. The difference between the sum of the project contingency durations (2.5 months) and the program's (4 months) would be a reserve (i.e., hold back on commercial promises).

However, purely sequential projects are rare; most program projects are done in parallel to some extent. For example, a program may have four projects that each take two years, but the overall program duration may be three years. The program's critical path may pass through all of its projects depending on the logic (if the program critical path is known at all, the project schedules are often not integrated – see Griffith).[13] In that case (or in the sequential case), you might choose to do only a program run for a total program schedule contingency; that would then be parceled out to buffer key project interfaces. CPM-based analysis would provide more information as to how to work contingency into the logic.

Later we will discuss quantification of program-specific integrative risks to be quantified using the expected value method and funded as appropriate to each specifically identified risk.

Summary

This Chapter presented the parametric modeling method for quantifying systemic risks. Because they are the foundation, I reviewed the original Rand models in depth. Parametric methods will be new to most decision makers. Therefore, by understanding the original research, practitioners can more credibly explain their approach. More recent research was reviewed on systemic risk

---

13 Op. Sit. (Griffith).

drivers such as project control, scheduling, and team development. Finally, this research was pulled together into working models for cost growth and schedule slip, including the generation of distributions adjusted for bias. My hope is that these models, and those that evolve from them, make it into wide usage.

However, this is just the starting point of a full cost and schedule risk quantification toolset. The next chapter covers the Expected Value method with MCS for *project specific* risks (i.e., probability of occurring times impact if it occurred) in which the outputs of the parametric models are inputs; i.e., systemic risks are Risk #1 with 100% probability of occurring.

As a final note, Chapter 15 reviews accuracy studies for non-process industries and assesses how well these parametric models apply. It concludes they are generically applicable to projects in any industry that revolve around construction. It also covers the applicability of the methods to contractors.

Questions

1) If your company has little historical data with which to create parametric RQ models, how can one proceed?

2) Describe at least one plus and one minus (strength/weakness) for using the John Hackney model as a starting point for in-house parametric RQ modeling.

3) Describe at least one plus and one minus (strength/weakness) for using the 1981 and 1986 Rand Corporation models as a starting point for in-house parametric RQ modeling.

4) How do the adjusted parametric models that are provided address weaknesses in the Rand models?

5) The adjusted model adds some systemic risks to the Rand models; how much additional contingency on average does this add to the Rand model outcomes?

6) Describe the approach that the Chapter takes to quantifying the model outcome probabilistically (i.e., values at various confidence levels)? How were these derived?

7) Parametric model inputs are ratings of systemic risks. What challenge must one be prepared for in eliciting systemic risk rating information from senior (business) management?

8) Describe why modeling of uncertain outcomes of Early Definition phases (Assess and Define) and Start-up is challenging.

9) Briefly describe how the parametric models can be applied on a
Program and how this can be used in funding a program level
reserve or contingency.

In regards to expectations, there is a quote by Alexander Pope that goes, *"Blessed is he who expects nothing, for he shall never be disappointed."* However, with risks as the object of the sentence, this would read, *"Cursed is he who expects nothing, for he shall always be disappointed."*

12

Project Specific Risks and the Expected Value Method

Some find the journey through systemic risks and parametric modeling a challenging one. The risks and methods are unfamiliar, the risk impacts are more significant than imagined, and communicating the systemic risk "story" can be difficult. Analysis results may not be well received by the business that owns most of the risks. And then there are the dreaded statistics. However, with all of this behind us, we move on to the Project Specific (PS) risks and Expected Value (EV). This is more familiar ground because it is similar to traditional risk analysis workshop practices.

Project specific risks are conditions and events specific to the project scope and strategy such as strikes, weather, soil conditions, and so on. Some call these *event* or *tactical risks*.

In addition, the recommended method for quantifying PS risks, namely expected value with Monte Carlo Simulation (EV-MCS), is familiar to most analysts because it uses a relatively simple extension of the standard risk model used for qualitative risk analysis: probability times impact.

The EV-MCS method for PS Risks was introduced in Chapter 7. In Chapter 10 the statistical basis for MCS was covered, and in Chapter 11, the Parametric method, which leads into the EV-MCS method, was described. This background and general familiarity brings us to the practical ways of applying the EV-MCS method for realistically quantifying PS risks for your project or program.

Before we proceed, it is suggested that you not call this the "Monte Carlo" method because there is some anti-MCS prejudice and because the important quality of a method is that it is explicitly risk-driven; MCS is secondary. Call it the "expected value" or "EV" method (because that is what it is).

Start with the Standard Risk Model

The expected value method has been called the standard risk model or method because of its long history. Its origins go back at least to Swiss scientist Jacob Bernoulli in the 18th century. There is a probability distribution bearing his name (the Bernoulli distribution) that deals with conducting a single experiment (n = 1) with two possible outcomes: success or failure. The probability of success is p and the probability of failure is then $(1 - p)$. If you conduct many experiments with failure counted as 0 and success as 1, the outcomes would average out to be equal to p. Plot this and you have a binomial distribution.

Likewise, if failure was scored as 0 and success was scored as 100, and the probability of success in this case was 10%, we would expect that the outcomes of many trials would average out to a score of ten. Said another way, the *expected value* is ten. Putting this in a risk event context: if we have a risk event with a cost impact of $100 if it occurs, and a 10% probability of it occurring, the expected value of the impact would be $10. Note, however, that the outcomes with respect to this risk are *never* the expected value – either the event happens ($100 cost), or it does not happen ($0 cost).

This is the basis of the expected value model, which has the following format as introduced in Chapter 7:

Cost or Schedule Impact of a Risk = Probability of Occurrence x Impact if it Occurs

A good question to ask is whether expected value is a practical and realistic model. In answer, its form is certainly consistent with the principal of quantifying the impact of the specific risk at hand; there is no ambiguity there. And for most non-systemic risks for which you have some experience (for example, the impact of a significant weather event), it is a reasonable expectation that a team could determine approximate cost and schedule impacts as well as an approximate probability of the risk event occurring. So, it passes the practicality test.

However, for a single risk on a single project, you *cannot* say that it is realistic. For example, for the $100 risk with a 10% probability of happening, if you fund the mean of $10 (0.1 x $100), there would be too much money in the budget if the risk did not happen and nowhere near enough money if it did. However, if there were ten such $100 potential risks in the register, and we funded each with $10, the overall amount of funding of $100 (10 x $10) would be enough to cover the impact of the occurrence of one of the risks. In that case, it would pass the realism test. The expected value model for a project then is a summation of the analyses for each individual risk:

Cost or Schedule Impact = $\sum$ (Probability of Occurrence x Impact if it Occurs)

However, quantifying every possible risk event, no matter how inconsequential or unlikely, is neither practical nor realistic. The EV method used alone and taken to its extreme leads teams to develop long risk registers in the mistaken belief that getting more risks included will get them closer to reality. *What this really does is take attention away from the risks that matter*. And the more trivial the risks, the less likely they are to be independent – they are likely to be manifestations of some larger risk driver that we are missing or counting twice (usually systemic risks). A limit must be placed on EV application to maintain fidelity with reality. That limit is to apply the method to *only* critical risks; the rest are statistical noise. This distinction is consistent with the Pareto principle whereby the vast majority of project-specific risks have negligible overall impact (noise), while a few have significant impact worth quantifying.

Focusing on the critical risks does not mean we forget about the noise. In fact, an empirically-based parametric model method deals with the noise inherently. A regression-based analysis of actual data provides us with a model of the mean impact of the systemic risks. It also provides us with a description of the noise of project cost and schedule uncertainty, i.e., the standard error of the prediction. In addition, the mean parametric model outcome for a "strong" system has less predicted cost growth or schedule slip in large part because the strong system is doing its jobs of managing the smaller day-to-day risks. A weak system has worse outcomes because it is more likely to be overwhelmed by the same smaller day-to-day risks. So by combining the empirically-based parametric method and the assumption-based EV method for critical risks, we are covering all the risks that matter.

The Rand models in Chapter 11 are based on cost growth and schedule slip after removing the impact of escalation and major risk events such as significant regulatory changes or catastrophic storms (to the extent project records recorded or teams recalled them). So from an empirical viewpoint, by applying the MLR-based parametric model first, and then allowing for these critical risks, our method should be historically valid and limited only by the extent of our ability to predict these critical risk events and conditions.

Considering Practicality and Realism

Critical Risks

AACE International has given us a definition of critical risks.[1] The AACE definition was borrowed from the work of Michael Curran, an early leader in project risk quantification.[2] While AACE and Mr. Curran speak of critical risks in the sense of critical "items" in an estimate, we can use their viewpoint of criticality for the impact of risk events as well.

> At AACE, a *critical item* (or *risk*) is "one whose actual value can vary from its target, either favorably or unfavorably, by such a magnitude that the bottom line cost (or profit) of the project would change by an amount greater than its critical variance," with the bottom line critical variance being specified as follows in 40R-08:
>
> ♦ Cost change: plus or minus 0.5%, and
> ♦ NPV change: plus or minus 5%.

---

1   AACE International Recommended Practice 41R-08, "Risk Analysis and Contingency Determination Using Range Estimating," AACE.

2   Curran, Michael W., Range Estimating: Measuring Uncertainty and Reasoning with Risk, Cost Engineering Journal, AACE International, March 1989.

For example, if the impact of a risk event is $1M and the project capital cost is $100M, this would be a critical risk because the impact is 1% of the total capital, which is greater than 0.5%.

The profit or NPV criterion is affected not only by capital cost, but by change in timing of the start of the revenue cash flow (execution and startup schedule slip). For example, if the scheduled completion and start of revenue slipped by 14 months and reduced the NPV from $5M to $4.6M (greater discounting of revenue due to slip), the risk would be critical because the NPV dropped by 8%, which is greater than 5%.

Typically, each project establishes its own definition of what the critical capital cost and project schedule duration threshold levels are, depending on a project's objective and its strategic importance. These thresholds do not need to be hard and fast rules. While critical risks will usually include all the "red" risks from qualitative risk matrix screening, they will likely include some "yellow" ones too. As a general rule-of-thumb, for a moderate to large project, expect to find between five and twenty critically significant project-specific risks. If there are more than twenty risks, this may be indicative of systemic risks and bias. For example, the analyst or the team may be overly conservative and/or the risk management process is weak, so risks are not being mitigated as they should prior to the decision gate. In the worst case, a large number of critical risks and their interaction with systemic risks may push the project towards disorder and a blowout (see Chapter 14).

Considering Overwhelming Risks

Previously, we discussed ten risk events with potential impacts of $100 each, expected values of $10 (10% probability of happening) each, yielding a total contingency funding of $100 with that total conveniently covering the cost of one of the $100 risk events happening. This approach works well for contingency quantification when you have between five and twenty risks and each has only nominal impacts (plus the allowance obtained from our parametric analysis of systemic risks).

But what happens if one of the risk events would consume all of the contingency funds (and then some) if it occurred? For example, say one of the ten risk events had an impact of $1,000 and probability of 1%. This yields an expected value of $10 just the same as a $100 risk event at 10% probability. However, if this *low probability/high impact risk event* happens, our $100 contingency allowance would not have anywhere near enough money to cover it. The EV method would therefore not be realistic.

The solution for dealing with these low probability/high impact risks is to not fund them with contingency at all but to quantify each one separately (possibly developing its own causal model) and fund them (or not) on their own using management reserve funding. Safety risks often fall into this category. Minor incidents are addressed by the parametric model, but major incidents can be overwhelming and should be covered by manaement reserve. On most large projects, there are usually one or two reserve risks worthy of special consideration and funding. We will discuss contingency versus management reserve considerations later.

Considering Risk Response

To this point, we have been addressing impact cost and time as deterministic or point estimates, e.g., the $100 risk event of the prior example. However, the impact is always uncertain. Further, the cost and time impacts are not natural or given attributes of a risk event, but result from cost and time of our *responses* to the risk event.

For example, if the risk is "lightning damages the main transformer," the cost and time impact if it happens depends on whether the project team decides to repair it, buy a new replacement-in-kind, buy new but of a different type because it can be expedited, or whether it is sitting in someone's warehouse, and so on. There are usually several logical response alternatives to consider. Therefore, estimating the impact requires some team and analyst effort to perform conceptual contingency planning, which takes some time (this is another good reason to limit the number of critical risks to evaluate).

The first contingency planning question is:

"Once the risk event happens, what activities will we do and what resources and time will we expend to deal with it?"

The next question, particularly since there is usually a range of possible risk responses, is,

"What is the range or distribution of possible impacts including the cost and time of our response?"

One alternative is to analyze these alternatives and impacts in a CPM risk model, but this requires probabilistic branching, which is usually not a practical approach (see Appendix A). But it is practical to perform estimates of cost and time, including three-point ranges, using conceptual estimating and scheduling approaches (keep in mind that impact estimates are "Class 5" estimates). *In all cases, the response will depend on the project's objective*, i.e., is the project cost or schedule driven? Will we choose the fastest or the least cost risk response?

As an example, consider a hydropower project. A temporary cofferdam is being used to allow foundation work to be performed in a riverbed along one bank of the river. If the risk event is a flood overtopping the cofferdam, the impact may include lost time for stopping work, cost to remove equipment from the area, work to shore up the cofferdam if it is safe and reasonable to do so, pumping water out the work area, remobilizing, repairing any damage, and possibly adding to the cofferdam. If the project is schedule driven, there may also be impacts of re-sequencing and/or accelerating later activities to recover lost time. All of this must be considered in the cost and time impact range estimates.

Applying the Expected Value Method

We have covered the fundamental math behind the expected value (probability times impact) method and considerations to assure its application is practical (focus on critical risks) and its outcome is reliable (consider critical risks and risk response). That brings us to applying the method. As outlined in Chapter 7, the expected value method using MCS has eight basic application steps as follows:

1. Screen the risk register,
2. Identify critical risks,
3. Quantify the probability of occurrence,
4. Assess risk responses,
5. Quantify impacts,
6. Run the Monte Carlo Simulation,
7. Screen for over-whelming risks and determine management reserve, and
8. Complete MCS and determine contingency.

The primary output of this quantification approach is integrated cost and schedule distributions from which contingency can be determined. Because the systemic risk outcomes from parametric modeling are applied in the EV method as the first critical risk, the expected value method output will include all contingency risks, plus a list of quantified reserve risks. Figure 12.1 illustrates this

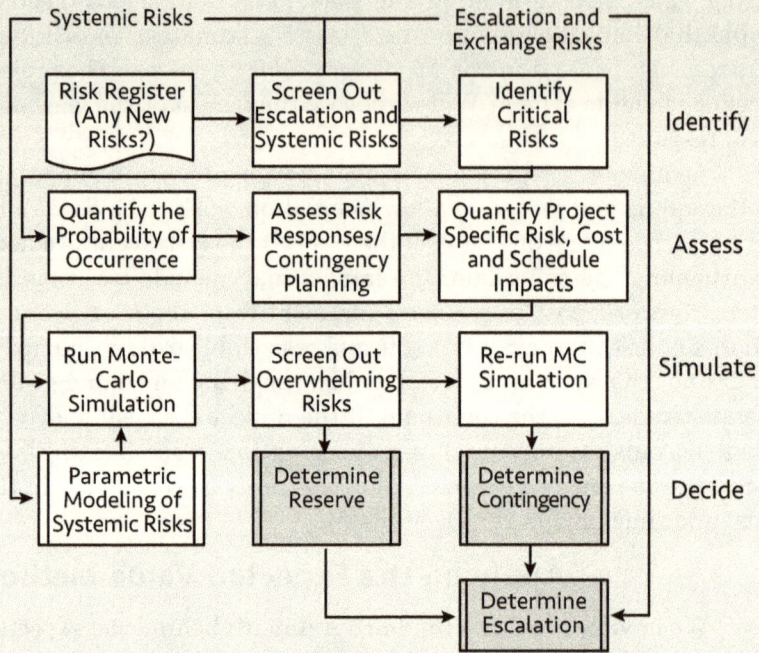

Figure 12.1: Expected Value Method Flowchart for Project Specific Risks

analysis process in a more specific flowchart. This is followed by a description of each step.

Steps in the Expected Value Quantification Method Process

The steps in the expected value method flowchart from Figure 12.1 for project specific risks are discussed in more detail below.

1. *Screen the Risk Register*

Readiness: Make sure that any new or modified risks (since the last risk management identification was done) are captured. If additions are extensive, delay the risk quantification workshop until the risk register can be updated to accurately reflect current status.

Characterization: Screen the risks to characterize each with *quantification type*, which can be registered with one of the following designations:

 ◆ Systemic,
 ◆ Project specific, or
 ◆ Escalation/Exchange.

Often team risk descriptions in registers are ambiguous. If so, the definition must be clarified before proceeding. The rule-of-thumb for quantification type designation is that if the risk description is not specific with respect to who, what, when, where and how, then it is likely a systemic risk. If a systemic risk is found that was not well considered in the prior systemic risk analysis (e.g., the business thought the team development was excellent, but the team itself raises all sorts of issues), then the systemic analysis may need to be revisited before completing the project specific risk quantification.

In regard to escalation, if the price-related risk is about a general price trend driven by economic conditions, it is escalation. If instead it is driven by company or project procurement or contracting practices, it is either systemic or project specific.

Issues: If your risk management process moves issues to its own register, these will need to be reviewed as well. Anything that may result in uncertainty going forward must be quantified (most issues are systemic risks).

2. *Identify Critical Risks*

Having screened out the systemic and escalation risks, sort the register's remaining project specific risks by their qualitative probability and impact ratings. Usually red risks are critical. The threshold criteria for criticality were discussed previously. Once the critical risks are noted, the workshop agenda can be reviewed to decide on the order in which to assess them (e.g., make sure construction risks are covered while construction leads are present). Also, verify that there is enough time in the agenda to discuss all of the critical risks.

3. *Quantify the Probability of Occurrence*

At this point, each critical risk's probability of occurrence should be refined into a specific percentage value. If the team is having trouble coming to consensus on a value, my suggestion is to lean to the conservative side (i.e., the higher probability) or assess the situation further off-line. A related input needed for MCS is whether the occurrences of any of the risks are correlated. For example, if one risk is a 100-year storm event and another is for a flood damage event (e.g., the cofferdam), these tend to go together (although not perfectly).

Often related risks can be reasonably combined for quantification purposes. For example, if there are multiple risks to the start of construction due to not receiving one or more permits, risks for permit A and permit B might be combined. They both have the same potential impact (it is not cumulative) but the probability of at least one of them occurring can be approximated as the sum of their individual probabilities.

With respect to permits, most projects have a high probability of delay from somewhere in a series of permits. In fact, permit risks are not so much risks but a fact today. It is often more efficient and cost effective to just plan for permitting delay.

4. *Assess Risk Responses*

In this step, a conceptual contingency plan (or set of plans) is developed. The operative question is, "How will we respond if the risk event happens?" The response actions should be aligned with the project cost and schedule strategy (i.e., cost versus schedule driven). Regarding a decision during the analysis, the project's PM should have final say on the answer, but the lead of the phase (e.g., construction) will have significant planning input. In general, the less clear and specific the response, the wider the range of potential impacts will be. This is because the cost and schedule range must cover all possible responses (or lack thereof).

5. *Quantify Impacts*

Based on the physical or other impacts of the risk and the projected project response(s), estimate the impact on the integrated cost and schedule. There is not enough time in a workshop to do this well, so the goal is to obtain enough team input so that the risk analyst working with the estimator, scheduler, and others can finalize the analysis offline. The outcomes are typically expressed as 3-point estimates.

Schedule impact is usually based on project completion impact because with risk quantification at decision gates, this is the metric of interest. The cost impact has two parts; direct costs to respond to the risk (e.g., repair the cofferdam) and the time-driven costs of delay, if any. A conservative approach for estimating the time delay cost is to assess a labor and indirect cost burn-rate (cost per day) for the project phase affected and multiply this by the delay duration (which is a 3-point estimate).

6. *Run MCS (Including Parametric Outcomes)*

Systemic Risks: The first risk in the EV-MCS model will be the outcome of the parametric model for systemic risks. This risk has

100% probability of occurrence and its impact distribution is the outcome of the parametric model itself.

Project Specific Risk Distributions: For each uncertain variable for the project-specific risks, the expected value model must have a distribution assigned. For practical analyses, these are usually triangle or PERT distributions based on 3-point inputs. The uncertain variables are the cost and schedule duration impacts.

Dependencies: In MCS, correlation between the occurrences of any of the risks must be identified and quantified as inputs for the MCS software. Arguably, the impact of the risks may be correlated but this is often because of a weak system. When the response to a risk goes poorly, all of the responses seem to go poorly. Assure that the system is rated appropriately in the systemic risk, and flag interaction risks with the tipping point indicator (which will be discussed later).

Simulate: Once the model with distributions and dependencies is set up (usually in an established tool to facilitate one's approach), the MCS can be executed.

7. *Screen for Overwhelming Risks and Determine Management Reserve*

After running the MCS, overall distributions of cost and schedule outcomes can be reported in a tabular (i.e., a *p*-table) and/ or graphical format. An *initial* contingency estimate (depending on the probability of underrun that management desires for its cost outcome and duration) can be set. However, this initial contingency should first be compared to the most likely and high values for each project-specific risk impact to see if any of the risks are overwhelming – if a risk happens, would it consume most of the contingency? Tornado diagramming can help in this determination. If so, decide on whether and how to fund that risk as a decision in its own right (i.e., a management reserve item).

8. *Complete MCS and Determine Contingency*

After removing any risks to be treated as reserve items, the MCS is rerun and the final cost and schedule outcome distributions are obtained, from which management can set the contingency. There will also be a list of quantified reserve risks.

Application Tool

There is no commercial tool currently available for the hybrid quantification approach described above (albeit I have my own). However, it is relatively easy to create a spreadsheet tool and use a commercial MCS add-in. Table 12.1 provides a *narrative* guide to constructing a spreadsheet-based tool. Each cell in the table represents a spreadsheet entry. It is up to the analyst to elaborate on it within Excel (or whatever system is being used) and design reporting tables and charts.

SPREADSHEET TOOL ENTRIES TO MAKE	EXPLANATION
Critical Risk (typically 5 to 20)	Describe the risk (note: systemic risk is always Risk No. 1). Combine risks where appropriate.
Probability of Occurrence	Enter a percentage. The systemic risk probability is 100%.
Dependency	Identify if any risks are correlated. If so, the dependency must be quantified using the MCS add-in capability for correlation.
Risk Responses	Describe the assumed risk response(s).
Direct Cost Impact (considering response)	Enter 3-point (Low, Most Likely, High) impacts as inputs to the MCS distribution selected. The Systemic risk impact distribution is the distribution output from the Parametric model.
Schedule Duration Impact (considering response)	Enter 3-point (Low, Most Likely, High) impacts as inputs to the MCS distribution selected. The Systemic risk impact distribution is the distribution output from the Parametric model.
Burn Rates ($ per day, week, or month)	Enter approximate burn rates for key phases of the projects impacted by risks (e.g., engineering, early construction); these can be treated as 3-point entries.
Time-Driven Cost Impact	Calculate Schedule Duration Impact above x applicable Burn Rate (does not apply to Systemic risks).
Total Cost Impact	Sum the Direct (including Systemic) and Time-Driven Impacts.
Total Schedule Duration Impact	Sum the Systemic and other Schedule Impacts.

Table 12.1: Elements of an Expected Value Risk Quantification Spreadsheet

Table 12.2 is a representation of a risk entry item in an Excel worksheet with a MCS add-in that applies the elements above. Note that the "Schedule Months (EV)" and "Non-Time Driven $ (EV)" cells include MCS distribution functions (the add-in displays the mean of the distribution). Note that the example risk had a probability of 40%, which is reflected in the EV results (i.e., EV = probability x impact).

The dark-shaded cells in Table 12.2 are the output calculation cells from the MCS. The lightly-shaded cells in Table 12.2 are inputs specific to this identified risk.

Risk 032	Major rain event during site preparation		Contract:	2	Site Prep Contract	
Risk Response:	Added gravel to improve working conditions, but otherwise accept productivity impacts					
Schedule Impact:	Months	Time Driven Cost Burn Rate:	$x1000/ Month	Non-Time Driven Cost Impact (x1000)		
Low	3.0	General & Service contracts	$512	Low	$1,000	Total Cost Impact (x1000)
Most Likely	5.0	Site Prep Contract	$196	Most Likely	$5,000	
High	7.0	Burn Rate (can override):	$708	High	$20,000	
Schedule Months (EV)	2.0	Time Driven $ (EV)	$1,416	Non-Time Driven $ (EV)	$3,467	$4,883

Table 12.2: Example of Part of an Expected Value Risk Quantification Spreadsheet

The Risk Quantification Workshop

In the process outlined above, steps three to five require information to be gathered from the project team and other stakeholders about the nature of the risks, their probability of occurrence, the likely risk responses, and their potential impacts. While general information about these topics should have been captured all along during the ongoing risk management process (which is focused on treatment), the quantification process requires more detailed input, i.e., information that is somewhat analogous to initial project planning with the focus on specific risks and not general project scope. The typical approach for obtaining that more detailed input is through a risk quantification workshop.

Most risk quantification workshops take place just prior to project investment decision gates. Qualitative risk management, including risk identification, has been ongoing up to this point, with risks being treated as appropriate. The team is left with the risks remaining at the gate, i.e., a snapshot in time of the residual risks that need to be quantified. The sections below provide guidelines for planning and conducting such a workshop, including facilitation, attendees, venue, timing, agenda, and follow-up.

Facilitator/Risk Analyst

A project-specific risk quantification workshop is similar to a traditional risk identification workshop; however the focus is on critical risks and quantitative analysis considering risk responses. As such, the session involves obtaining input from the project's lead planning, scheduling, and estimating personnel, as well as those who might be expected to decide upon risk responses (e.g., execution leads). Because discussions get into specifics, the facilitator must be experienced at knowing how much information is enough to get the analysis started (some of the detailed analysis will be done offline) and at keeping the dialog flowing within the time allotted. A scribe (content recorder) will be required to capture the workshop discussions and findings. A project control person may be a good scribe because they usually have a good understanding of the information being recorded.

Information Providers and Subject Matter Discussed

Table 12.3 lists the types of information to be obtained and the people who will typically be able to provide it.

INFORMATION TO ELICIT	TYPICAL INFORMATION PROVIDERS
Criticality Thresholds and Risk Response Determination	Program and Project Managers (PM) and Phase/Discipline Leads (Engineering, Procurement, Fabrication, Construction, and Commissioning leads)
Risk Characterization	Risk Owners who best understand the critical risks (usually the same lead participants who participated in ongoing risk analysis workshops)
Planning and Scheduling and Estimating of impacts considering risk responses	Cost Engineering/Project Control planning and scheduling and estimating leads

Table 12.3: Risk Quantification Workshop Topics and Attendees

Venue

Project-specific information is usually initially gathered and assessed in a group workshop. However, it is common for the quantification of specific risks to be completed offline, calling on input from other people and applying planning tools as needed.

Register This

"Risk Register" development is a Risk Management practice that most are familiar with. It's a simple concept – identify the risks and then manage them. The trouble is that risk descriptions are often not actionable and the risk owner can do little about them except worry. They are also not readily quantifiable if you cannot say specifically what the risk is. So, much of a quantification workshop's time will be spent on risk description clarification.

Here are examples of poorly described risks, followed by some questions I might ask about them (who, what, when, where, why) and some examples of improved, more specific wording. If the team cannot be specific, the risks are likely systemic or escalation. For example, the generic risk of "late deliveries" likely is caused by weak engineering and procurement systems and poor team development that will require overall organizational improvement for the company's project system, which is outside of project team control.

"Late delivery of long lead equipment"

- ♦ Questions: What equipment? What is making it late?
- ♦ Improved: Inadequate owner resources to review tower drawings result in fabrication delays.

"Skilled labor availability"

- ♦ Questions: What contract? What trades? When? Exacerbated by labor strategy?
- ♦ Improved: Shortage of journeyman welders for alloy work in the hydrotreater area results in low productivity and rework.

"Decisions by the business are delayed"

- ♦ Questions: What type of decisions? Who or what organization? Why are they delayed?
- ♦ Improved: Delay in supplier selection by the Refining group due to limited resources results in delay of refining process design.

"Corporate processes are changed"

- ♦ Questions: What processes? By whom? Why are they changed?
- ♦ Improved: Increased errors in and delay of process design due to midstream changes of design tools and processes and misalignment with suppliers.

Timing

The workshop immediately follows the systemic risk elicitation workshop(s). The EV workshop will usually require one or two days. Assume five to twenty critical risks will need to be quantified with about thirty minutes of discussion for each. Final quantification will take place offline with the facilitator working with the PM and the planning, scheduling, and estimating personnel. As to workshop scheduling, make sure there is time in the project schedule before the decision gate milestone for the project to thoroughly discuss complex issues, resolve conflicts, make reserve determinations, and so on.

Agenda

The workshop session starts with introductions and review of the purpose and objectives. It then proceeds with a check/update on the current status of the risk register. It then follows the flow diagram's (see Figure 12.1) "Identify" steps for the overall register, and then the "Assess" steps for each critical risk.

Actions/Follow-up

The session should conclude by summarizing open questions and issues with action items to close them. For some or all of the risks, it may be necessary in follow-up to elaborate on risk response planning and quantification.

After the workshop, the risk analyst enters the gathered information into the risk quantification tool described previously and runs the simulation with iterations for reserve risk handling. In Chapter 16, methods for communicating the analysis outcome are discussed.

Considering Programs

In Chapter 7, a flowchart diagram showed how the risk quantification methods can be applied to assess programs. As was stated, at the program level, the emphasis is on assessing commonalities and interactions between the projects in the program and the risks to those projects. There is inherent added complexity in a program that increases to the extent that its constituent projects are related.

Generally, the program will benefit from having its own risk funding to deal with interaction risks and to assure that the enterprise is prepared to intervene with project management if required. This often means a separate pass through the EV workshop process focused on interactions of project level risks. Note that risks may occur simultaneously on different projects and cascade or compound from project to project.

For example, consider a Program including three projects A, B, and C, with Project A taking place first. Project A, which is environmentally sensitive, included the risk of a one month schedule delay caused by a permit agency making an adverse determination. However, Projects B and C, being less sensitive (but also needing a permit from the same agency) did not consider this risk to be critical. However, considered from a Program perspective, we judge that this permit agency's behavior and interpretations tend to reflect a bias; i.e., the later projects will likely suffer for the sins of the prior. In that case, in terms of the Program completion milestone risk, a permit delay in Project A of one month might indicate two months delay for the Program. Having made that judgment, the Program should assure that Projects B and C learn from Project A as a mitigating action.

Speaking of schedule delay risks, there is one more impact not addressed in the discussion above and that is escalation costs incurred because of the delay and/or change in cash flow pattern. It is recommended that the escalation cost impact be quantified using the methods covered in the next chapter. However, if escalation is not addressed as a separate risk in your project system, it can be factored into the burn rate allowance for time-dependent cost impacts.

Questions

1) Why might some call the expected value method the "standard risk model"? And what is its basic form?

2) What are some conditions that have to be met for the Expected Value to be a realistic model?

3) What is a critical risk?

4) Why does focusing on quantifying critical risks only not lead to underestimation of the risks?

5) How would a potentially catastrophic risk event be quantified and funded?

6) List the procedural steps of performing risk quantification for Project-Specific risks using Expected Value with MCS

7) How is the Expected Value model applied to schedule risk and integrated with cost risk?

8) Describe two types of cost impact for most risk conditions or events if they occur.

9) For a project-specific risk quantification workshop, what are the three general categories of risk information that must be obtained?

10) How might project-specific risks be evaluated for Programs?

"A trader listened to the firm's chief economist's predictions about gold, then lost a bundle. The trader was asked to leave the firm. He then angrily asked his boss who was firing him, 'Why do you fire me alone and not the economist? He too is responsible for the loss.' The Boss replied, 'You idiot, we are not firing you for losing money; we are firing you for listening to the economist...'
–Joke credited to Nicholas Taleb

13

Probabilistic Escalation and Currency Exchange

For almost a generation from the oil price collapse in 1986 through 2003, escalation was a sleeping tiger. The oil price bounced around $20 per barrel. Commodity and project prices crept along with inflation in the historical 3% per year range. If risk is uncertainty, escalation seemed not to be a risk. However, in 2003, the escalation tiger woke up with the start of what we now call the commodity "super-cycle."

When I started working as an independent consultant in 2005, projects were in the midst of devastating price increases, particularly for steel, copper, and other commodity driven materials. But a short time later engineering and construction service prices in general increased significantly (services tend to lag). It kept me busy as an estimator and as a risk analyst. I seem to have been the rare person with experience quantifying escalation (from my prior job in benchmarking). Oddly, inflation hardly budged throughout this whole period. What I found at client companies were intense debates:

♦ Between finance and projects about the difference between *escalation* and *inflation*,

♦ Between estimating and controls about whether to address escalation directly as a control account or spread it around, and

♦ Between risk analysts and everyone else about how to quantify escalation and whether to treat it as a risk.

Then, in 2012 for metals and in 2014 for oil, the super-cycle ended as quickly as it began. However, currency exchange rate volatility remained significant as global currencies dropped against the US dollar. In short, escalation and exchange rates and their forecasting and uncertainty quantification are not "settled science" and they can be the greatest cost risk on a project. In addition, high or increasing escalation adds stress to projects that may already be on the verge of failure; blowouts are most prevalent in times of high escalation.

For better or worse, the science, such as it is, falls in the field of economics – a field that largely failed to forecast the timing of the beginning or end of these recent cycles. However, before we laugh at Mr. Taleb's joke about economists, please keep in mind that as project risk analysts, our experience with risk quantification has been about the same. We have been ineffective at predicting actual project cost growth.

In any case, it is not debatable that escalation and exchange are major risks for large projects of extended duration. As such, this cost risk must be estimated probabilistically (with an economist's help).

Escalation and Exchange Base Estimating

In Chapter 7, the base methods of quantifying escalation and exchange costs were covered. Escalation is estimated by applying forecast price indices against a cash flow forecast by cost type. Exchange is estimated by applying exchange rate indices against a cash flow by expended currency. Forecast price indices for various material and labor items are obtained from economists who use econometric models that tie pricing to general economic behavior.

This approach is described in AACE Recommended Practice 58R-10.[1] Below is an example of a deterministic escalation estimate for a single cost type (e.g., steel) with cost estimated in the current

---

1   AACE International RP 58R-10: "Escalation Estimating Principles and Methods Using Indices."

year (2016) and forecast to be spent in a given year (2022). This calculation would be done for each cost type and for each year in the cash flow and then summed to obtain the escalation total:

Cost Item A $ (Escalated)   = Cost Item A $ (2016 basis) x (2022 index) / (2016 index)

                                       = $2,000,000 x 1.20 / 1.10

                                       = $2,180,000 (2022 basis)

Escalation   = $2,180,000 – $2,000,000 = $180,000

Currency exchange cost estimating uses a similar method. The exchange rate impact comes about when we estimate a project in one currency (e.g., $USD) at current exchange rates, but expect to pay out funds in another currency (e.g., $CAN) at some future exchange rate. The question is, "How many $USD do I need to fund now in order to pay out the $CAN in year *X*?"

For example, assume $US and $CAN dollars are at par (exchange rate of 1.00 $USD per $CAN) at the time of the estimate (2016), but in 2022 when the money will be spent the $US is expected to weaken relative to the $CAN (exchange rate of 1.20 $USD per $CAN), not considering escalation.

Cost ($CAN) in 2016   = $CAN 2,000,000

Cost ($USD) in 2016   = $USD 2,000,000 (at 1.00 exchange rate)

Cost ($CAN) in 2022   = $CAN 2,000,000

Cost ($USD) in 2022   = $CAN 2,000,000 x 1.20 $USD / $CAN

                                      = $USD 2,400,000

Exchange to fund (or hedge) = $USD 2,400,000 – $USD 2,000,000

                                      = $400,000

While these base estimating algorithms are straightforward, the following sections discuss some complicating issues that the estimator and risk analysis method must consider. These issues revolve around what the indices represent and how they line up against the cost you are applying them to.

Escalation/Exchange Estimating: Principles of Good Practice

A price index includes much information within a single number. Make sure that the index represents the right information for your needs. This idea is captured in AACE RP58R-10, which highlights the generally accepted principles of good practice in escalation estimating as follows:

◆ Differentiate between escalation, currency, and contingency.

◆ Leverage economist's knowledge (based on macroeconomics).

- ◆ Use indices appropriate to each account.
- ◆ Use indices that address levels of detail for various estimate classes.
- ◆ Leverage procurement/contracting specialist's knowledge of markets.
- ◆ Ensure that indices address the specific internal and external market situation.
- ◆ Facilitate estimation of appropriate spending or cash flow profile.
- ◆ Calibrate or validate data with historical data.
- ◆ Use probabilistic methods (*see later discussion*).
- ◆ Use the same economic scenarios for both business and capital planning.
- ◆ Apply in a consistent approach using a tool that facilitates best practice.

In addition to these principles, estimators are cautioned not to expect much accuracy from escalation and exchange estimates. They are always Class 5 approximations intended to represent the average trends for a large group of projects in a broad region. The indices are generic and conceptual in nature and judgment must be used in any given situation. There is a diminishing return in trying to identify highly specific indices. Similarly, spending a lot of time allocating minor costs into each cost account is rarely worthwhile.

Estimating future cash flow patterns (e.g., exactly when the money will be expended) is another source of inaccuracy. Also, suppliers do not change their prices instantaneously with economic events or in lock step with trends; there is usually a lag that is difficult to predict (often as much as a year for many services).

Finally, economists, let alone estimators and engineers, have difficulty accurately predicting future price levels. All of these point to the need for probabilistic estimates. In short, there is significant inaccuracy in escalation estimating, and the longer the project duration, the greater it is.

Limitations of Index Sources

There is no industry source of historical price indices that meet the principles above. For North America, the two main sources of indices are the U.S. Department of Labor, Bureau of Labor Statistics (BLS at www.bls.gov), and Statistics Canada (Statcan at www. statcan.ca). Their indices are survey-based and they only survey major commodity and service markets for items that are purchased directly.

For example, there are no published price index forecasts for process plant engineering or construction services that are bid. The government only tracks wages and compensation for technical staff and construction trades. Similarly, the BLS surveys pipe mills as to the cost of bare pipe they sell, but they do not survey or have indices for shop fabricated pipe spools that our estimate's piping cost includes. Another challenge is that some cost items come from small, poorly documented markets where a small number of suppliers (oligopolies) have pricing power (such as for combustion gas turbines or a massive heavy walled vessels).

Finally, the government agencies do not publish long-term forecasts; these must be obtained from economics consultants (more on that later). Economists in turn derive their forecasts from macro-economic models that are correlated to the government provided historical price series; the government and consultant efforts are symbiotic.[2] Where this leaves us is that we must start with the economist's forecasts, but then construct "proxy" indices for the specific types of items that we estimate and how the item's market behaves.

Proxy Indices: Creating Weighted Composite Indices

Because published price indices often do not match the content of what we estimate, we have to create weighted composite indices from indices for the constituent parts of what we are estimating. For example, estimators may estimate process plant piping on a unit cost per meter basis with the meters derived from P&ID and plot plan drawings. We know that the piping includes bare pipe, fittings such as flanges and bends, and the welding to join these together in pipe "spools" in a shop. However, we do not quantify or list these parts or steps separately in preparing a Class 3 estimate. Estimators do know from history what the average frequency of bends and welds are per 100 meters of pipe "spool." And from that you can approximate that the material cost of process piping is, for example, 50% bare pipe, 20% fittings, and 30% shop costs (these will vary of course). Then you can create a weighted piping index with these proportions of the respective indices from the economists. Again, note that there is much uncertainty in the weighting process.

---

2   Hollmann, John K, and Larry Dysert, Escalation Estimation: Working With Economics Consultants, AACE International Transactions, 2007.

Adjusting Indices for CAPEX Market Demand

As stated above, the government agencies provide indices for common, generic items that are purchased directly. And for labor, it only measures wages and compensation. However, for specialty items and for services that are bid upon, the price to the owner will vary significantly depending on what markups the bidding market will bear at any given time, regardless of the supplier's raw material and wage costs. Prices are correlated with the seller's market leverage: high demand plus limited supply results in seller pricing power.

However, reliable price indices for these types of items can be derived if you have a forecast of the market demand; economists do have CAPEX forecasts for various industries and regions. For the EPC market it has been shown that changes in measures of CAPEX in an industry and region correlate with changes in service pricing in that industry and region.[3] The higher the amount of capital spending, the more the suppliers will charge (and vice-versa). We can use indices of CAPEX spending to derive a "demand factor" for adjusting the impacted price index:

CAPEX Market Adjusted Index = Base Index (i.e., BLS) x Demand Factor

The demand factor is the CAPEX index change taken to an exponent. For example, assume the economist's index for Labor (wages) increases by 8% from 2016 to 2017 (labor index change from 1.00 to 1.08). During the same time period, the CAPEX spend in the region increases by 20% (CAPEX index change from 1.00 to 1.20). From research of past trends, we determine that the CAPEX exponent (i.e., CAPEX market demand factor) is 0.4. Using this information, we can adjust the 8% wage cost increase to reflect service bid price increase for the uncompetitive market as below:

CAPEX adjusted price increase = Wage Increase x CAPEX Demand Factor

CAPEX adjusted price increase = $1.08 \times (1.20)^{0.4} = 1.08 \times 1.08 = 1.17$ or 17%

The concept of time-lag in pricing come in to play here – after a CAPEX bust or boom cycle, it may take six to twelve months for suppliers to change pricing and this lag can be incorporated in your algorithm. Again, this is an approximation that carries significant uncertainty.

---

3   Hollmann, John K, and Larry Dysert, Escalation Estimating: Lessons Learned in Addressing Market Demand, AACE International Transactions, 2008.

The Goodyear Rule

The megaproject reported below is a good example of what escalation can do in a boom. The project's cost increased 110% from 2004 to 2007 due to a regional labor shortage in Western Australia (WA).

What caught my eye in the report is the statement by BHP's CEO Mr. Goodyear, "Each major resources project approved in WA adds 10 per cent to the cost of every other project." This is a great non-technical description of the "CAPEX Demand Factor" covered in this chapter.

In the chapter example, the escalation cost increase due to market CAPEX increase is the CAPEX increase factor to the 0.4 power. Hence, a 25% increase in market CAPEX results in about 10% cost escalation ($1.25^{0.4} = 1.09$). If there were four big projects in the WA region, and one more was added, there is Mr. Goodyear's 10% increase – his rule looks pretty good! Further, if the WA CAPEX increased by 600% from 2004 to 2007, that's a 110% cost increase for Ravensthorpe. If CAPEX spending decreased from 2012 to 2015 by 50%, that would equate to a 25% de-escalation in costs ($0.5^{0.4} = 0.75$). This sounds reasonable.

"BHP Billiton yesterday revealed a further 64 per cent cost blowout at its Ravensthorpe nickel laterite project under development in Western Australia. The group had warned the market of a second cost blowout of at least 30 per cent and possible delays at the project – but few were expecting an overrun of such magnitude. BHP said it would cost $US2.2 billion ($2.8 billion) to build the project, up from a revised $US1.34 billion figure released last September. When the project was approved in March 2004, BHP said it would cost $US1.05 billion to develop. At full production, it should produce 50,000 tonnes of nickel a year. BHP also announced a timetable setback yesterday, postponing the estimated first production date to the first quarter of 2008. It had originally planned to be producing metal by the end of September 2007. The world's biggest mining company attributed the delays to lower-than-expected labour productivity and late deliveries of some materials and equipment." The article continues, "...The resources boom has placed particular pressure on major developments in WA. Earlier this year, BHP chief executive Chip Goodyear said each major resources project approved in WA adds 10 per cent to the cost of every other project under development in the state. BHP and Rio Tinto's iron ore expansion projects and the North-West Shelf expansion have tied up thousands of workers amid a nationwide skills shortage."[1]

---

1   Freed, Jamie, "Cost of BHP nickel project leaps to $2.8b," Sydney Morning Herald, December 1, 2006.

Probabilistic Approaches

Escalation and exchange estimates are highly uncertain, which means that using probabilistic approaches to estimating them are needed. Chapter 7 introduced the method in the section on "Escalation/Exchange Using CAPEX Market Adjusted Price and Exchange Indices." The probabilistic method is also defined in an AACE Recommended Practice 68R-11.[4]

Probabilistic analysis requires treating uncertain inputs to the estimate as uncertainties (distributions) rather than point values and then running a Monte Carlo simulation. The primary uncertain variables in an escalation estimate include:

- ◆ Price indices,
- ◆ Cash flow spending (spending peak is different than expected in a given time period),
- ◆ Cash flow duration (cash flow is extended over a longer time period),
- ◆ Cost contingency (which is subject to escalation), and
- ◆ Exchange factors (applied after the escalation estimate).

If you understand application of MCS to a spreadsheet, this is a simple concept. However, because escalation and exchange estimates deal with time-series (indices by period over the cash flow duration) it can become complicated. Try to keep it simple; the objective is to communicate to decision makers and finance that it is uncertain. Because decision makers and finance are probably working with economists already to forecast the market price of their product (e.g., oil, copper), this approach can be explained credibly. Point out that if uncertainty is being considered in revenue in the project's NPV, it only makes sense to consider uncertainty in the CAPEX as well (both CAPEX and revenue are affected by the same economic scenarios). This will help business management understand that cost and revenue can be affected by uncertain escalation and exchange rates.

The following section describes how to model uncertainty of inputs for escalation and exchange estimates. There are other ways to do this; some are highly sophisticated (particularly with respect to time-series), but this method is relatively simple and effective. I use a base escalation tool that includes a cash flow "generator." This is an Excel worksheet that applies pre-determined spending pattern distributions to each cost account. The distribution can be adjusted to reflect early or late spending patterns. MCS can then be readily applied as discussed below.

---

4   AACE International, RP 68R-11: "Escalation Estimating Using Indices and Monte Carlo Simulation."

Price Indices

Start with a fixed table of adjusted price indices by account and time period in the base estimating tool. You could replace each index with uncertainty assessments; however, that implies that each year is independent (which is not true). If prices are trending up in one or more years, that increases the probability they will trend downward later. While MCS tools can deal with time-series, I chose to treat each value in the index table as independent, my main goal being to incorporate uncertainty into the equation. In the very long term, the price trend tends to regress to the mean long-term inflation of about 3%.

For the uncertainty, I use a PERT distribution with the adjusted index as the most likely value, and the high and low based on the historical high and low ranges. For example, if the economist forecasts a 15% increase next year, and the historical max/min for any prior year has been 18% to −14%, the high, most likely, and low inputs will be 18, 15 and −14% for this uncertainty. This is an approximation, but it does introduce the range and respect history. The trend for each cost account in any given year will tend to be correlated, e.g., if structural steel price increases more than expected, it is likely that electrical materials will too (which has copper and aluminum inputs).

A good, but pricey alternative to the above is to pay the economist for an evaluation of the index ranges. Economists often provide clients with economic scenario evaluations (i.e., best/worst) with probabilities of the scenario's occurrence. They can link this economic model scenario to the price indices and provide ranges. If they have done this on the revenue side of the NPV equation, it makes sense to also do this on the CAPEX side.

Cash Flow Spending

My base estimating model has defined s-curve spending patterns. For example, the estimator may pick from spending patterns one through five. Pattern three is symmetrical, pattern 1 is early biased, and pattern five is late biased. To use these patterns, replace the fixed value in your model with an uncertainty that can range by one pattern earlier or later than entered. The patterns for each cost account will tend to be correlated. For example, if materials are ordered earlier than planned, this would imply that construction spending may start a bit earlier as well.

Cash Flow Duration

This uncertainty is the same as schedule duration uncertainty from the contingency quantification. My base estimating model has a cash flow section in which the user inputs the start and end date of spending. Treating cash flow duration as an uncertainty is simple – instead of entering a fixed value for the end date in the escalation model, apply the distribution outcome from the probabilistic schedule contingency analysis. (I use the "riskcumul" function of @Risk that converts the p-table to a PDF.) For simplicity, apply this schedule slip to all accounts (recognize that this assumes they are perfectly correlated). Note that schedule slip is usually the most significant escalation uncertainty driver after the price indices themselves.

Cost Contingency

Apply escalation to contingency because contingency is by definition expected to be spent and was originally estimated using nominal costs (i.e., the year of the estimate basis). Treating cost contingency as an uncertainty is simple. Instead of entering a fixed value in the escalation model, apply the distribution outcome from the probabilistic contingency analysis. (I use the "riskcumul" function of @Risk that converts the p-table to a PDF.) This will be somewhat (but not highly) correlated to the cash flow (schedule) duration (i.e., if schedule slips, contingency costs will likely be higher as well).

Exchange Factors

The base estimating model for exchange impact starts with the output of the escalation model. Exchange is an extension to the escalation model where the exchange factor impact is applied to the escalated estimate. In the probabilistic version, the same is true; the only added uncertainty beyond those above is that of the exchange factors. Address this in the same way as the escalation indices: use a PERT distribution with the economist's exchange factor as the most likely value. Base the high and low on the historical high and low for that currency pair.

Combining All CAPEX Risks – Universal CAPEX Risk Quantification

Because both cost and schedule contingency uncertainty are addressed in the probabilistic escalation model, its output can report not only probabilistic escalation and exchange account estimates, but a single "universal" total CAPEX cost distribution. This distribution can then be used in an NPV model. Most NPV models only have one line for CAPEX, so it must address all the cost and schedule risks: systemic, project specific, and escalation and exchange. This becomes important when the business asks the question, "What is the worst case for CAPEX?" You cannot simply add the $p90$s of separate contingency and escalation estimates (only the "means" are additive) – if you do, you will overstate the risk because cost contingency and escalation are somewhat independent. On the other hand, if you do not include schedule contingency risk in the escalation estimate, you understate the escalation risk. The probabilistic approach described in this chapter is the most practical and realistic CAPEX risk quantification approach I am aware of.

Obtaining Input Information

Unlike contingency, there is generally no need for an escalation/exchange quantification workshop. All the escalation and exchange estimating inputs are obtained from prior contingency estimates plus the addition of the economist's index inputs. These are external risks relative to the project team. Therefore, running the model requires only dialogue with the economics department or consultant (and finance, which tends to be involved in escalation/exchange issues). However, there should also be a dialogue with the business from an NPV point of view to assure that the revenue economic assumptions are consistent with those used for the CAPEX escalation and exchange estimates.

If finance risk treatments such as hedging are involved, finance will likely take ownership of the exchange risks. In that case, the project's estimate will likely serve as a rough indicator to give finance an advance indication of the approximate scale of the risk. If hedging is not a usual practice, it is a good way to alert finance of the potential need for it.

Procurement and contracting input is needed to discuss whether and how escalation has been addressed in supplier contracts, purchase orders, and agreements. For example, if there is a fixed-price construction contract already issued with no escalation clause (the contractor is responsible for escalation), then the escalation risk is removed for that account (but only if the contract is truly awarded or fixed; a bid that may expire before the project decision is not really fixed).

Pricing agreements usually allow for the vendor to recover escalation in accordance with some formula; this may differ from the

278 *Project Risk Quantification*

indices provided by the economists. Finally, the procurement and contracting functions usually have very good insight as to pricing trends in the short term (six to twelve months out) or with respect to certain labor agreements and so on. Their input may be used in lieu of or in addition to the economist's input, particularly for short duration projects.

Having analyzed the systemic, project-specific, and escalation/exchange risks, our quantification effort is close to complete. However, there is one more risk that history tells us is very real and is economically destructive, particularly for complex projects. That is the risk of a project entering a disorderly or chaotic behavior regime where the risk impacts are not linearly related to the risk inputs. So far, all our analyses assumed "orderly" project behavior and control. The next chapter outlines an approach for warning of, if not quantifying, the risk of chaos.

Questions

1) Briefly describe the base (non-probabilistic) method for estimating future escalation costs.

2) Briefly explain what exchange risk is.

3) What are some limitations to the historical price index data available from government sources?

4) What are some common adjustments that often need to be made to price indices obtained from economists or others?

5) List four variables in an escalation cost estimate that are uncertain and need to be treated as distributions in probabilistic (MCS) approaches.

6) What project team function should be interviewed to get information from in respect to escalation and why (other than economists and estimators)?

7) Describe why it is important to work closely with business and with finance when quantifying CAPEX project escalation and currency risks.

8) Describe a feature of the recommended escalation quantification method that improves probabilistic NPV analysis.

"The Jemima Principle[1] tells us that very large projects are fragile. They do not tend to simply degrade toward poor outcomes; they tend to collapse instead."
—Edward Merrow from *Industrial Megaprojects*

14

The Tipping Point: Risk Analysis at the Edge of Chaos

The Bi-Modal Nature of Risk Impacts: Order vs. Disorder, Linear vs. Non-linear

In my benchmarking experience, I was sometimes called in to help analyze *blowout* projects. In blowouts, it was typical to find that labor costs had grown by 50%, 100%, or even 200% over the budget in engineering, construction, and start-up. These projects were usually large and complex, but otherwise, despite their atypical cost outcome, they often appeared normal in terms of their project management practices. However, by "normal," I mean mediocre. On smaller and less complex projects, mediocre practices usually result in merely mediocre outcomes, i.e., 10% or 20% overruns, which hurt but don't destroy the project's economics. But with the large complex projects, the initial mediocre performance would compound and accelerate. Clearly, complexity exacts a terrible price on poor practices and system weaknesses. And if risk events and/or other stresses happen, it adds to the problems.

---

1   *Jemima* by Henry Wadsworth Longfellow
There was a little girl, who had a little curl—Right in the middle of her forehead,
And when she was good, she was very, very good—But when she was bad she was horrid...

What Chaos Looks Like

Most risk analysts are focused on interviews and reports at the home office. Some will ask me what a disorderly or chaotic project looks like in the field, literally speaking. Can you tell it's in trouble at a glance? What would you look for at a construction site?

It is hard to visibly see problems until construction is underway – the steel work is ramping up and piping is starting. At that point (about 30% construction), visible signs appear at the site as follows:

First, disorder results in increased head counts and labor hours (there is never a shortage in labor, only specific skills). So when you pull into the project site of a chaotic project, you can't find a parking space even though work is not at its peak (assuming labor is not all bussed). The safety orientation room for visitors will be standing room only. In the office trailers, there will be no place to sit; every desk is taken if not shared and meeting rooms are always full. The coffee pot will be empty with no cups anywhere.

Second, disorder often results in out-of-sequence fabrication and construction work and delays in installing materials and equipment. So, the lay-down yard or warehouse where materials are temporarily stored will be literally overflowing. I recall one plant where pipe-spools lined the entrance road on both sides for hundreds of meters. But there will be lots of activity as crews hunt for things to install, seemingly at random, so they can report some progress. I rarely see the caricature of idle crews leaning on their shovels; everyone is busy, just not on what was planned.

Third, people will be in foul moods; you can feel and see the stress. At worst, they are not speaking to each other. I recall one benchmarking visit where I had to interview each owner and contractor team member separately because whenever they got together in a meeting room, all they did was argue. By the time you start the interviews and review the reports, you know the story.

In more technical language, these blowouts were occurring when project behavior transitioned from an *orderly* state (where traditional project control is effective) to a *disorderly* or *chaotic* state (where traditional control fails and intervention is required to restore order). In Chapter 4, a "tipping point" was described where complexity, combined with systemic weakness (business indecisiveness, poor team development, poorly defined scope) and confrontation with high stress (aggressive requirements, multiple risk events, adverse markets), breaks the project (or per Mr. Merrow's "Jemima principle," results in a collapse). In Chapter 4, I showed how this manifests itself in bimodal project cost growth outcome distributions with a group of projects centering on merely mediocre outcomes and a second smaller group of projects with very large cost overruns.

In terms of risk quantification, we model projects that stay within an orderly regime with linear cost and schedule risk/impact relationships. Projects in a disorderly state require non-linear models (e.g., reflecting compounding or exponential risk impact). While the behavior of disorderly or chaotic projects is by nature unpredictable (i.e., the path to failure varies from project to project), the outcome or destination is clear in the historical record: approximately a doubling of labor related costs.

Blowout Risk Quantification Tools

I have developed two blowout risk quantification tools:

♦ One tool provides a metric that warns if the project is nearing the tipping point into disorder.
♦ The other tool uses this metric to introduce non-linear, bimodal behavior into the underlying Monte Carlo simulation. The tool's predictive value is well supported by theory and is consistent with my benchmarking experience; however, keep in mind that its predictive power is not confirmed by research.

As blowouts are very destructive to project economics, risk management needs a "tipping point metric" (an alert or early warning system) and a toolkit of associated responses. The first risk objective must be "Thou Shalt not Blowout!" If the alert happens, risk management must monitor for known disorder signs and apply crisis intervention and containment treatments. As stated in Chapter 4, traditional control does not work in a disorderly regime. Using the tipping point metric in risk quantification is less critical than detecting an impending blowout. Once a blowout is fully encountered, effective remedial action becomes increasingly difficult. However, quantifying this disaster is a good way to help communicate why management should pay attention to the qualitative warning (assuming management is still employed after the blowout).

Complexity and Stressors: Agents of Disorder

As discussed, complexity, combined with systemic weakness and confrontation with stressors, are the drivers that push project behavior into a disorderly regime. In a 2015 article, I described these risk drivers in detail.[2] My model of complexity risk – based conceptu-

---

2   Hollmann, John, "Risk Analysis at the Edge of Chaos," *Cost Engineering Journal*, AACE International, Jan/Feb 2015.

ally on the models of Baccarini[3] and Gul[4] – describes the elements of complexity with their typical attributes in projects (some attributes apply to multiple elements) as shown in Figure 14.1.

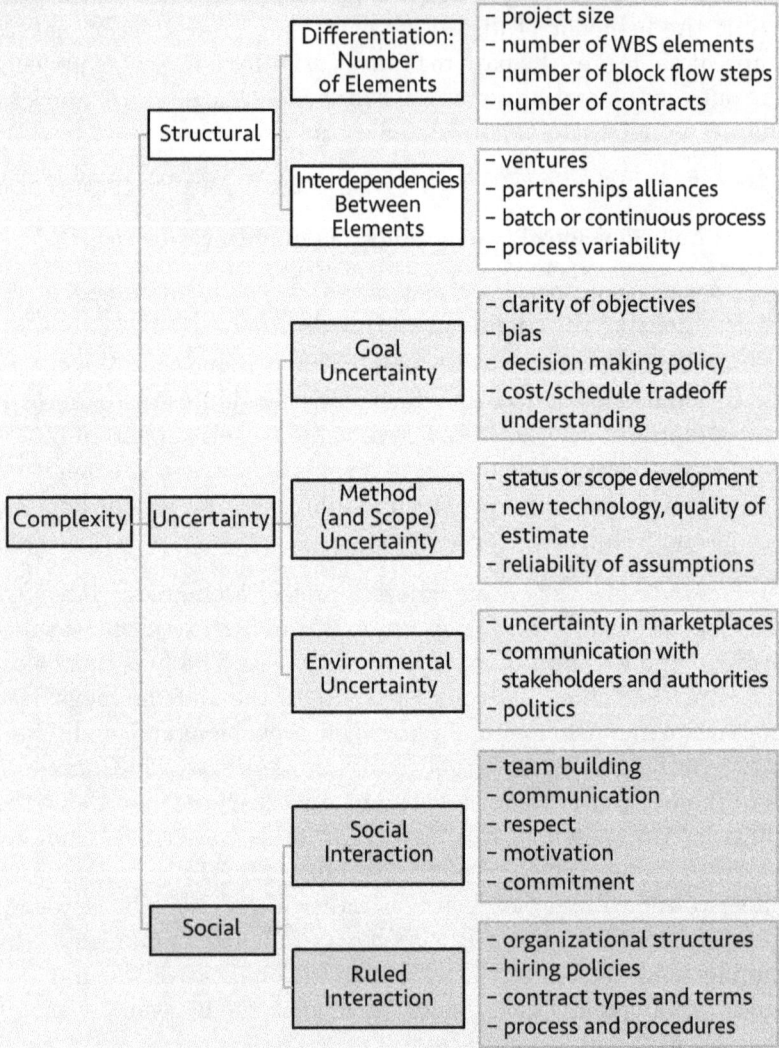

Figure 14.1: Breakdown Model of the Elements of Project Complexity

---

3   Baccarini, David, "The Concept of Project Complexity: A Review," International Journal of Project Management, Volume 14, 1996.

4   Gul, Saleem and Shahnawaz Khan, "Revisiting Project Complexity: Towards a Comprehensive Model of Project Complexity," Proceedings, 2nd International Conference on Construction and Project Management, ACSIT Press Singapore, 2011.

To this, you must add the components of stress on a project. Arguably, these stressors are just more elements of system complexity, but they reflect elements that tend to act on a system once it is in place (e.g., occurrence of a risk event). Figure 14.2 outlines the stressors (based in part on Bertelsen's construct of stress and decision power,[5] with the author's addition of risk events).

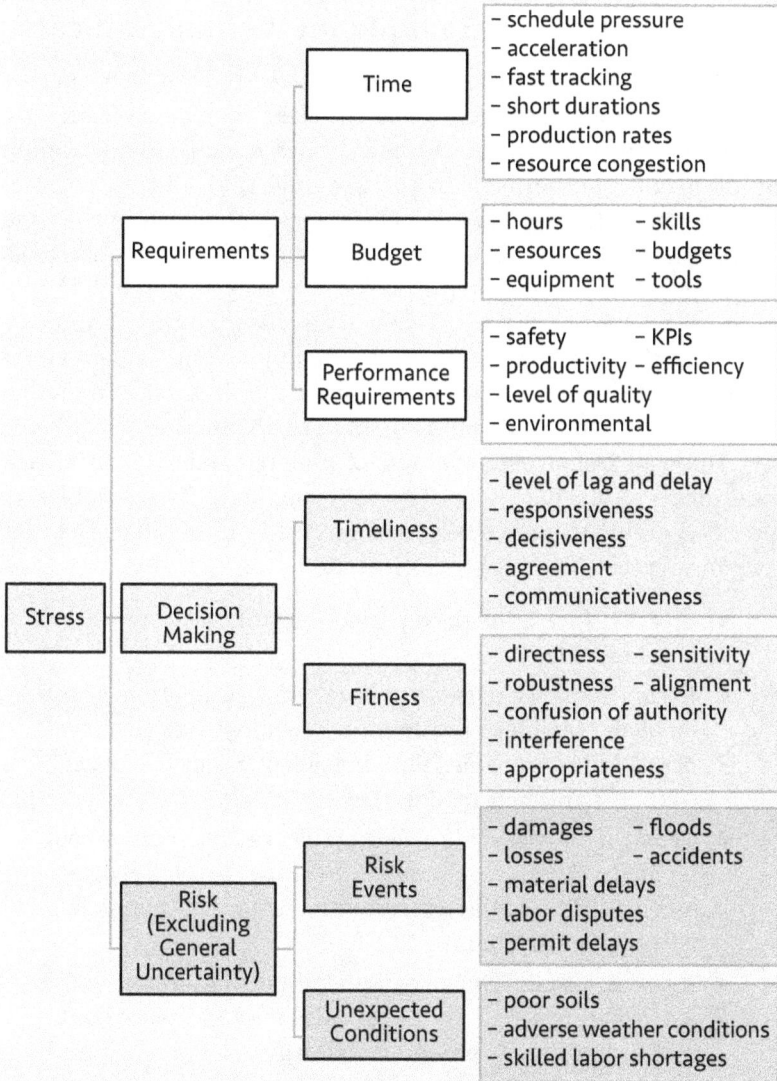

Figure 14.2: Breakdown Model of the Elements of Project Stressors

---

5   Bertelsen, Sven and Lauri Koskela, "Avoiding and Managing Chaos in Projects," 11th Annual Conference on Lean Construction, Blacksburg, VA, July 2003.

Note that all of the factors listed in the right hand tables are systemic and project-specific risks. It uses the recommended risk quantification practices laid out so far. You do not need to measure anything new in order to measure the "tipping point" – it is a matter of how the measures are applied. Pre-tipping, these risks have one impact; post tipping they have quite a different one.

A Tipping Point Warning Indicator

Based on the conceptual complexity/stressor breakdown above, and using systemic and project-specific risks that we have already identified and quantified, you can create a qualitative tipping point warning mechanism. In the example that follows, some of the systemic risk categories described were not shown in the base parametric models in Chapter 11. The author's parametric tools further sub-divide the systemic risks. The way to sub-divide risk measures in the parametric models is discussed in the Chapter 11 pie analogy; it is a fairly simple adjustment so long as you do not add more net risk impact by adding a risk sub-division. Where this sub-division was done, it is explained in the example.

Table 14.1 shows an example of a metric indicator from risk quantification models. Note that the complexity/stressor factors described previously have been summarized in six categories that work in this tool. The categories include:

♦ *Size*: This uses the total project capital cost (a measure of complication).

♦ *Decisiveness*: This uses a systemic risk rating from a tool labeled: "Business Leadership, Ownership & Decisiveness." This is an added sub-division of 'Scope Definition" in the Chapter 11 model.

♦ *Team*: This uses a systemic risk rating from a tool labeled: "Team Development, Staffing, Roles/Responsibilities." This is the same as the "Team Development" adjustment in Chapter 11.

♦ *Aggressiveness*: This uses an average of systemic risks ratings from a tool (based on validation of the estimate and schedule) labeled: "Cost Aggressiveness" and "Schedule Aggressiveness." This is the same as the "Bias" adjustments in Chapter 11.

♦ *Complexity*: This uses an average of systemic risks ratings from another tool labeled: "Process/Facility Complexity" and "Execution Complexity." These are added sub-divisions of "Complexity" in the Chapter 11 model.

♦ *Project Specific Risks*: This uses the percent contribution of project-specific risks to the percentage contingency (rated at the mean of probability x impact).

COMPLEXITY/STRESS FACTORS (TIPPING POINT FACTORS)						
Systemic Risk Factors	Size	Decisiveness	Team	Aggressiveness	Complexity	Overall
System Risk Indicators	◯	◯	●	◉	◯	◯
Project Specific Risks	Considers whether top risk events or conditions might consume contingency					◯
OVERALL						◯
EXPLANATION: The distribution of project cost outcomes is bimodal or discontinuous. At some point, certain risks may push a project into a chaotic regime with significantly worse outcomes than forecast. The factors above represent complexity/stressor risks associated with the *tipping point* into chaotic, unpredictable behavior. The base contingency does not cover chaotic outcomes; the potential occurrence of such outcomes is flagged by this indicator.						

Table 14.1: Example of a Tipping Point Indicator (Qualitative)

Note that *Size, Team,* and *Complexity* are "complexity" measures while *Decisiveness, Aggressiveness* and *Project Specific Risks* are primarily "stressor" measures. These are combined into an overall weighted tipping point metric:

♦ If the traffic signal is *red* (black in Table 14.1), this is a serious threat that warrants further risk treatment or intervention.

♦ A *yellow* (shaded in Table 14.1) metric is one to monitor closely, and

♦ *Green* (white in Table 14.1) is not a likely blowout factor.

My recommendation to an owner client is that if the overall warning is red, the project should not pass the decision gate as is. It is a blowout waiting to happen.

Behind each signal is a quantitative value. Other than the size and project specific risk values (which are objective values), the numbers vary depending on the systemic risk rating that you use (e.g., scale of 0 to 10 or 1 to 5). For example, the ratings I use are shown in Table 14.2.

TIPPING POINT RATING SYSTEM	GREEN	YELLOW	RED
Size	<$500M	$500M to $1B	>$1B
Decisiveness: *Business Leadership, Ownership,* and *Decisiveness*; scale of 0 to 10	>5	4 to 5	0 to 3
Team: *Team Development, Staffing, Roles/Responsibilities*; scale of 0 to 10	>5	4 to 5	0 to 3
Aggressiveness: Average of *Cost Aggressiveness* and *Schedule Aggressiveness*, each on a scale of 0 to 10	0 to 2	3 to 5	>5
Complexity: Average of *Process/Facility Complexity* and *Execution Complexity*, each on a scale of 0 to 10	0 to 3	4 to 6	>6
Project Specific Risks	<5%	5 to 10%	>10%
OVERALL (average, see text)	1 to 1.66	1.67 to 2.33	>2.33

Table 14.2: Example Tipping Point Rating System

For the *overall systemic* risk rating, each of the five systemic measures is converted to one, two, or three (green, yellow or red). The average is computed, and projects from 1.0 to 1.66 are green, 1.67 to 2.33 are yellow, and greater than 2.33 are red. The *overall* averages the systemic and project specific ratings. Depending on the company culture, project system, and management's understanding of what this warning means, the qualitative indicator (green, yellow, red) may not be enough. This leads to quantifying the impact of these measures.

The Tipping Point in a Quantitative Model

Incorporating the tipping point into an MCS model is fairly simple. The tipping point represents crossing over from an orderly to a disorderly regime, an either/or situation. So, in a Monte Carlo Simulation, we need two new variables:

♦ A trigger that tells each MCS iteration whether that sampling observation crosses the tipping point into a disorderly outcome, and

♦ The "disorder cost penalty" (e.g., a doubling of labor related cost).

The trigger uses the tipping point metric described previously. For example, the metric may have an overall value from one to three, with one being all green and three being all red. This one to three metric is converted to the percentage of MCS iterations that cross the tipping point. For example, if the metric is three, then 30% of the runs will blowout. Next, a random number generator is applied [in @Risk this is RiskUniform (1,0)] such that if the random value in a given iteration is less than the trigger percent (e.g., <0.3), that iteration's expected value will include the disorder cost penalty.

Figures 14.3 and 14.4 are from actual megaproject risk evaluations and illustrate the effect of this addition to the Expected Value model. In Figure 14.3, the project was red on several of the tipping point metrics. This resulted in many of the MCS iterations suffering the blowout penalty. A second mode plus a long tail began to appear in the MCS cost outcome distribution such that at the worst case (*p*90), the project would be a blowout (i.e., 77% over the budgeted amount). This would render most projects uneconomical.

In Figure 14.4, another megaproject was green on most of the tipping point metrics, but a few were yellow. This resulted in some of the MCS iterations suffering a blowout, but so few that the distribution has not so much a second mode but a narrow long tail. In this case, the worst case (*p*90) outcome was bad, but not enough to render the project uneconomical.

The hope is that a quantification number and picture will reinforce the tipping metric warning. The question the decision makers had to face for the first megaproject (in the example, the project was

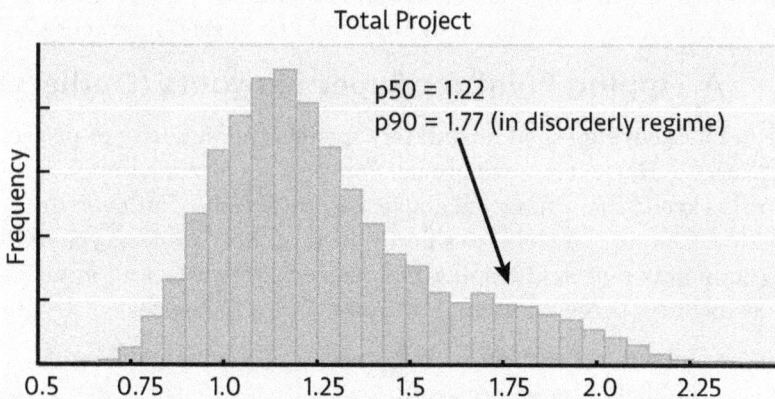

Figure 14.3: Example Expected Value Model Output for Cost Growth (Actual/Estimate) With High Tipping Point Risk

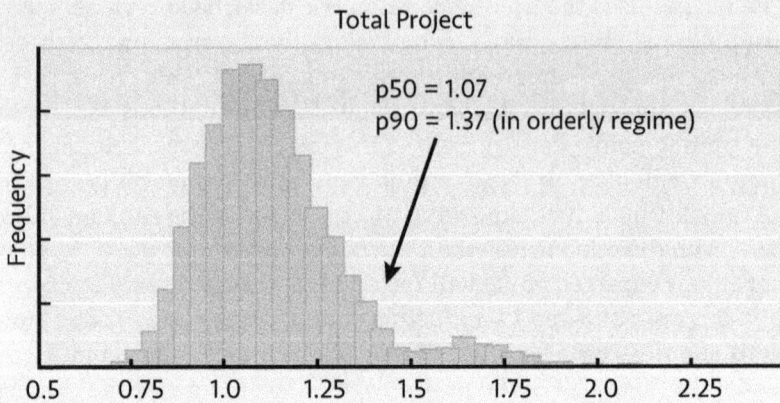

*Figure 14.4: Example Expected Value Model Output for Cost Growth
(Actual/Estimate) With Low Tipping Point Risk*

a "super-mega") was whether they wanted to stake their company's
valuation, not to speak of their personal reputations or careers, on
the risks that Figure 14.3 represents. Plus, if the company funds at
*p*80 as policy (as is common in the mining industry), an outcome such
as Figure 14.3 will likely kill the project. In fact, most of the mining
and other complex mega-projects during the commodity super-cycle
would have a risk profile similar to that shown in Figure 14.3 (high
systemic risks plus stress factors). It is no coincidence that many of
the top mining company CEOs were replaced by the end of 2012.

I have tested this MCS modeling approach to see if it can replicate the bimodal cost growth outcomes actually observed in empirical
research – and it can. I cannot say, however, whether the risk drivers
I picked or the ratings and evaluation I assigned are the whole story,
but this is closer to reality than anything I have seen in practice.

A Tipping Point for Super Blowouts (Outliers)

The above method adequately models the majority of project
situations. However, some projects have cost overruns that significantly exceed those modeled above; i.e., total costs that overrun by
>300%. Chapter 15 includes a description of those project types and
recommends a second tipping point model indicator and adjuster
that includes three additional "strategic" risk measures:

♦ Likelihood of Political Influence (e.g., as in monumental
   publicly funded projects),

♦ Likelihood of Regulatory Change (e.g., as in nuclear) , and

♦ Susceptibility to corruption.

In an Expected Value model this is applied the same way as the base model described in this Chapter. This second super blowout adjuster adds to the nominal blowout.

Anatomy of a Blowout

Many have not experienced a project blowout. They ask, "How can labor double without scope change and/or with stable prices and/or with major EPCs?"

It is difficult to imagine, so here is an example. This case is a process plant expansion in a developing country. The flow sheet was ordinary, but the plant is large and crowded. The owner has weak systems and is light on staff, so they use what they view as a conservative approach. They start with a major contractor for basic engineering. Next, they award an incentivized reimbursable EPC contract to another major contractor. The owner hires a third major as a Project Management Contractor (PMC) to help cover for their weaknesses. How badly can that go? As the construction manpower chart below shows – very badly – more than twice the planned labor and two years late. This chart could apply to any number of mega-projects that I have reviewed over the years.

The cause, as is common, was an insidious combination of systemic risks. The risk register was unremarkable. Start with an owner with weak systems and a weak team. Add to that complexity (which is inherent to most megaprojects). Then add the stress of shortages of skilled labor (which was a given from the start). A tipping point measure, if it had been done, would be nearing "red" at this point. But those are just facts; the dismaying part comes next.

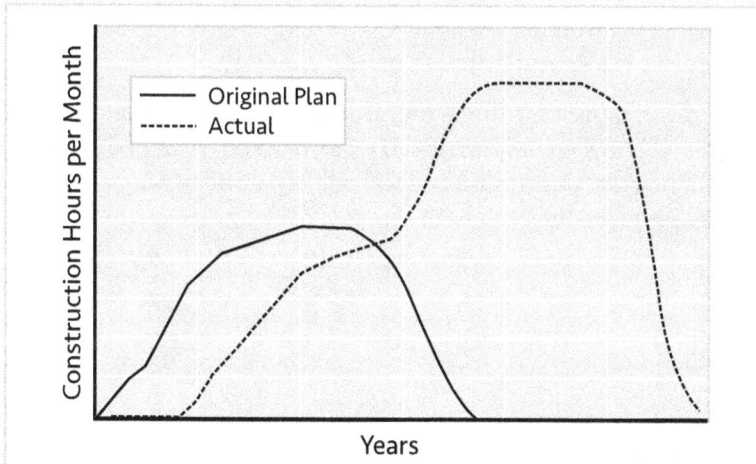

The EPC contractor mobilizes a "B" team and an unintegrated, untested mix of project control systems. The schedule logic is not sequenced properly. Engineering delays become fabrication delays that become construction delays. In construction, incentive stress distorts change control. Progress is overstated and actual progress is obtained via out of sequence work. The PMC makes suggestions, but the "disorder" nature of the risk is unrecognized, so there is no meaningful intervention – only hyped up control. For many months the team forecasts that the project's extremely low productivity will magically become 1.0 the next month.

Several years into the project, the over-reporting is recognized, but again, the real nature of the risks is not. Punishment is meted out on the owner side, resources are injected, and schedule stress is added in an unrealistic re-baselined plan. The tipping point is irretrievably crossed and a project blowout commences. Several more years after the re-baselining, the project is completed. The parties arbitrate disputes. The unknown-unknown cards are played. The asset is written down. The experience is written off as an exception (until their next project...).

Questions

1) Describe what is meant by the "tipping point" in this chapter.

2) What is the characteristic cost outcome of a project that has crossed the tipping point?

3) In general, what are the three drivers that push a project behavior toward a disorderly regime?

4) What six specific risk measures are compiled in the Tipping Point Indicator metric? Which measure complexity and which measure stress?

5) What two variables are added to an Expected Value MCS model to incorporate tipping point behavior?

6) For a company that funds projects and runs NPV economics on a $p80$ CAPEX confidence level, what is likely to happen when realistic risk quantification methods are applied on a complex megaproject subject to high stress?

"The more things change, the more they stay the same."
(plus ça change, plus c'est la même chose)
–Jean-Baptiste Alphonse Karr

15

Estimate Accuracy (and Outliers) for Various Industries and for Contractors

Chapter 4 began with a historical review of cost growth in 19th century transportation infrastructure projects, specifically canals and railroads. That review highlighted the fact that cost and schedule estimating accuracy and risk quantification is important in all industries. However, to this point the book has focused on the process industries such as oil and gas, chemicals, mining and metals and so on. The main reason is that the best empirical research and modeling available is for the process industries; it is the foundation. However, there have been many empirical accuracy studies for other industries.

The book has also focused on accuracy and investment decision making from the owner's perspective. This is because the sum total of capital risk to owners is greater and more extensive than to EPC contractors. Also, public data and research on accuracy from the contractor perspective is largely non-existent. However, depending on the risks that contractors accept (particular in lump sum contracts with liquidated damages), they are just as concerned about estimate accuracy as owners and sometimes more so because contractors are less able to absorb major losses.

To fill the gaps above, this chapter reviews published accuracy data for various industries and describes the contractor perspective. It also assesses how well the methods in the book apply for those sectors and entities. It is not an exhaustive review or assessment, but is sufficient to broaden the applicability of the risk quantification methods in Chapter 11 (Systemic Risks and the Parametric Method) and Chapter 14 (Tipping Point).

Accuracy References and Data for Various Industries

This section reviews a sample of empirical estimate accuracy studies for industries involving construction but not tapped by the Rand/Hackney/CII process industry research roots.[1] The selected industries differ in being either structure/civil centric and publicly funded or regulated (transport and hydropower), or outside the core oil & gas/chemical/mining/metals arena (nuclear, wind, solar energy, power transmission, and pipeline). There are many studies available.[2]

However, this sample was selected to support comparisons to the Chapters 11 and 14 methods from several risk perspectives. Some of the studies are referenced in a meta-analysis article that I published in 2012.[3] The studies covered in that article had the following attributes that apply to most sources that depend on published data and do not originate from cooperative benchmarking organizations (e.g., IPA, CII):

---

1   Military, aerospace, and IT projects are excluded. There is a wealth of data on those sectors; however, they have unique attributes and their own expert cost world. They are worthy of their own texts; however, the principles of this text apply there.

2   For example, the Lundberg study on transport to be covered later summarizes twenty studies in that sector.

3   Hollmann, John, "Estimate Accuracy: Dealing with Reality," Cost Engineering Journal, AACE International, Nov/Dec 2012.

♦ Projects were big enough to be relevant to the success of the company (i.e., a few million $US up to megaprojects),

♦ In response to a perceived preponderance of overruns, the studies asked, "What is the accuracy of our estimates and why?"

♦ The quality of the study data sets was generally poor; the researchers lament the poor state of historical project records and data, and

♦ The statistics are presented in ways that make them difficult to understand or apply.

In short, few studies provide useful data for realistic risk modeling. Most provide only summary descriptive statistics. In terms of causal inputs or risk drivers, they capture general project attributes such as project type, location, size and timing, but rarely include practices. For outcomes, they provide cost growth means and sometimes standard deviations, but rarely useful distributions other than charts that one may or may not be able to obtain useful data from. The basis of the estimate used for cost growth metrics (actual/estimate) are rarely known, including how much contingency the estimates included (i.e., when a project comes out on budget is it due to good practices or did they just allocate contingency for their poor practices, and vice-versa). Some apply inferential statistics (for example, regression of cost growth versus attributes), but they are unable to control for dominant risks such as the level of scope definition, system maturity, team development, or project-specific risks. In short, most studies are useful only as rough indicators. The researchers apply the best statistical rigor they can, but even the best studies are of statistically limited value. That is not a criticism of the researchers – as discussed in Chapter 18, industry historical data practices are dismal.

Table 15.1 shows the selected estimate accuracy study comparison sample. Each published study provided statistics on the distribution of cost growth outcomes for its sample of projects. For example, reference "F" calculated the cost growth for each of its 24 projects and then reported the $p10/50/90$ for the distribution of cost growth values (in that case, the p-values were from a fitted distribution). Often studies provide a mean and a standard deviation; in that case $p90/p10$ values can be approximated by transforming the reported data to an estimate/actual ratio and then assuming a

STUDY ATTRIBUTES				ESTIMATE ACCURACY OF SAMPLE		
REFERENCE	PROJECTS	REFERENCE POINT	Adjusted?	p10 or Similar	p50 or Mean	p90 or Similar
[A] Figure 1	258 Transport, Global	"Decision" estimate	Time	~–15%	~+15% μ = +27%	~+100%
Flyvbjerg, Bent, Mette Skamris Holm and Søren Buhl, "Underestimating Costs in Public Works Projects; Error or Lie?," APA Journal, 68:3, 279-295, 2002.						
[B] Table 2	167 Transport, Swedish	Varied reference	No	~–32%	μ = +15%	~+62%
Lundberg, Mattias, Anchalee Jenpanitsub and Roger Pyddoke, "Cost Overruns in Swedish Transport Projects," CTS Working Paper 2011:11, Centre for Transport Studies, Stockholm Sweden, 2011.						
[C] Various	250+ Transport, US compilation	From "Planning"	?	~0%	~+20% μ = +40%	~+100%
Harbuck, Robert, "Are Accurate Estimates Achievable During the Planning of Transportation Projects?" AACE International Transactions, 2007.						
[D] Pg. I.3.4	56 Hydropower, World Bank	From "Appraisal"	Time	–15%	μ = +24%	+65%
Merrow, Edward W. and Brett R. Schroeder, "Understanding the Costs and Schedule of Hydroelectric Projects," 1991 AACE International Transactions, 1991.						
[E] Figure 2	245 Hydropower, Global	From "Budgeted"	Time	~–20%	+27% μ = +96%	+300%
Ansar, Flyvbjerg, Budzier and Lunn, "Should we build more large dams? The actual costs of hydropower megaproject development," Elsevier Ltd, 2014.						
[F] Table 2	24 Hydropower, Canadian	Est By Phase (Cls 5,4,3)	Scope & Time	–11%	+14%	+53%
Hollmann, John. et. al., "Variability in Accuracy Ranges: A Case Study In the Canadian Hydropower Industry," AACE International Transactions, 2014.						
[G] Various	61 Hydropower	Ambiguous ("Estimated costs")	Time	?	μ = +71%	?
	180 Nuclear			?	μ = +117%	?
	35 Wind			?	μ = +8%	?
	39 Solar			?	μ = +1%	?
Sovacool, Nugent and Gilbert, "Construction Cost Overruns and Electricity Infrastructure: An Unavoidable Risk?" The Electricity Journal, May 2014.						
[H] Database	188 US Pipeline	FERC filing	No	–21%	0%	+34%
Oil & Gas Journal Online Research Center, US Pipeline Study 2009; Actual vs. Estimate (database for fee), Penwell Corporation, Houston TX, 2009.						
[I] Figure 1	? Process Plant Turnarounds	From "Budget"	?	–11%	+9% μ = +16%	+59%
Lawrence, Gordon, "Analysis Yields Turnaround Benchmarks for Allowance, Contingency," Oil & Gas Journal, April 2, 2012.						

Table 15.1: Selected Industry Estimate Accuracy Studies

normal distribution for which the $p90$ and $p10$ values are the mean plus and minus 1.28 times the standard deviation, respectively. For some, the $p90/p10$ values were roughly scaled from figures of distributions of varying quality.

Note that the tilde (~) symbol means approximate and the Greek letter mu (µ) is the mean. Hydropower is included because while it includes power generation (a process element), its costs are dominated by civil work (site work, excavation, and concrete) and these projects are publicly funded and/or regulated.

At first glance, the $p90/p10$ ranges in Table 15.1 exhibit wide variability. They range from +34% to –21% for US pipelines (and similar for wind, solar, and power transmission) to about +300 to –20% for global hydropower (and similar for nuclear). The questions of interest here are:

♦ Would the process industry model of Chapters 11 and 14 predict these outcomes?

♦ If not, what is driving the accuracy differences?

For any new risk drivers, how might we factor them into the Chapter 11 and 14 models?

Interpretation of the Industry Data

The following are assessments of the comparison studies to answer the questions about what they are telling us with respect to the process-industry base case.

Scope Definition

Most studies do not control for the level of scope definition at sanction. This is problematic because process industry research shows that the level of scope definition is a dominant risk driver.

REFER-ENCE	PROJECTS	REFERENCE POINT	$p10$ or similar	$p50$ or mean (µ)	$p90$ or similar
[D]	56 Global (uncontrolled)	From "Appraisal"	–15%	µ= +24%	+65%
[E]	245 Global (uncontrolled)	From "Budgeted"	~–20%	+27% µ= +96%	+300%
[F]	24 Canadian (controlled)	FEL 3/Define	–11%	+14%	+53%
		FEL 2/Select	–6%	+28%	+97%
		FEL 1/Assess	+12%	+64%	+186%

Table 15.2 : Comparison of Hydropower Estimate Accuracy Studies

The Table 15.2 study comparison shows why this is important. It compares two uncontrolled global hydropower studies to a controlled Canadian hydropower study. Looking at the *p*90 values, the high ranges for the studies vary significantly.

On closer inspection, the cost growth in the controlled Canadian study for FEL 2/Select estimates is close to the cost growth in study [D], while the cost growth from the FEL 1/Assess estimates is close to the cost growth in study [E]. Further, the differences in the *p*50 values of studies [D] and [F-FEL 2] and the mean of study [D] are not statistically significant. As to the *p*90 differences, the large sample in Study [E] had a small number of extreme outliers that pulled its mean and *p*90 far away from the median (it included a group or projects centered at about 500% overrun and one project that overran by more than 5,000%).

The conclusion that the uncontrolled study [E] drew from its data was that hydropower cost overruns were so dire that, *"Policymakers, particularly in developing countries, are advised to prefer agile energy alternatives that can be built over shorter time horizons to energy megaprojects."* The implication here is that big is bad. On the contrary, the statistically controlled study [F] showed that if you define hydropower project scope well before sanction (or allow for empirically valid contingency such as from this book's methods), the outcomes can be reasonably reliable. However, study [E] was swayed by outliers that raise questions that we will examine later.

The controlled study, which included all the large projects built in the participating Canadian provinces, was designed to determine if process industry accuracy applied to the hydropower industry. The finding was, *"The Canadian hydro experience is similar to that of other process industry projects, as well as of hydropower projects in other regions funded by the World Bank."* In other words, the model in Chapter 11 appears to be self-correcting for the differences in the technology, complexity, and so on between process plant and civil oriented/regulated hydropower projects. The next section explores that conclusion further.

Complexity, Technology, and Process Severity

Study [G] in Table 15.3 included power industry projects of all types using similar statistical review methods of published data. That study shows wide variability in mean estimate accuracy between different power project types. For hydropower, the mean project cost overrun is about the same as study [E] that we reviewed in the last section. However, nuclear, wind, and solar projects display quite different mean overrun values (the study did not report useful distribution data). The question is, can the difference be explained by the process industry model?

REFERENCE	PROJECTS	MEAN (μ)
[G]	61 Hydropower	$\mu = +71\%$
	180 Nuclear	$\mu = +117\%$
	35 Wind	$\mu = +8\%$
	39 Solar	$\mu = +1\%$

Table 15.3 : Comparison of Estimate Accuracy for Power Projects

To compare the studies to the Chapter 11 parametric model, we need to assume model inputs. The initial assumption is that, on average, the projects were sanctioned at FEL 2/Select equivalent scope definition (as indicated in the previous section analysis). Next, based on my experience working on these types of projects, nuclear and wind/solar are opposites in terms of their complexity, technology, and process severity. In physical and execution terms, nuclear projects are much more complex (although subsea elements of offshore wind are challenging). Likewise, nuclear has more technology (particularly regarding safety and the environment) and process severity challenges than wind or solar. Table 15.4 shows these and other rating assumptions for application in the Chapter 11 parametric model:

RISK DRIVER	NUCLEAR RATING	WIND/SOLAR
Scope Definition	Average 4	Average 4
New Technology	15%	5%
Process Severity	9	1
Complexity	9	2
Team Development	Poor	Poor
Project Control	Poor	Poor
Estimate Basis	Good	Good
Equipment	15%	35%
Fixed Price	<10%	20-30%
Bias	Low	Typical

Table 15.4 : Systemic Risk Ratings for Nuclear versus Wind/Solar Power Projects

Based on the Table 15.4 inputs (and also assuming that the study projects included 10% contingency in their budgets), Table 15.5 shows the Chapter 11 model outcome compared to study [G] for nuclear.

INDUSTRY	REFERENCE	P50	MEAN	P90
Nuclear	Study [G]	?	+117%	?
	Parametric Model	+32%	+36%	+115%

Table 15.5 : Nuclear Study versus the Parametric Risk Model

At first glance, nuclear projects have higher mean cost growth than predicted. However, we should consider the effect of extreme outliers that we saw in the hydropower study [E]. That study had a similarly high mean of +96%, but its median (*p*50) was only +27%! If study [G] had analogous outliers, which is not unlikely in a sample of 180, the study *p*50 and parametric model *p*50 would likely be close, which implies that the process industry model works. That will remain speculation because study [G] had no useful range data. However, we will revisit the outlier issue later.

Next, wind and solar projects were evaluated as shown in Table 15.6 (again, assuming the projects included 10% contingency in their budgets). Wind and solar are combined because of their similar outcomes and risk driver attributes relative to the model.

INDUSTRY	REFERENCE	P50	MEAN	P90
Wind and Solar	Study [G]	?	+1 to 8%	?
	Parametric Model	+4%	+8%	+47%

Table 15.6 : Wind and Solar versus the Parametric Risk Model

In this case, the study [G] and the predicted means are similarly low (+/-10% is within most finance department's expectations for capital discipline). Lower complexity, technology, and process severity impacts are particularly noticeable in the model's *p*90 value, which is about 1/3 the *p*90 of the nuclear case. Based on the scant study statistics, we can reasonably conclude that the parametric model applies.

We can also use this table in considering the pipeline projects in study [H]. Pipeline projects are fairly similar to wind and solar in terms of complexity, technology, and process severity ratings (i.e., the inputs would be similar to Table 15.4). The study [H] mean cost growth of +0% appears to be similar to wind and solar, and also the process model. Also, the major pipeline company referenced in Chapter 8 uses the methods described in this book successfully.

Transportation (Proxy for Infrastructure)

This section discusses transportation projects – an industry that differs greatly from process plants and power. Transportation includes road, rail, and urban transit. These projects (with the exception of freight rail) are usually taxpayer funded and owned by the government (although public-private arrangements are becoming more common). I used study [A] as our comparison because it is perhaps the most widely referenced study on cost estimate accuracy in any industry.[4] Parametric model inputs were assumed to test this data against the process model as shown in Table 15.7.

RISK DRIVER	TRANSPORT RATING
Scope Definition	Average 5
New Technology	0%
Process Severity	n/a
Complexity	3
Team Development	Poor
Project Control	Poor
Estimate Basis	Good
Equipment	0%
Fixed Price	>40%
Bias	Typical

Table 15.7 : Systemic Risk Ratings for Transportation Projects

For the level of scope definition at funding, reference [C] says that the first published and initially funded number (as opposed to later control estimates) is typically the conceptual or appraisal estimate; this is roughly analogous to FEL1/Appraise or Class 5. Next, it was assumed that their complexity and technology are relatively low, dominated by road projects. However, if you were to model only high-speed rail or urban transit projects, higher complexity ratings

---

4   Study [B] also included a table of twenty other international accuracy studies in transport. The unweighted average overruns of those twenty study averages is about 30%, with rail and urban transit projects being closer to 50% average and roads being closer to about 10% average.

would be justified. Process severity is not applicable and it was assumed that none of the projects were new technology (e.g., maglev). I have assumed that transport projects are also more likely to use fixed price strategies or unit price (such practices are not quantified in the study).

Table 15.8 shows the Chapter 11 model outcome, based on the Table 15.7 inputs (again, assuming the study projects included 10% contingency in their estimates). This is compared to study [A] range for transport as follows (note that the study *p*-values are approximated):

INDUSTRY	REFERENCE	P50	MEAN	P90
Transportation	Study [A]	~+15%	+27%	~+100%
	Parametric Model	+15%	+21%	+71%

Table 15.8 : Transportation Study versus the Parametric Risk Model

In this case the model *p*50 values appear to reasonably predict the study outcomes. The mean values are close although the study's mean value is pulling away from the *p*50. The *p*90 values are high; in the model the low level of definition assumed drives this. However, as with the other studies, study [A]'s mean and *p*90 value are affected by outliers; there were several in the study in the +200% to +300% overrun range. The issues of outliers will be covered later. From this scant data, and accepting that outlier premise, we can again reasonably conclude that the parametric model applies.

Conclusion: The Process Industry Model is Generic

While the studies and analyses above are by no means the final word, they all indicate that the process industry parametric cost growth model discussed in Chapter 11 can be applied across most construction-related industry projects. Unfortunately, the studies also all indicate that the contingencies being allowed for by industries of all types are similarly unrealistic (5% to 15% contingency versus 15% to 40% that the realistic model predicts). If realistic risk quantification methods had been used, the mean overruns would be closer to 0% in all cases.

This analysis also shows why analysts must interpret estimating accuracy studies with skepticism if the studies are not controlled for known risk drivers, particularly the level of scope definition. That factor alone explains much of the poor accuracy noted in studies of publicly available data. Other than for outliers, industry data does not support *strategic misrepresentation* as being the primary risk driver, even for public infrastructure projects. However, that may not be true if politicians understood our profession's failure to address the level of scope definition and other systemic risks in risk quantification. They could then play us all for fools just by getting funding as early as possible.

Another caution is not to focus on mean values. They are often sensational which makes them useful if your purpose is to make a point or get press coverage, but alone they add little to understanding (standard deviations add little to true understanding either). That said, outliers drive mean values and that makes them deserving of special attention.

Outliers: Beyond the Pale (Beyond *p*90)

In the hydropower, nuclear, and transport studies, the mean and *p*90 cost overrun values were pulled to the high side by outliers. I call outlier projects "beyond the Pale"[5] because their outcome is beyond the *p*90 boundary that we often consider as the worst case in economic evaluations. If you focus on the median values (and the mean when not distorted by outliers), the parametric model works reasonably well for all the industries examined.

It is tempting to call the outliers "unknown-unknowns" or "black swans" and discard them from studies, or say they are beyond the *p*90, so why care? However, a premise of this book is that we must quantify the risks that matter and these matter greatly. If you have a large portfolio of projects, a few outliers can ruin overall return-on-capital (and demonstrate what finance would call "poor capital discipline"). There are two hypotheses as to what causes massive overruns:

♦ Strategic misrepresentation (and its cousin, corruption) (Chapter 5), and
♦ Crossing the Tipping Point (Chapter 14).

An example of the former is hydropower study [E] in which the distribution of its 245 projects had a very long tail (median = 27%, mean = 96%). The distribution was bimodal, with a small group of outlier projects with overruns ranging from about 450% to 625%. A few projects overran by even more; the maximum was 5,142%! Among that study's authors is Dr. Bent Flyvbjerg, who is the leading

---

5   "The Pale" was an area of Ireland once under the authority of English law; being "beyond the Pale" meant outside the rule of English law and order.

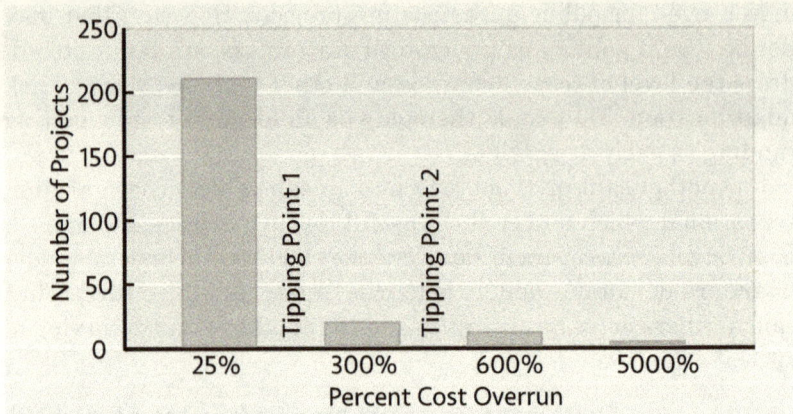

Figure 15.1: The Dual Tipping Point Concept as a Discrete Distribution

proponent of the theory that optimism bias and strategic misrepresentation ("*psychological delusion and political deception*" in the
study's words)[6] are largely to blame for the large average overruns
of public infrastructure project cost.

I propose rather that study [E]'s long tail is caused by a combination of misrepresentation *and* the tipping point risks, acting in a
combined and sometimes stepped fashion. The wide part of the tail
nearer the mean is made up of overruns of 100% to 300%. These are
common to tipping point behavior on megaprojects and the tipping
point model in Chapter 14 predicts this. However, the much smaller
group of projects at about 450% to 625% overrun (small in number,
but large in effect on the mean) appear to have crossed a second
tipping point driven by the blowout drivers covered in Chapter 14
and misrepresentation and/or corruption.[7] (See Figure 15.1.)

In addition, blowouts can be exploited by another risk driver.
After punishments are doled out for the initial failure (e.g., firings,
elections), the new overseer, free from fault, discovers an opportunity – *de facto fiscal stimulus* (albeit unsanctioned and ripe for
corruption). In weak economies, some economists promote spending
money on infrastructure using debt as a good thing (although not
in this way). I would suggest that an overrun of 300% or more is an
economic program, not a project. As Rahm Emanual, US President
Obama's former Chief of Staff said, "*Never let a serious crisis go to*

6   Op. Sit., Flyvbjerg, et al.

7   There is no doubt that there is misrepresentation in the public sector
     because politicians confess to it. As shared in Chapter 4, Mr. Willie
     Brown, former mayor of San Francisco wrote; "*In the world of civic
     projects, the first budget is really just a down payment.*"

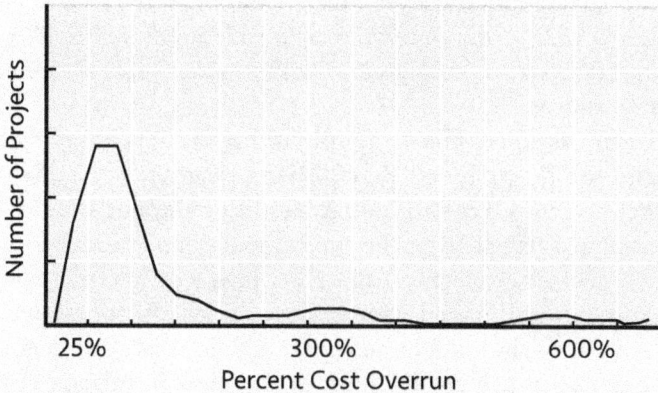

Figure 15.2: The Dual Tipping Point as an Example Continuous Distribution

waste. *And what I mean by that it's an opportunity to do things you think you could not do before.*"[8]

One example is Petrobras's Comperj refinery/petrochemical project in Brazil. A report stated, "*Comperj project is riddled with delays, cost overruns and reckless management, a state audit found, as it listed numerous modifications that raised the cost of the project from $6.1bn to nearly $50bn.*" That is about 800% with the project starting in 2004 and finishing in 2014. The report continues, "*In the audit, the TCU (Brazilian Federal Accounting Court) did not mention corruption, embezzlement or theft. However, it did find excessive risk-taking and a disregard of standard operating procedures.*" The article adds: "*The audit warned that the project is threatening Petrobras with heavy losses.*"[9] Granted, the project also made repeated "*massive revisions*" to scope, but I would posit that scope change is a risk when a project becomes something other than a project by any traditional definition.

To illustrate the dual tipping point thesis, Figure 15.1 depicts a simplistic discrete distribution of 245 projects including 214 orderly but mediocre projects with 25% overrun, 20 blowouts with 300% overrun, 10 exploitive disasters at 600% and one ridiculous project at 5,000%. This distribution has a median of 25% overrun and a mean of 100%. This is by design to replicate study [E]'s overall statistics. Of course, the actual distributions are continuous. There are no discrete sub-groups as such and the peaks and valleys vary

---

8   Seib, Gerald, "In Crisis, Opportunity for Obama," Wall Street Journal, Nov. 21, 2008.

9   ICIS News, "Overruns, Recklessness Riddle Petrobras Comperj Project – Audit," Oct. 20, 2014.

from sample to sample. The actual distribution would look something like Figure 15.2. A quote by a subsea contractor summarizes this effect as, *"When a project begins to have problems it is often followed by more problems."*[10]

In any case, both charts highlight that outliers are truly exceptions and are "beyond the Pale." Misrepresentation, exploitation, and corruption are real and must be mitigated, but should not be overstated as representing the typical state of *any* industry.

For nuclear projects in the US there was also a second tipping point, but in the nuclear industry, the risk factor is regulatory change or churn that is common when public safety and health and environmental concerns are high and project durations are long. This risk impact is not inevitable; for example one study pointed out that France did not share the US cost overrun experience because they *"had only one utility (EDF) and one builder (Areva) working closely together. They settled on a few standard reactor designs and built them over and over again, often putting multiple reactors on a single site. That allowed them to standardize their processes and get better at finding efficiencies."* The study continued: *"France's regulatory process was also less adversarial than America's – and, for better or worse, doesn't allow legal intervention by outside groups once construction gets underway."*[11] In the US, government and industry have formally recognized this risk mitigation approach and efforts are being made to standardize designs.[12] As climate change concerns increase, this type of risk increases for many other types of projects.

Two recent projects by the Southern Company in the U.S. provide examples of complexity, technology, and regulatory risks acting together. These are the Vogtle nuclear power project and the Kemper clean coal power project.[13,14] At 60% completion, Vogtle was projected to be three years late and its costs had already increased

10 Siem, K., "Update on Guará-Lula NE Project Offshore Brazil," Subsea7 conference call transcript, June 27, 2013.

11 Plumer, Brad, "Why America abandoned nuclear power," VOX, February 29, 2016.

12 U.S. NRC, "Backgrounder on New Nuclear Plant Designs," December 2015.

13 Overton, Thomas, "Even More Delays and Cost Overruns for Vogtle Expansion," Power Magazine, Feb 2, 2015.

14 Samuelson, Darren, "Billions over budget. Two years after deadline.," Politico, May 26, 2015.

21% over budget (a larger schedule slip than cost).[15] Kemper was also three years behind and its costs had tripled as it approached completion at the time of this writing.

In the case of the transportation study [A], there were no outliers exceeding 300% overrun. As bad as those were, these overruns were within the first tipping point blowout range. However, one can find anecdotes of infrastructure or civic projects elsewhere with greater overruns.

Possibly a better candidate for the second tipping point in public projects would be the Olympics; three games since 1960 overran by more than 300%.[16] Another candidate is monumental buildings for which the Sydney Opera House is the poster child, overrunning by about 1,400%.[17]

These hypotheses represent my opinions and experience; however, there is adequate evidence to propose a second tipping point adjustment model. This MCS model adjuster would be developed in the same way as described in Chapter 14, the difference being that the added risk factors/stressors to rate are the following:

♦ Likelihood of political influence (e.g., as in monumental publicly funded projects),
♦ Likelihood of regulatory change (e.g., as in nuclear and high carbon), and
♦ Susceptibility to corruption.

Some have fittingly called these "strategic risks." They can be rated with a 5-level Likert scale, e.g., ranging from 1 = very low to 5 = very high. Political influence would be difficult to rate objectively; perhaps past project outcomes for that government entity could be used as an indicator if historical data are available. The corruption rating could be measured using something like Transparency International's Corruption Perceptions Index (CPI) as referenced in Chapter 2. In a tipping point model, as the combined rating score increased, it would increase the percent of MCS iterations subject to this risk's impact multiplier.

---

15 Some may call 21% overrun a victory given nuclear's history; however, expectations were high for this project.

16 Flyvbjerg, Bent and A. Stewart, "Olympic Proportions: Cost and Cost Overrun at the Olympics 1960-2012," University of Oxford; Saïd Business School, 2012.

17 Hall, Peter, *Great Planning Disasters*, Weidenfeld & Nicolson, London, 1980.

This would be both practical and realistic – an objective way to model and explain the full reality and flash a "red light" for investors and stakeholders when appropriate. It is not a good idea to read too much into a few studies with vague statistics. However, they indicate that a rough estimate of the probability of "red" projects crossing the second tipping point is in the 5% range (i.e., beyond the $p90$ Pale) and a rough estimate of an impact multiplier of three times or more based on specific assessment that could vary widely. Such an impact also implies a significant schedule overrun.

Schedule Risk

The focus so far has been on cost overruns; however, schedule slippage has been studied as well. As with costs, the quality of schedule data in studies of public sources varies. For example, the start and end date definitions are not always clear. Most studies look at the duration from funding (there are few reliable rules as to how and when that takes place) through commercial operation (again, there are few rules of when a project is done). This differs from the Chapter 11 models focused on the Execution phase. As was discussed in that chapter, the startup phase duration can be highly uncertain on a percentage basis and is more susceptible to outliers (i.e., when are you done if you do not reach design capacity or there are lingering operability issues?).

REFERENCE	INDUSTRY	P50	MEAN	P90
Study [E]	Hydro	+27%	+44%	?
Study [G]	Hydro	?	+60%	?
	Nuclear	?	+60%	?
	Wind	?	+8%	?
	Solar	?	+1%	?
	Transmission	?	+8%	?

Table 15.9 : Overall Project Schedule Duration Slippage

However, a general conclusion of most studies (and as applied in Chapter 11's models) is that schedule slippage data is less skewed than cost overrun data. If we assume a somewhat poorly defined project at funding, the data in Chapter 3 from Rand and CII predict execution phase schedule slip of about 20-25%, increasing to about 40% for new technology projects excluding outliers (percent slip is the actual duration/estimated duration minus one, expressed as a percent). This can be compared to the sample studies shown in Table 15.9.

Study [E]'s p50 value is in the same approximate range as the Chapter 3 mean values of 20-25%. The mean slippage values of wind, solar and transmission projects appear to reflect low complexity (as with cost overrun). However, as with cost, the high mean values of hydropower and nuclear projects appear to be swayed by outliers.

Hydropower study [E] had a distribution chart that showed a group of projects (the schedule distribution, as with cost, was bimodal) with slippage averaging about 150%, and one project that slipped by 750%. While this analysis is very limited (most studies focus on cost), it confirms that schedule slip is similar between industries because the operative behavior is to preserve the planned completion date to obtain revenue. This suggests that the schedule slip model in Chapter 11 can be reasonably relied on for construction related projects. Schedules are also subject to tipping point behavior, albeit with a lessor impact multiplier than cost (perhaps half the cost values subject to assessment).

Contractors and Contractor Data

Contractors, to align themselves with their owner clients, apply phase-gate scope development processes as described in Chapter 3. They make economics-based decisions as described in Chapter 5 albeit without life cycle operating cost considerations (an exception may be warranty obligations). They also perform project cost and schedule risk quantification using the same methods as the owners. Unfortunately, use of line-item and activity ranging (LIR) is prevalent. What is different from owners is the priority given to certain risks in their quantification. However, the range of risk types they face are the same: systemic risks (level of scope definition, team development, complexity, and so on) and project-specific risks, escalation, and exchange.

Prioritization of risks to support management risk allocation decisions in alignment with the bidding strategy is the first objective of contractor risk analysis and quantification. The second objective is to support bid or tender price determination. In other words, they screen requests for quotations (RFQs) at one level (preparing a proposal can be costly), then make pricing decisions at another. As stated previously, contractors often have limited ability to absorb major losses. So when faced with the same project as an owner, they are more motivated to reduce the probability of a major overrun in

Contractors: Taking One's Lumps

This article provides a good example of the risks that contractors face when they bid on complex, schedule driven projects. The loss for Samsung C&T was about 18% of the $5.6 billion EPC lump sum contract value.

"The head contractor responsible for the development of Gina Rinehart's Roy Hill project, Samsung C&T, says it wants to 'focus on the future' after revealing it expects to book almost $1 billion of losses on the iron ore project. Samsung C&T said it expected losses of about 850 billion South Korean won ($993 million) on Roy Hill." The article adds, *"...The massive blowout was announced alongside Samsung C&T's fourth-quarter earnings on Thursday, in which it reported a net loss of 161.7 billion won for the three months to the end of December. It said its results for the full year reflected 2.6 trillion won in potential losses on projects, including Roy Hill."*

The article provides this background, *"Samsung began work on the iron ore mine, rail and port development in 2013 after winning a $5.6 billion performance-based, fixed price and time, head engineering, procurement and construction contract. After a delay, the first two cargoes from the $10 billion Roy Hill project were dispatched in December. Under the original contract, Samsung was liable for liquidated damages of about $55.9 million a month, applied daily for each day the first shipment was delayed after the end of October. The first shipment set sail on December 10... At the time of the first shipment Samsung said Roy Hill was one of the most complex and challenging projects completed in the company's history."*[1]

♦ Given Samsung C&T's statement about this being a "most complex" project, what do you think their bidding strategy and pricing approach might have been for the project?

♦ This project was 1/3 of Samsung C&Ts "losses on projects" in 2015. What does that imply regarding bidding strategy and pricing approach as a company?

♦ The first shipment was only delayed by 6 weeks, which was about 5% of the overall duration. What role might liquidated damages have played in the cost overrun being 18% and schedule only 5%?

---

1   Ingram, Tess, "Samsung-C&T-Reveals $1b Loss on Roy Hill," Sydney Morning Herald, Jan 29, 2016.

general and a blowout in particular. The models in Chapters 11 and 14 identify the risks that increase these probabilities (the systemic risks of the level of scope definition, complexity, and technology and the "stressors" of aggressiveness and critical project-specific risks).

Contractors are very aware of these risks. For example, team development is another difference between contractors and owners. Contractor managers may dedicate their entire careers to project execution. They often start as young engineers rotating though office and field assignments and through various discipline roles. They are assigned to increasingly more challenging projects, advancing to project engineer, to project manager, and then to director (or variations of the theme in different roles such as maintenance, procurement, or fabrication). So, when it comes to the risk allocation decision when screening RFQs for acceptable or unacceptable risk, they tend not to depend on quantitative methods as described in this book – they just know. They also know that some risks are opportunities – for example "change" is not necessarily a threat to contractors in certain situations and with the right contract risk allocation. That is not to say that contractors do not study the risk and perform assessments to support risk allocation decisions and RFQ screening; it is just that experience and judgment are depended on more.

Typically before the risk analyst joins the project team to quantify the risks for the purpose of bid or tender pricing decisions, the big risk allocation questions have already been decided. If the first or second level tipping point risks are significant in an RFQ, the contractor will not bid. If scope is poorly defined, complexity is high, technology is new, schedules are aggressive, skilled labor is hard to find, and/or many critical project-specific risks are present, the contractor is probably going to negotiate a reimbursable form of contract. If for some reason they do accept any of these risks in a fixed price contract, then the price to the owner will be very high, usually to the extent that the cost is uneconomical to the owner (e.g., if the contractor prices it reasonably at the $p80$ level). An exception is the high-change gambit where a contractor sees scope holes, weak contracts, and/or an indecisive or an undisciplined owner as an opportunity to benefit from change orders – a common but sometimes risky strategy.

In any case, once the decision has been made to bid, the contractor's risk quantification for pricing purposes is greatly simplified. If the contract is reimbursable, there is little cost risk to the contractor. The more that project costs overrun, the better the income to the contractor (incentive schemes only partially offsetting) unless the owner goes bankrupt. I have seen contractors who had no data as to how much their client projects overran the owner's budget; it is not the contractor's main concern (they do care, just not enough to measure). What matters most is how much they were in the red or black on the contract. I have also read stock analyst conference transcripts where contractor executives speak positively of increased backlog that in large part resulted from overrunning major reimbursable contracts.

On the other hand, if the contract is lump sum, that usually means that management has concluded that tipping point risks are low and the risk analyst's concern is mostly variability (or inside) risks around the contractor's estimating (e.g., takeoffs, rates), subcontractor, material and equipment pricing, and contractor performance (e.g., productivity). Project-specific risk events with major impacts tend to be reimbursed by the owner in any case (e.g., permit is delayed, site was flooded) in part because contractors have strong expertise in contract and claims management.

Almost all contractor risk analyses are of the LIR variety focused on variability or CPM-based methods. The risk quantification outcomes are usually in the +25% to −10% range ($p90$ to $p10$) typical of variability risk. The fact that LIR produces this outcome regardless of the risks is of less concern when variability is the only real risk. This practice should be a concern for owners that depend on FEED contractors for their project risk quantification. Many owners become focused on variability risks to the exclusion of the systemic risks that matter, because that is what matters to their contractors.

Contractor Data

I have found no reliable published empirical data as to contractor cost overrun experience (i.e., contract revenue/contract cost where revenue is the original contract plus all income from changes, claims recovery, and so on). The topic is commercially sensitive because to a contractor overruns speak directly to profit and claims practices; it is not something likely to be shared. The only data available is anecdotal. We see contractor overruns mainly when the company is publicly held and the overrun is large enough to become financially material. Accountants have formal thresholds for what is material and hence must be reported such as project losses exceeding some percentage of pre-tax income. Examples of such stockholder reporting (or in one case, a publicly reported court case) are:

♦ The Samsung story in this Chapter – they lost about 18% of the $5.6 billion EPC lump sum contract value.

♦ The Bechtel story in Chapter 15 about liquidated damages on a power plant projects: "...*claims between the parties (the owner and Bechtel) exceeding $500 million*."

♦ A report by Seimens about, *"€310 million in project charges related primarily to two high-voltage direct current (HVDC) transmission projects in Canada."*[18]

♦ A report by Subsea7 on an a Brazilian offshore project at about 60% completion said, *"Re-evaluation of the offshore risks based on experience to date, and the extended time line of the project, has resulted in us increasing the estimate full-life project loss by between $250 and $300 million."*[19]

A study of these reported contractor overruns, from the contractor's viewpoint, would be of great interest if available, but these anecdotes speak loudly of the applicability of all the risks and impacts discussed in the book.

Contractor Risk Quantification

While the data are anecdotal, contractors do at times accept major cost overrun and blowout risks (usually for lump sum contracts, as was the case for the examples listed). One can only speculate on why the contractors did that, but a contributing reason is likely the contractor's reliance on management's subjective judgment as to the probability and impact of the tipping point or strategic risks listed previously. *Optimism bias is not limited to owners.* Few have reliable risk quantification methods; they focus more on variability risks and claims recovery (many of the world's finest planners and schedulers are to be found in the claims and dispute resolution field).

Contractors can apply the same risk quantification methods that owners do. An example of an EPC contractor using the methods covered in this book was provided in Chapter 8. The difference is not in the methods, but in application procedure. Contractors should first use empirically valid methods to provide objective support to their risk allocation deliberations. Can we accept these risks? Do we invest in a proposal? Then, when the final bid or tender pricing decision is at hand, the methods can effectively quantify the variability risks that dominate reimbursable contracts, as well as the more potentially damaging systemic risks and stressors that come into play for fixed price contracts.

---

18 Siemens AG, "Mixed performance, outlook confirmed," Munich, May 7, 2014.

19 Siem, K, ibid.

Summary

This Chapter reviewed published accuracy data for selected industries and discussed the contractor perspective. While not an exhaustive review, it is sufficient to show that the parametric model of systemic risks covered in Chapter 11 for the process industries is a reasonable basis to quantify risk for construction projects. The same principles apply to military, aerospace, and IT projects. The assessment also found that a second tipping point MCS adjustment model, developed the same way as the model in Chapter 14, would be beneficial for projects that are highly susceptible to political influence, regulatory change, and/or corruption. Finally, this assessment noted that contractors, while having different objectives and application procedure than owners, would benefit equally from the methods in this book.

The metrics, charts, and examples associated with the risk quantification methods and studies in Chapters 11 through 15 were designed to help communicate the risk story to project managers and business sponsors. The next chapter talks a bit more about communicating risk quantification outcomes.

Questions

1) This chapter concludes that the parametric models in Chapter 11 are generally applicable to all construction-related projects regardless of the industry they are in. What was meant by saying the models are "self-correcting?"

2) What must you be concerned about with studies of estimate accuracy that provide only the mean cost growth or schedule slip for a set of projects, or that study conclusions are based primarily on mean outcomes?

3) What must you be concerned about with studies of estimate accuracy that measure only physical, cost, and time attributes of projects and not project practices?

4) What three added risk factors/stressors are hypothesized as a second tier of risk drivers in the dual tipping point concept?

5) Briefly describe the main difference in how contractors apply risk quantification (RQ) in making bidding decisions from how owners apply RQ in making an investment decisions.

6) Given the differences between how contractors and owners view risks, why must an owner be cautious in having a FEED contractor perform contingency estimates on the owner's behalf?

"A man who tells secrets or stories must think of who is hearing or reading, for a story has as many versions as it has readers. Everyone takes what he wants or can from it and thus changes it to his measure. Some pick out parts and reject the rest, some strain the story through their mesh of prejudice."
—John Steinbeck, *The Winter of Our Discontent*

"If you have an important point to make, don't try to be subtle or clever. Use a pile driver. Hit the point once. Then come back and hit it again. Then hit it a third time - a tremendous whack."
—Winston Churchill

16

Communicating Risk Quantification Outcomes

I have shared a few anecdotes of troubles I have had communicating analysis findings: the business sponsor who resented advice on asset management, the project manager in fear of his job going down with the project, and the functional executive not understanding statistical jargon. This is part of the learning experience; in my early years of analysis I was not the greatest communicator. Like many engineers and technical people, I was into the technology and the jargon, and not so much the people, their perceptions, and feelings. Like many, I wanted to focus on the "dashboard" with its p-tables, cumulative distributions, and tornado diagrams. But frankly, they don't work alone. By that, I mean the numbers and charts generally do not make a difference relative to the investment gate decision being made. The charts are necessary, but what I learned was to *tell the risk story,* and that is what this chapter is about.

People acting alone and as a group make investment gate decisions based on their general understanding:

- ◆ Colored by instinct, experience, biases, and personal interests,
- ◆ Rationalized to align with stated company objectives and policy, and
- ◆ Battled out through group dynamics.

In short, it's messy business. Finally, the analyst is typically not invited to participate in all of the discussion. We are usually just the messenger – a messenger the decision makers may or may not know well or trust highly. While charts and graphs are necessary, good communication of the risk quantification message comes down to understanding the people involved, their culture and situation, and telling them a convincing, reality-based story.

If you are a decision maker, understanding of the story is greatly helped if you understand risk quantification concepts (the fact that you are reading this book is a great sign). Also, your expectations for information to support your decision from the project manager, planners, analysts, and others involved need to be made as clear as possible. As was noted in Chapter 14, "Business Leadership, Ownership, and Decisiveness" or lack thereof is not only a source of uncertainty, it is one of the main contributors to project blowouts.

From the perspective of the analyst, here is how to approach the communication part of the work.

Telling the Story

Most risk analysts will have three main chances to communicate the project cost and schedule risk story on a project:

- ◆ During the risk analysis workshops and interviews as we start to frame the situation (in which the decision makers need to participate at some level),
- ◆ At the briefing of the analysis outcome, and
- ◆ In a written report and its executive summary (which we will describe later).

However, trust and credibility must come *before* meetings and reports.

First Build Trust

I recall a former employer once telling the staff, *"Without trust, consultants have nothing to offer."* Consultants work diligently to maintain trust with their clients and add value by providing an independent, objective, and confidential view, building on a foundation of skills and knowledge. This applies to all risk analysts, whether in-house, consultant, contractor, or sub-contractor status.

The starting point for building trust is *competency*: analytical ability that is backed by sound research, correct logic, and experience. Reading books (like this one) is a good sign that you are working to develop your own skills and knowledge (and this book offers a balance of techniques based on both research and practical experience).

Sharing your knowledge is also a great way to gain trust; it is no coincidence that most subject matter experts (SMEs), senior analysts, and consultants have articles, publications, and courses in their resumes. Most of us do a lot of research about our topic before we present; we share to learn. Done well, this builds trust with your audience. I spend a lot of time working in professional associations on committees, boards, and product teams; this is another good way to build confidence and trust.

Beyond sharing your competence-based knowledge, building trust requires good listening. Too often, experts come to over-value their own experience and opinions in comparison to the other party's. I pointed out in Chapter 2 that as a first rule we must remain humble about our ability to identify risks and forecast their outcome. The same is true as to our knowledge and how we communicate. We cannot understand the other party's needs without listening, and we will *never* gain trust if the other party does not feel their experience and opinions are respected and given a fair hearing, putting our own agenda and opinions aside. We learn and gain mutual understanding by listening.

The Workshop and Interviews

As was covered in the description of the systemic risk quantification methods, you need input from the project's business sponsor and other senior managers. As discussed, they own most of the systemic risks (e.g., responsibility for implementing project systems, organizational development). These people are also generally invited to the investment decision-making discussion and will be the recipient of the message at the end of the analysis.

Even though an executive's time is usually limited, while interviewing them, try to gauge their personal biases, the decision making culture they are working in, the pressures they are under, and so on. At the same time, they have likely never heard of "systemic risk" (likely not being a party to initiating the analysis or developing the process), so you must concisely educate them. The better you can prepare them at this point, the better the message will be received at the later briefing.

In project-specific team risk quantification workshops, while the executives are generally not present, there will typically be influential SMEs in the room. Again, time is short, but as with the executives, you need to gauge the SMEs' biases and situation as well as educating them about the risk analysis. The better you can prepare them at this point, the better the communication is when the executive asks the SME's opinion off-line.

The Briefing: So What?

At the conclusion of the analysis, the project sponsors and managers will want a briefing as to its findings. This is usually in two parts:

- An initial on-site briefing shortly after the workshops based on the analyst's immediate impressions, and
- A later formal briefing, face-to-face if possible or by teleconference if necessary.

Many senior managers will not have time to read the full report. The briefing itself will likely be between twenty minutes and one hour. So, you are left with the Churchill method: "use a pile driver." The more you have developed trust and prepared the executives and the SMEs, the better this briefing will go.

Hopefully the project is a good one with low complexity, minimal stressors, and a strong system to support it (this *does* happen occasionally). However, the project system often needs improving in one way or another and if the project is of mega-scale with significant time pressure and other stressors and risks, there is a significant risk of blowout. In this situation, remember that our briefing is indeed brief, and the decisions in front of the company are major: "*Do we proceed past the gate or not?*" If the answer is "no," then the company has to decide whether to cancel or recycle the project. In a recycle situation, the question is, "*What do we need to do to proceed through the gate?*"

In these cases, spending a half hour with distributions and a tornado diagram is probably not going to answer their questions. After my father retired from being a steel industry senior executive, he handed down to me a rubber stamp that said "*So What?*" in very large type (this was from the day of the paper memorandum). This was a good early lesson.

Later, I could hear his voice in a senior executive who asked, "*What am I supposed to do with this information?*" The executive was speaking about a p-table and a laundry list of ranked risks and impacts provided by the team. This information was useless to her. You *must* focus on the important conclusions (which can be communicated in the following meta-language):

♦ There is a (low, moderate, high) chance of meeting (cost and/or schedule) objectives...

♦ With a worst case of (cost and time impact),

♦ Because of factors a, b, and c,

♦ Which require x, y, and z to mitigate the risks to the extent possible.

Reserve talk about the contingency until after management clearly understands the risk story and why it matters at this gate decision. In fact, once the executives understand the risk story, they don't even ask about contingency because the conversation has switched to taking action to address the situation. In other words, a task that often starts as "do a contingency analysis" becomes, "recycle," but this time the decision is based on reality.

Similarly, the project analysis may find one or more management reserve risks. As discussed, these are risks such that, if they occur, they will overwhelm the contingency. Often the response to the risk will be major enough to be considered a change of scope. Each of these risks requires its own decision as to how to treat it:

♦ Accept it and fund it in full as a reserve,

♦ Accept it and don't fund it, or

♦ Some other treatment.

Each of these risks has a story, so if there are reserve risks, plan for time in the briefing to discuss them. Again, these often result in recycling the analysis back through the scope development and risk management processes.

The Report

The formal report will include an executive summary, the body of the analysis (including tables and figures, see the next section), and attachments (risk register summaries, simulation printouts, and so on). Of these elements, the executive summary is most important. It should have the same succinct message as outlined for the briefing.

I personally prefer to also prepare extensive detailed reports, including the story narrative. These reports are not always read. However, I do know that some executives do prefer a full report (good airplane reading), so I follow through accordingly unless the project has been recycled such that the analysis will be redone on a different basis quickly. In regulated industries and/or those with strict quality assurance (e.g., nuclear), the report and its content may require special consideration and care.

Tables and Figures

Quantitatively, the purpose of the analysis is usually to provide a basis for funding contingency and reserves. At most companies today there is a capital decision-making and/or project control policy for funding large project contingency at some percent probability of underrun (depending on the company's risk attitude and tolerance). Even though schedule contingency durations are less commonly incorporated into baseline plans, the company will also want to know what duration contingency is required at various percent probabilities of underrun.

This information can be reported in tabular and graphic formats using histograms (and/or cumulative distribution diagrams) and what I call "*p*-tables." The histogram provides insight into the risk story. Therefore, I usually present the histogram first. There are other types of diagrams used to illustrate the outcome's sensitivity to critical risks and/or to flag those critical risks. While the technicalities are in the realm of statistics per Chapter 10, the following descriptions focus on how the diagrams speak to the story.

Histogram

A histogram is a bar chart with vertical bars representing the frequency that MCS outcomes fell within the bar's span. For example, if there are 10,000 MCS iterations, and 1,000 fell between 20% and 25% contingency, that bar height (y) would be 0.1, and so on for each equal increment of x values. Often the vertical axis has no

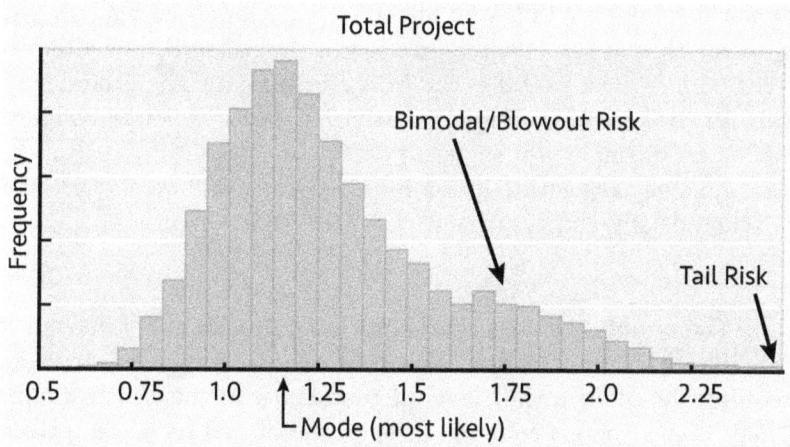

Figure 16.1: Example Histogram with Story Features

quantities shown; all is relative. The *x*-axis may be the contingency, total cost, or some other metric such as a ratio of the analysis outcome/reference estimate (e.g., 1.15 would indicate a 15% overrun). As shown in Figure 16.1, this chart helps because it clearly shows the risk story in its mode (most likely outcome), range (best/worst case), and the general profile (e.g., bias, bimodality, long tail). Always highlight the key story elements in your chart.

S-Curve

This is a cumulative probability diagram that is based on the same data as a histogram. It sums or accumulates the probability of each value from left to right or least to most money or time. S-curves

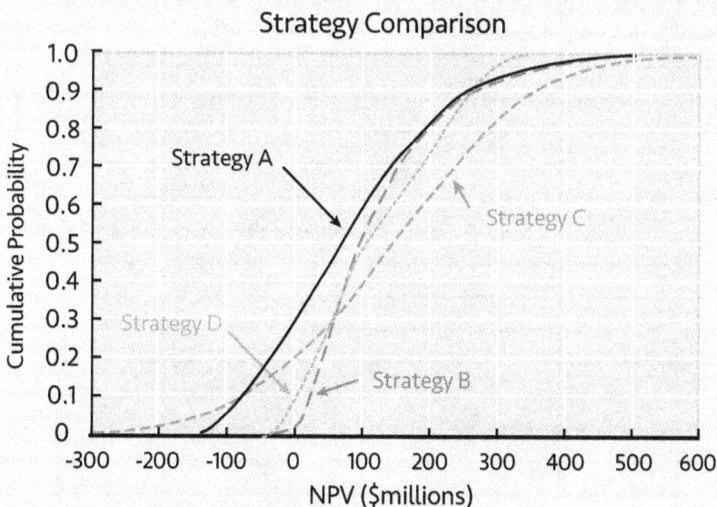

Figure 16.2: Example S-Curve for Comparisons

do not display long tails and bimodality as clearly as histograms; however, they are excellent for comparing the risk profiles of alternatives. This is most useful at the FEL 2/Select gate when there may still be two or more viable scope alternatives being decided on. Figure 16.2 is an example of using s-curves to compare multiple alternatives, in this case with NPV as the *x*-axis rather than cost growth or schedule slip metrics (this was Figure 5.5 in Chapter 5.)

P-table

The *p*-table is a simple table with the probability of underrun (confidence level) in the first column, and the respective contingency required to achieve that level of confidence in the next column. There may also be a column of the total cost and schedule including the contingency in a third column. Show these in increments of 5% confidence, with a min/max of 5% and 95%. Outside this range numbers go asymptotic; however, that does not mean that outliers are irrelevant (see Table 16.1).

EXECUTION DURATION RANGE TABLE			
PROBABILITY OF UNDERRUN	RISK ADJUSTED DURATION (MONTHS)	ESTIMATED SCHEDULE CONTINGENCY (MONTHS)	PERCENT OF BASE DURATION
5%	45.8	−2.2	−4.5%
10%	47.4	−0.6	−1.2%
15%	48.5	0.5	1.1%
20%	49.4	1.4	3.0%
25%	50.2	2.2	4.7%
30%	51.0	3.0	6.1%
35%	51.6	3.6	7.6%
40%	52.3	4.3	8.9%
45%	52.9	4.9	10.2%
50%	53.5	5.5	11.5%
55%	53.5	6.2	12.9%
60%	54.8	6.8	14.2%
65%	55.5	7.5	15.7%
70%	56.3	8.3	17.2%
75%	57.1	9.1	18.9%
80%	58.0	**10.0**	**20.7%**
85%	59.0	11.0	23.0%
90%	60.4	12.4	25.9%
95%	62.5	14.5	30.3%

Table 16.1: Example P-table with Highlighted Contingency

As discussed in Chapter 15, outcomes beyond the *p*95 range may be very important when certain 'strategic' risks are present. If they are, an asterisk should be added to the p-table directing the audience to the story of those extreme risks. Finally, the policy levels (e.g., funding policy is *p*50) should be highlighted. I sometimes also show the mean value, as this is the risk neutral funding point (whether the company policy recognizes it or not).

Tornado Diagram

This type of chart is used to highlight specific risks that drive the cost and schedule outcomes, i.e., they highlight the sensitivity of the outcome to the risks. The tornado diagram is a special type of bar chart where each risk is listed in rank order with the risk affecting the outcome the most at the top. The risk's high and low impact relative to a base value is shown on adjacent horizontal bars. To tell a story, show those risks that matter most to the decision. For example, Figure 16.3 was intended to communicate to a manager that cost contingency was very sensitive to base estimate bias, and the impact of bias was about the same as the level of scope definition for this business unit's types of simple projects (this example chart most definitely does *not* reflect complex projects).

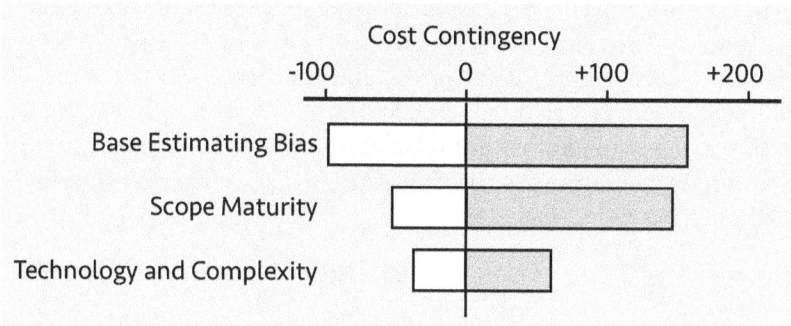

Figure 16.3: Example Tornado Diagram of Selected Systemic Risks

MCS add-ons allow you to generate such sensitivity charts with relative ease for those variables that are in the MCS model (e.g., the project-specific risks). However, in the hybrid parametric/expected value approach recommended by this text, the systemic risks are incorporated in the MCS model as a single distribution, i.e., the output of the parametric model. Once reserve risks are taken from the picture, even the most critical project-specific risks (e.g., permit delays) in the MCS tend to be overwhelmed in impact by the overall systemic risks. And, this does not consider the compounding nature of systemic risks in the presence of complexity. In other words, the risk story is almost always about systemic risks such as scope definition and team development, and blowout risk if present, and not the events or minor variabilities that traditional analyses and tornado diagrams tend to dwell on almost exclusively.

Without the aid of the MCS add-on sensitivity tools, you must create your own sensitivity charts of the systemic risks such as in Figure 16.3. One advantage of this is that you must think about what you want to show. Another is that you can include escalation and exchange that are not in most MCS models. Figure 16.3 also illustrates that you should focus on *what really matters* – in the example case only the top three risks are shown.

Flags

Another type of chart is qualitative traffic signals. The "Tipping Point" indicator shown in Table 14.1 is an example. In Table 14.1, systemic risks (which by name are the same for every project) each have a green/yellow/red indicator to quickly highlight what is important. In that case the importance is relative to the complexity/ blowout risk story.

There are of course other charts that can be created (e.g., spider diagrams). There are many general texts and MCS user guides on the topic of graphics, dashboards, and the like. But in a 20 to 60 minute executive briefing, you are limited on what you can show. It is very easy to get lost in tables and figures and if you do, it will not help to communicate the risk story, which in the end should be a compelling narrative.

Dealing with Show Stoppers

When empirically valid risk quantification methods are used, it is more likely that the worst case (i.e., $p90$) CAPEX and/or completion (first product) date will be a "show stopper" than if traditional ranging methods are used. This is particularly so if the project is nearing the tipping point. The analysis will result in an IRR that does not meet the company's threshold for capital project investments or it will have a negative NPV. This situation is even worse if the company has a policy of funding at, say, $p80$ because past analyses were not empirically valid and its $p50$ results were negligible and $p80$ contingencies only moderate. Communicating bad news is, of course, a classic communication challenge. In most cases, everyone

Hard News

The following is an edited excerpt from a risk quantification report for a mining megaproject during the peak of the commodity super-cycle boom. At the time, many projects were schedule-driven. The owners had never tried the hybrid risk quantification methods of this text; they depended on FEED contractors to provide them with "line-item ranging" analyses.

"The following are risks that the team feels are virtually certain to occur and for which the impact is not included in project plan assumptions and for which no contingency plans are in place:

♦ Permit X delays (pre-construction), and

♦ Staff Shortages.

Beyond this, all critical risks on this project (except X) have a significant likelihood of occurring. Likely compounding these project-specific risks are high systemic risks and schedule stress. As such, this project is a strong candidate for business failure (although this is by no means certain). It is assumed that unless the revenue side of the business case is outstanding, there is too much CAPEX risk at the $p90$ confidence level (70% cost overrun and 14 month delay in mechanical completion) to sanction as-is.

"My recommendation is to develop a risk-tolerant plan that optimizes the construction schedule for the weather, adds a time buffer before field mobilization to be confident in permit X receipt, fully and effectively resolves the housing situation before mobilization, and completes the geotechnical studies and process system X design. The estimate and schedule would be re-baselined to this strategy. This would add some define phase costs ($\$X$ to $\$Y$ million), but should reduce the worst case CAPEX and schedule outcome to economical levels. In any case, the pre-construction burn-rate needs to be carefully managed while the recommended work is completed."

Before going on, consider these questions:

♦ Did this meet my four criteria for telling a succinct risk "story?"

♦ What do you think the owners' reaction was?

After I presented the report, the owners did not call me – no questions or comments. I assumed that I had failed to communicate the story and that trust was not established – maybe a step too far for a company that had seen only +25% worst case in prior analyses.

However, several months later they did call and asked, "We did everything you recommended; now what?" Shortly thereafter, commodity prices collapsed and the project, still pre-sanction, was shelved. This was a success. Their restraint avoided pre-mature field mobilization costs and commitments (at a minimum). At worst, escalating commitment bias could have led them to follow through on a low or negative return project.

from the business unit VP to the project manager to the project team (and down to the contractors and suppliers) really, really want this project to go forward.

As noted at the beginning of this chapter, we must have the decision maker's trust to succeed in communicating the risk story. They have to believe that we are not biased and that we are not trying to "kill" their project. We are trying to help them improve the project, and, since most systemic risks are owned by the business, improve the company's project system. Our methods are empirically grounded, and we need to be ready to explain the technical basis for our work clearly and concisely. This is much easier if the company already participates in benchmarking through independent firms or through research consortia such as CII or COAA.

We also need to have solution ideas ready for when the question is asked, *"What am I supposed to do with this information?"* Unfortunately, the solutions are usually painful.

For example, if an absurd completion date target stresses the project, it needs to slow down. I call this "buying certainty." I don't mean perfect certainty, but there is a clear trade-off of adding, say, three months to duration to reduce the blowout risk to a much lower probability.

The most difficult cases are companies with weak systems and teams; this is often a company taking on a mega-project alone for the first time. Strengthening systems and organizations often requires organizational development projects, which are difficult to do. However, if the company can find a more capable partner and use that experience to learn from, or if they can break the job down into smaller projects in a program, they can decrease their risk of a blowout. There is rarely a clear or easy answer, but there are usually viable options.

Once we have communicated the story and improvements are made, and there is a decision to move forward with executing the next phase or the entire project, the next step from our quantitative perspective is to support the accounting and control of the approved risk monies and time; this is covered in the next chapter.

Questions

1) What are some of the toughest challenges for technical risk quantification analysts when communicating with management and stakeholders about their investment decision or project?

2) What is required before any communication can be effective and what personal attributes help analysts meet that requirement?

3) What are the common venues or mechanisms where risk communication takes place?

4) What are the four basic elements (or meta-language) of a *risk story* to communicate in a briefing?

5) What quantitative information does a histogram convey at a glance that is difficult to convey in words?

6) How does the development of a Tornado diagram of a systemic risk (e.g., rating of team development) differ from that for a project-specific risk (e.g., a weather delay event) and what different story does it tell?

7) For a risk that is difficult to communicate as a quantitative measure or graphic, what visual device is useful instead? Describe a risk measure for which this would be useful.

"O to be self-balanced for contingencies! O to confront night, storms, hunger, ridicule, accidents, rebuffs, as the trees and animals do."
–Walt Whitman from *Leaves of Grass*

"A budget is nothing more than a mathematical confirmation of your suspicions."
–The Colorado Engineer, 1943

17
Budgeting for Risks and Account Control

The risk analyst's primary risk quantification role is to provide decision makers with the information they need to make an investment decision considering cost and schedule risk. The preceding chapters provided methods and tools to support that role. However, once the decision is made and the project work is authorized, there is still the quantitative matter of accounting and control of the approved money and time. As was pointed out in Chapter 2, this last step is not so much about uncertainty and risk as it is about numbers, i.e., fixed values. This chapter summarizes how and why money and time are set as budgets for control purposes and how they are managed during project execution. The scope covered here may be the responsibility of project controls. During execution (with the exception of quantification to support change control decisions), risk quantification is more about policy than it is about analysis.

Risk Funds and Time Accounting

At the decision gate, using the practices laid out in this book, we will have quantified the cost and time elements of contingency and management reserves for cost and schedule and escalation and exchange for cost. For each, we will have provided the project manager and decision makers with probabilistic distributions showing values at various confidence levels of underrunning. In addition, we will have flagged any overwhelming risks that are not amenable to contingency funding. And if applicable, we will have also done this at a program level.

Now it is management's responsibility to select the project's overall budget in accordance with policy or however they see fit to do so, hopefully in consideration of the risk story. There are four principles of best practice, however, that we should remember with respect to this final valuation or accounting:

- ◆ *Contingency is expected to be spent.* Literally speaking, this is the mean of our expected value contingency analysis (however, the *p*50 level is often used).
- ◆ *Contingency excludes the impact of business scope change.* This is the purpose of reserves – either for overwhelming risks that imply scope change in risk response, or for management discretionary purposes such as optional scope or to address risk aversion. Business scope is the basic premises of the business case.
- ◆ *Contingency is only meaningful in aggregate.* Given the uncertainty inherent in our analysis methods, it is inappropriate to allocate or spread contingency around to other accounts. There is only one contingency per project management authority. An exception may be made for escalation funds, especially for short duration projects.
- ◆ *Those with change control authority should have funds to exercise this authority.* The project manager and program director (if applicable) have authority to use contingency at their level to address risk impacts as they occur. They do have a responsibility to report this use.

Not applying these principles carries certain risks that should be considered – in particular, diminished control discipline, team development, and decision making (all elements of tipping point concern). For example:

♦ *Over/under funding contingency*: Under funding (aggressive budget) results in inappropriate corrective actions and/or risk responses (a tipping point factor). Over funding invites added "urban renewal" scope.

♦ *Allocating contingency to various WBS elements or accounts*: The work or accounts impacted by actual risks will have insufficient contingency; others will have too much. This encourages competition between work packages rather than coordination and effective team development (a tipping point factor). This causes inappropriate and/or ineffective corrective actions and/or risk responses.

♦ *Allocating escalation to accounts*: This inflates the budgets and early earned values and cost performance indicators. If actual escalation differs from the estimate, budgets are corrupted and control metrics become suspect.

♦ *Not giving the project manager authority to decide on contingency*: This results in change control delay and less timely risk response (a tipping point factor). It also institutes mistrust in leadership as policy, another tipping point factor.

Some argue that these rigorous contingency management principles are a nuisance. It is true that this approach requires more control effort, but that is also exactly the point. By not allocating to everyone a bit of contingency, escalation or slack for inclusion in their work package budgets or activities, it forces the work package leads to communicate performance deviations and risks to the project manager; there is no obfuscation. Having set these principles, the following sections define approaches for risk money and schedule duration accounting.

Cost Contingency

For each project (and program), assign contingency at the expected value (mean), for which the project manager (and program director) will have spending authority. The $p50$ level is somewhat aggressively biased (the longer the high side tail, the more aggressively biased *p*50 will be) and is not additive at a program level. There should be no punishment of managers for a project overrunning – only for not knowing why it is overrunning, lack of appropriate assessment and reporting and/or effective corrective actions.

Schedule Contingency

Apply the concepts in AACE RP 70R-12. It recommends including an explicit amount of time in the project and/or program schedule to allow for the impact of risks and uncertainties. The RP's principles are that schedule contingency:

♦ Must be visible in the schedule,

♦ Is time only and does not contain scope, resources, or costs,

♦ Is only established based upon an analysis of schedule risk,

♦ Is not float (i.e., neither project float nor total float),

♦ Is not lag/lead (relationship durations),

♦ Is not hidden artificial lengthening of schedule activities,

♦ Is not the improper use of what some term as "preferential logic,"

♦ Is not a non-work period in the software calendar, and

♦ Is not management reserve.

As with cost contingency, the duration contingency should be assigned at the mean value. Note that the RP does not say where in the logic to include the contingency or buffers. It assumes that contingency is applied judiciously. For example, in a project where all soils excavation must be completed in the winter while the soils are frozen, a buffer may be allocated at the end of the winter season to ensure the soils work is done before the spring. Buffers are also common when a project is integrated with "turnarounds" (major maintenance) during mid-execution. When there is no explicit schedule contingency, it is common for schedulers to estimate the activity durations at a conservative confidence level (for example, *p*80), which, unfortunately, will likely lead to mediocre schedule performance (an argument for using the critical chain method instead).

Planet Budgeting

Contingency is too often treated as a pre-determined value. It is difficult to overestimate the distortion of project control and the destruction of asset value that comes from failing to recognize the nature of project risk, how to quantify it, and how to manage it. Too many projects treat contingency as politically radioactive – don't touch it – set it at 10% and step away. Others treat it respectfully as the manifestation of uncertainty that it is. Having geology training, I developed a planetary analogy that represents the views of contingency relative to the rest of the control budget.

The left figure in Figure 16.A depicts contingency as an assumed fixed solid core (usually 10%) of the project budget planet; all uncertainty is radiated out to the mantle – the rest of the project budget. This makes the budget mantle a hot amorphous thing (of uncertain state and hence uncontrollable). The right image puts all uncertainty in formation of the contingency; uncertainty configures its shape, which may vary (be it 5% or 50%). It is hard to quantify, but it is contained in a solid control budget mantle; a mantle we can touch, work with, and build on (though an occasional earthquake or volcano occurs).

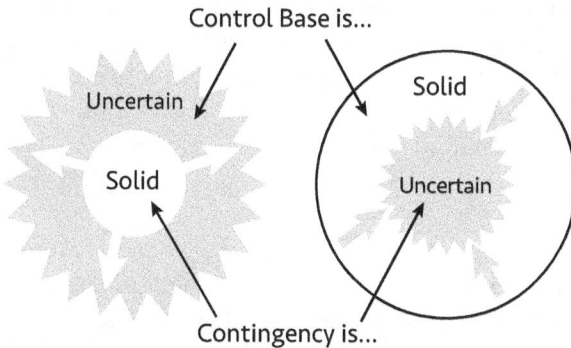

Figure 16.A: Two Views of Contingency

Which Planet Budget would you rather live on? The one where the control budget mantle is magna with a solid contingency core? Or one where the control budget is solid and contingency is magma?

Management Reserves

In general, there are several types of reserves for cost or time:

◆ Reserves for specifically identified risk events (see the expected value method) that are not amenable to contingency funding.

◆ Reserves to address specific business objectives, for example, a buffer before the first product milestone to facilitate early negotiation of commercial agreements with customers.

♦ Reserves to address the company's risk attitude. For example, some risk averse companies may fund the project at $p70$ or $p80$. In this case, the difference between the contingency (i.e., the mean or $p50$) and the higher level, will be funded as reserve.

♦ Reserves set aside for management discretion.

In all cases, reserves have a specific purpose and designation, with the expectation that these funds or time will be used only for the designated purpose. For each reserve item, the person authorized to make its disposition is identified. Note that some use the term "contingency reserves." I do not recommend this wording because it conflicts with the principles of expecting to spend the contingency and that the project manager has spending authority.

Finally, the prevalence of funding at high levels ($p70$ or $p80$) and setting aside reserves (the difference between $p80$ and $p50$) is often a symptom of endemic unrealistic risk quantification. If the methods in this text are applied, you must be prepared to deal with analysis outcomes where the $p80$ regularly threatens project economics (as noted in Chapter 14).

Escalation

For larger projects (durations of greater than two years) and for short projects with high likelihood of economic and market volatility during the duration, escalation should be funded, like contingency, as a separate account that is expected to be spent. Escalation should be set at the mean of the probabilistic escalation estimate.

Escalation is managed like contingency during change control. When the economy impacts prices, the project draws from the escalation account. The exception is when a cost account is truly fixed at the time of authorization. Note, however, that firm quotes are not fixed unless the scheduled purchase or contract issuance will happen before the quote expires. For short duration projects and in stable economic times, escalation may be reasonably allocated to the various control account budgets as indicated by escalation estimating practices.

Exchange

On larger projects when there is significant money spent in non-basis currency, finance should apply hedging or other mitigation strategies. If so, the project must work with finance to report and account for impacts from these risks (e.g., cash flow by currency). For small projects and stable economic times, as with escalation, exchange impacts may be reasonably allocated to the various control accounts as applicable.

Risk Funds and Time Control

Once the budgets are set and decision authorities are defined, the project (or project phase) starts execution activities. The recommended approach to the control of risk funds and time is described in this section.

Change Management (Including Risk Quantification)

During execution, the risk management function should work in close coordination with the project control function. Project control oversees the change management process and tracks performance trends and risk event occurrences. Risk management and project control should provide analysis to support corrective actions and risk responses. Project control tracks budget, escalation, and contingency expenditures.

A challenging aspect of this process can be determining what is a change to contract scope, particularly for fixed price contracts. The cost and time for some risk events and responses may be considered a change. If it is a contract change, the money and time is allocated from the owner's risk allowances; if not, the contractor will have to cover it with their risk allowances.

As the risk register is updated, project control addresses impact on the project. Any risk treatment action (even a study) during execution is an in-scope activity that consumes project resources. Therefore it must be budgeted and tracked.

During execution, the project manager should have full authority to make contingency disposition decisions unless the identified trend, deviation or change is specifically out of scope or it is one of the distinctly identified management reserve items. In that case, disposition will be by the designated higher management authority.

Drawdown

The change management process includes making decisions to allocate cost and schedule contingency (and escalation for cost) to the accounts and/or activities impacted by a risk event or condition. The principle is that the current budget and schedule control base must reflect work activity accurately. As the money and time are shifted from the contingency and escalation accounts to the other accounts, track this drawdown over time.

If the drawdown appears to be happening faster than expected, update the risk quantification analysis at that time (see the next section). If the drawdown is slower than expected, the risk quantification is usually updated at the end of the fiscal year to determine whether some of the contingency funds can be returned to the business, and in the case of schedule duration, whether completion commitments can be adjusted. Reserves are only allocated at the discretion of the appropriate authority; the change control process will inform the higher authorities promptly of the need.

Risk Quantification during Execution

As discussed above, the drawdown process, or forecasting exercises, will flag the need for risk quantification during execution. In addition, the project may establish periodic or special milestones for re-quantification. For example, update the risk analysis at about 90% engineering completion (which usually corresponds to about 30% construction completion), because if the tipping point is nearing, this is the latest point in time to make effective interventions without creating severe stress on the project. Also, at about this time start-up planning will be advanced and risks to that phase need to be carefully considered and quantified. At the beginning of start-up, especially if there is a turnover of authority from a project to a start-up manager, there should be a reevaluation of the risks for that phase and any budgetary and contingency considerations.

The quantification methods for updating the analysis during execution are the same as for the decision gates. The difference is that the base project cost and schedule are the current budget and schedule for the work remaining and the risks to quantify are for those going forward. If change management has not been effective up to this point (the budget and schedule model are corrupted or otherwise suspect), then the base plans will need to be reviewed as part of the quantification (re-baselining).

As part of change management, project control must quickly analyze cost and schedule impact of each significant trend, notice, deviation, or change. This analysis should include analysis of risks. During execution, watch for cumulative risk impacts; they tend to compound and accelerate (which can lead to a tipping point). Also, identify any secondary risks resulting from changes made and from recommended corrective actions.

At project completion, as decided at the completion gate or when capitalization is being finalized, if any contingency or reserve funds are remaining after allowance for back-charges, claims, and other lagging obligations, they can be returned to the company. At or just prior to completion, there should be a project close-out process that captures historical information and lessons learned. That takes us to our last chapter on "closing the loop" on risk quantification.

Questions

1) Briefly describe how the role or focus of risk quantification changes from pre-sanction to the start of execution.

2) What four principles are highlighted in respect to budgeting for contingency?

3) What are some systemic risks that may be created when the risk funding principles in the prior question are not followed?

4) Rigorous change control processes can be viewed by some as a nuisance as the team makes frequent requests for contingency or escalation funds; why might this be a good thing?

5) What are some circumstances that would favor escalation being allocated to the various project budget accounts?

6) What project function should risk management work particularly closely with during project execution and why?

7) When should one perform robust risk quantification during execution?

"History doesn't repeat itself, but it does rhyme."
—Attributed to Mark Twain

18
Closing the Loop

A central theme of this text and the methods described is that realistic risk quantification must be empirically based. Everything must be based to some extent on actual experience of risks and their impacts. This is the Janus view to the past. That is not to diminish the value of expert opinion – judgment is crucial to risk response planning and other inputs, but as discussed, our experience with respect to cost and schedule outcomes and forecasts is strongly influenced by optimism bias. Establishing an empirical basis for any cost engineering method or tool is one of the most difficult challenges of our profession.

Unfortunately, very few owner and contractor companies capture, analyze, and use project historical data. I have been working in the historical data analysis field for decades. When I wrote a paper on historical data and metric practices in 1995, I did not find a single practical reference in the cost engineering literature.

When I was a project control engineer for an EPC firm during a slow spell, I was "on the bench" (which means that I had no billable project work). My manager, knowing my quantitative leanings, told me to, "See what you can do with our project data." I was led to a large storeroom with scores if not hundreds of boxes of project files and close-out reports that nobody had ever done anything with (to the firm's credit, I understand they have since made improvements in this area). That is not to say that nobody collects and analyzes this data – Chapters 3 and 4 cover many studies – but they are usually special one-off efforts by academics or researchers who are given the proverbial keys to the storeroom for a few months.

The reason for industry's failure is not lack of recognition of the need for data and learning (everyone wants it). What is lacking is what I call "stick-to-itiveness." Many companies start to do something with their data, but a year or two into the effort, reality intervenes: CAPEX workloads and staffing are cut, departments are reorganized or outsourced, project sponsors retire or get promoted, IT strategies change, and so on. What everyone learns is that implementing a system takes more time and resources than expected.

The other learning is that data captured by Enterprise Resource Planning (ERP) systems (e.g., SAP, PeopleSoft, JD Edwards, or similar ERP systems) does not meet project planning needs. The reason is that we do not estimate, schedule, or analyze risks using the types of data captured by these systems. Our planning data comes from reverse engineering of what is in those records. My saying is, "There is no such thing as actual data. There is only our interpretation and estimates of what that data represents."

The good news is that in recent years, some notable project historical data successes have found their way into the literature. Still, most database efforts are focused on supporting cost estimating tool calibration or accounting purposes with little consideration for risk management. The rest of this Chapter highlights the knowledge management process and best practices with respect to risk quantification.

Capturing Historical Project and Risk Information

The process and practices for project data or knowledge management are well outlined in the AACE International Total Cost Management Framework.[1] Figure 18.1 is derived from that text; it illustrates that project data and learning underpins all aspects of planning methods and tool development, including risk quantification.

For risk quantification of cost and schedule, the following data and information are most important to capture (note that outcomes such as operability can and should be added, but this book is focused on cost and schedule; the principles are the same):

---

1   Hollmann, John, editor, *Total Cost Management Framework*, Section 10.4 "Project Historical Database Management" (first edition), AACE International, Morgantown, WV, 2006.

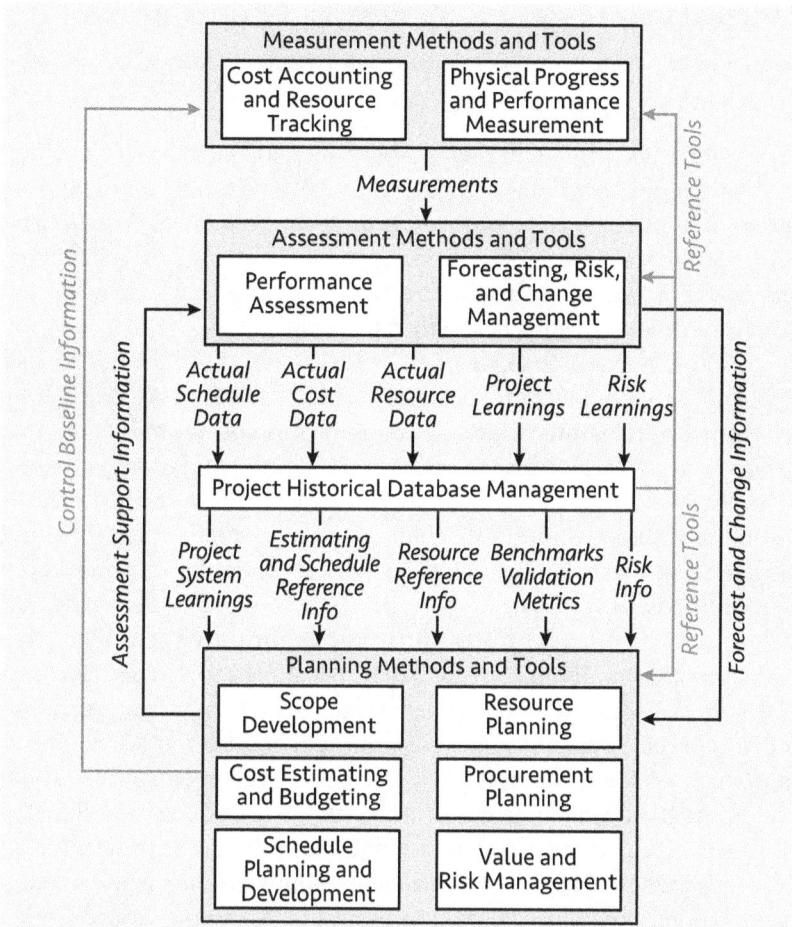

*Figure 18.1: Project Historical Management Flow Chart
(derived from AACE's TCM Framework)*

Processed Information

- Project scope (including attributes related to systemic risks),
- Cost and schedule, actual and estimated (by phase) data,
- Resource actual and estimated (by phase) data,
- Systemic risk ratings (by phase),
- Critical project-specific risks identified and actual occurred, including impacts, and
- Lessons learned.

Original Records (searchable electronic format is optimal)

◆ Risk analysis reports and risk registers, and

◆ Change control logs.

You might ask why I don't list metrics such as "percent of identified risks that occurred" or other metrics about the risk management process. This is because *most cost growth and schedule slip is driven by systemic risks,* so a focus on risk register metrics is of less importance. Data to support predictive modeling of risks and overall cost and schedule outcomes is the first priority.

The eventual outputs of the process will be parametric risk quantification models and data and metrics to calibrate them, plus checklists and lessons learned to support the expected value method. Also, the data will be used to calibrate escalation and exchange tools. The outputs and analysis to create these tools are described in later sections but keep in mind that most of this data is for modeling and as such needs to be quantified or coded. For example, for project type we will need to set up codes for each type of project of interest.

As to the system for capturing this data, this is difficult because commercial applications are not designed to do this. Successful efforts require custom coded systems or heavy customization of commercial systems. Database management often starts out in spreadsheet form. This usually works out well because initial development is a time of learning and change. But once the system is well framed, getting it coded in a database system is preferable.

The following are brief discussions about capturing and managing the key risk quantification data inputs. As mentioned above, in early development, data collection is often via spreadsheet forms; this can later be shifted to database entry vehicles. The sooner you can start capturing data the better; don't let information from good projects go unused (a room full of boxes may be where things start).

Project Scope

In terms of risk quantification, we need to capture scope attributes as defined at the gate that are also systemic risk drivers. Project size and dates will be captured by cost and schedule data. The types of information that may be correlated to uncertainty and hence amenable to modeling include, but are not limited to:

◆ Cost/Schedule Objectives (cost or schedule-driven, strategic importance, bidding strategy if for contractors, etc.),

- Location and proximity to labor and other resource supply,
- Asset and technology type and capacity (e.g., power generation versus transmission, and HvDC or AC in transmission),
- Ownership information (business unit(s), venture partners, alliances, etc.),
- Management approach (e.g., plant-based versus major project and turnaround),
- Project type (greenfield, add-on, expansion, revamp, turnaround, etc.),
- Contract strategy (EPC lump sum, reimbursable), and
- Execution strategy (e.g., modular, phased, fast track, or shift strategy).

Note that these attributes define business scope as understood by the project sponsors and hence if any of these were changed at a gate or during project execution, that fact must be captured in the risk occurrence data below.

Cost Actual and Estimated (by phase) Data

These are the source data for calculating the primary cost outcome metric – cost growth – usually expressed as a ratio of actual/estimate or estimate/actual (which is more normally distributed). The raw data is captured first along with information that will allow for normalization before modeling later (e.g., dates and currency). Capture each estimate at the phase-gates (Class 5, 4, 3), as this reflects the level of scope definition. Usually, estimates are nicely coded with the cost accounts and work breakdowns that we need (e.g., concrete for powerhouse), but actual expenditures are a different story.

Actual expenditures ("actuals") are usually a mess as captured in accounting, ERP, or control systems. They are useless in raw form (e.g., "civil contract for north area"). In addition, we want to capture owner's cost, which accounting may have called expense but that we may need to capture as CAPEX per our planning metric definitions. The actuals need to be transformed to standard breakouts and this will always require estimating intelligence and informed allocation. We capture various project phases to help us understand costs and where risks are most impactful, even though a final model may just include the overall capital cost. We are likely to capture discipline data (e.g., concrete) for estimating purposes; however, for risk, we look at higher-level breakouts of capital spending by owner and suppliers as listed below. (Note that these also align with the schedule data we will collect.)

♦ Front-End Loading (FEL): pre-sanction including FEED and owner's cost,

♦ Project Management: owner and contractor general management costs,

♦ Construction Management: owner and contractor management of construction excluding field and shop supervision,

♦ Engineering: detailed engineering, post FEED,

♦ Procurement: purchased materials and equipment except major fabrications,

♦ Fabrication: cost of modules or other major fabrications,

♦ Construction: direct and indirect installation including field supervision, and

♦ Start-up: post mechanical completion including owner's cost.

For estimates we capture the above from the base estimate and capture contingency, escalation, and reserve costs separately (these are embedded in the actuals of the other accounts).

Schedule Actual and Estimated (by phase) Data

These are the source data for calculating the primary duration outcome metrics – schedule slip is usually expressed as a ratio of actual/estimate duration or its inverse. Schedule is captured as milestone dates from which durations can be calculated. The dates planned at each phase-gate (e.g., Class 5, 4, 3) should be captured. However, note that prior to sanction, schedule is somewhat amorphous and is not highly amenable to prediction. The focus is on execution duration (sanction to mechanical completion) and then to start-up completion (first product).

We capture various phases to help us understand the schedule and strategy and where risks are most impactful, even though a final model may just include the execution phase duration. The dates for the following key milestones are usually captured:

- Pre-sanction gates: the end of FEL 1/Assess and 2/ Select,
- Full funds sanction: FID, the end of FEL 3/Define,
- Start and completion of detailed engineering: post-FEED to last major release,
- Start and completion of procurement: first major order and last major delivery,
- Start and completion of fabrication (particularly if modular): first major order, and last major delivery,
- Start and completion of construction: first foundation to mechanical completion,
- Start and completion of start-up: mechanical completion to achieving steady-state production even if not salable quality, and
- First product: first output of salable product.

Resource Actual and Estimated (by phase) Data

While we will generally not be modeling quantities and hours, this data will provide us with understanding of risk impacts. For example, the doubling of hours is a common feature of blowouts, and capturing the hours will help risk story understanding. As with cost, this data is usually easy to get for estimates, but difficult for actuals. Owners generally do not fully understand what was invested in their assets other than the cost totals. Much of this should have been collected for estimating database purposes (so it should not be an added risk concern). The following data are useful to capture:

- Major equipment count (may be the only thing known at early phase),
- Module counts,
- Quantities of key trades (tonnes of steel and piping, volume of concrete, etc.),
- Total Project Management hours (owner and contractor),
- Total Construction Management hours (owner and contractor),
- Total Engineering hours (detailed engineering),
- Total Fabrication hours (if modular, often hard to get), and
- Total Construction hours (directs and indirects).

Systemic Risk Ratings (by phase)

Once you have a parametric risk quantification methodology in place for systemic risks, these ratings will reflect those assigned at the time of risk analysis that you have performed on the project (assumed to have taken place at each decision gate). Otherwise, these ratings have to be backfilled based on the team's best recollection. I will not list them here as they are thoroughly described in Chapter 11.

Critical Project-Specific Risks Identified and Actual Occurred and Approximate Impacts

The nature of critical risks is discussed in Chapter 12. For the purposes of research, capturing up to ten of these risks in the database is adequate. A risk breakdown coding structure is useful for classifying common risk types (e.g., permitting risk). The code, brief description, and expected value of cost and schedule at the time of sanction are captured. The same is then captured for risks that actually occurred (which will likely differ from those predicted). Reserve risks or scope changes need to be noted as such with a code or captured in a separate data collection table.

Lessons Learned

Lessons learned are typically narrative (albeit coded) information from a defined learning process. The company should have a database to capture and retain lessons learned. What we need for risk quantification is to extract key learnings as to the cause of risks that occurred and the selection and effectiveness of corrective action decisions and risk responses. If the risk manager can help design the lessons learned process, it will help assure we get what we need out of it. This will particularly help risk analysts facilitate project-specific risk workshops.

Risk Analysis Reports and Risk Registers

This will usually consist of capturing PDF or similar copies of quantitative analysis reports and the risk registers that were in place at the time of the analysis (not monthly risk management reports). Also, the final risk register should be captured. This is particularly useful for understanding outliers during model building and calibration, and will provide explanations of various risk ratings and risk determinations. While risk registers may be in the database of your risk management system, there is a tendency to recode these over time and change systems, so a PDF print may seem redundant, but it is a more permanent record.

Change Control Logs

In my experience, risk registers often only tell about half of the risk story. The project control staff capture trends, deviations, and changes of all types, corrective actions, and contingency drawdown (impacts) in the change control process records. If these are done well (often not the case), project outcomes (particularly outliers and blowouts) can be investigated and understood.

If completing all of the above activity sounds like a lot of information and work, it is. However, good reference literature as to successful industry applications is available. In particular, one major owner company reported on its extensive custom-coded Project Knowledge Management System (PKMS) including risk quantification elements that, in their words:

> "...allows users to investigate the reasons of the cost variances through additional tabs that inform users regarding scope changes and risk events recorded in the different stages of the project... Also, through review of the "Major Risk Events/ Risk Management" tabs, users can compare the different risks assessed in the different project stages and relate this to the cost variance being assessed."[2]

Developing Risk Models and Tools

After the data has been captured, it needs to be processed for application. There are three main tools to do so: checklists for risk workshop facilitation, references to support analyses, and parametric models.

Checklists and References

Chapters 11 and 12 outline the parametric and expected value methods and the workshops or interviews used to obtain input information for risk quantification. Tools such as checklists can help guide the analyst regarding questions to ask, issues to watch out for, and risks and impacts that typically occur in various situations. As a company develops a legacy of experience, there may be classic stories in the lessons learned database or report files that the checklists can highlight (e.g., *In this situation, refer to...*). It adds credibility if the analyst can bring up useful anecdotes, stories, and insight during discussions.

---

2   Figueiredo, Cristina, and Ray Philipenko, "Taking a Project Knowledge Management System (PKMS) to the Next Level", AACE International Transactions, 2011.

Cleaning and Normalization for Models

As was discussed, raw actual data tends to be messy. The key outcome metrics we model for parametric analysis are cost growth and schedule duration slip. For cost growth, we want to first separate out scope change impact. Then we want to separate the growth (which could be negative) caused by escalation, currency exchange, and contingency risks, because we will develop or calibrate models for each of these.

Scope changes (and reserve risk occurrence) should be highlighted in the change control report and captured as such in historical data collection. Cost and duration impact of these are subtracted from the actuals. However, this can be difficult because the records usually capture only the direct impact and not the secondary impact (e.g., knock on effects to productivity). If the secondary impacts can be objectively removed, they should be, but if not, it is best to leave them alone so as not to introduce bias in the record.

Escalation and exchange impacts to cost can be removed using your escalation and exchange tool in backward looking mode. Enter the actual costs incurred by account and by period and the tool should be designed to apply historical adjusted indices to calculate how much of that spending was the result of escalation. This capability can be built into custom coded database systems.

After normalizing cost and duration for scope change, and cost for escalation and currency, you are left with the impact of contingency risks, both systemic and project-specific combined; this should be captured. However, because we want the parametric model to forecast systemic risks alone (allowing for noise), we should subtract the impact of significant or critical project-specific risks as we would for scope change.

Modeling

At this point we have normalized actual costs and adjusted schedule durations. Usually the schedule focus is the execution and start-up phases. The metrics we will analyze are:

- ◆ Cost Growth = Estimate (base estimate cost at the FEL gate of interest excluding contingency, escalation and reserves) / Actual (normalized to the estimate scope, year and currency)
- ◆ Execution Schedule Duration Slip = Plan (base schedule duration at the FEL gate of interest excluding contingency allowance if any) / Actual (normalized to the plan scope).

Note that these ratios are the inverse of what many usually look at. Most look at actual/estimate and if it is 1.20 for example, this means a 20% overrun. We use the inverse (i.e., 1/1.20 = 0.83) because we know from experience that this metric is approximately normally distributed and is hence amenable to linear regression analysis.

Regression analysis based modeling is covered in Chapter 10 in general and in Chapter 11 with respect to recommended parametric models. You do not need to restrict your analysis to only the variables in Chapter 11. Your projects may have attributes that significantly drive outcomes that are masked when looking at overall industry values. However, a challenge for most owners is getting enough data points, say ten projects, for every variable examined.

If possible, try modeling against quantified measures of the project scope attributes listed earlier in this section. In particular, look for differences between projects managed by the plant or operations (small) versus major project organizations (large). This will usually highlight estimate bias.

For small project systems or company cultures focused on predictability and biased to over-estimation, the analysis of cost growth data presents a special challenge. In that case, the cost-growth distribution will reflect not only the impact of risks, but the impact of programmatic bias. Appendix B addresses how to deal with this special situation in historical data analysis and model building. The goal is to isolate the impact of the risks and the impact of the over-funding practices.

Calibrating and Maintaining Risk Models and Methods

Many will start with an industry model such as Rand, or the updated one in Chapter 11. These have the advantage of having some credibility as they are backed by references. However, as you collect internal data, you can run your own models, likely starting with the same variables in the Rand or updated model in Chapter 11. The fact that your model results differ does not mean you are wrong. If you have enough data and modeling know-how, add and test additional variables to see if you can explain differences. If you find rational new drivers, or different coefficients, you can update your base model.

If your data or abilities are not robust, the base model can have some simple bottom line calibration factors built in. For example, a distribution expressed in a lognormal function in an Excel para-

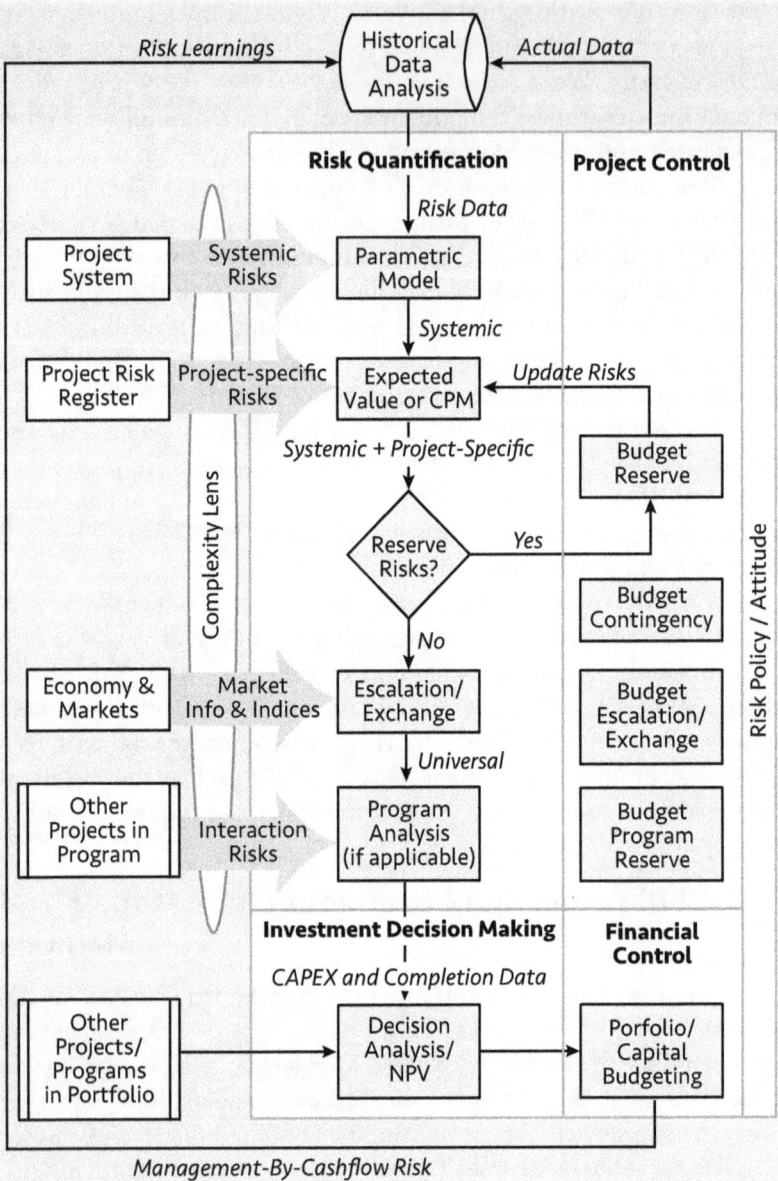

Figure 18.2 The Risk Quantification Process (Figure 7.1)

metric tool has two variables that can be adjusted: the mean and the standard deviation (in "logspace" for lognormal). A factor can be used to shift the mean higher or lower (bias) without changing the shape. Another factor can be used to modify the standard deviation to change the width of the curve (more or less uncertainty).

Improving the Project System

Risk quantification per se is focused on forecasting the impact of identified risks on a given project or program, and highlighting risks for treatment when the quantification output does not meet project objectives (for example, the project is uneconomical given the company's risk attitude). However, systemic risks are difficult (if not impossible) for any given project to change; they reflect the company culture, processes, policies, systems, tools, and competencies. To treat systemic risks and improve project outcomes, you must improve your project system. Continuous improvement should be the long-term objective of risk quantification.

Conclusion

The loop is closed on the cost and schedule risk quantification process by a project historical system that supports methods improvement. Figure 18.2 shows that feedback loop and summarizes the set of methods described in the book.

As shown, the methods are integrated with all cost and schedule risks being quantified (systemic, project-specific, escalation, and exchange) including their interactions in the face of complexity (the tipping point into chaos) and at a program level. This starts with validated base estimates and schedules developed in accordance with a strategy.

The methods are also realistic. Part One of the book detailed over fifty years of process industry research on project cost growth and schedule slip from Hackney, Rand, CII, and others. It pointed out that the dominant risks are usually systemic in nature and how empirically-based parametric methods are needed to quantify that type of risk realistically. Chapter 15 covered accuracy research in other industries and shows how the methods are universal in nature for any projects involving construction. Stories and examples were provided throughout the book to reinforce the research.

Each method is designed to be practical as well. They can be applied on the entire portfolio of projects from small to large with reasonable requirements for in-house competency in risk management and quantification for owners or contractors. Further, they do not require ideal base estimates and schedules in order to apply them (but for those using CPM-based risk modeling, Appendix A provides guidelines to improve that method). For those without project history to build on, research-based parametric models for systemic risks are provided that can be put into immediate action!

Do We Want To Change?

Companies whose projects experience repeated and large overruns will usually want to improve their systems. But what if the system regularly *underruns* their estimates? Figure 18.A below is from a study of a company's "small" project system. The study's purpose was to calibrate the industry model (similar to Chapter 11) and provide a baseline for possible project system improvements. About 400 projects from the prior five years were studied. They averaged about $10 million each and on average they underran their base estimate by 5% (15% less than the funded amount, which almost always included 10% contingency). As can be seen, the actual/estimate distribution was wider than for industry large projects of low complexity.

Actual / Base Estimate Calibration
Company X versus Large / Low Complexity Industry Projects

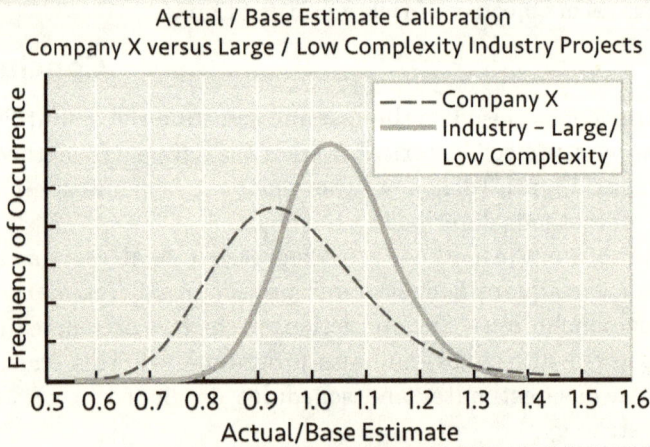

Figure 18.A Small Project Performance

Because of the project underruns, they also underran their annual capital budget. Business management and finance read the underruns and variability as lack of "capital discipline" (see "Capital Strategy? What Strategy?" in Chapter 6). The questions coming out of the study then were:

♦ What is the cause?
♦ How could it be corrected?
♦ What would it cost to correct?

The questions were fairly easy to answer; the decision on what to do was not so easy.

The cause, as for many small project systems, was biased estimates prepared by engineers as one task in their varied roles. The correction was more disciplined estimating, including risk quantification. The price would be added resources, competency development, and process improvement. But what savings would they get for that price? The chart shows little evidence of waste. The projects gave back their unused funds (implying defacto capital discipline). A stronger, less biased system would add stress (more overruns, more overhead), which is a new risk in a long entrenched, low overhead culture. The situation raised several questions that remained unanswered at the end of the assessment:

♦ Could the company change an entrenched practice without adding more risk?

♦ Should the company just stop adding 10% contingency, skip the addition of estimators and process change, and just move the fat curve to the right via the contingency reduction?

♦ Is this company's project management system broken or just biased?

Finally, the methods are aligned with project phase-gate scope development processes. In that way, the end result is more profitable capital investment decisions based on a clear risk story as well as more effective risk responses and project control during execution with budgets including appropriate contingency and management reserves.

The methods covered *will* help you and your company better face risk reality and consider what works and what does not – how to avoid the "Alice in Wonderland rabbit hole." We should strive for the wisdom of Janus with one face looking into the future and one looking back to the past. In that way we will not be overly swayed by the fire of hope, opportunity, and added value or the fear of failure and lost value and entropy. While we need to remain humble as to our methods for prediction (like rabbits with a watch), we have to try to make the best of it. Only then can outcomes be improved.

Questions

1) What are some reasons that companies often do not have effective project historical data or knowledge management processes and tools?

2) What types of "processes" information are recommended for capture in a database to support risk quantification (in addition to traditional cost estimating and schedule support data)?

3) What types of original records are recommended for retention in a database to support risk quantification?

4) What does Normalization mean and why does it need to be done as part of a historical database process?

5) Why are ERP systems not recommended as one's sole database in support of risk quantification?

6) Considering the nature of systemic risks, what should be the long term objective of the risk quantification process and methods?

Appendix A

The Hybrid CPM (Critical Path Method) with MCS (Monte Carlo Simulation) Method

Chapter 7, "Introduction to Risk Quantification Methods," includes a section titled, "The CPM-Based Model Alternative if Applicable." That section briefly mentions that systemic risks can be addressed objectively using parametric modeling and then those results can be incorporated into the CPM model where project-specific risks are added and further quantified (a hybrid of Parametric and CPM-Based methods). This Appendix further describes that method.

While the base CPM with MCS method, and the hybrid approach to be described here, are not my first choices for practicality reasons described in Chapter 7, there are many experts who do recommend the base CPM method. For those who use that approach, this Appendix offers a way to better quantify systemic risks and to incorporate the tipping point concept into CPM with MCS practice.

Base CPM with MCS Method

AACE International describes the base method in its Recommended Practice 57R-09, "Integrated Cost and Schedule Risk Analysis Using Monte Carlo Simulation of a CPM Model."

The Recommend Practice (RP) summarizes the method as follows: "The methods presented in the RP are based on integrating the cost estimate with the project schedule by resource-loading and costing the schedule's activities. The probability and impact of risks/uncertainties are specified and the risks/uncertainties are linked to the activities and costs that they affect. Using Monte Carlo techniques one can simulate both time and cost, permitting the impacts of schedule risk on cost risk to be calculated."[1]

---

1   "Integrated Cost and Schedule Risk Analysis Using Monte Carlo Simulation of a CPM Model," Recommended Practice 57R-09, AACE International, Morgantown, WV. This RP is available for free to AACE members, and at a nominal price to others (visit http://www.aacei.org/resources/rp/).

While some steps in the RP method are described here (those steps affected by linking it with parametric modeling), the 23-page RP should be read in its entirety as there are many important procedural details that are too extensive to repeat or summarize. I also recommend that those wanting to learn more about the CPM method study the text titled *Integrated Cost-Schedule Risk Analysis* by the AACE RP's lead author, David Hulett.[2]

A key feature of the base method is that the *risks are linked to the activities*. It is "risk driven," which is a first principle of good risk quantification practice. That makes the base RP method a realistic model for quantifying *project-specific* risks. In the risk driven method, the impact of each critical risk is incorporated into the model as multipliers of impacted activity duration and cost. The multipliers are entered as a distribution.

For example, a risk's duration impact multiplier might be entered as a triangular distribution of 0.95, 1.10, and 1.20 (low, most likely, and high). Each risk has a percent probability of occurrence, so when MCS is run, that percent of iterations is impacted by the risk, with MCS sampling from the multiplier distribution when the risk occurs. For each risk, the analyst defines multipliers of impacted activity duration (or a group of activities), which will also proportionally impact its time-dependent costs that have been loaded into that schedule activity. They will also enter multipliers of non-time dependent cost associated with impacted activities (e.g., a material purchase).

The RP specifies two types of risks that are quantified in somewhat different ways. This is where this hybrid approach varies from the RP. The RP's risk types are:

♦ Risk Events: The RP definition is synonymous with *project-specific* risks.

♦ Uncertainties: The RP calls these "ambiguities" that are 100% likely to occur. What that includes is more or less synonymous with *systemic* risks as covered in this text, at least in terms of how their impact is modeled.

The RP calls for the uncertainties to be represented by traditional 3-point estimates of multipliers on duration and resources. The impacts are usually applied broadly; for example, a single "duration estimate uncertainty" risk multiplier might be applied to all activities or a related group of activities. In the RP, the multiplier estimates

---

2   Hulett, David, *Integrated Cost-Schedule Risk Analysis*, Gower Publishing, Burlington VT, 2011.

are based on subjective input from traditional risk workshops and/ or interviews with team members. Optimally, these workshops will discuss all the key systemic risks.

The Hybrid Approach

In our modified method including parametric modeling, we are going to make the following variations to the RP method:

♦ Eliminate all subjective "uncertainty risks" or decouple their impact from the activities and costs (also delete escalation risks if any).

♦ Add a "systemic" risk activity to the schedule that starts with the as-is completion milestone (may re-label it as "pre-systemic" completion or similar) and finishes with a new total completion milestone. Our interest in the outcome will be focused on this total completion date.

♦ Assign a duration and non-time dependent cost to the "systemic contingency" activity equal to the $p50$ or mean of the systemic risk parametric model outputs (or whatever level of confidence is used to fund contingency – see Chapter 11).

♦ Convert the parametric model's distributions of absolute duration and cost impact values to factors relative to the $p50$ or mean, and apply those factors as custom impact multiplier distributions to the "systemic risk" activity (see example Table A-1). These have 100% probability of occurring (i.e., they are not an event, but a given attribute of the system that results in uncertainty).

In summary, this replaces the various subjective uncertainties with an objective, empirically-based quantification that covers systemic risks. Note that systemic risk and its quantification in the parametric model includes what is sometimes called "variabilities." These are just artifacts of the system.

It should be noted that the RP includes an example analysis with a table of eight risks. Four are systemic risks (design complexity, capable management, cost estimate inaccuracy, and duration estimate inaccuracy) and one is escalation risk (suppliers may be busy). While these were simplistic examples for the purpose of the RP, this is consistent with my experience that most risks found in risk registers are systemic or escalation, which are not realistically quantifiable by brainstorming (although the team will have opinions).

	PARAMETRIC MODEL		CONVERT TO FACTORS	
PROBABILITY OF UNDERRUN	COST	SCHEDULE	COST	SCHEDULE
10%	-12.5%	-3.8%	(0.96)	(0.26)
15%	-8.2%	-0.4%	(0.63)	(0.03)
20%	-4.5%	2.3%	(0.35)	0.15
25%	-1.3%	4.6%	(0.10)	0.31
30%	1.7%	6.8%	0.13	0.46
35%	4.6%	8.9%	0.35	0.60
40%	7.4%	10.9%	0.57	0.73
45%	10.2%	12.9%	0.78	0.87
50%*	13.0%	14.8%	1.00	1.00
55%	15.9%	16.8%	1.22	1.13
60%	19.0%	18.9%	1.46	1.27
65%	22.2%	21.1%	1.70	1.42
70%	25.7%	23.4%	1.97	1.58
75%	29.6%	26.0%	2.27	1.75
80%	34.0%	29.0%	2.61	1.95
85%	39.4%	32.5%	3.02	2.19
90%	46.6%	37.0%	3.57	2.49
* Contingency Level				

Table A-1: Example Conversion of Parametric Outcomes to Factors

In summary, this replaces the various subjective uncertainties with an objective, empirically-based quantification that covers systemic risks. Note that systemic risk and its quantification in the parametric model includes what is sometimes called "variabilities." These are just artifacts of the system.

Example Application

The following is an example of how to apply the above steps to a schedule. We will start with Table A-2 which is an extract from the RP 57R-09 example schedule (Figure 1 of the RP) but showing only the final "Commissioning" activity and completion milestone.

ID	Description	Remaining Duration	Start	Finish	Cost	
0050	Commissioning	100	20-Jan-13	29-Apr-13	$16,500	
0060	Project Turnover	0		29-Apr-13	$0	

Table A-2: Example Schedule from RP 57R-09 (Figure 1)

Table A-3 adds a "Systemic Risk" activity and a new total completion milestone. This new activity is assigned a duration of 30 days and non-time dependent cost of $3,000 based on the *p*50 output values of systemic risk parametric models.

ID	Description	Remaining Duration	Start	Finish	Cost	
0050	Commissioning	100	20-Jan-13	29-Apr-13	$16,500	
0060	Project Turnover	0		29-Apr-13	$0	
0070	Systemic Risk	30	29-Apr-13	29-May-13	$3,000	
0080	Final Completion	0		29-May-13	$0	

Table A-3: Example Schedule with Added Systemic Risk Activity

Next, Table A-4 shows our modification of the RP's risk and impact factor table (Table 4 in the RP) to delete the "inaccuracy" risks and replace them with Systemic Risk factors. The factor values are from the Table A-1 example *p*-table. In the RP, the inaccuracy risk factors had been applied to the Commissioning activity duration and cost (and other activities) – all those "uncertainty" risks and links are removed. The "Systemic" factors in Table A-4 are applied to the new Systemic Risk activity duration and cost.

Risk	Probability	Duration Impact Ranges			Cost Impact Ranges		
		Min	ML	Max	Min	ML	Max
6 Activity duration estimates are inaccurate	100%	90%	105%	115%			
7 Cost estimate is inaccurate	100%				95%	105%	115%
6 Systemic risk duration	100%	75%	100%	249%			
7 Systemic risk cost	100%				4%	100%	357%

Table A-4: Example Risk Table Replacing "Uncertainties" with Systemic Risks

Having made these changes, the CPM model MCS simulation will now include the parametric systemic risk impacts for cost and schedule. Note that the systemic risk impacts are additive to any critical project-specific risks that were incorporated in the model.

Risk Response Treatment

Chapter 12 described how realistic risk quantification requires that impacts be estimated in consideration of the risk response assumed. For critical risks, the response often involves a change in the schedule logic. In the Expected Value method, this situation is quantified through conceptual assessment by the team of the possible range of responses and impacts to completion.

In the base CPM method, a risk response that changes logic is modeled using "probabilistic branching." This requires adding risk response activities to the CPM model. While the response may be quite complex, it can usually be simplified to a few activities. The RP provides an example of probabilistic branching and shows how the MCS outcome of such a model may be bimodal.

For probabilistic branching, many references use the example of a test activity failing. However, critical project-specific risks tend to be more serious in nature, such as "river flood overtops the cofferdam" from which the recovery could be quite an undertaking and quite uncertain as to severity and scope of how the team will respond and recover. The impact of risk responses to critical risks also tend to spill over into other activities (e.g., move all cranes on site to recovery area), making for a complex CPM modeling challenge. Unfortunately, I do not have an alternate, practical approach to probabilistic branching to recommend, but it is necessary for realistic analysis.

Tipping Point

Chapter 14 describes how projects enter a disorderly state (i.e., loss of control or chaotic) when a combination of complexity factors and stressors push it over a "tipping point." It also defines a way to model that situation in the Expected Value method. In essence, blowout is a risk event that may or may not exist as indicated by the tipping point rating. For example, we might determine that a tipping point metric of three on a scale of one to ten equates to a six percent probability that the project will cross over into a disorderly mode of behavior. This approach can be applied in a similar way in a CPM model.

In a CPM model, a blowout activity can be added after the systemic contingency activity described earlier. The blowout activity's cost and schedule are entered as 3-point estimates. However, this activity will be invoked or exist in only a set percentage of the MCS iterations (e.g., 6% probability per the example). The resulting MCS cost outcome will be bimodal, depending on how many iterations include the blowout and the scale of the blowout impact entered. Schedule impacts may be more limited.

A blowout is manifested primarily in a collapse of productivity resulting in a doubling or more of labor related costs. It affects the cost of every activity after the point where the productivity collapse begins (often evident at about 30% construction completion). It may result in schedule delay (and a 3-point estimate of that delay can be assigned to the blowout activity) but in the usual case it is primarily a cost event.

In fact, schedule aggressiveness is a tipping point stressor. Management sets an unrealistic schedule target, it then does everything it can to complete on time, productivity declines, so more schedule stress is added, productivity declines some more, and so on. Eventually the schedule will give way (the team will not report or confess to a completion delay until they give up and acknowledge the problem late in the project), but the initial economic impact is the increased CAPEX. In other words, this is not a risk whose impact on individual activities is worth studying (eventually, if the risk happens, you will have to re-baseline upon capitulation). The cost outcome finally gets management's attention that there is a problem so that action can be taken.

Communicating Risk Outcomes

The CPM RP describes traditional tornado diagramming as an approach to communicating the priority of risks. As discussed in Chapter 16, for a project with typical systemic risks, a tornado diagram generated by MCS software for a hybrid model will usually show the impact of systemic risk as a whole as being dominant, often by a wide margin over most project-specific risks. If management wants to know the influence of any one systemic risk factor (e.g., scope maturity or team development), then a sensitivity analysis needs to be conducted. Managers who are familiar with traditional methods may want to know the specific contribution from estimating uncertainty or any of the myriad of uncertainties that they are used to seeing tabulated.

This is the opportunity for the analyst to explain the nature of systemic risks and why estimating uncertainty is a symptom of scope development, system maturity, team development, and other drivers. Systemic risks affect every practice on a project in over-arching ways, not just estimating. Focus on the root causes and improve the system. It is not estimating's problem – the risk belongs to senior management. Finally, if there is tipping point risk, the bimodal cost outcome is shown as covered in Chapter 14. That should motivate management to manage the blowout risk.

Summary

With the application of the hybrid approach in this Appendix, the analyst gets the benefits of CPM-based analysis (detailed insight to schedule behavior in an orderly project) plus the realism of objective, empirically-based analysis of systemic risks. The drawbacks are its day-to-day practicality – the need for a high-quality, resource loaded schedule and the expertise and time to apply rigorous methods such as probabilistic branching. But if you have schedule quality, expertise, and time, this hybrid approach can be valuable, particularly for strategic projects applied along with the Expected Value method for validation.

Appendix B

Addressing Bias in Project Systems Focused on Predictability

Chapter 4 described how small project systems tend to overestimate projects (i.e., costs tend to underrun the budget). Figure B-1 (Figure 4.5 from Chapter 4) illustrates the typical distribution of cost growth data in these systems; i.e., the "cresting wave" where most projects come out on budget, a few overrun by more than 10%,

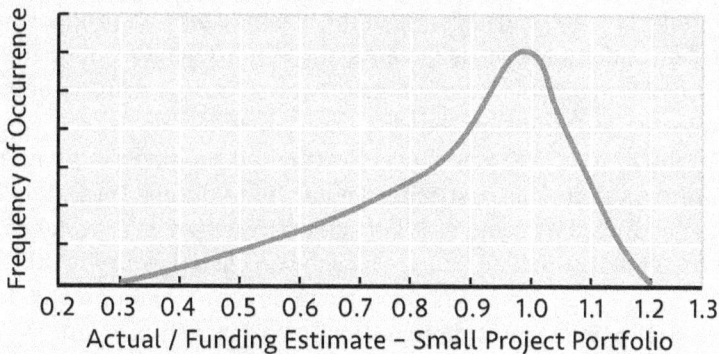

Figure B.1 (Figure 4.5): Typical Accuracy for a Small Project Portfolio

but many more underrun the budget, often by very large margins. This is driven in part by a focus on achieving "predictability" in outcomes – often accompanied by a culture in which overruns are punished. This behavior is not unique to small project systems; it can be found in government projects where there is political pressure to avoid inquisition and also where favorable economics (e.g., low feedstock cost) take the pressure off of capital cost competitiveness.

This Appendix addresses the special situation of interpreting historical accuracy data for these project systems. This is needed because the "cresting wave" distribution of cost growth data for these projects is not natural. It is not primarily a reflection of the impact of risks, but of a combination of risks plus programmatic (e.g., finance, procurement, and/or control) biases. It reflects a practice that can be viewed as buying predictability through increased estimates (intentional or otherwise). This distorts project control behavior because it creates an option for teams to spend any extra funds (deliberately or through poor performance) or to return the excess to the business. The following sections describe how to interpret historical data to segregate the natural impact of risks from the more or less intentional impacts of providing and using excess funds.

Natural Cost Growth Behavior versus the Cresting Wave

Typically, base cost estimates and funded amounts for large projects tend to be "competitive" – only as much money as needed to do the job is provided assuming reasonable if not stellar performance. In that situation, the distribution of cost growth data is well represented by a lognormal distribution skewed toward overruns.[1] The distribution of actual data will generally be a smooth continuum that reflects the natural range of labor behavior (i.e., productivity) and the randomness of risk events and conditions. Parametric risk quantification models based on history are typically going to employ a lognormal distribution that fits this behavior and risks.

However, if the project is not estimated competitively and has extra funds in its base estimate and/or in its funded total, there is a good chance that some or all of the extra money will be spent. In fact, in a finance-driven culture focused on cash flow predictability, the team may be rewarded for coming out exactly on budget.[2] So, instead of a lognormal distribution with smooth continuum, the historical cost growth distribution (actual/estimate cost) of such systems will have a sharp peak at about 1.0 with few overrunning by more than 10% (the amount allowed for by finance before triggering an inquisition) such as shown in Figure B-1. There may be a significant number of projects that underrun and that is good because it means extra money is being returned to the business. The worst case is where there are very few underruns because this means that all the money is being spent on poor performance, budget shifting between projects, and/or "urban renewal" scope.

---

1   Hollmann, John, "Estimate Accuracy: Dealing with Reality," Cost Engineering Journal, AACE International, Nov/Dec 2012 (that article describes the typical distribution of cost growth for large industry projects).

2   Many companies base employee performance evaluations and/or bonuses on its projects coming out within +/-10% or similar. This practice guarantees only one outcome: *overestimation.*

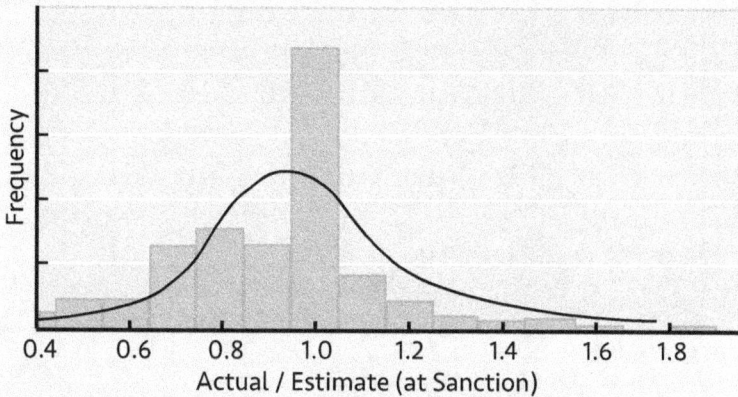

Figure B-2: Typical Best Fit Distribution to an Actual / Estimated Cresting Wave Histogram

Interestingly, the best-fit for a cresting wave distribution will still be a lognormal or similar distribution because there is no natural cresting wave distribution in the curve repertoire of our statistical tools. Figure B-2 shows a typical comparison of an actual cresting wave histogram and a best-fit curve.

It is immediately obvious that the "fit" curve in Figure B-2 is not a close representation of the actual data's extreme central tendency at 1.0 and its truncation at 1.10. The question then is, *"How is performance that is naturally lognormal or similar in distribution transformed into a "cresting wave" via our programmatic practices?"*

The transformation starts with the fact that our system is biased towards overestimation. A reasonable assumption in that case is that the estimates are about the *p*80 level of a competitive reality. With that assumption, we can shift the log curve to the left until the histogram peak (actual / estimate = 1.0) is at the natural (best-fit) curve's *p*80 level as in Figure B-3. At this point, the curve and histogram are still not visually comparable. However, the last transformation step is to shift project outcomes that would normally be underruns by having them spend their entire budgets. Figure B-3, shows this shift of the projects that should have been less than 1.0 to equal 1.0.

This can occur because the funding was on a generous fixed cost basis, which means the supplier enjoyed the underruns, or the funding was on a reimbursable basis with a generous budget that tended to be spent for better or worse (noting that not all the underruns spent the extra). The few overruns (>1.10) are now

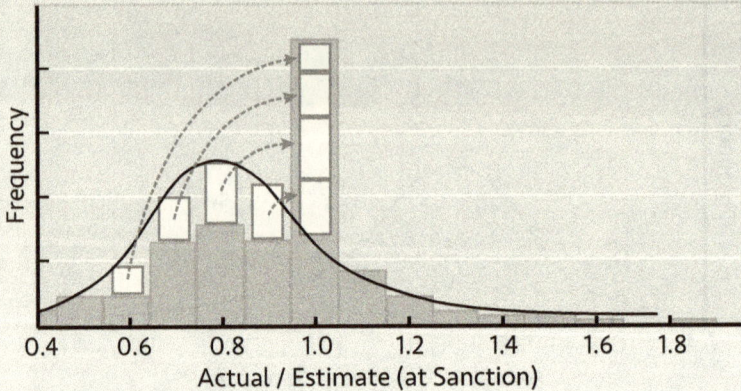

Figure B-3: Curve Fit Showing Transformation to the Actual / Estimated Histogram

consistent with natural uncertainty and risk behavior (they fall on the adjusted curve; funding would have to be extremely uncompetitive to encompass these cases). Neither the fixed nor reimbursable scenario is a cost "competitive" approach but they are typical for project systems where "predictability" is the main objective (e.g., small project systems).

Finally, note that the best fit curve's actual/estimated mode (peak) is about 0.8 or 0.85, which implies the overestimation or funding is about +15 to 20% on average which is a consistent with the experience of the author and others for small project systems.[3]

Addressing Overestimation Bias in Historical Analysis and Modeling

When a project system is focused on "competitiveness" (or at least not biased to over-estimation), which is common for large projects, the historical analysis of data through MLR analysis will work well. Parametric models of systemic risk can be developed using "natural," best fit lognormal, or similar distributions.

For project systems driven by "predictability" with bias to over-estimation (as characterized in cresting wave histograms), the historical analysis of data through MLR analysis still works, but requires some adjustment. Parametric models of systemic risk can still be developed using "natural," best fit lognormal or similar distributions (as in Figure B-2). However, before hard-wiring a biased

3   Kulkarni, Phyllis, "Stop Punishing the Overruns," InSites, IPA, InC-, Sept 7, 2011.

result into base forecasting models, we need to ask ourselves if we want to accept "fat" estimates as our mean expectation and lose sight of the fact that this outcome is not competitive. There are two options to consider:

1. Tighten up base estimating practices to make sure it is competitive (have a base estimating strategy) and then, if conservative funding is desired for predictability, do it explicitly by funding at say $p80$ of our risk analysis.

2. Accept biased base estimating (e.g., historical norms strategy) and then fund at the mean or $p50$ of the risk analysis. This loses sight of the base estimate's competitiveness and our project control effectiveness.

If option 1 is chosen, then "shift" the cost growth distribution curve to remove the historical bias as in Figure B-3. My recommendation is that the shift adjustment be equal to moving the curve to the left until the histogram peak (actual /estimate = 1) is at the best fit curve's $p80$ level. The difference between the curve's peak and the curve $p80$ will be approximately the average over-estimation (in essence, this is a form of "validating" our estimating practice).

Having plotted the adjusted curve and actual histogram as in Figure B-3, your job as risk analyst is then to communicate with business management about the behaviors resulting in this bias (what is the story?). The following questions should be considered;

♦ For estimating future projects, should we estimate competitively, and then fund at a high level (e.g., p80) and provide all these funds to the PM?

♦ Is this cresting wave consistent with a practical priority and explicit strategy to get projects done quickly and safely while minimizing planning overhead? (This is not economical for large projects.)

♦ Are projects well controlled and returning any over-funding (the peak at 1.0 is not overly exaggerated as in Figure B-1)?

This can be a very difficult conversation because it may uncover uncompetitive and/or undisciplined behavior if overfunding is not being returned. If project system key performance indicators (KPI) for cost are predictability based, this may also show how they are possibly increasing capital costs and inappropriately rewarding and/

or penalizing employees. Usually management will say they want *both* competitiveness and predictability, but it needs to be pointed out that one cannot have both if the system they are responsible for developing is not top-notch (i.e., systemic risks are minimized).

Glossary

Note: Where an AACE definition is referenced, the source is *Cost Engineering Terminology*, Recommended Practice 10S-90, AACE International®, Morgantown, WV (www.aacei.org).[1] Readers should refer to the latest version of that Recommended Practice (RP); it is updated regularly as Industry practices evolve. While I tend to favor AACE terminology, unless otherwise indicated, these definitions are my own or the source is cited.

AACE (AACE®, AACE International®), aka the Association for the Advancement of Cost Engineering. Key products include their risk quantification RPs, the TCM® Framework, and the DRMP® Certification. See http://www.aacei.org. A list of technical products is included on page 392.

Accuracy/Accuracy Range per AACE is *"An expression of an estimate's predicted closeness to final actual costs or time. Typically expressed as high/low percentages by which actual results will be over and under the estimate along with the confidence interval these percentages represent."* It is Industry's shorthand for expressing the uncertainty of estimates.

Allowance per AACE is *"...resources included in estimates to cover the cost of known but undefined requirements for an individual activity, work item, account or sub-account."* Specificity of the item differentiates this from contingency, which is for general uncertainty.

Base Estimate per AACE is an *"Estimate excluding escalation, foreign currency exchange, contingency and management reserves."* This is sometimes called a "Point Estimate." The only uncertain items in the base are allowances. This is the starting point for risk quantification; a key concern is bias in the base. Optimally, the base estimate will be prepared in accordance with a base estimating strategy (see Strategy: Cost and Schedule). Considering bias and allowance treatment, the following definition is suggested: "Estimate excluding escalation, foreign currency exchange, contingency, and management reserves *and prepared in accordance with a documented base cost strategy."*

Base Schedule per AACE is a *"Schedule excluding risks (i.e., excluding contingency)."* The only uncertain activities or durations in the base are allowances. This is the starting point for risk quantification; a key concern is bias in the base. Optimally, the base schedule will be prepared in accordance with a base scheduling strategy (see Strategy: Cost and Schedule). Considering bias and allowance treatment, the following

---

1   Excerpts from RP10S-90 with permission of AACE International, 1265 Suncrest Towne Centre Dr., Morgantown, WV 26505; http://www.aacei.org, Copyright ©2016 by AACE International; all rights reserved.

definition is suggested: "Schedule excluding contingency *and prepared in accordance with a documented base schedule strategy*."

Basic Engineering is usually the phase of engineering work associated with Class 4 or FEL 2/Select of project phase gate processes (for example, complete the PFDs) when multiple options may still be under consideration. This is followed by Front End Engineering and Design (FEED) on a selected option during Class 3 or FEL 3/Define.

Basis of Estimate or **Schedule** per AACE is "*Written documentation that describes how an estimate, schedule, or other plan component was developed and defines the information used in support of development*." This should not only include descriptions of the base estimate and schedule, but also how risks were analyzed, quantified, and accounted for. It is an essential document for communicating to the team and decision makers what the estimate or schedule represents.

Bias per AACE in a behavioral sense is a "*Lack of objectivity based on the enterprise's or individual's position or perspective*" (for example, *optimism bias* and i*mmediacy bias*). From a statistical sense, it means systematically over or under estimating a cost or duration.

Blowout is vernacular to describe a project cost overrun or schedule slip outcome that is well beyond the typical range of expectations and is usually damaging to project and capital effectiveness, profitability, and often reputations and careers. Blowouts often result from project performance tipping into a chaotic or disorderly mode of behavior (loss of control).

Branching: Conditional or Probabilistic: per AACE for a CPM schedule is "*...schedule analysis that allows for changes in schedule logic and/ or durations depending on the occurrence of risk events or conditions*." A conditional branch has an "if/then" form. For example, if activity X duration exceeds ten days (in a probabilistic model), then perform conditional successor activity Y. In risk modeling, preparing contingency plans (alternative activity branches) reflecting each risk response can be very complex.

Business Case per AACE is a deliverable that "*Defines a project's or other investment's justification for business decision making purposes*." The basic premises of this justification form the business scope (for example, X capacity, of Y quality, on Z date).

CII, CII® (Construction Industry Institute®): a key CII product is their PDRI® or Project Definition Rating Index® (www.construction-institute.org).

CAPEX: Capital Expenditure per AACE are costs "*...which are not carried as a current expense on the books of account and for which depreciation is allowed*." Capital expenditures are made through the performance of capital projects. In NPV analysis, the CAPEX cash flow usually begins at the time a single project option is selected and ends to turnover to operations control. In finance, the CAPEX value is booked in the asset register at project completion and capital cost is depreciated against income over time.

Capital Budgeting per AACE is *"A systematic procedure for classifying, evaluating, and ranking proposed capital expenditures (CAPEX) for the purpose of comparison and selection, combined with the analysis of the financing requirements."* This procedure usually involves phase Gate or Stage Gate processes.

Capital Project per AACE is *"A project in which the cost of the end result or product is capitalized (i.e., cost will be depreciated)."* As covered in this book, the project usually involves engineering and construction and the end result is usually a new or modified capital asset (for example, a facility such as a building, road, process plant, or manufacturing plant).

Cash Flow refers to capital or expense expenditures and revenues spread out over time (usually an annual time frame for finance and risk evaluations). Cash flow is used to complete engineering economics evaluations (NPV and IRR) as well as escalation and currency risk evaluations.

Causation (also see **Cause**) per AACE is *"An explanation or description of the facts and circumstances that produce a result."* In statistical modeling, it is important to remember that correlation does not imply causation.

Cause (also see **Risk Driver**) refers to a condition (for example, a project system attribute) or potential event that results in cost and schedule uncertainty in planning and ultimately in project cost or schedule impacts.

Change Control/Change Management per AACE is a *"Process of accepting or rejecting changes to the project's baselines."* The process includes analysis of proposed changes, deviations or trends, including of their risks. Poor change control is a significant systemic risk.

Change Log (Trends/Deviations/Notifications/Changes) refers to records kept to help manage identified changes and other deviations from project baseline plans. If done well, these are important records for empirical research of risks and their outcomes.

Chaos/Chaotic (see **Blowout**) is vernacular to describe project performance (particularly labor) that has become disorderly or "out of control." Speaking more statistically, the outputs are not linear with the inputs; i.e., risk impacts become disproportionate to risk driving conditions and events because of compounding and other effects.

Classification (Class) refers to the mechanism recommended by AACE International to rate the level of scope definition upon which a cost estimate or schedule is based. AACE provides for five classes aligned with typical phase gate project processes. Increasing scope definition and class correlates with improving accuracy, but there are no standard accuracy ranges associated with class levels. Class corresponds to Front-End Loading (FEL) ratings (for example, Class 5 aligns with FEL 1/Appraise).

Class Creep refers to the tendency of those who self-rate their level of project scope definition (Class) to take credit for better scope definition than can be objectively supported.

Complexity refers to the interrelation and interaction of parts in a project or system. The more elements there are (i.e., complication) and the more they interact, the more complex and difficult it will be to manage. Complexity can be measured and used in risk quantification models; it is a key driver of non-linear, disorderly, or chaotic behavior.

Complication (versus Complexity) is an element of complexity that reflects the number of elements in a system. Complication alone does not mean something is complex; however, with enough complication this may become the case (for example, megaprojects tend to be complex regardless of strategy, process, technology, or other complexity elements).

Conditional Branching per AACE for a CPM schedule is "*...schedule analysis that allows for changes in schedule logic and/or durations depending on the occurrence of risk events or conditions.*" A conditional branch has an "if/then" form. For example, if activity X duration exceeds ten days (in a probabilistic model), then perform conditional successor activity Y. In risk modeling, preparing contingency plans (alternative activity branches) reflecting each risk response can be very complex.

Confidence Level is a statistical term that defines the percentage probability or "confidence level" that an estimated value will be underrun. It is often expressed as a "*p*-value." For example, the $p80$ value would be that which has an 80% chance of being underrun (or 20% chance of overrun). Be careful to be clear as to whether you are speaking of the level (will cost less than) or interval (will cost between).

Confidence Interval is a statistical expression of a range bounded by low and high (+/-) confidence levels or *p*-values. For example, an 80% confidence interval reflects the width of the range bounded by the $p90$ and $p10$ levels (90% − 10% = 80% confidence interval).

Contingency: Cost per AACE is "*An amount added to an estimate to allow for items, conditions, or events for which the state, occurrence, or effect is uncertain and that experience shows will likely result, in aggregate, in additional costs.*" Note two key phrases,

♦ "*experience shows will likely*" means the amount is *expected to be spent*. It is not fat, but the mean of empirically valid analysis, and

♦ "*in aggregate*" means "in total" or "bottom-line." There should be only one contingency value for a project.

Cost contingency specifically excludes major (business) scope change, escalation, currency, and management reserves. The only uncertainty in a base estimate then should be allowances (see respective definitions).

Being likely or expected to be spent, contingency is under the authority of the project manager to use so he or she can respond to risks in a timely and efficient manner.

Contingency: Schedule per AACE RP 70R-12 is *"...an amount of time included in the project or program schedule to mitigate (dampen / buffer) the effects of risks or uncertainties identified or associated with specific elements of the project schedule."* The AACE RP further specifies that schedule contingency must be visible in the schedule and is not float.

Contingency Planning (also **Risk Response Planning**) refers to planning as to potential responses if and when a critical risk condition becomes evident or a critical risk event occurs. Successful mitigation of the risk event depends on the scope, cost, duration, and effectiveness of the response.

Control (Statistical) in reference to regression analysis refers to including known risk drivers (for example the level of scope definition) as independent variables in the analysis to avoid ascribing outcomes to the wrong cause. Most published articles on estimate accuracy fail to control for known risk drivers because of the lack of project practice data.

Correlation (versus Causation) is a statistical term indicating relationship between variables in a model – the variables have some sort of dependence. "Correlation Coefficients" are a measure of the degree of the relationship and are used in Monte Carlo simulation models. Analysts must remember that *correlation does not imply causation.* However, if there is causation, the concept allows for models that can make predictions, such as cost growth and schedule slip.

Cost Cutting/Savings/Reduction Exercise is an effort to lower the cost of a project, often late in project scope development or during execution. Unlike Value Improving Processes (VIPs), these efforts tend not to give full consideration to either value (impact to asset life cycle cost) or risk (impact to uncertainty of cost or schedule outcomes).

Cost Engineering per AACE is that *"...area of engineering practice where engineering judgment and experience are used in the application of scientific principles and techniques to problems of business and program planning; cost estimating; economic and financial analysis; program and project management; planning and scheduling; cost and schedule performance measurement, and change control."* This includes risk management and quantification. Cost engineering adds most value to the performance of investment decision making, working closely with business and design engineering to develop asset and project scope.

Cost Growth is vernacular for an increase in cost of an item or the project itself during the life of a project. If the growth is from the base cost estimate, it may be termed "contingency usage." If the growth is relative to the FID amount, it may be termed cost "overrun." The value can be negative. This is commonly the dependent variable of parametric cost contingency models.

Cost/Schedule Integration refers to methods that analyze and quantify cost and schedule together. This is done because cost and schedule interact and can be traded (time is money). Cost and schedule risk should not be analyzed separately and there should be a cost and schedule strategy that reflects the owner's preferences regarding tradeoffs between cost and schedule.

Cost/Schedule Tradeoff refers to the fact that the selection of project options (including likely risk responses) depends on cost and schedule strategy. Options may be high cost and fast (schedule driven), low cost and slow (cost driven), or some compromise. Research shows that project cost growth is typically worse than schedule slip. This is typically due to projects being schedule driven and choosing costly risk responses (for example, attempting to accelerate by adding more workers, regardless of their productivity in order to get revenue started).

CPM (Critical Path Method) per AACE is a *"Technique used to predict project duration by analyzing which sequence of activities has least amount of scheduling flexibility."* It applies *"Network scheduling using activity durations and logic ties between activities to model the plan to execute the work."* A CPM network model can be used as a base for integrated cost and schedule risk quantification modeling.

Critical Risks per AACE RP 41R-08 are risks that could cause cost or duration to *"...vary from its target, either favorably or unfavorably, by such a magnitude that the bottom line cost (or profit) of the project would change by an amount greater than its critical variance."* The critical variance is a cost or time threshold that would make a material difference to the investment decision or to perceived project success. For example, the team may decide that risks that result in a total project cost increase of more than 2% if they occur are "critical" and therefore should be included in project-specific risk analysis.

DRMP® (Decision and Risk Management Professional) is a certification available from AACE.

DA (Decision Analysis) per AACE is *"A systematic and typically quantitative process for selecting the optimum of two or more alternatives in order to address a problem or opportunity."* The evaluation step in the DA process often incorporates probabilistic modeling addressing risks.

 ♦ Skinner defines DA as, *"...a methodology and set of probabilistic frameworks for facilitating high quality, logical discussions which illuminate difficult decisions and lead to clear and compelling action by the decision maker."*[2]

 ♦ Leach defines DA as, *"A process through which companies and teams can gain insight into the key issues that drive value on their projects and in their teams."*[3]

2   Skinner, David C., *Introduction to Decision Analysis*, 3rd Edition, Probabilistic Publishing, Gainesville, FL (2009).

3   Leach, Patrick, *Why Can't You Just Give Me The Number?*, 2nd Edition,

♦ Charlesworth defines DA as, *"Decision Analysis is a set of tools (frameworks) that can help people and/or groups of people clarify and reach alignment on their goals and objectives, develop and examine alternatives, systematically examine the effect of uncertainty, and maximize the probability of achieving their goals and objectives."*[4]

Decision Criteria/Threshold/Hurdle Rate refers to a deciding factor or metric that is considered in making a decision. The business or project team may establish a metric value (a threshold or hurdle rate such as IRR) that must be exceeded in order for the option to be selected or the project to be approved. This hurdle rate may be a matter of organization decision policy.

Decision Gate/Gates refers to milestones in defined phase gate processes at which a group (chaired by a gate keeper) reviews the project scope development for further direction and/or decision and funding (a gate review). The gate review team often does not have funding authority but advises those with authority as to their findings.

Decision Policy per AACE is a *"Definitive position of an organization on how investment or project decisions will be made. Policy establishes the basis for decision models. Provides a basis for consistent and appropriate decision making and defines authority and accountability within the organization."* It usually establishes decision criteria and is a key guideline for gate reviews.

Distribution (see **PDF**) is a statistical term for the observed frequency of occurrence of values in an actual or model sample. The distribution may be plotted as:

♦ A histogram (frequency diagram) with bars whose height (y) corresponds to the percentage of observations with value x (or range of x values), or

♦ A cumulative distribution diagram where the y-value is the percentage of observations less than the x-value.

Drawdown (Contingency Drawdown) refers to project control measurement of contingency usage by time period during execution. This may be compared to planned usage, keeping in mind that a plan for risk impact is never deterministic (i.e., not a reliable control baseline). A drawdown or usage rate that varies significantly from expectations will indicate the need to update the risk analysis and quantification.

EMV (Expected Monetary Value) is a measure resulting from a multi-criteria decision model in which non-monetary inputs or decision criteria (for example, company reputation) are valued in monetary terms, allowing the objective selection of alternatives.

Probabilistic Publishing, Sugar Land, TX (2014).

4   Charlesworth, David, *Decision Analysis for Managers*, Business Expert Press, New York (2013).

EVM (Expected Value Method or **Standard Risk Model)** per AACE is a risk quantification "*...method that employs the product of a risk's probability times its impact.*" For example, if the impact if a risk occurs is $100 and the probability of occurrence is 10%, the EV is $10 ($100 x 0.1). This book recommends EVM for quantifying critical *project specific* risks.

Econometric Modeling refers to statistical methods used by economists to model the relationship between various economic drivers (supply and demand) and economic outcomes (prices). Economists usually use econometric models for a particular market to derive the price indices used in escalation risk modeling.

Empirical refers to methods based on or validated against actual historical experience. Empiricism implies that knowledge should be based on experience – demonstrated to actually work. This is a driving concept behind this book's recommended methods.

Engineering Economics refers to methods for studying the economic viability of potential project options. These traditionally include NPV and IRR methods that consider cash flow streams and the time value of money.

Escalation (versus **Inflation**) per AACE is "*A provision in costs or prices for uncertain changes in technical, economic, and market conditions over time. Inflation is a component of escalation.*" Per AACE, "Inflation" is "*A persistent increase in the level of consumer prices or a persistent decline in the purchasing power of money, caused by an increase in available currency and credit beyond the proportion of available goods and services.*" Escalation tends to vary by cost item, region, and market and is typically much more volatile and uncertain that inflation, particularly for commodity pricing.

Execution is a phase in phase gate systems that starts at the FID or sanction and includes detailed engineering, fabrication, and construction. Execution ends with mechanical completion and turnover of the facility to operations.

FID (Final Investment Decision or **Sanction)** gate in phase gate systems is when authorization is granted to the business and project team to obtain and expend the full capital funds needed. FID is usually at the end of FEL 3/Define and supported by a Class 3 estimate and schedule.

First Product/First Sale Milestone in phase gate systems refers to the completion of start-up and commissioning and delivery of the first product. It is the start of the revenue cashflow stream in NPV calculations. Commercial terms with customers, often set before project scope is fully defined, may include penalties for late delivery (a stressor risk on project schedule).

Fit-for-Use refers to methods that are practical or value-adding considering the quality of inputs, the capability of practitioners, and how the outcomes of the method will be used. The methods recommended in this book are fit-for-use – they are practical and reliable for internal use by most companies and teams.

FEED (Front End Engineering and Design) is usually the phase of engineering work associated with Class 3 or FEL 3/Define of project phase gate processes (for example, complete the P&IDs). This usually supports the FID or sanction and is followed by detailed engineering and design.

FEL (Front-End Loading) and **FEL Index** refers to the phase gate process first defined by IPA, Inc., and its clients (FEL 1, 2, 3). The term is now in general use. The IPA FEL Index is a proprietary measure of project scope definition. AACE Classes were designed to align with FEL phases and gates (for example, FEL 1/Appraise corresponds to AACE Class 5).

Gate Keeper refers to a person assigned in a phase gate process who assures that procedures and protocol are followed, facilitates gate review group efforts, and interacts with investment decision making authorities.

HAZOP (Hazard and Operability Study) refers to a systematic study of a designed process or operation to identify risks to people or the asset and risks to the efficient operation of the asset. P&IDs and the engineering model are key focuses of the study (some may consider HAZOP conduct to be part of P&ID development). In the US, HAZOP is an OSHA-approved method of completing a Process Hazards Analysis (PHA), which is a necessary part of Process Safety Management (OSHA 1910.119). Other approved PHA methods include What-if Analysis, Failure Mode and Effect Analysis, and Fault Tree Analysis.

IPA, IPA® (Independent Project Analysis, Inc.) is a project system benchmarking company that focuses on empirical research of project practices designed to improve its client's project outcomes. The company and its methods evolved from ground-breaking research of project risks by the Rand Corporation.

IRR (Internal Rate of Return) is the interest rate that makes the NPV of all cash flows for an alternative equal to zero. This calculated rate should exceed the company's hurdle rate for projects. It does not indicate the benefit of an alternative in absolute terms.

Intervention (also **Re-baselining**) refers to risk treatments applied when a project is headed towards disorder. Elements of complexity or stress driving the disorder need to be mitigated immediately to avoid project blowout. Intervention often involves adding external resources to the team to implement immediate changes. A common change is to recast (*rebaseline*) the budget and schedule from scratch so that it reflects what is actually happening in the project. Unrealistic plans lead to loss of control and add stress on the system (better an orderly overrun than a chaotic blowout).

Investment Decision Making (Capital) is vernacular for a Decision Analysis process that may or may not be rigorous in nature. This is usually strategic in nature with specific senior managers of the company or enterprise being vested with capital spending decision authority. This is distinguished from project tactical decision making where spending is usually within the authority of the project director, project manager, or equivalent.

Issues are risks that have already occurred or are sure to occur. Some take issues off of the risk register because they are day-to-day management concerns and are handled outside of risk management. This is *not* recommended because issues are then not quantified as risks. However, most systemic risks are issues (and most issues are systemic risks). Research shows that systemic risks are often the risks that most significantly affect a project's outcome.

Knowns/Unknowns is a philosophical approach to categorizing risks. In Donald Rumsfeld's words, "*...there are known knowns; there are things we know we know. We also know there are known unknowns; that is to say we know there are some things we do not know. But there are also unknown unknowns — the ones we don't know we don't know.*"[5] This leaves out the risks that matter most – what we know but do not want to know (i.e., unknown-knowns or inconvenient truths), which applies to many systemic risks. This book does not recommend this risk classification. It sounds logical but is too easily used to cover for poor risk quantification practices and outcomes.

Lessons Learned/Knowledge Management/Closeout refers to systematic efforts to capture practices and experiences at the end of a project to support improving project systems and future project outcomes. Knowledge management and closeout include capturing and analyzing actual quantitative data and metrics that can be used in tool development (for example, risk modeling). This is essential for parametric risk quantification methods and understanding systemic risks.

Line-Item Ranging (LIR) and **Ranging** refer to risk quantification methods where costs of items in an estimate or durations of activities in a schedule are replaced by 3-point estimates. MCS is then applied to obtain a probabilistic cost or schedule outcome. In this method, risks are not explicitly incorporated in the model and the 3-point estimates tend to reflect only the "inside view" of risks. Research referenced in the book has shown that its use is ineffective where systemic risks are present.

Lognormal Distribution is often a best fit probability distribution for cost and schedule outcome distributions (for example, actual/estimate cost or duration metrics). Lognormal means the logarithms of sample values are normally distributed. This facilitates regression analysis, which works best with normally distributed data.

---

5   Plain English Campaign (http://www.plainenglish.co.uk/)

MBC (Management by Cashflow) refers to project systems where the financial objective of predictable cashflow becomes paramount and the uncertainty of final outcomes is less important than hitting annual cost targets. This is a systemic risk because it breaks down project control discipline as work is accelerated or slowed to meet spending goals rather than focusing on optimal performance and cost effectiveness.

Maturity/Maturity Rating refers to how well a project process or system has been defined and developed, how much experience the organization or team has with its performance, how it goes about improving the system, and how effective the system is in meeting its objectives. Maturity can be objectively measured and used as an input to parametric systemic risk models.

Megaproject refers to a project that is so large that it is difficult to manage. IPA, Inc. has suggested that projects that require more than $2 Billion (2016, US) to complete are megaprojects. However, the underlying cause of the poor outcomes associated with megaprojects is *complexity*, which considers more than just size. Size is a measure of only the *complication* aspect of *complexity*.

MCS (Monte Carlo Simulation) is a modeling technique that introduces random sampling to inputs of a model to obtain probabilistic model outcomes. The simulation involves running and recording the outcome distribution of repeated sampling iterations of the model. The modeler assigns PDFs for each uncertain input to the model and these distributions are sampled. How realistic the method is depends largely on how well the underlying model and input distributions represent reality (for example, line-item ranging models are generally not realistic).

 ♦ Leach defines MCS as, *"A process in which a probability distribution is given for each of the inputs to some algorithm (say, one that calculates NPV), and then a computer runs the algorithm many times (usually hundreds or thousands of times). On each trial, the computer selects a different value for each input parameter, honoring the range and probability distribution given for that parameter. Thus, the computer generates a different value for each output of interest (say, NPV) on each trial. At the end of the simulation, a histogram for each output of interest is created from the list of possible values that has been generated, and statistics are calculated for that list."*[6]

NOC (National Owned Company) is a company whose main stakeholder (owner) is the government. NOC projects have political and socio-economic objectives that tend to differ from those of private companies and result in unique biases as well as uncertainty in decision making and project control behavior and outcomes.

NPV (Net Present Value) is a common decision making criteria that per AACE is *"The value of a benefit or cost found by discounting future cash*

---

6   Op. Sit., Leach (2013).

flows to the base time. Also, the system of comparing proposed invest-ments, which involves discounting at a known interest rate (represent-ing a cost of capital or a minimum acceptable rate of return) in order to choose the alternative having the highest present value." It is a core method of Engineering Economics.

Normalization per AACE is *"...a process used to modify data so that it conforms to a standard or norm (for example, conform to a common basis in time, currency, location)."* In developing parametric risk mod-els, normalization is used to remove the impact of escalation, foreign exchange, business scope changes, and catastrophic risk event impacts from actual cost and schedule outcomes so the resulting model repre-sents only contingency risks.

Operability refers to measures of the degree that asset operation objectives are achieved by a project (for example, percent of nameplate capacity, reliability). Many of the systemic risks that drive cost and schedule also drive operability (good scope definition, complexity, etc.).

OPEX (Operations Expenditure) per AACE are the *"...expenses incurred during the normal operation of a facility."* In NPV analysis, the OPEX cash flow usually begins at the time of asset turnover to operations control. Finance expenses OPEX in the current period.

Opportunity/Threat per AACE an opportunity is an *"...uncertain event that could improve the results, or improve the probability that the desired outcome will happen."* Conversely, a threat *"...will have an adverse or downside impact on an objective or objectives."* In project management, risks include both opportunities and threats. However, in safety and insurance, risks are limited to threats. If recognized late in a project, opportunities may also be threats (i.e., may result in uncertainty due to stress on control discipline).

Order/Disorder refers to project behavior that does not respond effectively to traditional project control (out of control or chaotic). Intervention (change) is needed to restore order. Speaking statistically, the outputs are not linear with the inputs and risk impacts become disproportion-ate to risk driving conditions and events because of compounding and other effects.

Outside/Inside View refers to the perspective of those who are quantify-ing risks or the perspective of the risk quantification method itself. *Outside view* implies broad consideration of uncertainties in external projects such as a parametric risk model based on industry research or benchmarking might bring. *Inside view* implies narrow consideration of only the uncertainties in the quantifier's experience. The traditional +/-10% cost uncertainty range often quoted reflects an inside view; i.e., it usually includes only the uncertainties in the estimating process (take-off uncertainty, etc.) and excludes the impact of critical risk events, systemic risks, and so on.

Overrun/Underrun is vernacular for actual cost or duration that is or will be more (*overrun*) or less (*underrun*) than the base or reference amount. For cost, the expected amount is usually the FID amount or current approved budget for individual items. An overrun that exceeds the high end of traditional ranges (for example, greater than +20%) is often called a *blowout*. Schedule duration overrun is often called *schedule slip*.

PDF (Probability Density Function): Wikipedia's definition is concise and applies, "In probability theory, a probability density function (PDF), or density of a continuous random variable, is a function that describes the relative likelihood for this random variable to take on a given value."[7] In MCS, the analyst must define PDFs for each uncertain input variable in a model.

PFD (Process Flow Diagram) refers to diagrammatic drawings (sometimes called flowsheets) developed during Front End Engineering and Design (FEED) that show process steps and major equipment and the general flows in and between them. It supports calculation of material and energy balances. It does not show piping or other details. These are complete by the end of FEL 2/Select and support Class 4 estimate and schedule development in phase gate project systems.

P&ID (Piping and Instrumentation Diagram) refers to diagrammatic drawings developed during Front End Engineering and Design (FEED) that shows process plant piping and instrumentation. It does not show details that are defined during detailed engineering (for example, piping isometrics). P&IDs are completed (issued for detail design) at the end of FEL 3/Define and support Class 3 estimate and schedule development in phase gate project systems. P&IDs are necessary for completing Process Hazards Analyses, sometimes referred to as HAZOPs.

Parametric Analysis refers to stochastic estimating or risk analysis methods developed by analyzing a sample of actual data statistically. The usual analysis method is multiple linear regression (MLR) of normalized project or system input and output data.

Parametric Risk Model: Based on regression analysis of the data, a parametric model quantifies the relationship between inputs (risk drivers) and outcomes (cost growth or schedule slip). It is probabilistic in that it also provides statistical information for determining accuracy of the model (i.e., root mean square error or RMSE). It works best with normally distributed data. Using logs or inverses, most cost and schedule risk outcome metrics can be transformed to a normally distributed form.

Phase Gate/Stage Gate refers to project management processes for the systematic staged development of project scope (phases) with decision gates between each phase at which decisions are made (selection of options, funding of the next phase, recycle, cancel, etc.). The purpose of using a

---

7   en.wikipedia.org/wiki/Probability_density_function.

phase gate system is to reduce risk by requiring an adequate level of scope definition before progressing to the next phase of a project.

Plant-Based Project System (Small Projects) refers to organizations and processes designed to manage many small capital projects at an operating facility. They are characterized by using shared resources, having quick turnarounds, and applying less rigorous or detailed control discipline. While small project costs can be very uncertain, there is also a tendency to bias (over-estimate) the base estimate to cover for this (i.e., they often underrun).

Portfolio/Capital Management refers to a group of projects and programs under the purview of a business unit (for example, refining). The projects are often aligned under an overall business strategy and hence are not entirely independent. The projects in a business's capital budget are often called the project portfolio. At the portfolio level, there are integrative risks that may not be evident at a project level.

Price Index/Cost Index/Proxy Index refers to how economist's price forecasts are presented. The price in the reference year is presented as an "index" of 1.00 and the price index for other years indicates the percentage change from the reference (for example, an index of 1.25 means the price in that year is 25% more than the reference year). If the economist cannot provide or model an index for a specific or unique item, one can assign or develop a "proxy" or substitute index that is believed to represent applicable trends.

Probabilistic Branching per AACE for a CPM schedule is "*...schedule analysis that allows for changes in schedule logic and/or durations depending on the occurrence of risk events or conditions.*" A conditional branch has an "if/then" form. For example, if activity X duration exceeds ten days (in a probabilistic model), then perform conditional successor activity Y. In risk modeling, preparing contingency plans (alternative activity branches) reflecting each risk response can be very complex.

Productivity: LABOR refers to the effectiveness of labor performance (output relative to input). Labor (management, engineering, construction, etc.) is often one of the largest project costs and is generally the most uncertain because human behavior is hard to predict and performance is susceptible to becoming disorderly or chaotic (out of control).

Profitability (see **NPV** and **IRR**) of companies is often measured in terms of return on capital. Therefore risk management practices that improve capital effectiveness improve profitability. NPV or IRR metrics used in investment decision making in part measure the effective use of capital to generate returns.

Program/Program Management refers to projects grouped, usually under the purview of a program director, in order to achieve a specific business strategy. The projects are generally somewhat dependent. Megaprojects are often a type of program albeit with highly dependent projects. At the program level, there are integrative risks that may not be evident at a project level.

Project Control refers to the project organizational function typically responsible for estimating, scheduling and cost/schedule control. Project control, in particular its change control function, should work closely with risk management during the project execution phase. Project control, which in general seeks to minimize (or at least carefully manage) change, does not work well when a project becomes disorderly and intervention is required.

PMI, PMI® (Project Management Institute) is a "*...not-for-profit professional membership association for the project, program and portfolio management professionals.*"[8] PMI covers risk management, but AACE International products (TCM and RPs) are referenced in this book because they are better attuned to the owner's interest in life cycle capital asset management, investment decision making, and quantitative approaches in general.

Project Objectives (Cost/Schedule Trading) must be considered in project-specific risk quantification because the risk response that a project makes when a risk event occurs depends in large part on whether the project is cost or schedule driven. A schedule driven project is likely to make costly but quick risk responses (trade cost for schedule). Given the importance of the first product milestone on most projects, percentage cost growth is usually greater than schedule slip.

Project System refers to the project organization and its capabilities, processes, procedures and methods, and tools that work together as a system and interact with external systems. Viewing projects as a system helps one understand why *systemic risks* and *parametric analysis* are so important to risk quantification. If a system is immature and/or broken, uncertainty will be ubiquitous and not amenable to quasi-deterministic approaches. Project *system maturity* can be objectively measured for consideration in systemic risk quantification.

Project Teams refers to the project organization: a key element of the project system. Having a weak team in terms of clarity of objectives, roles filled, level of competency, and so on is a key systemic risk. Project team development can be objectively measured.

***P*-Value/*P*-Table** is shorthand for the confidence level (or table of confidence levels). The confidence level is the probability of the cost or schedule being less than the amount shown (for example, the *p*10 value is the value for which there is only a 10% chance of underrunning).

QA/QC (Quality Assurance/Quality Control): *quality* is *conformance to requirements*. *Assurance* refers to the practice of assuring that processes are well defined, while *control* refers to the practice of measuring a process's performance. Because systemic risk analysis involves

---

8   See www.pmi.org.

measuring project system attributes, it could be viewed as a quality assurance practice. QA/QC is also a function in a project system and team and its effectiveness is an element of systemic risk. Poor quality, and resultant rework, is usually a significant project risk.

QRA (Quantitative Risk Analysis) refers to the quantitative analysis step in the Risk Management process. This is different than the qualitative risk analysis step (for example, application of a risk matrix). Risk Quantification (RQ) is not about the RM process, but the methodology. The AACE TCM Framework process for Risk Management is the only one that explicitly highlights a unique QRA step.

RBS (Risk Breakdown Structure)/Risk Types per AACE is *"A framework or taxonomy to aid risk identification and for organizing and ordering risk types throughout the risk management process."* Risk registers need to include a breakdown category for the applicable risk quantification method for each risk – systemic, project-specific, escalation, or currency exchange.

RPs (AACE International **Recommended Practices**) are developed by AACE technical committees and describe practices that in the general consensus of the subject matter experts can be reliable and effective. Many of the methods in this book are aligned with RPs, which are referenced as appropriate. A list of RPs is included on page 392.

RCF (Reference Class Forecasting) is a forecasting method that (1) identifies a comparison set or "reference class" of past similar projects, (2) determines the distribution of the set's outcome of interest (for example, unit cost), and (3) uses that as the forecast of the most likely outcome for the project. It is *not* recommended because it does not appropriately consider *why* past projects performed as they did – it inappropriately uses descriptive rather than inferential statistics to make predictions.

ROC/ROA (Return on Capital/Return on Assets) as used here is not a specific measure, but refers to profitability metrics that consider how well a company manages its capital investments. ROC/ROA increases if assets cost less (or are written-down) and decreases with cost overruns. ROC/ROA decrease if the schedule slips (late revenue) and cost increases (interest and escalation). In short, risk quantification is critical to profitability metrics.

Rand® Corporation is a research company that developed groundbreaking parametric project cost and schedule risk models for the process industries in the 1980s. That research used actual data from many participating companies, but because it was sponsored by the US Department of Energy, the research results are available to the public in Rand publications.

Ranging (includes **Estimate Line Item Ranging [LIR]** and **Activity Ranging**) refers to risk quantification methods where costs of items in an estimate or durations of activities in a schedule are replaced by

3-point estimates. MCS is then applied to obtain a probabilistic cost or schedule outcome. In this method, risks are not explicitly incorporated in the model and the 3-point estimates tend to reflect only the "inside view" of risks. Research referenced in the book has shown that its use is ineffective where systemic risks are present.

Re-baselining refers to a risk treatment applied when a project is headed towards disorder. Elements of complexity or stress driving the disorder need to be mitigated immediately to avoid project blowout. Intervention often involves adding external resources to the team to implement immediate changes. A common change is to recast (*rebaseline*) the budget and schedule from scratch so that it reflects what is actually happening in the project. Unrealistic plans lead to loss of control and add stress on the system (better an orderly overrun than a chaotic blowout).

Recommended Practices: see RPs.

Regression/ (MLR) Multiple Linear Regression is a inferential statistical modeling method that quantifies the relationship between two or more independent variables (for example, risk drivers) and a dependent variable (for example, cost growth, schedule slip, operability) by fitting a linear equation to the actual, normalized data. It is typically used to develop parametric risk models for systemic risks. It is important to *control* for known risk drivers by including them in the analysis to avoid ascribing outcomes to the wrong cause.

Reserves (Management Reserves) per AACE is "*An amount added to an estimate to allow for discretionary management purposes outside of the defined scope of the project, as otherwise estimated. May include amounts that are within the defined scope, but for which management does not want to fund as contingency or that cannot be effectively managed using contingency.*" *Management* in this term means levels of management above the project manager or director. Some sources use the term "contingency reserve" for what AACE calls just "contingency." This usage is *not* recommended because it implies that the project manager is not authorized to spend contingency to respond to risks in real time.

Revenue refers to the incoming cashflow stream from the sale of products. It is usually the variable with most influence on NPV. The first product milestone is therefore a key focus of business sponsors. This often results in stress being put on project schedule completion, which in turn results in increased risk to both cost (due to cost/schedule trading) and schedule, particularly for megaprojects.

Risk (Uncertainty) per AACE is "*an uncertain event or condition that could affect a project objective or business goal.*" As such, it includes both opportunities and threats. However, in safety and insurance, risks are limited to threats. If recognized late in a project, opportunities may also be threats (i.e., may result in uncertainty due to stress on control discipline).

Risk Analysis: Qualitative versus **Quantitative** refers to a Risk Management process step that follows risk identification. Qualitative analysis (Risk Matrix, Risk Register) is focused on prioritizing risks for treatment. Quantitative analysis (QRA) is applied at decision gates or anytime a significant decision must be made. The AACE TCM Framework risk management process is the only industry process that has a specific step for QRA.

Risk Assessment refers to a broad Risk Management process step that includes both risk identification and risk analysis.

Risk Attitude/Appetite/Tolerance refers to the explicit policy or implicit bias an organization or decision maker has toward taking risks in decision making. Policies or biases may include being risk seeking, risk neutral, or risk averse. The attitude can influence the project system culture. For example, risk-seeking companies may underestimate risks while risk averse companies may be punitive and overestimate risks.

Risk Control refers to a Risk Management process step that follows Risk Treatment. During execution, risks are monitored and responded to as appropriate. This process should be tightly integrated with project control during execution because the control function must observe and address risks and their impacts in near real time.

Risk Driver: see **Causes**

Risk Elicitation refers to the process and methods of obtaining risk information from stakeholders and teams (workshops and interviews). Understanding biases is important to successful elicitation. (For more information, see Skinner Chapter 10.)[9]

Risk Events and Conditions refers to sources of uncertainty with *events* implying uncertain actions (for example, a strike, storm, permit denial) and *conditions* implying uncertain state of being subject to discovery (for example, weak project system, poor soils, corroded tank). Events are always project-specific risks, but conditions may be systemic or project-specific risks.

Risk Impact is the consequence of a risk event occurring or uncertain condition having a different state or effect than planned. This book focuses on project cost and schedule impact, although the same risks might also affect safety, operability, and other outcomes.

Risk Management (RM) refers to an asset and project management process that in the AACE model (the TCM Framework) has the steps of Risk Planning, Assessment, Treatment, and Control. Risk Assessment includes Identification and Analysis, including Risk Quantification. Its objective is to increase the likelihood that the project will meet its objectives (risk being anything that might cause those objectives not to be met).

Risk Matrix (Probability Impact Matrix) per AACE is "*A method used in qualitative risk analysis to rate or rank the severity of risks in terms*

---

9 Op. Sit. Skinner (2009).

of their combined impact (or consequence) to some output measure that is at risk and the risk's probability of occurrence. The matrix has impact on one axis and probability on the other with each intersecting node given predetermined severity rating designations (e.g., high, moderate, and low)." Probability multiplied by impact is also the basis of the Expected Value (EV) method of risk quantification; therefore, the use of EV has the benefit of continuity in qualitative and quantitative analysis.

Risk Owner per AACE is *"A person(s) or entity charged with planning and implementing a specific risk response."* Systemic risks (for example, maturity of a project system, level of scope definition) tend to be owned by senior management outside the project team or business unit. This is part of the reason why systemic risks are unfortunately often not included in risk registers.

Risk Policy per AACE is *"...the enterprise's or decision maker's established and preferably documented risk tolerance and general approach to treatment of risk in decision analysis."* Policies can sometimes conflict with actions. Company mission statements may express a tolerance for risks in terms of revenue and income but capital project team behavior reflects risk aversion (overly tight accuracy expectations and standards and punishment of overruns and schedule slips).

Risk Quantification (RQ) as covered in this book is integrated project cost and schedule risk analysis practices focused on providing probabilistic cost and schedule values for consideration in phase gate decision making. RQ may support strategic investment decisions during scope development or tactical project change and risk response decisions during execution. RQ may be called Quantitative Risk Analysis or QRA. RQ differs from qualitative risk analysis that is focused on risk management prioritization (however, in the case of Expected Value, may reflect continuity in approach).

Risk Register per AACE is *"A formal record of identified risks, typically including additional summary information as regards assessment, treatment and control of the risks."* It is a risk management tool. Risk registers should also identify the risk type in respect to the applicable risk quantification method (for example, systemic, project-specific, escalation or exchange). In some companies, risks that have already occurred are called "Issues" and are moved off of the register (this is not recommended).

Risk Responses (Corrective Action/Intervention) per AACE are *"Strategies or actions identified and planned in the risk treatment process to address risks."* It also includes actions taken immediately, planned or not, when a risk occurs. In project control practice, these are called corrective actions. Plans for responses if an accepted risk occurs are called contingency plans. If a risk threatens to result in disorder (loss of control), the appropriate risk response may be Intervention.

Risk Treatment refers to the Risk Management process step that follows risk assessment. In this step, action is taken on identified risks to avoid, reduce, share, or accept them. At decision gates, risks for which treatment actions are pending or are incomplete (residual risks) must be quantified as if they were accepted (do not assume actions will be done and successful until they actually are).

Risk Workshop/Interviews refers to methods of obtaining (eliciting) risk information (characteristics, potential risk responses, risk impacts, etc.) from stakeholders and project teams. Workshops may be for periodic risk assessment (focus is identification and treatment) or for quantitative risk analysis at the decision gates (focus is on probabilities, responses and impacts). Group discussions tend to be best, but interviews are helpful when there are difficult group dynamics, sensitive topics, or not all stakeholders can be present. Individual interviews can also help counteract Groupthink[10] and bias introduced by management.

Risks: Compounding/Interactions: a risk that occurs alone will have one impact, but if they occur together with other risks or in sequence with them, the impacts can compound and the nature of the risk may change due to interaction. Impacts are often not additive; they become non-linear (chaotic). This is more common on complex projects. One way to model the outcome without considering each possible interaction is to measure complexity and use that measure to drive non-linear or bimodal functionality in the model algorithm.

Risks: Integrative refers to risks identified in program and portfolio risk analysis. These risks may result from the interaction of projects in the program. For example, labor shortage risks may arise because projects in the program are competing between themselves for limited resources. Programs tend to add complexity and often slow decision making.

Risks: Overwhelming refers to project-specific risks that, if they occur, have impacts that consume much of or the entire contingency. These are typically discrete or binary risks; i.e., they either occur with large impact or not. Contingency is intended for day-to-day risks that have nominal (albeit critical) impacts. These risks should be analyzed and funded in their own right with dedicated Management Reserves as appropriate.

Risks: Project-Specific (Tactical) per AACE are risks *"…related to events, actions, and other conditions that are specific to the scope of a project (e.g., weather, soil conditions). The impacts of project-specific risks are more or less unique to a project."* Quantify project-specific risks using the Expected Value Methods (EVM).

---

10 Wikipedia defines Groupthink as follows: "Groupthink is a psychological phenomenon that occurs within a group of people, in which the desire for harmony or conformity in the group results in an irrational or dysfunctional decision-making outcome."

Risks: Residual per AACE is *"That portion of risks that remain after risk responses (or treatments) are implemented in full or in part."* These are the risks that are quantified at the decision gates (do not assume a risk treatment has been done or is successful until it is completed).

Risk: Secondary per AACE are *"Risks that occur from actions taken to treat other risks."* These should be considered in risk analysis, but are often unforeseen. These are more common in complex projects and are similar to integrative/interaction risks (i.e., a compounding effect).

Risks: Systemic (Strategic) per AACE are risks *"...that are an artifact of an industry, company or project system, culture, strategy, complexity, technology, or similar over-arching characteristics."* Quantify systemic risks using empirically based parametric modeling.

Risks: Tail (or Bimodal) refers to the fact that most actual cost and schedule outcome distributions have many more overruns than underruns and the overruns can be extreme (two or three or more times the original budget; i.e., blowouts). As such, the lognormal distribution is often a good fit from a statistical perspective. Further, these overruns tend to "bunch" at the extremes; i.e., the distribution is bi-modal and in some cases tri-modal. Multi-modal behavior is believed to reflect orderly projects crossing a tipping point into disorder.

SAVE® (SAVE International) is the international society for the advancement and promotion of the value methodology (also called value engineering). See Value.

Scenario Analysis per AACE is defined as, *"Methods to assess a range of events, conditions, and outcomes employing specific scenarios. An alternative to simulation methods for assessing ranges."* For example, a scenario may be "China Hard Landing." You would then assess how that scenario would play out in the relevant CAPEX market, and then consider the chance of the "hard landing" occurring.

Schedule Delay/Activity Delay is a risk impact where project and activity schedule duration (time) is increased and completion is late. Businesses and NPV analyses are very concerned with the first product date. Delays of activities will only affect the first product date if the activity is on the critical path or the risk impact puts it on that path. The risk response to address a delay is often to change the network logic; logic-change behavior can be addressed in CPM models using conditional or probabilistic branching but that difficult.

Schedule Milestone per AACE is *"A zero duration activity or event which is used to denote a particular point in time for reference or measurement."* The FID (FEL 3) and first product milestones (start of revenue) in a phase gate process are example key milestones for NPV analysis. Schedule contingency is generally included in CPM schedules as an activity right before critical completion milestones.

Schedule Slip refers to a measure of execution phase delay duration (or sometimes execution plus start-up and commissioning phases), usually expressed as a percentage of total duration (for example, schedule slips of 20% are common). Its cost counterpart is cost growth.

Scope pre AACE is *"The sum of all that is to be or has been invested in and delivered by the performance of an activity or project.... Generally limited to that which is agreed to by the stakeholders in an activity or project (i.e., if not agreed to, it is 'out of scope')."*

Scope: Business refers to the scope "agreed to by the stakeholders" which in this case is the business unit that owns the asset and funds the project. Their agreement with the project team includes the key premises of the business case (for example, X capacity, of Y quality, on Z date). Anything that does not change these premises must be covered by contingency, escalation and exchange (for example, a change from a 100 hp to a 500 hp pump is not a business scope change if it does not change the overall business case premise of X bbls/day production capacity).

Scope: Contract per AACE *"...includes all that an enterprise is contractually committed to perform or deliver."* A risk treatment option is to transfer risk as appropriate between the owner and contractor. If a risk is designated a contract scope change (and contractors often pursue such designation) the impacts may not be considered overrun or slip in the contractor's database (their perception of risk quantification and contingency is different than for owners).

Scope Change is a change to that which was originally "agreed to by the stakeholders." For the business, this is a change to the business case premise. For a supplier, this is a change from the terms of the contract. Contingency for each party excludes scope change in their view.

Scope Creep per AACE is *"Gradual progressive change (usually additions to) of the project's scope such that it is not noticed by the project management team or customer."* This is often caused by weak project systems and poor project control discipline – a known systemic risk that is predictable as such.

Scope Definition/Level of Scope Definition refers primarily to the deliverables that define the project scope such as analyses and studies, plans, designs, specifications, estimates, and schedules. The level refers to the extent or status of defining activity or deliverable completion. The required levels are specified in phase gate systems; for example, IPA FEL 3/Define which correspond to AACE Class 3. Decades of research have shown that the level of scope definition (and efficacy of the project system) is a predominant systemic risk.

Sensitivity Analysis per AACE is *"A test of the outcome of an analysis by altering one or more parameters from an initially assumed value(s)."* Tornado diagrams are common way to display the outcomes of sensitivity analyses. One purpose is to prioritize risks for treatment.

Shutdown(s) refers to a shutdown of unit or plant operations so planned maintenance can be performed (i.e., a maintenance shutdown). Their costs are usually expensed. A Turnaround (TAR) is a more extensive shutdown in which planned revamps and upgrades are also made.

Stakeholders per AACE are *"Decision makers, people or organizations that can affect or be affected by a decision."* Stakeholder expectations, perceptions, and biases are uncertainties to consider in risk quantification analysis and communication.

Start-up/Commissioning in phase gate systems refers to the phase during which the asset is transitioned from mechanical completion to production of salable product. The product may not be produced at planned capacity or quality; operability is a measure of the degree that operations objectives are achieved (percent of nameplate). The cost and duration of this phase are often more uncertain than the execution phase and have different risk drivers (for example, technology-driven) and therefore warrant their own parametric risk models.

Statistics: Descriptive (Mean, Mode, Skewness, Standard Deviation) versus **Inferential** (Regression and MCS) distinguishes statistical analyses to aid understanding (descriptive) versus those directed more to prediction and forecasting (inferential). Inferential statistics are essential for empirically-based risk quantification methods.

Strategic Misrepresentation is a politically correct term for consciously lying about the estimated cost and/or schedule of a project in order to assure that a project or program is sanctioned. This is most common in public infrastructure projects (i.e., taxpayer funded). It is different than optimism bias, which is subconscious. Where this practice is common, Reference Class Forecasting (RCF) has been suggested as an analysis technique when "professional forecasters" cannot be trusted.

Stress/Stressor (see **Tipping Point**) refers to conditions or actions that put pressure on a project system and increase the chance that it will fail (for example, overly aggressive schedule requirements). The combination of complexity and stressors can cause a project to cross from orderly to disorderly (chaotic) behavior (i.e., cross the tipping point).

Systems Engineering (SE)/Systems Dynamics (SD) is an interdisciplinary engineering field focused on understanding and improving systems. Capital and project management should be viewed as a system in risk quantification (for example, systemic risks). Systems Dynamics is a method to model complex systems, including non-linear behavior, using internal feedback loops and time delays. While applicable to risk quantification, the models are difficult to build for each project and they assume an orderly system.

TCM/TCM® (AACE International's **Total Cost Management**)/**TCM Framework®** is an asset and project life-cycle process for the practice of Cost Engineering. It centers on Investment Decision Making with ongoing capital asset management preceding the decision and project control following the decision during execution. Risk management and quantification are processes in TCM.

Tipping Point refers to the point in a project when the combination of complexity and stressors cause it to cross from orderly to disorderly (chaotic) behavior (i.e., cross the tipping point). Orderly projects respond to traditional project control, while disorderly ones require Intervention to restore order.

Tornado Diagram per AACE is *"a graphical bar chart of quantitative risk analysis data that ranks the key risk drivers in descending order of impact or severity."* These are a common form or illustration of sensitivity analysis. (For more information, see Skinner, Chapter 11 and Leach, Chapter 4.)

Transformation refers to changing the mathematical expression of a parameter so that it is more amenable to statistical analysis. For example, actual/estimate data usually has a highly skewed distribution, but transformed to estimate/actual form, the same data is more normally distributed and amenable to regression. Similarly the logarithms of cost and schedule metrics are often normally distributed (i.e., lognormal).

Turnaround(s) (TAR) refers to a unit or plant shutdown in which planned revamp and upgrades are also made. The revamp and upgrade elements are generally capitalized, and the turnaround is often coordinated with other capital projects and programs. TARs are usually schedule-driven and add complexity to any project coordinated with them.

Uncertainty is synonymous with risk in the project management field and this book. However, some differentiate uncertainty from risk.

♦ The "Knight" definition (economist Frank Knight) is that *risks* are those uncertainties governed by known probability distributions (can be measured) while *uncertainties* are more or less unmeasurable.

♦ For others, *risks* are events and conditions (items listed in the risk register), while *uncertainties* are expected variations in our work process outcomes (i.e., budget quotations have a range of +/– *X*%) that can be quantified step by step (as in line-item ranging).

VIP (Value Improving Practice) is a term coined by IPA Inc. and its clients to describe specific planned, actionable practices, usually performed early in project definition, that improve value (get better outputs with less input). Some of the most common VIPs are Constructability Analysis and Value Engineering. Cost or time savings exercises that are not focused on increasing value, particularly done during project execution, are generally *not* recommended because they usually do not consider the increased risks.

Validation per AACE *"...confirms that a product or service satisfies user or stakeholder needs."* For risks, the base cost estimate and schedule are quantitatively assessed to confirm that they meet the cost and schedule strategy (are they competitive? aggressive? conservative?). Validation compares the plans to a variety of benchmark metrics, internal and external. Contingency estimates can then objectively allow for biases observed in the base.

Value in a general sense is about getting more for less. For example, increased production capacity or operability for the same or less CAPEX and/or OPEX over the asset life cycle without sacrificing other objectives such as safety adds value. Value Engineering and other VIPs are applied during early project scope definition. The pursuit of value tends to push limits, which increases uncertainty. Therefore, value and risk analysis must be done together. Cost savings alone are not synonymous with value.

Value Management (VM) refers to a defined sub-process within a phase gate system designed to help the team assure and maximize value. VIPs are the fundamental tools of Value Management in projects. Risk Management (RM) works with VM; i.e., opportunities are steered to VM to capitalize on them, and potential VM threats are steered to RM for analysis and treatment.

WBS (Work Breakdown Structure) per AACE is a *"Framework for organizing and ordering the activities that makes up a project. Systematic approach to reflect a top-down hierarchy with each lower level providing more detail and smaller elements of the overall work."* The WBS helps guide risk analysis to assure the risks are considered for the entire project scope. A complicated WBS contributes to complexity and hence risk.

Write-Down/Write-Off: a write-down is when the booked value of an asset is reduced because the fair market value is less; write-offs remove the asset from the books entirely. Net income is reduced by the write-down/write-off value. Blowout projects often result in a write-down. Write-downs are often grouped to put mistakes in the past and to make future return on assets look better (asset book value having been reduced).

AACE International Technical Products

The following are AACE International technical products related to Decision and Risk Management (DRM). Please note that these products are updated and added to regularly. At this writing, the TCM Framework and the Recommended Practices are available to AACE members for free from: http://www.aacei.org/resources/.

GENERAL REFERENCE
Total Cost Management (TCM) Framework
Professional Practice Guides (PPG)
Decision and Risk Management Professional (DRMP) Certification Study Guide

RECOMMENDED PRACTICES (RP)			
RISK MANAGEMENT PROCESS STEPS		**COST ESTIMATE AND SCHEDULE CLASSIFI-**	
72R-12	Risk Management Planning	CATION (LEVEL OF SCOPE DEVELOPMENT)	
62R-11	Risk Assessment	17R-97	Generic (the following are industry-specific versions)
63R-11	Risk Treatment		
67R-11	Contract Risk Allocation	*18R-97*	• Process Industries
77R-15	Quality Control/ Assurance for Risk Management	*47R-11*	• Mining and Mineral Processing
RISK QUANTIFICATION PRINCIPLES		*56R-08*	• Building and General Construction
71R-12	Skills and Knowledge of a DRM Professional	*69R-12*	• Hydropower
10S-90	Terminology (including DRM terms)	*87R-14*	• Petroleum Exploration and Production
		27R-03	Schedule Classification System
40R-08	Contingency Estimating (RQ) – General Principles	**ESCALATION RISK QUANTIFICATION METHODS**	
66R-11	Selecting Probability Distribution Functions	58R-10	Escalation Principles and Methods Using Indices
SYSTEMIC RISK QUANTIFICATION METHODS		68R-11	Escalation Estimating Using Indices and MCS
42R-08	Risk Analysis and Contingency Determination Using Parametric Estimating	**DECISION MAKING**	
		85R-14	Use of Decision Trees in Decision Making
43R-08	Example Models as Applied for the Process Industries (includes functional Excel-based Hackney and Rand models)	**RISK CONTROL**	
		70R-12	Schedule Contingency Management
PROJECT-SPECIFIC RISK QUANTIFICATION METHODS			
41R-08	Risk Analysis and Contingency Determination Using Range Estimating		
44R-08	Risk Analysis and Contingency Determination Using Expected Value		
57R-09	Integrated Cost & Schedule Risk Analysis Using MCS of a CPM Model		
64R-11	CPM Schedule Risk Modeling and Analysis: Special Considerations		
65R-11	Integrated Cost & Schedule Risk Analysis & Contingency Determination Using Expected Value		

Index

www.ingramcontent.com/pod-product-compliance
Lightning Source LLC
Chambersburg PA
CBHW021844020426
42334CB00013B/179